MOZART

AND HIS

PIANO CONCERTOS

CUTHBERT GIRDLESTONE

DOVER PUBLICATIONS, INC.
NEW YORK

This Dover edition, first published in 1964, is an unabridged and corrected republication of the second (1958) edition of the work first published in 1948 by Cassell & Company, Ltd., London, under the title *Mozart's Piano Concertos*.

International Standard Book Number: 0-486-21271-8
Library of Congress Catalog Card Number: 64-8198

Manufactured in the United States of America

Dover Publications, Inc.
180 Varick Street
New York 14, N.Y.

To
Dame Myra Hess

Contents

CONTENTS

Preface

I HAVE attempted in this book a study of Mozart's piano concertos. This important part of his work has never received the attention it deserves and, until within the last few years before the war, orchestras and executants had neglected most of his great concertos, whereas less personal compositions, such as his piano sonatas and trios, were known to everyone. The only studies of his piano concertos, at the time when this book was written, were those found in works dealing with him or with the genre as a whole, such as those of Abert or Engels,[1] or in articles like those of Fr. Blume.[2] No study had been devoted to them exclusively.

I have sought to observe the growth of Mozart's form and inspiration throughout his twenty-three piano concertos. From one period to the next, sometimes from one work to the next, I have sought to understand the unfolding of his art by using the piano concertos as landmarks in my journey. Their importance in the history of music is generally recognized; there remained to define their part in his work as a whole.

I have insisted perhaps a little more upon the growth of his inspiration than upon his technique. But as in the last resort the two are inseparable, both have their share in these pages. Moreover, as it is arbitrary to isolate this or that category of an artist's work from its context, I have related the concertos to the most representative of his other compositions.

My aim has been to follow the unfolding of his genius throughout his piano concertos and to give them their place in his work. It is not for me to judge with what success this aim has been attained; it is enough that there should be no doubt of the excellence of the aim itself.

In making an English translation of this book, the original of which appeared in French in 1940, I have shortened a few passages

---

[1] H. Engels: *Die Entwicklung des deutschen Klavierkonzerts von Mozart bis Liszt* (Leipzig, 1927).

H. Abert: *Mozart* (Leipzig, 1919–21).

[2] Fr. Blume: *Die formgeschichtliche Stellung der Klavierkonzerte Mozarts* (*Mozart Jahrbuch*, II, 1924).

A*

and corrected a few mistakes in the examples. The chief change in the text concerns the remarks on pp. 49–50 about the origin of the sonata rondo.

C. M. G.

THEME GUIDE

FOR MOZART'S PIANO CONCERTOS

PART I

1. *Introduction*

THE twenty-three concertos that Mozart wrote for his favourite instrument play, in the history of their genre, a part comparable to that played by Beethoven's nine masterpieces in the history of the symphony. Just as Beethoven's works established the form of the symphony for nearly a century, so Mozart's piano concertos, owing to their number and the great beauty of most of them, were at the source of the modern concerto and laid down the lines along which it was to develop for many years. The structure of most concertos of the last century is fundamentally the same as that of his own and even modern works show proof of his influence.

Mozart has enriched the concerto form with a larger number of masterpieces than any other of the great composers. In the work of most of them concertos have occupied but a small place, much smaller than that held by symphonies or quartets. With him, on the other hand, they are more numerous than any other kind of composition except symphonies, and he has left in all some forty for instruments or groups of instruments of all kinds. The partial neglect of the form by most of the masters has thrown his into greater prominence, especially those which he wrote for the piano.

Nevertheless, for the music-lover who is less concerned with the history of the form than with the personality of each work, with the thought that inspires it and the joy it gives, his twenty-three concertos are still more precious. They are an inexhaustible spring of delight. Their diversity corresponds to our most varied moods, from the state of quiet content in which all we ask of art is entertainment, exquisite rather than deep, the exuberance of animal spirits, the consciousness of physical and moral health, to melancholy, sorrow and even revolt and to an Olympian serenity breathing the air of the mountain tops. The comparative uniformity which we notice between them at first sight disappears with closer scrutiny. The feeling is never the same from one to the other; each one is characterized by a personality of its own and the variety of their inspiration shows itself ever greater as we travel more deeply into them.

Thanks to this variety, Mozart is one of the few composers who can become one's daily bread. Formal diversity matters little; what we demand is diversity of inspiration. Many composers have a more varied form than he and yet their work, when we steep ourselves in it, soon brings on a tedium which his greater works never cause and from which we suffer only when we persist in studying him in compositions where he did not express his full being.

It is this privilege of giving lasting satisfaction to mind and spirit, even more than their historical importance, that causes his concertos to rank among the masterpieces of their art. We shall therefore seek above all to discover the inner character of each one of them and the nature of the emotion which makes it what it is. Formal study cannot be neglected, however, for form is never separable from matter and formal analysis often reveals beauties of an emotional order. Formal studies exist already[1] but no one has attempted to show how rich and deep is the inspiration of these works. The tendency has been rather to underestimate their inspirational value, to consider them as "drawing-room music", and to put them below his symphonies and chamber music. We hope to show that they deserve a higher place and represent as worthily and as fully as these the personality of their creator.

Not only in the work of Mozart but in general, musical critics have been inclined to deny the concerto an exalted position and to regard it as an inferior genre, unworthy to stand beside the symphony. Such an attitude is seen in definitions like that of Ebenezer Prout in the first edition of Grove[2] and in pronouncements like that of Paul Dukas: "The concerto, compared with the symphony, is an inferior genre since its only object, generally speaking, is to show off the talent of an instrumentalist."[3]

Similar definitions are still current and depreciate the genre by accusing it of placing the executant's muscular agility and his vanity above artistic expression. They are just when they apply to the virtuoso concertos of certain soloist composers, but it is unfair to take the poorest representatives of a form as its models. Mozart, Beethoven, Schumann, Brahms, Franck never devoted their genius to satisfying the

---

[1] A. Schering: *Die Geschichte des Instrumentalkonzerts*, Leipzig, 1906; H. Engels: *Die Entwicklung des deutschen Klavierkonzerts von Mozart bis Liszt*, Leipzig, 1927; H. Abert: *Mozart*, Leipzig, 1919-21.

[2] "An Instrumental composition designed to show the skill of an executant."

[3] Quoted by J. G. Prodhomme: *La question du concerto*, in *Zschrft. der Internat. Musikgesellschaft*, 1904-6.

vanity of a virtuoso, to helping an "executant" to "show his skill".
The numerical preponderance of bad concertos is alone responsible
for these definitions; there lies the reason why the mass of the public,
when it hears a concerto, whatever be its value, admires first of all
the accomplishments of the soloist, and why the meaning of its
applause is less "How beautiful this music is!" than "What a lot of
notes this performer gets in!"

def.

The essence of the concerto lies in the struggle between the
orchestra on one hand, and the solo instrument, or group of instruments, on the other. The struggle is broken by truces during which
orchestra and solo collaborate on friendly terms, and it ends with a
reconciliation—but it is none the less a struggle. Sometimes the
weapons are common to both sides—the main themes which return
in solos and tuttis; sometimes each side has its own—themes reserved
for the solo and others that belong to the orchestra. There are
vicissitudes; the strife may remain indecisive, and solo and orchestra
may toss the chief subjects from one to the other; the tutti may win
a momentary victory and loudly proclaim its triumph, or the soloist
may see his endeavours carry the day by dint of chords, scales and
arpeggios, and spurn the vanquished orchestra with a series of scintillating trills. But, whatever the temporary issue, we know that in
the long run neither side will win and that the final cadence will conclude peace and alliance between the former adversaries.

For this result to appear likely, the forces must be evenly balanced.
The orchestra uses its polyphony, its mass, its colour; the soloist, his
virtuosity. Semi-quavers and demi-semi-quavers are his only means
of defence against the weight and colour of the band. Take away
this defence and his instrument is just one among fifty; the orchestra
crushes and absorbs it. Virtuosity is not a mere display of "skill"; it
is a source of beauty and the very condition of survival for the solo
instrument. The orchestra is not forbidden to exploit its colour and
its mass; why forbid virtuosity to the soloist? The fact that certain
composers of concertos have misused the weapon is irrelevant; the
soloist must have recourse to it or succumb.

The danger of absorption by the band is a real one for the solo
instrument, and it is often by reaction against it that so many mediocre
concertos fall into the extreme of limiting themselves to being just
series of runs, preceded, interrupted and followed by interventions
of the tutti. This danger threatens especially concertos for string and
wind instruments; those for the piano fear it much less, for the tone
of the instrument stands out clearly against the orchestral background.

For this reason, the piano concerto is perhaps the ideal of the form. The battle between a single fiddle and the whole host of strings, woodwind and brass always appears unequal, but with the piano we know that the orchestra will find its match.

If, then, we consider the concerto as a struggle between two forces, one simple, the other complex, it ceases to be an "inferior genre" and becomes as worthy of study as the sonata, quartet or symphony. Now, of all the concertos that exist, those of Mozart form the largest group of masterpieces. That is one of their claims to a special study. There is another. Nowhere in all the composer's work is there a form wherein he has expressed himself so completely. His twenty-three piano concertos, extending from his eighteenth to his thirty-sixth year, reveal him at all ages; they are the most varied and most extensive witness to his artistic life. We find in them his joys and sorrows, his hopes and disappointments; we penetrate through them into the inner sanctuary where the harassed and overworked man found afresh the radiant life which never ceased to spring up within him. Not that his finest concertos are greater than the best of his other works; the four great symphonies, certain of his quartets and quintets and many other compositions are in every way their equals. In almost every one of the manifold genres within which he poured forth his treasures one finds one or two works which are among his finest, but none of these genres show so abundant a succession of masterpieces as his piano concertos. He wrote some fifty symphonies, but thirty-eight of these were composed before the age of twenty-one and only the last four of the remaining ten can be called great. He composed also some thirty quartets, but only the last thirteen date from his maturity; the others were all written before he was twenty-three and most of them much earlier. The eight quintets, too, do not form a homogeneous group. One is very early; the horn quintet and that for piano and wind belong to his twenty-eighth and twenty-ninth years; the next two were written at thirty-one; the clarinet quintet at thirty-three; and the two others right at the end of his life. It is the same with the rest, except the operas which space out fairly equally over the years of his maturity, and are the only group which might vie with the concertos in reflecting fully the personality of their creator. If only one part of his instrumental work had survived,[1] the one which would give us the completest picture of

---

[1] The idea is not far-fetched. It happened with Clementi whose piano works have alone survived, whereas his symphonies, overtures and concertos have almost all been lost.

him, the one whose survival would come nearest to consoling us for the loss of the rest, would be the group of the piano concertos.

Mozart's life is so short that it does not seem possible to give to his work the threefold division which, since Lenz, we recognize in that of Beethoven and which, according to Vincent d'Indy, can be found in the life of every creative mind. In his life of thirty-six years it seems impossible to distinguish the ages of initiation, of maturity, and of full self-possession which mark the "law of the three periods". Is it reasonable to suppose that Mozart could have reached before the age of forty the point which most artists reach only after fifty? Moreover, in a work which seems so uniform, how can one discover three "periods"? The opinion once prevalent that all his works are alike and show no sign of development would make it seem arbitrary to divide into three periods the music of a composer who, from one end of his short life to the other, always harped on the same theme.

And yet, despite appearances, a deeper knowledge of his music shows that one can apply the "three periods" law to him without losing oneself in hair-splitting distinctions. To deny its existence in his work is to go against the facts. The notion that he never changed is due to the fact that so many people still know little of his work beyond the piano sonatas, often "interpreted" by the pitiless hands of children, and these are the weakest and least personal part of his output. When one gets beyond them and comes to the quartets, quintets, concertos and symphonies, the impression vanishes and one recognizes in him a variety indicative of growth.

If, therefore, we divide his work into three periods, the first, that of initiation and formation, will cover the years of his youth, at Salzburg, in Paris, and during his travels, from 1762 to 1780. The second, his maturity, begins at twenty-five with *Idomeneo* and finishes with the three great symphonies and the last quartets, at the moment when the silence of 1789-90 marks the lowest point of discouragement and wretchedness. The third is when the artist, overstepping the limits which had bounded him hitherto, enters new lands and walks under new skies; it is the culmination of his existence. True, with Mozart one hardly dares to speak of culmination; his career was checked too early for him to reach one, and this third period, which corresponds to the works of his last year, is incomplete. It is but the beginning of a period of which the *Magic Flute* and the *Requiem* show how magnificent the harvest would have been. None the less, his last year is distinguished from his earlier periods. After the almost complete silence of 1789 and 1790 it is a new and sudden

3 periods [margin note]

MOZART's work – too easy for children too difficult for adults. [handwritten note]

blossoming of masterpieces. His two "testaments", the *Magic Flute* and the *Requiem*, the one secular and humanitarian, the other Christian, bear indeed a stamp of finality. Their place is at the end of a life and they strike chords which Mozart had never touched so deeply till then. Other works of that year show this character to a lesser degree and justify our calling it his "third period".

For the composer's biography, two rather than three periods is the right division. The watershed is his departure for Vienna in 1781. Freed from the yoke of the Archbishop of Salzburg and from the guardianship of his father, against whom he rebelled, not only by leaving the Archbishop but also by marrying in the following year, Mozart asserted his independence as son and as servant, and his newly-won freedom was soon reflected in a greater originality in his music. The story of both his life and his work agrees in marking 1781 as the date of a deliverance, of a taking-off, and the turning-point of his career.

This taking-off happened at twenty-five. At an age when most artists begin to produce, Mozart reached his maturity. Although so young he stands almost alone in that his creative life up to this point is long enough to constitute a "period", and one which includes works of which several, notably some of the violin concertos, still survive in our concert halls and the mass of which is bulky enough to have provided material for the two large volumes of Wyzewa and Saint-Foix.[1] Schubert and Mendelssohn alone are comparable to him in this.

Nevertheless, despite this voluminous output, he was not an infant prodigy. The works of his youth contain neither a *Gretchen am Spinnrade* nor an *Erlkönig* nor a *Midsummer Night's Dream* overture. It is true that before he was twelve he had composed seven symphonies. But the symphony in 1760 was a slight thing, hardly more than "drawing-room music", and these symphonies are merely the playthings of a clever, imitative child, of quick sensibility, able to incorporate in his work anything that strikes him in what he hears. Most of what he wrote before eighteen is not more valuable than the sonatinas which Beethoven, it is said, composed at twelve, and Beethoven has never been looked upon as a precocious composer. On the contrary, he is always contrasted, as one who ripened late and whose growth never stopped, with the precocious geniuses who

---

[1] *La jeunesse de Mozart* (1756–77), Paris, 1912. These volumes have been republished and with three later volumes constitute *Mozart: sa vie musicale et son œuvre*, by Saint-Foix (Paris, 1937–46).

gave all they had to give at twenty and produced nothing later. This contrast is partly valid when it is applied to Mendelssohn; it is less so of Schubert who produced real masterpieces at an early age but continued, nevertheless, to evolve all through his short life; it is quite invalid for Mozart who wrote nothing great before his journey to Paris at twenty-two, and who went on developing to the very end, to the *Magic Flute* and the *Requiem*.

Mozart wrote his first concerto in 1773 at the age of seventeen. At this time the period of youthful journeys was over and the young man, who had visited Vienna, France, Holland, England and Italy (the latter country thrice), was back in Salzburg. Until his final departure, in 1781, his only absence was to be his journey to Mannheim and Paris, during which he wrote no piano concertos. We can therefore look upon his six first, written between 1773 and 1780, as belonging to one period.

But they were composed at dates too widely separated for them to constitute a homogeneous group. The first is distinct from the five others and, indeed, from all those that follow it; the second, third and fourth, on the other hand, are alike and are his best examples of the *galant* concerto; the fifth and sixth, again, stand out from their neighbours and can be included with them in a chronological sense only. But in spite of these differences it is convenient to class these six Salzburg concertos together and we can thus distinguish four groups.

The first group comprises the works composed at Salzburg between 1773 and 1780.

The second is made up of the three concertos written at Vienna during the summer of 1782.

The third, by far the most important and interesting, includes the twelve masterpieces written in 1784, 1785 and 1786; and the fourth, an arbitrary group, will serve to bring into this classification the two last concertos, composed at nearly three years' interval in 1788 and 1791.

The concerto, therefore, covers all Mozart's active life fairly evenly from seventeen onwards, and preponderates and produces its finest fruits between the ages of twenty-eight and thirty.

The harpsichord concerto had existed for more than half a century when Mozart first attempted it. Of all the concerto forms it had been the last to appear. The concerto for solo violin was known before 1700 but it was only towards the first third of the 18th century that the harpsichord began to figure as a *concertante* instrument. It had tried at first to play, all alone, arrangements of concertos written for other instruments[1]; then it had attempted concertos written for itself but without orchestra and imitating alternations of tutti and solo, like Bach's Italian Concerto. Finally, it came to play in concertos with stringed instruments, and here, again, among the earliest examples we find works of Bach.

Hardly fifty years separate Bach's concertos from Mozart's. The growth of the form during this half-century takes place in three main "schools": those of Northern Germany, of Vienna, and of London, whose chief representatives are respectively Philip Emmanuel Bach, Wagenseil, and John Christian Bach. It is curious that two of these three should be sons of John Sebastian, and if one adds that another son of his, Wilhelm Friedmann, also cultivated the harpsichord concerto, it may be said that before Mozart the form was almost a fief of the Bach family. In any case, it is possible to outline its history and enumerate its principal features without leaving that family, and no composer earlier than Mozart produced such fine examples of it as John Sebastian and his three sons.

The North German school and those of Vienna and London consider the concerto from different angles. In the first, the roles of orchestra and solo are fairly equivalent; the two work and strive together on equal terms and one is not subordinated to the other. The Viennese concerto and John Christian's English concerto, on the other hand, assume the predominance of the solo, to whom the orchestra acts as an accompaniment and as a framework to enhance its dignity, just as a crowd of courtiers enhances the dignity of a monarch. The tutti is limited to announcing the solo's entry and, by playing the part of ritornellos in an operatic aria, to allowing the soloist a moment's rest and to avoiding monotony by affording contrast of tone.

Of these two conceptions, the first is indisputably the more fruitful whilst the second is the cause of the unfavourable criticisms of the concerto form to which we have alluded. The treatment implied by the Viennese conception is bound to be limited and to degenerate quickly into mere virtuosity. But the combination of orchestra and soloist, as instanced in the concertos of Philip Emmanuel Bach, affords developments as varied and as rich as those of a symphony. The second of these two forms was destined to triumph towards the

---

[1] Such as those of various Italian and German composers arranged by Bach.

end of the century at the time when the cembalo was giving way before the hammerklavier. But in its very triumph the Viennese concerto was transformed and found in Mozart one who was to unite the lightness, brilliance and melody of John Christian with the concertante style of his brother. *mozart united the quality of lightness, brilliance (J.C. Bach) w. C.P.E Bach's concertante style.*

The period which precedes that of Mozart shows a great diversity in the concerto form. The three-movement plan is not yet predominant, neither is the tradition of the *rondo finale*, and the structure of each movement varies from composer to composer. Together with the form with three or four separate movements, which is beginning to assert itself, we find also works with two of the movements—and sometimes all of them—linked; we find, also, the more frivolous concerto in two movements whence the andante—too serious for the *galant* taste—has been banished. In his magnificent work in C minor[1] Philip Emmanuel has left a one-movement concerto, where the sonata form is combined with one in four movements, the exposition being followed by an andante and a minuet, after which the beginning returns in the subdominant as a recapitulation, all four sections being continuous. The original cadenza contains quotations from all three sections, rather in the manner of the ninth symphony. The works of Philip Emmanuel, a musician who ranks immediately after the greatest in his century, besides great formal variety contain many unsuspected treasures. The andante of a certain concerto in D is an ancestor of that of Beethoven's fourth; solo and orchestra converse in majestic phrases, each one keeping its theme and character; the orchestra, in E minor, speaking sorrow and tragedy; the harpsichord, in major keys, seeking to console with its bright, serene tones.[2]

This formal variety in the concerto before Mozart is more a sign of fumbling and hesitation than of riches. Each composer is looking for his path, and the differences between one and the other come less from great personal originality than from the absence of a type capable of acting as a model. They are in the manner and not in the matter; they are the disorder of primitive and transitional periods. The age of Philip Emmanuel has, indeed, characters which belong to both kinds; it is at once primitive and transitional. It is a transition

---

[1] A. Wotquenne: *Carl Philip Emmanuel Bach: Thematisches Verzeichniss seiner Werke* (Breitkopf und Hartel, 1905); no. 43, IV; published in two pianos arrangement by Steingräber.

[2] Wotquenne no. 43, II; published by Steingräber.

between the polyphonic and harmonic periods of instrumental music, and as, at the same time, it turns out to have been a preparation for a great classical age, it also appears primitive. One finds scattered in it the elements that the age of Mozart and Beethoven were to organize and blend into a well-moulded whole; one sees it feeling its way and trying to grow in many directions before finding the right one.

Philip Emmanuel himself is not devoid of these hesitations. His work is one long search for novelty and the quest is not always successful. Too often one is conscious in him of a straining which takes us nowhere and leaves the spirit unsatisfied. His thought is too often but a roughcast which fails to shape and express itself. In his music one finds veins of gold that he has not known how to exploit, and whose existence he does not appear to have suspected; sometimes from his composition there arises a sense of incompleteness that saddens. This does not detract from the value of some very fine works in which he rises above the transitional character of his age.

Philip Emmanuel is the only great composer whose active life fills the middle of the century. His father, Handel, Rameau, all belong to the first half; Haydn and Mozart to the second; the work of Philip Emmanuel, comprised between 1733 (the date of his first concerto) and 1788 (that of his death) fills the interval between the two groups. He might have accomplished the task that fell to Mozart, consolidated the gains of the new music and built up an orderly construction with them—in a word, given it a classical character. His own genius rather than circumstances prevented him. His work is sometimes the outcome of intellectual vagrancy; he is too much on the look-out for what is new and unheard-of to cultivate what he has already acquired. It is as if novelty stood him in the stead of all other virtues, and he identified originality and beauty. His object is too negative—to rebel against his predecessors, against the contrapuntal school of which his father had been the last representative, to avoid all they had done, and to refuse to incorporate in his work anything of theirs instead of building upon them to raise his new structure. Hence, not only hesitation but also a certain dryness repels us at times and discourages us from going into him further. Yet a deeper knowledge of his music, especially of his concertos, shows how unjust it is to extend this condemnation to all he wrote, and a critical selection of his compositions would give him the place he deserves.

The talent of John Christian, John Sebastian Bach's youngest son, is much inferior to Philip Emmanuel's, but his concertos lead up to those of Mozart. He who used to say, "Philip Emmanuel lives to compose; I compose in order to live," confined himself within the limits imposed by a frivolous society. His public wanted music that amused it and dispelled tedium; it feared earnestness and depth, "the great commotions of the soul", and its taste banished from the galant style the minor mode that expressed these things. John Christian has left a few robust pieces like his C minor piano sonata, Op. 5, VI, but they are rare and one seldom or never finds their like among his concertos. His music is a succession of graceful and refined melodies; his allegros are amiable and playful; his andantes, tender, sometimes languishing and idyllic, reflect the pastoral dream that enchanted the society of 1780; his prestos are not devoid of vigour, but everything is cloaked with a mask of smiling impersonality which expresses superficially the society for which he was writing and does not give one a glimpse of the composer's own feeling. John Christian is a soulless Mozart, with the external qualities of grace and measure, but without the deeper beauties which have made Mozart live. And yet, with all his levity, he has a sense of shapeliness and construction more highly developed than that of Philip Emmanuel. Taste replaces genius with him; his ideas are trifling but they are elegantly presented; he has no gold mines but he makes the most of his tinsel. He arranges and orders his ideas with art, and the different parts of his movements are well balanced. John Christian's music is more plastic than his brother's; its lines more clearly defined, even though what they circumscribe be less significant; its gestures are more regular, even though they betray no strong emotion. It is effortless, and so is our grasp of it. A vigorous spirit may have been slumbering in him, and if he had reached old age he might have blossomed out as did Haydn in his later years. But he died in 1782, at forty-six, without having been more than a society musician.

Mozart's first concertos show his influence. John Christian is, perhaps, not the first to make the piano "sing" nor give the solo a theme of its own, but melodic passages and special solo themes recur so regularly in his concertos that they owe their origin partly to him, for an art form springs less from the man who first uses it than from him who uses it consistently and bequeathes it to the common inheritance. The formal changes he made in the piano concerto bring it to the point at which Mozart takes it up. Between his Op. 13 and the young Salzburger's first concertos, the differences are in the personality, not in the climate or the form.

2. General considerations on Mozart's piano concertos: Structure

WITH all their variety of form and content, Mozart's piano concertos keep throughout certain features which never change. They all have three movements: the first always begins with an orchestral prelude; the second is nearly always an andante; the third generally a rondo. It will therefore be convenient to study them briefly as a whole before turning to each one separately.

The first movement is in sonata form modified according to the concerto formula. This suffers no exception. The second is generally an andante or an andantino; only once[1] do we meet with an allegretto. Its form is often that of a sonata in two or three sections, with or without a *development*, but variations and rondos also occur. The finale is a rondo in two or three episodes; the only exceptions are the first concerto, where it is a *sonata*, and those in G and C minor which end with variations.

In the classical concerto, as in the symphony, the first allegro is the chief movement, the one which sets its mark upon the work, and on it one is tempted to found one's judgement of the concerto as a whole. It begins with a fairly long tutti, at the end of which the solo enters. This prelude, which serves as a first exposition and contains the movement's main subjects, finishes in the tonic. The solo's entry starts a new exposition, usually longer, which ends, as in a symphony, in the key of the dominant or the relative major. Apart from this double exposition, a concerto first movement follows sonata form; the *development* comes next, then the recapitulation.

Post-Beethovenian concertos generally bring in the soloist with the very first bars, and Mozart does this in K.271. Elsewhere, he lets the orchestra play alone in an introduction which lasts from thirty to sixty bars.

[1] In K.459.

One tends to imagine that the opening tutti of a classical concerto corresponds point by point with a sonata exposition, except that the second subject is given out in the tonic. This conception has the advantage of being clear and simple but it is true in only a few cases. To limit ourselves to Mozart, out of twenty-three piano concertos only thirteen conform to such a scheme; all the others show "irregularities". Sometimes the second subject is in the dominant[1]; sometimes it is absent[2]; sometimes the phrase which in the first tutti appeared to be the second subject does not reappear till the *development*[3] or the recapitulation,[4] whilst the true second subject appears first only in the solo. One cannot generalize further than to say that the opening tutti opens with the first subject and contains some of the ideas which are to return in the rest of the movement.

Let us follow it step by step.

It begins, we have said, with the first subject. Slow introductions are unknown in Mozart's concertos, as in the classical concerto in general.[5] His last concerto begins with a bar of accompaniment before the violins attack the first subject—a practice followed also in the G minor symphony.

Once given out, the first subject is sometimes repeated, either in part[6] or wholly.[7] Of variable length, it generally ends on the tonic and has a well-marked conclusion. In a few movements it loses itself in what follows and links up by developments with the second subject. The concertos of the great 1785-6 period show some examples of this, but in most, as in Mozart's work in general, the inspiration takes breath before going on. The clear articulation which this gives the work is not a personal quality; only, whereas with lesser composers it often makes the music disjointed and patchy, Mozart gives his successions of phrases an internal unity which is felt but cannot be analyzed, and binds together, with a single flow of emotion, themes whose outlines are very different. However changeful their shape and however clear-cut the separation between them, the continuity of the emotion is not broken; we grasp it intuitively when analysis reveals but a series of apparently independent subjects. On occasions, however, Mozart uses external devices of development comparable to those of Beethoven.

The first subject once completed, there begins the phrase or series

---

[1] K.413, 449.   [2] K.415, 459, 466.   [3] K.365, 503.   [4] K.450, 467, 482.

[5] There are two in Philip Emmanuel's concertos: Wotquenne's catalogue nos. 41 in E flat and 43, V in G.

[6] K.449.   [7] K.242, 271, 414, 456, 459, 466, 491.

of phrases leading to the next stage, which is generally the second
subject. They form a continuous chain of subsidiary themes, nearly
all destined to reappear at one moment or other of the movement
and to assert the unity of it by reiterating passages already heard.
They are the links that connect the different parts of the movement,
the mortar of the building whose stones are the main subjects. Though
only mortar, many of them have nearly as pronounced a personality
as the main subjects themselves. In the first tutti, they do not move
far from the tonic and are generally content to lead to a dominant
chord, whence the second subject, or its equivalent, brings us back at
once to the tonic. A few of them visit rapidly the regions of the dominant,[1] sometimes approached via its own dominant,[2] of the sub-dominant,[3] less often of the relative minor[4] or major.[5] The presence of
remote keys is uncommon; E flat bursting in suddenly in the tutti of the
G major concerto, after the second subject, is unique.

We have just said how uncertain is the appearance of the second
subject in the opening tutti. In K.449 it is, quite exceptionally, given
out entirely in the dominant. Often it is absent and is then replaced,
either by a chain of subsidiary subjects[6] or by one whose importance
gives it the appearance of being the true second subject but which we
are later surprised not to find in the solo exposition[7]; in K.503, this
"mock" second subject reappears in the *development* and takes it over
completely.

The second part of the tutti joins on to the conclusion with a chain
of subsidiary subjects—passing thoughts, devoid of independent
existence but prolonging the idea, if not the form, of the main
subjects. Yet Mozart, like all his age, tends towards formal unity,
towards the use of a single theme which permeates the whole movement, and twice, towards the end of his career as a concerto writer,[8]
he repeats the first subject after the second and draws new developments from it before concluding his exposition.

There only remains to conclude the first tutti and prepare the
solo's entry. Here again there is as much diversity as with the second
subject. The conclusion of the tutti includes often a regular third
subject, of greater consequence than the subsidiary ones, which may
be utilized in the course of the movement and which comes back
at the end. When the character of the work does not forbid it, it
is readily playful and more rhythmical than melodic.

[1] K.415, 453.   [2] K.449, 503.   [3] K.246.   [4] K.449.   [5] K.466.
[6] K.415, 459.   [7] K.450, 467, 482, 491, 503.   [8] K.467, 491.

textbook solo entries

The moment of the solo entry counts among the most impressive in the movement. In the typical concerto, such as one imagines all classical concertos to be, the orchestra concludes and is silent at the end of the tutti; the solo then gives out the first subject. This is the "regular" form, as we find it in Beethoven's C minor concerto. But Mozart, much more "irregular" than is usually believed, follows the conventional practice in only fourteen of his piano concertos; the nine others, among which are nearly all his greatest, prepare an original entry for the solo and vary it from work to work. [Sometimes orchestra and solo overlap, the piano beginning the first subject before the instruments have finished the conclusion;[1] sometimes the solo's impatience is betrayed by a trill before the orchestra has completed its phrase and it breaks forth into brilliant fireworks as soon as it can[2]; sometimes it asserts itself by giving out a new phrase, unknown to the orchestra, which will remain its exclusive property[3]; sometimes the orchestra itself repeats the first subject and the solo accompanies it[4]; and sometimes orchestra and solo share the new phrase which will bring back the first subject at the beginning of the second exposition.[5] [So many different ways, so many unforgettable instants; Mozart's solo entries, when he leaves the beaten track, are among the loveliest moments in his music.[6]

The soloist's appearance, however original, ends always by leading back to the first subject, generally given out by the orchestra.[7] The second exposition is in its structure much more like the exposition of a symphony than the first, but the effect it produces on the listener is quite different from that of a true exposition. It gives one more the impression of a development. Some of the chief ideas are already known; they have been heard in the tutti, and the second exposition seldom reproduces them without change. The true *development* itself is so short compared with the rest of the movement, especially in Mozart, that one hardly thinks of isolating it from what precedes. The result is that, for him who listens without worrying about forms or formulae, the real development begins with the solo entry, and instead of dividing a concerto first movement into four parts as do

[1] K.413.   [2] K.271, 450.   [3] K.415, 466, 482, 491.   [4] K.467.   [5] K.503.

[6] We are thinking also of the shadowy and suggestive entry of the solo in the A major violin concerto, surely one of the most beautiful, and the first appearance of the solo violin and viola, hovering "above the tumult", in the *Sinfonia Concertante*.

[7] But in K.271, orchestra and solo give it out together, and in K.450 the solo, not content with a particularly long and brilliant introduction, attacks the theme alone without tolerating any intervention from the tutti.

the textbooks, it would be more sensible to keep a threefold division, as for the sonata and the symphony: tutti exposition, *development* (including the solo exposition and the *development* in the textbook sense), and recapitulation.

The second exposition[1] is therefore really the beginning of the development. Some themes, it is true, which we have not yet heard will appear in it; the solo's own subject, for instance, and sometimes the second subject; but the greater part of them are already familiar. The first subject we know; the concluding subject, heard at the end of the tutti, comes back at the end of the second exposition in about half the concertos, and several subsidiary themes are common to both expositions. Most of the thematic material has been presented by the tutti and comes back, not to be "expounded" any longer, but "developed", in this first solo.

The second section of the allegro, the longest and most interesting, comprises two landmarks which, however diverse the concertos, are found in all of them. They are the appearance of the second subject and the return of the tutti which concludes this part and leads to the so-called *development* section.[2] These two stages are constant; it is the intervening part that changes from work to work.

The piano's appearance settles the character of the composition. The opening tutti might have announced a symphony, but with the soloist's entry, however brilliant the orchestral part, the interest shifts and the orchestra henceforward takes second place. In vain does it start the first subject; the soloist nearly always takes it away[3] and forges ahead alone, or almost alone, through scales and arpeggios. From these bravura passages, occasionally interrupted by the band, there arise by degrees melodic ideas, subsidiary subjects already heard or new ones. Sometimes an echo of the concluding subject returns to link up the second exposition with the first; sometimes, too, the solo's special subject follows immediately on the first one. But generally, once the first outburst of the solo has calmed down, the orchestra intervenes with more authority, recalling fragments of ritornelli, repeating and altering the last phrases of the solo, starting

---

[1] Or first Solo.

[2] Or second solo.

[3] K.415 is an exception; after the exposition of the first subject by the tutti, beneath a solo trill, the piano follows completely new paths and leaves the first subject to one side.

new passages. Finally the agitation dies down altogether and from out of the confusion arises an independent subject, either the second strain of the opening tutti, or, more often, a new idea that the soloist gives out alone and that the orchestra will not seek to take from him. It is the solo subject which may just possibly deceive us and pass as the main second subject, especially as it often appears in the dominant.

To John Christian Bach has been attributed the notion of giving the solo instrument a theme which belongs to it alone. If he did not invent the device, he is probably the first to make a constant use of it. Mozart took it from him, but he gave the theme a more personal character and made it more prominent. With him, it really characterizes the solo instrument: instead of being, as with John Christian, a little ephemeral tune, it generally possesses an individual outline which distinguishes it from the two other main subjects and enhances the piano part by entrusting it with the expression of something all its own. One thinks of the witty, syncopated theme of the concerto in G, of the *minor* ones of K.467 and 482, and of the spacious subject of K.503.

The second subject marks a halt in the struggle between solo and tutti. The *galant* concerto, which had reduced the orchestra to being mere accompaniment, bestowed on the piano exclusively the privilege of announcing it, and the tutti did not raise its head whilst the solo pursued its triumphal progress towards the dominant trill which closes this part of the movement. Mozart, too, had begun that way. But Mozart, it cannot be repeated too often, started from the narrow conception of the *galant* concerto and raised the genre little by little to the level of those reputed "serious" by associating the tuttis with the fate of the work and giving them a symphonic character. If his first attempts conform still to the *galant* formula, the concertos of his maturity free themselves altogether from it. Its lazy ways soon cease to satisfy him and already in his second concerto he gives the orchestra a part in the exposition of the second subject. In his Viennese period nearly all his concertos do likewise. Of the nine where the tutti is left out at this point, six are earlier than 1783. On the other hand, when later he still gives the piano the duty of announcing the subject, the orchestra, in every case but one, takes it up again to the answering or the accompaniment of the solo instrument. In some of the 1784-6 concertos, we hear the subject actually given out first by the orchestra, and taken up by the solo only when the tutti has done with it. This happens in the flashing concerto in D, K.451,[1] among others, in the C minor, and in the last, in B flat. The equality between orchestra and solo which is at the base of the symphonic conception of the concerto, the "emancipation of the orchestra" once attributed to Beethoven, is already an accomplished fact with Mozart.

The end of the solo exposition which heaves in sight once the second subject is passed varies from one concerto to the next.[2] After the second subject a solo passage—or a succession of them—of rising strength and strain culminates in a triumphal affirmation of the dominant or relative major and in the customary trill; after which the piano rests, for a few moments, upon its laurels.

Thereupon the tutti enters with long-pent-up vigour. In about half the concertos, it brings back the concluding subject. Others tighten even more firmly the bonds of the movement and assert its unity still further by bringing back, not only the conclusion but also the first subject,[3] a survival of an earlier age when each part of the movement began with it. When neither concluding nor first subject is heard, the orchestra recalls a few subsidiary themes. It does not always enjoy a clear field, for the piano sometimes intervenes early and hastens on the second solo.

The section from here to the recapitulation bears the name of *development* by analogy with that of the symphony and sonata. In reality, five concertos only[4] offer *developments* containing material taken from the body of the exposition, and of these K.503 and 595 alone really develop this material. The work for two pianos, K.365, after a new passage, recalls a theme of the first tutti (the mock second subject); in the D minor, this section begins with the tragic lament which the piano had uttered on its first appearance; then, during the grand, stormy solo which follows, the orchestra punctuates the strong beats with a triplet motif taken from the first subject, and that is all that it owes to the rest of the work. K.503 builds its whole *development* on its mock second subject, a march theme which the opening tutti had given out, and develops it in a masterly way, but it builds it upon this theme alone and the many other ideas already expressed

---

[1] "Soldierly", is Tovey's epithet for it.

[2] The C minor concerto musters three distinct main subjects; the second and third correspond to the ordinary second subject and both are in the relative major. In the recapitulation they reappear in the tonic in inverse order.

[3] K.467, 491.

[4] K.271, 365, 466, 503, 595.

are left aside. K.595 confines itself to the first subject, which it varies and breaks up and treats contrapuntally under a running piano commentary. In the other concertos, the development is rather a fantasia, an improvisation, than a logical working out, and only the fact that it sometimes begins by playing with the last phrase of the exposition connects it with the rest of the concerto.

The relation between solo and tutti has made the repetition of material in the exposition specially impressive and characteristic, and the recapitulation and coda will make it still more so; and therefore the *development* needs to be more simple and more contrasted than it would be in a symphony or sonata, apart from the enormous difficulties of balancing solo against tutti in a *development* on ordinary lines. Accordingly, we find that in the finest classical concertos there is hardly an exception to the rule that the *development* is either based on the least weighty of the themes of the exposition, or on one that the solo had omitted (a most brilliant device of Mozart's), or it transforms the themes almost beyond recognition, or it has much episodic matter.[1]

It must, moreover, be owned that in Mozart as a whole the *development* ill deserves its name. True, there are works where he conceives it as do Philip Emmanuel Bach, Haydn and Beethoven. In addition to the concertos mentioned, nine out of ten of the "great" quartets, the four great quintets, the piano allegro in F (K.533), the string trio in E flat (K.563), and the four last symphonies afford examples of *developments* worthy of the name. But these are only some twenty instances against more than sixty sonata form movements of his Viennese period which show nothing of the sort.

Most often, Mozart looks upon the *development* as a transition. It is a return towards the tonic, the first subject and the recapitulation, rather than an autonomous section of the movement. In many cases it would be fair to say that the Mozartian sonata form is made up of two symmetrical parts, one of which repeats the other, joined by a transition passage or bridge. The first movement of the E flat serenade (K.375), for wind instruments, shows an extreme case of this. The *development* is limited to a few chords and a fragment of theme borrowed from the exposition which brings in at once the first subject and the reprise. In certain andantes, the device is pushed even further and the middle section drops out completely. The movement is then composed of two similar halves of which the second repeats the first with a few alterations of detail. In fact, Mozart's first movements belong to the tradition of the *da capo*

---

[1] D. Tovey, from an unpublished programme note.

aria rather than to that of really ternary movements like those of Philip Emmanuel and Haydn.

But though the *development* be brief, it often holds the finest bars of the work. The darkest hours come before dawn and Mozart's inspiration reaches its highest peak of sombre power in the bars just before the reprise. They are the critical moment, the climax of the movement; they reveal the maximum of intensity reached by the flow that carries it on. The most joyous and most serene allegros wear at this moment a melancholy or even tragic air; chromaticisms and *sforzandos* come piling up and the tempest appears to reach its highest point, despair seems to be complete, when suddenly the veil is torn aside and the radiant dawn of the first subject announces the recapitulation. One could quote numberless examples: the first movement of the violin sonata in E flat (K.380) where piano and violin chords follow on each other like thunder on lightning and make one think of Beethoven's Op. 111; the string trio, with its pathetic *minor* scales; and the quintet in C, one of Mozart's most majestic *developments*, where, after the sinister rising scales of the third subject and the poignant cries of the second, transposed into the minor, the cloud is riven and the great peaceful line of the opening theme appears on the landscape. One remembers also the reprise in the clarinet quintet: the arpeggios of the clarinet, crossed by the ascending and descending strings, hurrying ever more restlessly, ever more feverishly, sinking ever deeper into the minor; then, when the agitation reaches its highest point, suddenly holding their peace before the suave presence of the returning main theme. In the concertos themselves, those in D minor, C minor, A (K.488) and C (K.503; rondo) speak here in threatening tones which grip the soul like the forebodings of disaster.

The reprise with Mozart is therefore often a deliverance; it is never, as with Beethoven, a transfiguration. After the increased passion, accompanied by sorrow and anguish, of the end of the *development*, the return of the tonic and of the first subject relieves one like an arrival in port after a stormy passage. The reappearance of the first theme is a return to the fold, which closes a painful exploring of unknown lands; on seeing it one knows oneself to be on a friendly shore. With Beethoven it is not quite the same. The theme is unchanged but its presentation is often different. What a triumph in his violin concerto for the first subject, so retiring, so shy at first, with its almost inaudible drum taps, when the recapitulation brings it back *fortissimo* and the drums have become brass!

Such apotheoses are unknown in Mozart. And in his minor key

works the reprise is neither apotheosis nor even deliverance, but just relapse. The *development* of the G minor quintet and symphony sought to cast off the load of anguish which oppressed the work; weary, vanquished by the struggle, they fall back, and with the implacable return of the first subject the movement resigns itself to its fate and follows despairing the road along which it is driven.

One cannot reproach the concertos, as one can some of Mozart's works, with not varying their recapitulations. In his lesser pieces more particularly, the last section sometimes repeats almost note for note the first; it avoids merely passing into the dominant and it finishes, as it began, in the tonic.[1] That was no doubt an advantage when the sonata was a new and unfamiliar form. To-day, we notice only too easily the monotony of the procedure. No group of Mozart's works is more free from it than his concertos. Even the most bloodless, the most *galant*, vary the re-exposition, either by omitting themes already heard, or by introducing themes heard in the opening tutti, but not since, or by changing the order in which these themes appear and making solos and tuttis alternate. The concerto as a genre is much less a prey to the monotony of recapitulations than the sonata and the symphony; the variety is much easier to obtain; and if one allows that the object of literal repetition is to make it simpler for the audience to understand the new form, there is less risk of such variety confusing the listener here than elsewhere.

In a general way, Mozart cuts down very much the bravura passages in this part of the movement and here the 19th century concerto writers have followed him. The work hastens towards its climax and tolerates with difficulty what is not essential. Collaboration, too, becomes closer between solo and tutti. The solo, after the strain of the *development*, is somewhat exhausted and shows itself more accommodating towards its adversary, leaving it nearly always the first subject and only speaking again when this is complete. The most exquisite combinations of piano and orchestra are met with here, as in the E flat (K.482) where piano and first violins converse in phrases that interplay as if they were canons. And finally, we meet again the various themes which have played an outstanding part in the movement. The true and the mock second subjects jostle and link up, affirming their kinship;[2] the more characteristic of the subsidiary themes appear also, throwing light upon each other and

---

[1] Here again Mozart's sonata form is akin to the *da capo* aria.
[2] K.450, 482, 503.

acquiring their full significance. Mozart loves especially to keep back for this moment some subsidiary motif which had been given out in the opening tutti and not heard since.[1] In fact, this third solo is the meeting place of the sometimes very diverse elements that had made up the two expositions, and it is delightful to speculate concerning the manner in which this meeting will be managed. At length the movement reaches the awaited pause where begins the cadenza which Mozart never omits in his piano concertos. The conclusion is sometimes perfunctory, as in the D major (K.537), sometimes the ending of the opening tutti is repeated, as in the D minor where the voice of the orchestra, pathetic and sombre, re- sounds long after the solo has been silent; sometimes, too, a new conclusion follows the last trill of the cadenza, as in K.467. This, the most interesting, is also the rarest kind of ending.

Here should come the coda. Less numerous and less extensive than Beethoven's, fine codas are not uncommon in Mozart, especi- ally in works in a minor key. The opening allegros of the three great G minors, quartet, quintet and symphony, sum up in their codas, with passionate conciseness, the main thought of the movement; the C minor sonata likewise. The quartets in D minor, B flat and F, the E flat quintet, also crown their first movements with codas which epitomize all that has gone before; the C major quintet, before repeating the conclusion which had already served in the exposition, inserts a development full of mystery. The quintet in D begins over again the slow introduction which had opened the work, then inter- rupts it and, returning to a few bars of the allegro, ends abruptly on this joyful note. The sonata form finales of several quartets reach also great heights in their codas. The queen of all these perorations is, of course, that of the *Jupiter* symphony, incorrectly called Fugue, where the first subject returns inverted, the three chief themes re- appear and are given out simultaneously, with a skill and a vigour equal to those in the well-known passage of the *Meistersinger* overture but with that lightness and grace which only Mozart can ally with strength and intensity.

Mozart never enriched his concertos with such great perorations. The coda of the first movement of the C minor is the only example one can compare with the G minor quintet and symphony. The piano's re-entry right at the very end, very rare with him, closes this movement of storms and darkness and deepens still further the

---

[1] K.246, 413, 414, 415, 449, 450, 453, 595.

mysterious twilight which envelops it. In general, the endings of his concerto allegros contain nothing that has not already been heard and do not transform elements already familiar. They are not the equals of the much more original endings of the rondos.

We so seldom hear to-day works of the *galant* age other than those of Mozart and Haydn that it is difficult for us to admire with what perfection Mozart has embodied his thought in the form imposed by the æsthetic conventions of the time. To understand a great creative genius, one should be familiar with the average work of his period and thus be able to compare him with his inferiors, recognize the points of contact between them and measure the distance that separates them. Only thus can one eliminate what is of the time and reach to what is personal in a work.

It is for lack of knowing Mozart's lesser contemporaries that even an enlightened public credits him with features which are in no wise his own. The articulated form, the sections marked off by noisy cadences, the transitions so simple and swift as to appear rudimentary, all these belong to the *galant* style; Mozart should be neither praised nor blamed for them. What belongs to him is the craft with which he used these forms that were everyone's to express his thought without the one suffering by contact with the other.

He took over and made use of the current forms: sonata, variations, rondos, with such ease that if he had had to invent his own forms he would hardly have been able to find any better suited to his thought. The forms of the classical sonata are the Mozartian ones *par excellence*; he seldom uses others in his first movements. With him, they take on their full significance and answer, not only to a structural need, but to the claims of the feeling which quickens the work. The adaptation of the personal matter to the classical form is absolute, to such an extent that one is never conscious in his best work, as one is with lesser composers of the time, that certain themes come back at certain points, that such a development takes place at such a place, not because the composer felt the need for it but because his plan, laid down beforehand, required it of him.

Even in Mozart's lesser works, the slow movement remains generally above the level of a purely formal excellence. Never more than here does he show to what extent his self-expression complies with the form which the conventions of the age offer him. Seldom, under the clothing of the movement, does one feel the skeleton which supports it; seldom does one's attention settle more on the form than on the feeling. (We speak, of course, of the ordinary musical person, not of the critic whose habits lead him to look for the structure before all else in a work.) It may happen to us, in some of his weaker allegros and rondos, to be aware of the symmetry and regularity of a passage and to be more impressed with these features than with the thought; this seldom happens in an andante; inspiration and technique, lyricism and construction blend with such unity that nothing takes away our attention from the beauty of the music itself.

The concertos would not deserve in his work the highly representative place they occupy were not their andantes the equals of the best of those in his quartets and symphonies. No group of movements in his work surpasses them in variety. It is difficult to class movements according to their content and the result of such a classification risks being somewhat arbitrary; content escapes definition and it is only approximately that one can describe the general character of a movement. One feels well enough that some are gay, some sad, but the epithets that one can bestow thus are soon exhausted and when one has called a piece "joyful, melancholy, brilliant, amiable, vigorous, majestic, delicate", one is at the end of the list; to go any further is to fall into fancifulness.

And yet we feel that certain movements are akin to each other, that there are "families of movements" just as there are "families of minds". They are akin in the work of the same composer; they are also akin from one composer to another. This kinship of movements is really but one aspect of the kinship between the composers themselves. Just as between father and son, brother and sister, we recognize a family likeness difficult to define, so between works and composers we notice affinities which defy a precise analysis but are nevertheless indisputable.

The kinship which we notice between works of different composers is even more recognizable between works of the same man. Thus it is that Mozart's andantes, despite their richness and their diversity, can with a few exceptions be brought under four or five heads which we may label, for convenience, the *galant* andante, the "dream", the "meditation"; the "singing" andante or romance; the "tragic" or "dramatic" andante.

No one will be taken in by this classification to the extent of thinking it absolute, but it can help us to grasp more easily as a whole these slow movements into which Mozart has poured such precious music. Every classification is, by its very nature, approximate and arbitrary, especially when it deals with something as indefinable as the content of music. Let no one accuse us of seeking to break the most poetic of musicians upon a Procrustean bed! We only propose this division as a method which will lead us in the long run to a truer and finer understanding. Approximate and loose though it be, it is still too rigid to embrace all Mozart, and some of his best known andantes are impossible to fit into one or other of its categories.

With these strictures, and provided one interprets freely the terms we use as labels, we think that most of his movements justify this division.

The *galant* slow movements are those which belong least to their author. The taste of the time is more obvious in them than the personality of Mozart. Several of them might be signed John Christian Bach and, were it not for external evidence, one would have difficulty in fixing their authorship. They possess a certain sensual, languorous or idyllic charm which does not survive frequent hearing. They were the delight of an audience which would bear with a little emotion on condition it was neither strong nor personal and did not demand any prolonged concentration. Only at distant points does some deep beauty reveal the master's soul. This kind of andante is naturally found most often during his Salzburg period when he subordinated his originality to the requirements of his public with the greatest severity for himself and the greatest indulgence for his listeners. This was due, not only to his youth (he was but twenty-five when he left the town for good) but to his official position at the archbishop's court which obliged him to conform to his patron's tastes.

The *galant* part of his work is not much known and that is natural. Were it not for the nine lives of his sonatas which owe their longevity less to the beauty of a few of them than to their didactic qualities, nothing of it would be familiar to-day to the ordinary public. To find a *galant* andante known to everyone, it is to them one has to turn: to those, for instance, of the violin sonatas in C (K.296) and B flat (K.378). The famous and verbose *Haffner Serenade*, K.250, which dates from his twenty-first year and appears sometimes on our concert programmes, affords one of the best specimens of a *galant* slow movement: the andante in A, not undignified, with moments of spriteliness and even wit, but without much personality.

The period par excellence of these movements is the Salzburg one but they occur all through his life. The very year of the great symphonies saw the composition, during the summer when they were written, of two sonatinas, for piano in C (K.545) and violin in F (K.547). Their andantinos are pure *galant* toys, the last he was to produce. But at this stage he could no longer be only *galant* and even in these trifles the presence of the composer of the *Jupiter* is felt.

Long before this, the *galant* andante had undergone a transformation. The true *galant* slow movement was tender but lacked flame. Little by little, Mozart introduced into it his own personality. The first signs of this change are seen early. Already several years before he left for Paris, certain andantes and adagios had thrown off their pink and blue silk ribbons and were quite personal.[1] They were exceptional at the time, but as his life at Salzburg drew to its end personal accents became louder and more frequent, and we are thus led gradually towards the type of andante which, during his Viennese period, replaces almost entirely the movement of his youth. The andantino of the flute and harp concerto is a witness of this transformation. The work dates from 1778, the year he spent in Paris, that is, the decisive period in his career and his artistic growth. Its general appearance is that of a *galant* piece, with a slightly dreamy tenderness, a beribboned softness; but certain features are thoroughly Mozartian. It marks the passage from the impersonal idyll to the more individual *romance* of his maturer years.

It is the *romance* which corresponds to the *galant* andante in his work after 1780. He used neither the term nor the form before he went to Paris and the form does not appear regularly till his break with the archbishop had ensured his artistic freedom. He first gives the name to a slow movement in 1781, in his B flat serenade for wind instruments (K.361), and from this moment *romances* are more and more frequent and *galant* andantes fewer and fewer. The last piano concerto, the E flat quintet, both have *romances*;[2] at the end of his life's work, he finds in it his favourite type.

It is a far cry from the *galant* slow movement of his adolescence to the *romance* of his greatest period. And yet the descent is clear. The *romance* of his second horn concerto, the andantino of the E flat piano concerto (K.449) are still quite close to the *galant* style, and the personal accent is as yet not very pronounced. But soon, to the colourless sweetness of the fashionable *romance* there is added a more pungent feeling, tones of passing sadness, and the sweetness itself becomes more quivering; we feel in it that "passionate tranquillity"

---

[1] We are thinking especially of the C minor andantes of the E flat symphony (K.184), and the quartet in C (K.157).

[2] The title is not used in these movements but they are none the less clearly *romances*.

which is one of his most personal traits. [At the time of his master-pieces, from 1784 to his death, all his *romances* disclose now and again these depths of melancholy which his exuberant joy sometimes covers up but never fills.] The *romance* of the C minor concerto is so calm outwardly, with the broad and peaceful lines of its refrain, but how pleading are the strains of its episodes! The refrain of the *romance* in the *Coronation* concerto (K.537) is serene, too; but, once it is complete, the orchestra adds a phrase of heart-rending yearning. The *romance* of the last concerto is one long farewell, poignant yet resigned; and once at least a *romance* whose peace seemed unshakable breaks forth in its middle portion into tragic cries: we refer to that of the D minor concerto.

The transition from his slender *galant* andantes to the *romances* of his last years leads us from the imitative labour of his childhood to the awakening of his personality and the full blossoming of the end of his life. But it must not be thought that the term *galant* applies to everything Mozart wrote before the urge of his genius made him throw off the yoke of contemporary conventions. There is another group of slow movements which goes back to his years of childhood and into which he cast all the riches which the domination of an im-personal taste kept out of his sonata movements and rondos. It is that of his "dream" andantes. This title is but a label and we do not defend it on condition a better one is found. The name "noc-turne" would perhaps express the limpidity, as penetrating as moon-light, of certain andantes and adagios, but the word is linked to Chopin and might suggest between these movements and the Roman-tic composer a kinship which occurs but seldom.

The "dream" belongs to Mozart's childhood and the early part of his maturity. After giving of its best in the fine andante of K.467 it disappears. It is, therefore, mainly a youthful form and if the best example dates from 1785, the most numerous and most characteristic belong to Salzburg. The "dream" andantes of the violin concertos, of the G major especially, express best the ideal that Mozart sought to render in it, for that of K.467 mingles with the dreaming certain dramatic strains that carry us away from it and bring the movement nearer the *romance* and the "tragic" andante.

The true "dream" does not imply any strong emotion; it does not exclude passion, but the exquisite fancy of a fresh and rich nature is its chief character· True, the "dreams" of Mozart's early years in Vienna are deeper and richer than those of the Salzburg concertos, but fancy predominates over melancholy and when melancholy speaks it is not with a tragic voice. They are inspired by a spirit of fairyland, too far removed from reality to know sorrow. Their form is often that of a long, winding melody which cannot be broken up into phrases and follows on almost uninterruptedly from one end to the other, and Mozart's rhythms are found here at their freest.

Just as the *galant* andante gave way before the *romance*, so the "dream", by growing deeper and richer, loses a little of its fancy and unreality and becomes the "meditation" of riper years. The transition is even more gradual than with the *galant* slow movement. Some andantes, like those of the quartet in C or the *Prague* symphony could be classed in either group and already that of the concerto for three pianos, with the quivering motion of its *development*, announces a more concentrated vision than that of a mere "dream". The truth is that the two groups are closely related and if some works belong clearly to one or the other, like the adagio of the G major violin concerto, which is a "dream", or that of the D major quintet, which is a "meditation", many others mingle too intimately "dreaming" with "meditation" and "recollection" for one to label them without hesitation. It is better to recognize the mixed character of such movements, which nearly all date from Mozart's first years in Vienna, whereas the "dreams", pure and simple, come from his Salzburg time and the "meditations" from the years later than 1782 and especially 1785.

The "meditative" second movement, which is more often an adagio than an andante, is ordinarily less purely melodic than the "dream" and the writing is richer and given to polyphony. It is in his string quintets, that genre so peculiarly his, where few have followed him and none have excelled him, that we find his biggest and most searching adagios—the largest, too, both in dimensions and inspiration. The magnificent polyphonic adagio of the G minor quintet and the still more complex adagio of the quintet in D, the more vocal one of the quintet in C, with its hymn-like line, that of the quartet in D (K.499) contain what is most exalted in his thought, the firmest product of his craft, and it is to them, and to the andante of the concerto K.503, that we would refer those who are surprised that we dare place the amiable Salzburger on the same plane as Bach and Beethoven.

The four groups of andantes whose chief characters we have just been sketching correspond to fairly precise periods in his life: the *galant* one and the "dream" to his childhood and adolescence; the *romance* and "meditation" to his maturity. There is a fifth group the works of which spread out irregularly over most of his life: that of the "tragic" or "dramatic" andantes.

Mozart's slow movements in minor keys are distinctive enough to be set apart from the rest of his work. We have called them indifferently "tragic" or "dramatic" and both names distinguish them from his other slow movements. It may seem useless to speak of "drama" to distinguish one composition of his from another, since his whole work is habitually looked upon as dramatic. But this quality is most apparent in his allegros. His andantes show it much less. He has to be impelled by a keen and sorrowful inspiration to give them a dramatic character. Their themes appear, then, to be sung by ideal voices and to await words. All his minor key andantes are in this sense dramatic, whether they adopt the form of the variation, the sonata or the rondo. There are not many of them; a dozen between 1777 and his death, but nearly all are among his finest slow movements. Like his contemporaries, he uses the minor mode little, but when he does it is always to compose a masterpiece. His *minor* works occupy, amongst his finest works, a place quite out of proportion to their number, some twelve or so during his Viennese period, and yet these twelve contain a good part of the compositions that have made him live. And so with his andantes, when one thinks of the greatest, there come first to mind the D minor variations of the violin sonata in F (K.377), the G minor andante of that in E flat (K.380), the G minor variations and the F sharp minor *Siciliana* of the concertos in B flat (K.450) and A (K.488) and the C minor andantino of the *Sinfonia Concertante* (K.364) and C minor andante of the concerto in E flat (K.482).

His finest minor key andantes begin with that of the concerto K.271, in 1777, and finish with the prelude and fugue for string quartet (1788)[1] and the adagio of the first organ fantasia in 1790, but already several years before 1788 they become rare and the last work in sonata form where one is found is the A major concerto (K.488) which belongs to the early spring of 1786. The sadness is so transfigured in them that they leave no feeling of depression or disheartenment, but rather comfort and strengthen us as much as his most exuberant allegros. The beauty first glimpsed, then reached, through tears, is of such brightness that the listener is spell-bound and forgets the bitterness, forgets the suffering whence the movement sprang. These sorrows, which are nevertheless a young man's

---

[1] The fugue, intended originally for two pianos, had been composed in 1783.

sorrows, since Mozart was only thirty when he ceased composing "tragic" andantes, are rich and beautiful with all the strength of his throbbing, vital nature.\

The piano concertos offer some of the best examples of these five kinds of slow movements.   Mozart has left no more typical instances of *galant* andantes than the second movements of K.413 and 415. The *romance* produces some of its finest examples in the concertos in D minor, C minor and B flat, K.595. The "dream" of his twenty summers, which sweetens the hard brightness of many of his drawing-room works, is met with in the first concerto, in those for three and for two pianos, and in two of the "great" period, K.451 and 467. The "meditation" which succeeds the "dream" is found four times: in 1782, with K.414, one of its earliest appearances; in 1784, with the hymn-like variations of K.450 and the more tormented andante of K.453; and a last time with the superb andante in F, of K.503, one of the most spacious that he ever wrote. \

Hitherto, we have seen that the piano concertos represent as well as any other group the chief tendencies of his genius.   But when we come to his "tragic" andantes, we find they are almost the only ones at the period of his maturity, to reflect this side of it.   It is remarkable that from his first year in Vienna onward, from the time when his genius takes possession of itself, minor key andantes are rare in his chamber music and vanish completely from his symphonies.   Apart from the moving adagio for piano in B minor, an isolated piece, in 1788, and the adagio (introduction and conclusion) of the first organ fantasia, in 1790, and some other movements of lesser importance[1] the only ones are those of his piano concertos.   At earlier periods, minor key andantes had been commoner, but even then the best were those of K.271 and of the *Sinfonia Concertante*.   And after 1781, the year of his finest violin sonatas, two of which contain splendid minor slow movements (K.377 and 380), the expression of the shade of tragic emotion which needs a slow *tempo* for its embodiment is reserved throughout the greatest period of his creative life for the piano concertos.   There must we seek the dark and saddened Mozart of the slow movements.   What corresponds in his andantes to the

---

[1] Preludes for string quartet: K.546 in C minor, and for string trio: K.E. 404a, in F, G and D minor; a rather insignificant adagio in C minor, K.617, the first movement of the quintet for harmonica, flute, hautboy, viola and 'cello (1791).

allegros of the C minor serenade, of the G minor quintet and symphony is found in his concertos and there only.

It is tempting to look in Mozart's andantes for a relation between the nature of the emotion and the form used. If one could say, for instance, that "meditations" always adopt sonata form, how satisfying it would be for a systematic mind! Waste of effort! Such a relation does not exist, at least in the andantes. One can, it is true, discover something like it in certain allegros; some of them, inspired by the same emotion, show likenesses of form; thus, the *developments* of passionate *allegros assai* in minor keys tend to be more concise than others:[1] but in his slow movements such a parallel between form and matter is impossible to establish. The "singing" movements called *romances* are often rondos, but that is a merely outward likeness due obviously to the fact that the rondo is the most vocal of forms and that the *romance*, as its name implies, recalls an actual song. We must therefore resign ourselves to keeping separate matter and manner.

Mozart never seeks those contrasts of key between movements of which Philip Emmanuel and Haydn are fond and which have become almost obligatory since Beethoven. His second movements are generally in the sub-dominant. The quartet in G has its andante in C, the *Jupiter* symphony, in C, has its andante in F. Exceptions are negligible. When they exist, the sub-dominant has more than three accidentals and Mozart does not like heavy key-signatures. Four sharps or flats are rare with him; five one never finds save for an instant in the *minores* of a few variations or of minuets in B or E flat. Rather than write four accidentals in the signature, he prefers to give up the sub-dominant and have recourse to the dominant; he does it here and there in his E flat works, among them two of the four piano concertos written in that key, K.365 and 449. At other times he uses the relative minor (*Sinfonia Concertante*); more seldom, the relative minor of the dominant (quartet in F, K.158; violin sonata in E flat, K.380). Those works whose key is minor generally pass into the relative major in their slow movements.[2] Finally, once or twice, perhaps as an archaism, he retains the same key in all the movements. But these exceptions do not affect more than a third of his andantes.

---

[1] See the C minor sonata, the violin sonata in G, K.379 (second movement) and the G minor quintet.

[2] The D minor concerto is an exception; its *romance* is in B flat, the sub-dominant of the relative major.

The structure, on the other hand, is varied. For his first movements, he uses almost exclusively sonata form, occasionally replaced by variations in his Parisian works.[1] But for his andantes he has at his disposal several models, especially the variation which fits all movements, the rondo, another universal form, and the sonata whose ample and majestic outlines suit perfectly the meditative phrases of an andante or an adagio. This latter is sometimes in two sections, the *development* being absent, sometimes in three. Finally, several andantes follow no fixed scheme.

He did not use these moulds indifferently at all periods. He turned to the *sonata* in two sections after 1787. The *sonata* in three was common at the beginning and end of his life, rarer between 1783 and 1789. The rondo, which is found from time to time in the works of his youth, such as the early D minor quartet, K.173, did not become common till 1783.

The piano concertos prefer the three section *sonata*; out of twenty-three, eight make use of it, all of them belonging to the later half. The two section *sonata* is nearly as popular; five concertos at different periods use it. Two andantes in variation form belong to 1784 and two others of irregular plan, in 1784 and 1785, are modifications, one of the rondo, the other of the *sonata*.

The three section *sonata* appears in the first concerto and vanishes in 1786 after the A major, K.488; it covers therefore almost all Mozart's career as a concerto writer and it may be considered as the typical andante of his concertos. It goes with broad and ample themes which unfold slowly and melt one into the other. The sonata form is less clearly articulated than in the allegro; its divisions are less sharply distinguished; the elements of its structure less recognizable. Its texture recalls rather those masses of cement in which the Romans buried bricks and rubble and which form a compact and inseparable whole. It is, one might say, more monolithic than in the allegro. This is one feature. The aspect of the second section is another. This part is hardly ever a real development, recalling themes from the earlier part. Most of the time it is but a transition destined to lead us back to the beginning and sometimes its reduced dimensions make us hesitate to consider it as a separate section.

When the andante of a concerto is a three section *sonata*, the

---

[1] Sonata in A, K.331; quartet in A for flute and strings, K.298, a work in a French form, though composed in Vienna in 1787 (cf. Saint-Foix, op. cit., IV, 307).

movement nearly always begins with a tutti introduction, which contains the first member of the phrase. That of K.488, the structure of which is rather different from the others, is the only one to begin directly with the solo. Sometimes this introduction is of the briefest and only sketches the beginning of what will become the solo[1]; sometimes, and more often, the two themes are given out, as in the tutti of an allegro.[2] As for the phrase which will conclude the movement, it appears sometimes thrice.[3] In K.414 it also accounts for the *development*. Elsewhere it is content with two appearances, at the end of the tutti and of the movement[4] or at the end of the first solo and of the movement[5]; or it may appear at the end of the movement only.[6]

The two section *sonata* is a less familiar form. Mozart is the only great classic who has made much use of it; Haydn and Beethoven attached great importance to the *development* and one can understand that a form whence that section was absent did not attract them. But Mozart, as we know, lingered little over his *developments* and he uses the binary form without scruple. Towards the middle of his career it is one of his favourite moulds; after 1788 he comes back to the ternary *sonata* and henceforward his only binary movement will be the larghetto of his B flat quartet, K.589. The highest point of the binary *sonata* is reached in the three magnificent andantes of the C major concerto, K.503, and the quintets in C and in G minor.

The rondo andante is, with the ternary *sonata*, the andante par excellence in his concertos. It is found, we have said, at all periods, but it becomes common only after 1783 and even then Mozart keeps it chiefly for the smaller genres, sonata, trio, *Musical Joke*. It appears once, it is true, in a quartet[7] and one other time in a symphony,[8] in a modified form somewhat different from the rondo of the sonatas; the last quintet also uses it. With these few exceptions, the concertos are the only works where Mozart appears to treat it as a serious form.

The first rondo andante in a concerto dates from 1784; it is that of the D major, K.451. Three other great concertos use it, the D minor, E flat, K.482 and C minor. The concerto in D, K.537, and the last, in B flat, also make use of it, and towards the end it becomes his favourite movement in the genre.

The rondo andantes in his concertos have not the uniformity of

---

[1] K.415.   [2] K.175, 242, 246, 271, 365, 414, 453.   [3] K.242, 365.   [4] K.175, 415.   [5] K.242, 365.   [6] K.488.   [7] D minor, K.421.   [8] E flat, K.543.

structure of the sonatas. That of the D minor is distinguished by
the G minor prestissimo which interrupts it, a quick interlude in a
slow movement which is most uncommon in his work.[1] That of
the E flat, K.482, is quite unique in its varied refrain, which make it
a cross between rondo and variation. It is moreover characterized
by the couplets being reserved for the orchestra whilst the soloist
confines himself to varying the refrain; the coda unites both. Those
of the D major, K.451, and the C minor are more regular: a refrain,
given out at first by the solo, then by the tutti, two couplets and a
coda. The two last concertos recall the romance of the D minor,
without the prestissimo: refrain in the solo and the tutti, first couplet,
refrain and coda, new couplets, and return of all the first part including the coda (ABAC D ABAC). It is an application to the andante
of the masterly form of the sonata rondo which Mozart developed and
used so often in his finales.

Variations, a form of which the *galant* age was madly fond, are
always uncommon in his serious work. He considers them as an
amusement without significance and the great number of those he
wrote for the piano, though often charming, are not among those
pieces into which he put the whole of himself. Yet, now and again,
he uses this form in more important compositions. Those of the
violin sonata in F, K.377, a transformation of those in the divertimento, K.334, and forerunners of the finale of the second D minor
quartet, K.421, are among his most passionate movements; those of
the quartet in A lead to a grandiose coda, and the serenity of his last
months expressed itself in the variations of the second organ fantasia,
K.608.

The two concertos which have slow variations are both in B flat
and both date from 1784. Those of the first, K.450, are valuable
especially for their theme; those of the other, K.456, are akin through
their key, G minor, to great works; their richer and more tortured
inspiration drove Mozart to elaborate the form, and the interplay of
piano and orchestra, the transformations of theme and especially the
coda are of the first order.

Two concertos use free forms for their slow movements. The
andantino of K.449 is a kind of three-part *sonata* with the air of a
rondo; it could almost be looked upon as a series of variations.
The majestic concerto in C, K.467, has an andante whose "nocturne"

---

[1] There is another example in the *romance* of the B flat serenade,
K.361.

feeling proclaims the coming of Chopin. Five or six themes can be distinguished in it, but the order of their return and that of their keys do not correspond to any fixed plan and this magical andante proves that the "formalist" Mozart was as much a master of fantasy, when he wished, as the dreamiest of Romantics.

Into all these movements, so varied by their plan and their feeling, Mozart put the best of his soul. The qualities which make his best andantes and adagios precious to us are all found in these concertos to the same degree as in his works belonging to the genres deemed "serious": quartet, quintet, symphony.

It is seldom that the finale of a work is the equal of the andante and the opening allegro. How often are we obliged to own that the last movements of works whose first ones had pleased us have left us dissatisfied! This does not apply to one single age; it is common to all, and to all composers from the 17th century to our own days. There are, of course, exceptions; many works have in their last movement their best part; but, generally speaking, it remains true that a composer, for one reason or another, does not reach in his finales the height of his andantes and allegros.

How can we explain this? There are doubtless several reasons and they vary according to the period. At the time of Mozart and Beethoven the inferiority of the finale was deliberate. A *galant* public must have listened with difficulty to music whose character was unremittingly serious[1]; it felt more than we do the need for contrast, and two serious movements on end were no doubt enough. After an allegro and an andante, it needed relaxation, and this was provided by the light and skipping finale; it would not have tolerated a third serious movement. For the same reason Haydn inserted scherzo minuets in his quartets and symphonies and caused thus two serious pieces to be followed by two lighter ones. When Mozart started placing his minuets between his allegros and his andantes (as in several of his quartets and quintets), the alternation of the frivolous and the severe was assured.

The frankly superficial character of the finale is therefore intentional with *galant* composers. Haydn sometimes and Mozart often, nevertheless, reacted against it; but Beethoven, except in his minor key finales, generally kept up the tradition of the light-hearted rondo

----

[1] Possibly because its concerts were longer than ours.

and passed it on to the Romantic generations. Schubert, Schumann, Mendelssohn, even Brahms think fairly often of the finale as a relaxation rather than as a crowning of the whole, and the ideal of the "entertainment" finale is still alive to-day.

Out of some hundred finales in Mozart's "great" period, about forty rise above the merely recreative tone of the ordinary rondo and a score are in no wise inferior to the opening allegros. Such are those of the four last symphonies, of the quartet in A and the concertos in D minor, C minor and C major, K.503. In his greatest works he casts away the ideal of the happy ending and crowns them with finales of a serious and sometimes overcast mood. In a score of others the happy ending survives, but the emotion is deepened and attains grandeur, as in the quintets of 1787 and 1791, the quartets in C and G, and the concertos in G, K.453, and A, K.488. The proportion of last movements that place themselves definitely on lower ground and aim only at amusing and relaxing through a round of merry, skipping tunes hardly exceeds one half of the works of these fourteen years and one should remember that most of them belong to that part of his output that he composed for his fashionable *clientèle*, such as the trios and piano sonatas. Most of these are rondos; he keeps rather the sonata form and variations for his "serious" finales.

The frivolous conception of the concerto that prevailed in the *galant* age and with which Mozart himself had started, survives till the end in the use of the rondo. He transforms it, however, to such an extent that one has to be warned in order to recognize it. It is clearly his favourite form. Out of a hundred and eleven finales in his "great" period, seventy-six are rondos, eighteen sonatas and seventeen variations or minuets. The mere numbers show his preference. But it is proved also, and more decisively, by the care which he brought to the elaboration of the form and the infinite art with which he varied it from work to work. If, for his inspiration at its loftiest, one has to turn to his andantes, it is in his rondos that he shows himself at his greatest as master of form.

It is a far cry from the simple little rondos of the early 18th century to the sonata rondos of the quartets, quintets and concertos of Mozart's last years. It is a far cry, even, from the rondos that John Christian wrote for his London public and with which he ended at little cost sonatas, quartets and concertos, to the last rondos of his disciple. From the year of his childhood when his musical personality began to shine through, Mozart was never content with the dryness of the rondos which John Christian and all his contemporaries were turning out in tens and hundreds.

The Mozartian sonata rondo is not a development of the simple rondeau form used by Couperin. The rondeaux of Couperin do not go beyond a straightforward succession of couplets, or episodes, separated by returns of the refrain. Each couplet is independent and there is no repetition of earlier ones; the only organic link in the movement is the refrain, which usually comes back unaltered. The number of couplets is not fixed. This kind of movement occurs all through the century; some of Mozart's finales[1] show it in a form hardly more complex than that of Couperin.

The origin of the sonata rondo must be sought in the dances "*en rondeau*" of the French operatic composers. These differ from the simple rondeau in that there is generally only one couplet and seldom more than two. When a pair of such dances is combined we are well on the way to the sonata rondo. Many of Rameau's dances point in this direction. Let us, for example, examine the rigaudons and tambourins that close the first Entrée in *Les Indes Galantes* (1735). Each of these dances has the same plan. The first is a rondeau in G major with a single couplet that leads to the key of the dominant. The second follows the same course but is in the minor; after it, the first dance is repeated. The likeness in plan between such a pair of dances and a sonata rondo is easily seen.

A   G major.
B   Leading to D major.
A   G major.

C   G minor.
D   Leading to B flat. (This part closes in B flat in the tambourin, returns to G minor in the rigaudon.)
C   G minor.

ABA as before.

Often the second dance is in binary form (C D); even so, the analogy with the sonata rondo is close. The first dance corresponds to the refrain, exposition couplet and first return of the refrain; the second dance, to its *development* couplet; and the *da capo* to the further returns of the refrain and the recapitulation.

The main difference in the later form lies in the absence of hard

---

[1] E.g., those of his serenades in B flat and E flat, K.361 and 375.

and fast lines marking off refrain and couplets. But even these are not always pronounced in the earlier rondeau. Couperin seeks more than once to unify his rondeaux by the use of themes or motifs that recur throughout the movement and Rameau carried this practice further, as in the E minor tambourin for harpsichord, *Les Cyclopes*, *La Follette* and *La Villageoise*. In this latter, the first couplet opens with the same phrase as the refrain and, after the second episode, which has a semi-quaver bass accompaniment, the same figure is carried into the refrain.[1] *Les Cyclopes* carries us very near indeed to the Mozartian rondo, as the following analysis will show.

Refrain: A (a)   4 bars.
                   (b)   47 bars; a number of strains, with reminders
                            of (a).   All in D minor.

1st Couplet   B   33 bars.   D minor (13 bars); modulating
                            (6 bars); F major (14 bars).

Refrain: A (a)   4 bars.
                   (c)   8 bars; a new transition.   All in D minor.

2nd Couplet: C   27 bars.   D minor (7 bars); A minor (20
                            bars).

Refrain: A (a)   4 bars. }
                   (b)   48 bars. } Unchanged.

The long and complex refrain, the second part of which contains many reminiscences of the opening bars, would be comparable to an exposition if it did not remain in the same key; but it is quite like the rich, many-themed refrain of a Mozart or Beethoven sonata rondo. Only the first four bars are repeated between the first and second couplets and the return of the whole fifty odd bars of (a) and (b) gives one the impression of a recapitulation. In fact, were it not that these bars do not modulate to the relative major on their first appearance, *Les Cyclopes* might be considered as an early example of the sonata rondo. It is in any case one of the closest anticipations of that form.

The Mozartian rondo is, then, but an elaboration of the French combination of two dances "en rondeau" with a return of the first part.

[1] The same device occurs in the second half of the rondo of K.449.

We find it fully formed in the second piano concerto, a perfect example of that sonata rondo which he was to use in most of his piano concertos and which in all his work he adopts more often than any other form, for his finales, from 1778 to his death.

This movement repeats, like the dances "en rondeau", the whole of the first part after the second, and is thus nearly as closely unified as a true *sonata*. It turns all its last section into a recapitulation and for that reason we have proposed calling it a *sonata rondo*, to distinguish it from less organic rondos. One might say that it is a *sonata* where each section is separated from the other two by the same subject, the refrain, and where the exposition, instead of finishing in the dominant, returns to the tonic.

There are few "regular" sonata rondos in Mozart for, in this form which was so much his own, he has confined himself less than elsewhere to a fixed plan. That of K.451, in D, is one of the few which conform in every way to the type and it will be convenient to analyze it.

After the exposition of the refrain which consists here of two strains and does not depart from the tonic, there begins the first couplet or exposition. Two themes can be distinguished: the first extends over some forty bars, in D; the second is in the key of the dominant. It is a first section of a *sonata* up to the point where it modulates and returns at the same time to the tonic and the refrain. This latter is repeated unchanged, and the movement enters on its second couplet which, after giving out a third theme, in the minor, develops the refrain subject and the second subject of the first couplet. This section corresponds to the *development* of the *sonata*. Finally, the refrain is once more repeated; the whole of the first couplet returns with modifications of detail and without departing from the tonic. The refrain is heard once more; it brings in the cadenza, after which the movement, which is in 2-4, closes with a fairly long coda in 3-8. We have therefore the following outline:

Refrain: A } D major.
        B

1st or Exposition Couplet: C D major.
                            D A major.

Refrain: A } D major.
        B

2nd or *Development* Couplet: E   B minor.
                                    A and D: "developed", modulating.

ABCD AB EAD AB C D A cad. coda .

Refrain: A ⎱
         B ⎰ D major.

3rd or Recapitulation Couplet: C ⎱
                               D ⎰ D major.

Refrain (shortened): A D major.

Cadenza.

Coda: Continuation of the Refrain with change of time-signature.

This sonata rondo is perfectly regular and, what is more, comes close to the true *sonata* in that its second couplet is a real *development*, a feature which it shares only with the finales of the E flat string quintet and the concertos in B flat, K.450, and C, K.467. All Mozart's other sonata rondos show some kind of irregularity, sometimes small, sometimes pronounced, sufficient to give them as a whole a variety which appears the greater the more one considers them. Sometimes the refrain returns bereft of some of the themes which made it up on its first appearance; certain rondos, even, appear to be reduced to two couplets by omitting it altogether between the *development* and the re-exposition.[1] Sometimes the first couplet, instead of starting in the tonic to end in the dominant, sets out from the latter and unfolds in different keys more or less remote from the tonic. And sometimes, finally, the third couplet leaves out a part of the exposition or else brings in new subjects or yet again recalls phrases from the second couplet or the refrain; the possibilities are endless.

After the last couplet the refrain is often shortened; once it is even absent.[2] It is generally followed by a coda, long or short, and more or less new according to the composer's fancy.

Some rondos, moreover, cannot be reduced to any definite form, even when one allows for "irregularities". The finale of the *Kleine Nachtmusik* of the piano sonata in B flat, K.570, of the B flat quartet, K.589, are built on plans of their own, and this is true of some of the concertos.

After the slow measures of the andante, the piano springs forth joyously to meet the theme of the finale. The solo expounds it and claims it before the orchestra is able to put in a note; the strings just keep up a murmur of repeated chords, a misty and approving back-

---

[1] K.413, 414, 456, 459, 488; sonata for two pianos, K.448; E flat piano quartet, K.493; string trio, K.563; K.478.

[2] Piano trio in C, K.548.

ground against which the luminous outline of the refrain stands out radiantly. The tutti is seldom the first to take up the finale; it never does so with passionate themes; when the character of the movement is quiet and pensive or when the form is that of theme and variations the solo consents sometimes to leave the first place to the instruments.[1] In general, this first appearance is short; in K.271 it is unusually indiscreet in its length, some fifty bars long, but this is exceptional. The theme once outlined, the orchestra repeats it and adds several subsidiary motifs. This opening tutti is sometimes followed by a regular conclusion and leads to a full close on the tonic,[2] after which the piano opens the exposition couplet. For these concerto refrains are no longer the agreeable ditties of galant rondos but true developments with several distinct subjects[3] and a concluding codetta.

In the couplets, the foremost part belongs generally to the piano without the orchestra ever withdrawing completely. The traditional virtuosity of the rondo—traditional especially since the 19th century with its Hummels, Moscheles and Chopins—is as absent from Mozart's rondos as from his first movements. Pure virtuosity is almost unknown to him; the brilliant runs with which he embellishes his themes and thanks to which he develops them and links them up one with the other are always expressive and it is impossible to make the cuts in them which one can make with advantage in those of Dussek, Hummel, Cramer, Field, Steibelt, Kozeluch and other pianist-composers of the *galant* age. The exposition couplet unfolds, passing from tonic to dominant, allowing itself only seldom to drift into distant keys and hardly ever to change its *tempo*.[4] However, it readily inserts between the first and second subject a minor episode corresponding to the solo subject in the first movement which is also often in the minor. At the end of the couplet, the task of bringing back the refrain falls usually to the solo and the orchestra repeats it afterwards.

The middle couplet affords as much unexpectedness as the *development of the first movement*. It is the essential part of the rondo, the one for the sake of which, in certain cases, one listens to the rest.

---

[1] K.382, 386, 413, 414, 449, 453, 491, 503.

[2] K.488.

[3] Two or three; K.482 has four.

[4] K.415 inserts in this first couplet a short and moving adagio in the tonic minor.

In K.450, piano and wind enter upon a refined and witty conversation anent the refrain, sporting with it until it comes back for good. K.415 recalls and develops here the three motifs which make up its refrain; K.246 uses a theme of the first couplet as a bridge to return to the refrain and K. 271, one of the most eccentric, before proceeding to the minuet with variations which fills two thirds of this section, recalls in the minor the first strain of its refrain.

But most of the concertos, faithful in this to the tradition of the dance "*en rondeau*", bring new elements to the building of this second couplet and (another French trait) put it in the minor. These new elements are less definite themes than passages and runs, melodic as all Mozart's passages are, but not forming clear-cut tunes. They give this couplet the character of an extemporization and one recognizes once again that Mozart, sometimes so formal, is also a master of fantasy.

It is impossible to sum up the characters of these middle couplets. When Mozart has surprises up his sleeve, it is here that he springs them on us; it is here that, in the middle of a 2-4 presto, he unfolds a sinuous minuet which he varies up to four times[1]; it is here, in a 6-8 gallop, that he stops and recollects himself in an andantino in three time, like a huntsman who in the heat of his fiery course suddenly finds himself before a broad, poetic landscape and pulls up to contemplate it lovingly.[2] It is here, finally, that the tragedy, which is never as near as when he appears most carefree and most overbrimming with mirth, breaks forth and covers a whole section of the rondo with a dark minor hue. We are thinking particularly of the magnificent finale of K.503; its second couplet, an apotheosis of the modest *minore* of the French rondo, is one of the most stirring utterances of the great dramatist.

But little by little, dusky storm-clouds, minuets and andantinos, free fantasies, all scatter and vanish, and the familiar outline of the refrain brings us back to well-known lands. This return of the refrain, perhaps a little too well-known, is the weak point in the rondo and Mozart, in five concertos,[3] has strengthened the movement by omitting it and passing straight on to the recapitulation. At other times, it comes back so much curtailed that it is hardly recognizable,[4] or else in a key other than the tonic, as in the last concerto, K.595, where it is stopped before it can be finished and vanishes before the impatience of the recapitulation.

---

[1] K.271.   [2] K.482.   [3] K.413, 414, 456, 459, 488.
[4] Piano quartet in G minor, K. 478; clarinet concerto.

The third couplet, in which the piano plays a smaller part than in the first, is also very diverse from work to work. Most concertos shorten it by leaving out themes that had been heard in the first couplet, and realizing that it can easily become tedious, hurry it on towards the conclusion. The only reproach one can address to the splendid C major concerto, K.503, is precisely that this third section of its rondo is too long and too like the first; a slight weariness is the result.

The first movements seldom culminated in codas; the composer reserved them for the finale. The coda of K.450, through a repeated triplet motif in the bass, leads to a *strepitando* statement of the key of B flat and the reckless gallop of the rondo winds up in an increasingly frenzied stamping before the goal. That of K.595 is more peaceful; it carries on the motion of the finale without intensifying it and keeps the note of good-humoured but slightly saddened sweetness which belongs to the whole work. Some of them violate the rule that a concerto should end with a sound of noisy triumph and fade away to *pianissimo*. Two of the violin concertos had finished thus. That of the C major piano concerto, K.415, seizes a little piece of the refrain which had already played a certain part, and this fragment, tossed between piano and orchestra and multiplied *ad infinitum*, sails through the whole coda like a flight of fairies in a darkening wood; everything dies out little by little till it alone survives as a mere shimmer and ends by losing itself in its turn in the dusk.[1]

The external form of the Mozartian concerto is, in its main lines, roughly the same from one work to the other. The succession: *sonata* allegro, *sonata* andante, rondo or variations finale, is seldom broken. But when one goes beneath the surface the variety is boundless. We have enumerated some of the changes of detail that the passage from one concerto to the next holds in store for us; our enumeration has seemed long to us and we were sometimes afraid of bewildering the reader; yet it covers but a small part of the transformations which rondo and *sonata* undergo. We shall not regret this bewilderment if it helps to correct the very false idea one has of Mozart's sameness, but we will stop and leave to the examination of each concerto the task of revealing other aspects of his infinite multiformity.

---

[1] To be complete, one should add that two concerto rondos, K.415 and 449, are quite irregular and follow no definite plan, and that K.537 is a two couplets rondo, a form which, like the two section *sonata*, leaves out the *development*.

3. General considerations on Mozart's piano concertos: Relations between piano and orchestra

In the sorry midden of dead and buried concertos of the last century, there lie many which reduced the orchestra to being a mere backcloth against which stood out the lightning excursions, the "quips and cranks and wanton wiles", of the piano. In the 18th century one was still too close to the traditions of the *concerto grosso* for such a deformation to become the rule, but the school of John Christian Bach, at any rate, did not entertain a much more exalted idea of the orchestra's function. The disfavour into which polyphonic writing had fallen was accompanied by a general impoverishment of the style, betrayed in the concerto by an overweening preponderance of solo over tutti.

Mozart was one of the first to reconcile the fullness of the polyphonists with the new style. After a period during which he was only the pupil of John Christian he regained little by little the point from which the concerto had started, and placed solo and tutti face to face, not as monarch and courtiers, but as equally matched adversaries or collaborators. In a general way, his first nine concertos keep to the practice of John Christian whilst from the tenth onwards orchestra and piano fight with equal weapons, and the study of their relations, which is the subject of the present chapter, is full of interest.

One often reads that Beethoven was the first to "emancipate the orchestra" in the concerto. This has been contradicted more than once.[1] The study of each of Mozart's concertos will show again, we hope, that the older musician had already emancipated it. But he was not the first to do so since, without going back to John Sebastian, the orchestra is already as emancipated as it can be in some concertos of Philip Emmanuel. For the present, we shall limit ourselves to summing up the problems which Mozart, like all composers of

---

[1] E.g. by D. Tovey, *Essays in musical analysis*, III, 26.

concertos, had to face, and to sketching the general lines along which he solved them.

When an instrument breaks away from the mass of the orchestra and asserts its independence, either temporarily or, as in the concerto, for a whole work, it can take up several attitudes towards the others. In bad concertos, it sticks to one, the simplest and laziest: it attracts all notice to itself, drives into the shade the instruments which are playing at the same time and compels them to be content with accompanying. The polyphonic style of the earliest concerto composers had lent itself perfectly to diverse combinations of solo and tutti but the abandonment of polyphony led to a relative abandonment of these combinations and the orchestra took to subordinating itself to the solo.

Mozart's merit was that he reacted against this without, nevertheless, returning to polyphonic writing, and obtained thus once again the collaboration of solo and orchestra by using, not counterpoint, save occasionally, but the new symphonic style.

With him, as with all composers who have taken the concerto seriously, the relations of solo and tutti, of tutti and solo, are of three kinds. The tutti can submit to the solo and accompany it. The solo in its turn can submit to the whole or a part of the orchestra and accompany it. Both, finally, can be of equal importance and combine or converse without one lording it over the other or claiming a larger share than the other of the public's attention. It will be easier to study in detail the forms these relations take in Mozart when we come to each concerto in turn; we can, however, outline their general character here and now.

The natural state of a concerto, so to speak, is for the tutti to be subordinate to the solo. However much the orchestra "emancipates itself", the bars where the solo is to the fore are bound to be the most numerous. It is thus with Mozart as with John Sebastian and Philip Emmanuel Bach, as with Beethoven or Schumann or Liszt. In this respect Mozart's concertos are in no way remarkable. The role of the orchestra, even in his finest works, is often that of an accompanist. It accompanies, generally, by using the customary devices: sustained notes, repeated figures, rhythmical contrasts, arpeggios in contrary motion to that of the solo, chords containing the harmonies implied in the runs, rhythmical motifs opposed to *cantabile* themes: such are the commonest of the many shapes assumed by the orchestral accompaniment. None of these is peculiar to Mozart and there is no need to dwell on them. We will merely point out the presence, in half a dozen of his concertos of the "great" period, of thematic accompaniment, that is to say, of one which uses as its motif one of the main themes of the movement or a part of this theme. This device goes back to John Sebastian Bach who uses it often and to his sons Wilhelm Friedmann and Philip Emmanuel. Philip Emmanuel, especially, makes more of it than his father; in his magnificent D minor concerto,[1] he fills out a good part of the first movement with the opening subject, repeated and varied *ad infinitum* under the decorations of the piano.

Mozart has made less use of it. One can nevertheless quote several memorable examples in the concertos in D minor and A, K.488. Few moments are more exquisite than that when, in the finale of K.488, a passage of imitation is transformed by the simple action of the piano ceasing abruptly to answer and going off on its own, whilst the woodwind continue their calls which suddenly turn into a thematic accompaniment (ex. 1). The bars in the *development* of the D minor where, under the fiery piano arpeggios raining down on to the bass, there rumble in the depths the ominous triplets of the first subject, are of a kind which sum up a whole work in one lightning vision (ex. 239). Thematic accompaniments, used less dramatically, are found also in the concertos in C, K.467 (ex. 259), C minor and D, K.537. In some cases, the accompaniment is not far from being as important as the solo itself. One can trace a regular evolution from the use of a theme as an accompanying motif to its complete development, with piano accompaniment, as in the allegro of the last concerto, an evolution whose stages are marked by the finale of K.415 and the first movements of K.467, 491 and 503.

---

[1] Wotquenne no. 23. After several others, may we put in a word for this neglected musician? Some forty of his fifty-three piano concertos have never been printed, even in his lifetime. Out of a hundred and fifty cembalo sonatas, only a hundred have been printed, several for the first time in our own day. There should be a critical edition of his best work, based on a complete examination of all that is known, which would omit the second-rate compositions and keep only the very numerous masterpieces. There should be, above all, instrumentalists willing to take advantage of what is already published, of the admirable piano concertos edited by Riemann at Steingräber's, especially those in D minor and C minor, great works in all respects and admirable for pianists who have only a chamber orchestra at their disposal. The study of these concertos cannot be recommended too warmly to all pianists who are not deaf to the art of the 18th century.

Ex. 3 (suite)

The tutti's accompaniment, without borrowing any definite theme, may owe a certain originality to its outline or to its orchestration. More numerous than examples of thematic accompaniment are those where the subordinate parts, without asserting themselves as much as the solo, free themselves completely from conventional forms and develop independently, almost outlining melodies. No need to quote passages; they abound in the concertos of 1785 and 1786. This setting free of the accompanying parts is common also in Philip Emmanuel; one finds it in the first movement of his D minor concerto, W.23. What could not be found before the growth of orchestration at the end of the century was the colour due to the diversity of timbres which characterizes Mozart's accompaniments. One thinks especially of the woodwind chords that sustain the fiery triplets of the piano in the andante of the D minor (G minor interlude; ex. 243), of the chords climbing and descending in contrary motion to the piano scales in the *development* of the allegro of the E flat, K.482, of the agitated jumps of the bassoon and of the flute and hautboy scales passing like an Ariadne's thread through the labyrinth of solo arpeggios, in the first movement of the G major (ex. 155).

The tables are sometimes turned and the situation becomes even more interesting. One has a malicious pleasure in seeing how submissive the once conquering instrument has become and how the orchestra wins back the rights lost on the entry of the solo. But one has also another pleasure, a more artistic one, in seeing the solo reduced to accompanying the tutti, because of the increase of colour thus produced. Condemn the piano to accompanying the orchestra and you take from it momentarily its personality; you oblige it to lose itself in the mass of instruments and you enrich thus the palette of tone colours.

Mozart saw this early. In his first concerto he sometimes gave the piano a back place. Those that followed it till 1782 were devoid of interesting relations between solo and orchestra, but after this date he renewed the practice and varied it cleverly.

The simplest way to subordinate the piano is to give it a commonplace accompaniment formula, such as an Alberti bass, broken chords in triplets, or ascending and descending arpeggios. There are instances of this in most of the concertos of the "great" period (1784-6). Mozart has a fondness for clarinet solos accompanied by the piano which will be shared by Beethoven and Schumann.

Piano accompaniment becomes more original when it avoids the beaten tracks. It is already more enterprising when it doubles the melody given out by the orchestra. It seldom does this literally; it prefers to play round it, embroidering it, repeating it in broken octaves, treating it as a theme to be varied, but without moving far from it, as in the two fine pedal passages in the finale of the G major and the andante of the C major, K.503. The piano part, more brilliant in the first (ex. 173), differs less from that of the orchestra whose chords it is content to reproduce without breaking them. Broader and nobler in the C major, it consists in triplets spaced over two octaves, rising and falling like a swell as the harmonies descend majestically, one step at a time, to the unison which brings back the main subject.

Without being subordinated one to the other, solo and orchestra may collaborate.

We speak of collaboration, when the two adversaries play together and both appeal with equal force to the attention of the listener. They can do it in several ways.

In the repetition of a passage already heard in the opening tutti, the piano can take hold of a part previously granted to an instrument of the orchestra, and replace the instrument. Generally, it is a first violin part that is thus appropriated. Mozart has made it do this in his concertos K.449 and 450, after which the device is met with only occasionally and for a few bars. This substitution of the solo for an orchestral instrument causes a somewhat amusing surprise but it is an effect that soon wears off.

A more fruitful device is that of descants, or counter-subjects. Here, the theme is given out by the orchestra and the piano traces above it an independent line. These counter-themes are very diverse. Generally, they are melodic—a new melody being given above one already known; but when, exceptionally, they fall to the orchestra, they usually consist in scales. From K.451 onward after the solo's first appearance, Mozart likes to take up again unchanged fairly long passages from the opening section, adding to them a solo part which unfolds freely above or amidst the voices of the orchestra. This free counterpoint, this new personality mingling with the familiar ones of the tutti, has the effect of suddenly broadening and moving back the horizon of the work. From K.451 to 503, Mozart acts thus in almost all his first movements, but never with more genius than at the beginning and end of the series, in the D major concerto of 1784, K.451, and that in C, K.503, the *Jupiter* of the concertos, of 1786.

The andantes, too, offer good examples of this practice. One of

the most felicitous is at the solo entry in the poignant slow movement of the E flat, K.271; the orchestra opens with a grave, rhythmical
subject, not very melodic; the piano enters and the orchestra gives
out its theme again, whilst the piano superposes a quite different one,
lyric and *cantabile*, which ends after a few bars of collaboration by
assuming supremacy and reducing the orchestral subject to silence.
It is a beginning in an archaic style that recalls the andantes of older
concertos (exs. 17 and 19). Another example occurs in the D major,
K.451; it is a regular descant; one tune is placed above another and
each one keeps its independence (ex. 2). Other instances come mostly
from the conclusions of andantes; the orchestra is speaking, but from
time to time the piano puts in a word, almost like an echo, and without
interrupting the orchestral song. The concertos in G, A (K.488), C
minor, C (K.503) and B flat (K.595), all have andantes which end
thus. Two of them afford also examples in their finales, K.453 and
488; in the first, the passage is repeated, solo and tutti wittily exchanging their parts; in the second, the solo which has just given out a
pert tune catches up a fragment of it and sports with it while the
orchestra repeats the theme itself (ex. 319).

There are also some examples of imitative counterpoint. That
in three parts, between flute, bassoon and piano, in the G major
concerto; that, also *a tre*, in the finale of the F, K.459, between piano,
violin and 'cello; that *a quattro* between the two hands of the piano,
the hautboy and the bassoon in the andante of this same work, belong
to 1784, the contrapuntal period in Mozart's life. Let us note also
the exquisite moment just after the reprise in the allegro of the E flat,
K.482, where, over the Alberti bass of the second fiddles and the piano
chords, first fiddles and right hand mingle and imitate in lines of free
counterpoint, flowing and gracefully canonic.

Twice, in the first movement of the concerto in D, K.451, and the
finale of the D minor, we find another form of free counterpoint.
The material is here, in each case, one of the themes of the movement,
cut in two and shared between piano and woodwind, one half to
each. The finale of the D minor prolongs for some time this lively
situation and a little episode derives from it. This device does not
occur again and it seems to have been the result of a passing fancy of
the composer's, for we find it in the minuet of the A major quartet,
written a month earlier than this concerto.

Mozart, whose growth, contrary to what has so often been said,
never came to a stop, and who was developing strongly at the time
of his death, foresaw a still more fruitful use of the solo to which this

last practice could lead. The piano has dared to add itself to an already familiar orchestral passage; it will go further; it will mingle its embroideries and bedizenments with episodes entrusted exclusively to the orchestra.   In the middle part of the allegros of K.488, 503 and 595, the tutti returns to familiar subjects,[1] repeats them, varies them, plays with them, develops them, in short, then brings them back gradually to the recapitulation, whilst the piano spreads itself in arpeggios, scales, *fioriture* of all sorts, independently of the work of the other instruments.   The most remarkable of these three *developments* is that of the last concerto, a work which, despite its modest size, reveals unfamiliar and interesting aspects of its composer.   It is a *development* which Hermann Abert calls Beethovenian, but which it is not at all helpful to label thus, for no comparable example exists in Beethoven's concertos and this one is a very authentic possession of Mozart's.

A distinction must be made between collaboration and dialogue. It is not an idle one.   In collaboration, piano and orchestra combine simultaneously; in dialogue, they do it alternately.   It has seemed clearest to us to keep the two separate, especially as the second occurs much more often than the first.

The varieties of dialogue are more numerous and more diverse than those of collaboration. \ The orchestral link, the echo, the answer, phrases that alternate between solo and tutti, imitation: all these devices are found in most of the concertos after 1780.|

The most frequent and most commonplace form of dialogue is the orchestral link.   It is a little phrase or fragment of phrase interposed between two solos, which both separates and links them, and fulfils, most often, a purely formal function.   It is a punctuation mark, warning us that one passage is over and another about to begin.   The dialogue principle exists in it in only a rudimentary state; it is the "Yes, madam," the "No, sir" of the super.   But it happens now and again that these apparently inoffensive little phrases acquire a psychological import and an emotional as well as a formal value.   They then become short, incisive commentaries on the piano's doings and their effect is often that of a witty and mocking interruption.

At such moments, they are not far from being echoes, and it is

---

[1] In K.488, the theme had been given out for the first time at the beginning of the *development*.

indeed towards the echo, a device of which Mozart is very fond, that
the link tends.   In its simplest form, the echoing instrument repeats
unchanged the end of the previous phrase.   It matters little whether
it be a member of the orchestra which echoes the solo or vice versa;
in point of fact, the first is the more frequent.   Most often, the echo
answers by transposing the phrase, sometimes a third lower, more
often a second, a fourth or a sixth higher; more seldom it modifies
the fragment, but without transposing it.   It is naturally the wind
rather than the strings that make echo.

Pretty examples of echoes are fairly abundant in all the concertos.
We will quote three.   One of the simplest and most poetic is in the
G major where the piano reproduces the last three notes of the theme
without changing them or altering their value (ex. 3).   Another
is drawn from the finale of the C major, K.415; here, the echo is
entrusted to the hautboy and the bassoon which repeat the same notes
but augment them (ex. 4).   The andantino of the E flat, K.271, uses
the echo with more dramatic effect in the moving dialogue between
piano and first violins towards the end of the movement.   Here, the
echo is in the form of a canon, but the academic character of the
form does not detract from the emotional power of the passage
(ex. 5).

In these three examples as well as in some ten more, the echo
repeats the fragment without change.   On other occasions, more
numerous, it differs from it and gives the impression of an echo without really being one.   Thus, in the first movement of the concerto
for two pianos, it has the brevity of the echo and keeps fairly close
to the outline of the phrase which it answers; the hautboy plaint, in
spirit if not literally, is an echo of the second piano's sinuous line (ex.
23).   The very varied accompaniment in the andante of the C major,
K.467, fulfils at times the function of the echo (ex. 270) and repeats
in a simplified shape the piano's more ornate lamentations.   But
usually the relation of this half-echo with what precedes it is that of
an answer with a question, and it completes it or comments on it,
rather than repeats it.   Such is the case in the biting or pensive calls
made by the woodwind in the first subjects of the G and B flat concertos, K.453 and 595, and in the little flutterings of the flute in the
middle of the second subject in K.451 (ex. 6).   Sometimes the answer
goes as far as completing the meaning of the phrase; it then takes on
frequently the form of piano arpeggios that finish off the orchestral
theme.   Finally, it may end by constituting a true phrase of its own,
subordinate but distinct, as in the first movement of the E flat, K.449

Ex. 7

Ex. 8

(ex. 7) and the andante of the G major (ex. 8), but that is an uncommon use of the answer.

In all these forms of dialogue the game is unequal; the echo, answer, link are bound to be less important than the themes which precede and follow them. The dialogue is better distributed when the adversaries share a phrase of which each one takes a member. The phrase is usually given out only once; less often it is repeated twice or thrice, either unchanged or transposed. On two occasions, it is not only repeated but also developed, and in the finale of K.415 this development, shared between piano and tutti, provides an episode of exceptional beauty.

The different members of what appears at first to make up a single phrase may turn out to be so distinct and so well characterized that it is fairer to consider them as so many separate phrases, some belonging to the orchestra, others to the solo. This is a form of dialogue by alternate phrases, a less common form with Mozart than the preceding.

The phrases here are generally short and nearly always go in pairs; the coda of the finale in the E flat concerto, K.449, offers an example of phrases alternating in groups of three. Sometimes, they are alike and make up a symmetrical whole; sometimes, the solo is a scale or arpeggio passage. In several cases, nevertheless, all of them to be found in developments,[1] it is regular sections, and not just phrases, that alternate and answer each other. By alternating, the phrases can be modified, but here diversity is too great for one to generalize.

Finally, it is sometimes the same phrase which is repeated from one instrument to the other, unchanged or modified. Examples of this device which lends itself less to elaboration than the former, are not numerous. There is a masterly instance of it in the concerto in C, K.467 (development couplet of the finale, ex. 272).

To be complete one should add that imitation, of which we have already spoken, instead of being simultaneous, alternates sometimes between one part and the other and assumes the aspect of a canon; it then becomes "dialogue" rather than "collaboration". The finale of the G major shows an example of this; that of the D minor has a more remarkable one, where piano, flute and hautboy send back from one to the other the different fragments of a phrase taken from the preceding couplet.

It is hardly necessary to add that the distinctions we have made, not only between sundry forms of dialogue but also between dialogue and collaboration, between collaboration and accompaniment, are not rigid and exist only for the needs of clarity. Many passages can be classed in more than one of these divisions; we have adopted them only to show more easily what diversity of genius exists, in these concertos, in the relations between orchestra and solo.

The concerto's problem is to combine solo and orchestra without, on the one hand, the orchestra being treated as a simple accompanist, or, on the other, the solo losing its personality by blending too intimately with the mass of instruments. Balance of the two forces, struggle without triumph, collaboration without blending: such is the ideal of every concerto worthy of the name.

This intercourse between solo and orchestra, the modalities of which we have been studying in Mozart, is the soul of the concerto.

---

[1] First movements of K.466, 488 and 491, and finale of K.450.

Melodic ideas, modulations, development, poetic value: all this is common to it with other genres; what characterizes it is the struggle between two adversaries of equal strength. Progress for a concerto consists therefore in rendering more and more complex the relations between solo and tutti, in bringing the protagonists closer and closer together without ever uniting them or crushing one to the advantage of the other. This progress, of course, remains subordinated to the value of the content. It is clear that a concerto where this essential element is present but whose thought is mediocre will be less precious than one where the orchestral part is only an accompaniment, but where the thought is interesting.

When one goes through Mozart's twenty-three piano concertos in chronological order, one finds a progress in complexity and intimacy of relation between piano and orchestra. But this progress is not constant. It includes halts and even sometimes retrogression. Moreover, it does not correspond precisely to the no less unmistakable progress in significance and depth. To say that complexity of intercourse goes hand in hand with a heightening of musical significance would satisfy a tidy mind but it would be only partly true.

'Let us go quickly over the concertos considered from this double standpoint. The passages which are interesting for solo and tutti interplay are infrequent in the first nine (1773–82). Before 1784, Mozart does not tackle the fundamental problem which he resolves later on. But, though no work of these years is really *concertante*, two of them, the first in D, K.175, and the fifth in E flat, K.271, rise above the gentle heights of *galant* music and answer to an inner experience. Here, thought is ahead of technique.

From the tenth concerto to the twenty-first, K.449 to 503, there is, on the other hand, a marked though irregular growth. The first one of the great Viennese series, K.449, in E flat, a work of moderate size, has a finale which is rich in complex relations between solo and orchestra, whereas K.450, in B flat, of more ambitious dimensions and more brilliant virtuosity, tends to return to the level of the *galant* concertos and loses the ground gained with K.449. The distance is caught up with K.451, in D; the work is even more flashing than K.450 and its psychological import is greater; at the same time, the protagonists interplay elaborately. The gain is kept up with the G major, K.453; the thought is more intimate and more personal; the relations are as close in the first two movements as in K.451, and much more in the finale, which was rather poor in the D major. These early 1784 concertos form a group and the G major marks a stage in Mozart's progress. With it, musical import and richness of interplay reach similar points in their development.

The next four concertos also form a group, but merely a chronological one. They belong to the musical season of the winter of 1784-5 and spread out from September to March. In character they are not homogeneous; the first two go with those of 1784; the other two are akin to those that follow.

K.456, in B flat, is more intimate in character than K.450, 451 or even 453. Its lyrical tone makes it almost a chamber concerto. But this intimacy does not exclude depth and it turns to tragedy in the andante variations. It is less varied than the G major but quite as poetic. Technique, on the other hand, loses a little ground in it; piano and tutti intercourse is less sustained and the orchestra is ready to stand down before the solo instrument. But with K.459, in F, the complexity of the relations between the two again progresses; the interplay is, indeed, more continuous here than it will ever be again. The piano often plays a subordinate part; the orchestra, especially in the grand *fugati* of the finale, has a part of great richness, and one has at times the impression that one is listening to an orchestral concerto with piano accompaniment. On the other hand, the inspiration is on a lower plane than in the three preceding concertos; the first and third movements express a mainly physical vigour and high spirits; and it is the only concerto not to have a slow movement; a 6-8 allegretto takes its place. Mozart has not reached here the balance of the G major, which united richness of interplay and depth of feeling.

The immense psychological progress accomplished by the celebrated D minor, K.466, a work of a very different climate from the first fifteen concertos, does not restore equality. But here, the complexity of combination is sacrificed; carried away towards the new world of emotion he has discovered, Mozart has ceased for the time being to take interest in it. The examples of interplay that survive, however, are more original than in earlier concertos. The emotional value of K.467, in C, the antithesis of the D minor, is no less, and technique begins to catch up again. Moreover, in these two masterpieces the combinations of piano and orchestra, which had been hitherto of mainly formal interest, acquire dramatic value.[1]

The four concertos of the winter of 1785-6 are also masterpieces. In inspiration they are all on the same level as K.466 and 467, but

---

[1] This was already so in the andante of K.271 and, still more, in that of K.453.

their personalities are most diverse.   The E flat is as graceful and majestic as a queen; the A, "innig" and prone to sadness; the C minor, elegiac and, at moments, tragic; and the C major, Olympian.   The technical advance is kept up.   The moments of interplay are not numerous in the E flat but they are the most beautiful in the work; the coda of the andante shows at its highest point the art with which Mozart can express the dramatic nature of his genius in a symphonic form.   The A major, among the concertos of this year, corresponds to the B flat, K.456, among those of 1784; its feeling is nevertheless deeper and its interplay of piano and tutti as exquisite as in K.482. Finally, the last two of this series of twelve regain the balance broken since the G major; here, on the plane of the greatest masterpieces, there reigns absolute equality and unity between the interplay of the protagonists and the spiritual value of the music.   The C minor and C major, K.491 and 503, are on all accounts the highest peaks in Mozart's concertos.

With them finishes the development we are sketching.   Eighteen months later, Mozart wrote the concerto in D, the so-called *Coronation*, K.537, but, despite its size, the work is poor in both respects.   As for the B flat, K.595, of 1791, it might perhaps have opened a new period if death had not cut off the young composer eleven months later; in this last work for piano and orchestra, the same problems are again tackled, and solved in partly new ways, whilst the emotion is as earnest as in the great concertos of 1785 and 1786.

PART II

1. The Salzburg Concertos: K.175 in D; 238 in B flat; 242 in F (for three pianos); 246 in C; 271 in E flat; 365 in E flat (for two pianos)

IT is always with a certain reverence that one approaches the work of art which, not itself a masterpiece, is at the head of a series of masterpieces. Beethoven's first quartet, Wagner's first opera, Shakespeare's earliest tragedy may or may not have little value in themselves; their position at the entrance of a road along which stand great works is enough to make them venerable in our eyes. It is with a feeling of reverence, likewise, that we undertake the study of Mozart's earliest concertos. They are slight in comparison with those that follow; they are nevertheless their elders and, if only for that reason, they are entitled to our respect.

But it happens that Mozart's earliest concertos, and especially the first one of all, have no need of their seniority to interest us. They have a charm of their own and he who is willing to linger by their limpid waters and gaze at their beauties with an affectionate and searching eye will be well enough rewarded by the joys of the task, without needing to be heartened by the distant view of the grander concertos that are to come.

One cannot deny, however, that modern hearers need a certain good will—we would almost say, a certain training—to enjoy gems of so small a magnitude. Successive schools of music for the last century and a half have so well blunted our sensibility by the growing complexity of their productions that we easily pass these merits by without heeding them. And this is true, indeed, of all Mozart, if not of all older music. Mozart seems to-day to be the most discreet of the great masters.[1] He never forces his entry into our midst. He

---

[1] We say to-day, because the epithets of "Stormer and caresser" (*Stürmer und Schmeichler*), which were applied to him in his life-time, prove that some of his contemporaries held a different opinion.

comes without noise or show. If we will have him, well and good; if we ignore him, he will not thump the table, he will not raise his voice. He is reserve itself. His intimate meaning escapes us most easily. He allows us to penetrate him less readily than Beethoven and one remembers how Schumann saw in his G minor symphony only "that hovering Hellenic Grace" (*diese schwebende griechische Grazie*), perceiving, that is, in that work of passion, merely qualities of form. One almost regrets his exquisite plastic loveliness when one hears him reduced to the level of just a graceful composer, a pure stylist, and when so many ignore the life that pulsates in his music.

The fact is that the delight given us by his perfect form is such that we are tempted not to ask anything more of him. The casket is so fair that we are content to look on it without opening it. We recognize in him an admirable goldsmith; we overlook the thinker (in the sense in which this word can be applied to a composer). We even sometimes reproach him with lacking a soul; his music comes from his head; it is superficial; the words of the reproach vary with the critic but in all cases the complaint is that he wants warmth and emotion.

When one hears such statements, one's first idea is that, of all his works, the speaker knows only the too well-known sonatas. Now, whilst one renders full homage to the delicate taste and feeling of these torments of one's childhood and whilst granting readily that some half-dozen of them will bear comparison with his best compositions, it must be admitted that their average level is below that of all his other works except his trios and his lieder. Abert has very judiciously divided his output into three parts: what he wrote for his public; what he wrote partly for his public and partly for himself; what he wrote wholly for himself. Five-sixths of the sonatas belong to the first category; they show his most impersonal side. His reputation has suffered from his music being best known by its weakest part; it is as if one judged Shakespeare on *Titus Andronicus* and *Timon of Athens* and started from these plays to express a comprehensive judgement on him.

Yet even in his greatest works Mozart is never emphatic. He never dwells on his thought, and the swift and shimmering succession of emotions through his music runs the risk of slipping by without imprinting itself on his listeners' minds. On knowing him, one catches his least beauties as they fly past, enjoying them, but ears too exclusively accustomed to the Romantics perceive in him little that deserves to attract notice and inspire admiration. For that reason we say that he is one of the hardest composers to understand.

In 1773, young Wolfgang is back in Salzburg. For the third and last time he has left Italy, having composed there, for the stage of Bologna, *Lucio Silla*, the last opera he is to write for an Italian audience. He is crossing the threshold of adolescence and entering his eighteenth year and the passions which, in the operas of his childhood, *Mitridate*, *La Finta Semplice, Ascanio in Alba*, he so often depicted imitatively and from hearsay, as it were, now graze his youthful soul. Precocious in musical intelligence, in every other respect he has remained a child and he awakens to the life of the passions no sooner than less abnormally gifted men do. At seventeen, the composer of quartets, symphonies and operas is still little more than a boy, over whom passes for the first time a breath of Romanticism.

The awakening of his sensibility causes individual strains of hitherto unknown intensity to resound in his works. It is after his last stay in Italy that he begins to be himself. Before that journey, one could point out indications and promises of personality; from then on, one finds whole works that belong entirely to him. In a sense, he was to remain imitative for a long time to come; but the imitation was henceforward to be different and take the form of assimilation instead of copy. Before 1772, his work has a documentary interest; the quartets of this year[1] are his first compositions to enjoy a life of their own and to deserve survival in virtue of their beauty. It is significant of the importance of the piano concerto in his life that his first attempt in this genre should date from this very period.

The fine, youthful ardour of these works of 1772 and early 1773 dies down in the routine-laden atmosphere of Salzburg, with the return to the small town after the stay in the greater world outside, a depressing experience which everyone knows and from which we suffer more or less according to the strength of our ambitions and aspirations, according also to the ease with which we accept the domination of our surroundings. We cannot be certain that Mozart experienced, on his return to Salzburg, the impression of collapse which seizes us when drab reality succeeds the enthusiasm of illusions; but it is likely that he felt already what he was to feel in 1778, on another return home.

---

[1] K.155 to 160, and perhaps Köchel-Einstein *Anhang*, nos. 210-213.

Salzburg, with its circumscribed life, dominated, musically, by the narrow taste of Archbishop Colloredo, was a prison for him. He put up with it as best he could since he had to, but already at seventeen his genius, perhaps unwittingly, was compressed in it, and the five years that separate his return from Italy from his departure for Paris are characterized by an impoverishment in the quality of his music.

If there is a tradition more popular than any other and slower to die, it is that of a dapper, powdered, beribboned and bewigged Mozart, the darling of the court and drawing-rooms of Vienna and expressing in his music nothing more than the superficial elegance and frivolity of 18th-century aristocratic life. This is the Mozart of minuets and contredanses, charming, no doubt, but bloodless, empty, incapable of serious thought and feeling. Mozart's work, it is said—and one adds: Haydn's, for Haydn has suffered the same injustice—breathes the scent of the salons and boudoirs of the Ancien Régime . . . and little else.

It is needless to say that such a tradition could arise only at a period as prejudiced against "Classical" art as the first half of the 19th century. Appearing at the time when the gigantic shadow of Beethoven was throwing darkness over what· had gone before, it maintained itself largely because of the public's knowledge of his sonatas and relative ignorance of his masterpieces.

The period concerning which this traditional opinion, happily fast dying out, is least unjust is that which extends from his return in 1773 to his departure for Mannheim and Paris in 1777. During these four years, Mozart is no more than the musical purveyor of pleasures to His Grace the Prince-Archbishop of Salzburg. Succumbing to the debilitating air of his town, he endeavours to refine his style, but, save in a few adagios, under the graceful exterior he utters only commonplace thoughts.

Before yielding, however, to the lethargy of these four years, he knew an instant of wonderful creativeness. In March, 1773, he came back to Salzburg. He left again four months later and his summer was spent in Vienna, his final return taking place in the early days of October. Now, although the romanticism of his stay in Italy had quickly worn off in contact with Salzburg, the two months in Vienna brought new fuel to his energy and stimulated it with new influences. If the six quartets he composed there in August and September[1] no longer shine with the same flame as those he had written in Italy,

---

[1] K.168 to 173.

they bear witness to a serious conception of the genre and to an elaboration which would make them worthy of their predecessors, were it not that a certain awkwardness and the newness of the style sometimes hinder the inspiration. The curiosity and desire to explore and break new ground which mark them were to resist for some time the influence of Salzburg; they survive in the first piano concerto and traces of them persist in the bassoon concerto written in July of the following year.

Mozart's first concerto for a solo instrument and orchestra[1] dates from December of this year and is written for the harpsichord.[2] The young musician's interest in the genre goes back a long way. Not only is his first concerto composed for a keyboard instrument but the first evidence we have of the little man's musical activities concern a harpsichord concerto which he was writing in 1760, with manifold blots of ink, at the age of four. An old friend of the family, the trumpeter Schachtner, records the following dialogue:

Papa: What are you doing?
Wolfgang: A harpsichord concerto; the first part is nearly done.
Papa: Let me see.
Wolfgang: It isn't done yet.
Papa: Let me see; it must be something wonderful!

Schachtner goes on:

His father took it and showed me a scribble of notes, most of it written over blots which had been rubbed out. Little Wolfgang, out of ignorance, had dipped his pen to the bottom of the inkwell; the result was a blot, but he at once took his decision, passed the back of his hand over it, smeared it over, and started merrily writing again. We laughed at first at what seemed to be just nonsense, but the father then gave heed to the important part, the notes and composition, and he remained for a long time motionless with his attention fixed on the sheet. Finally he let fall some tears—tears of admiration and joy. "See, Herr Schachtner," he said, "how correct and regular everything is; only it isn't playable; it's so terribly hard that no one could perform it." "That's just why it's a concerto," interrupted little Wolfgang; "one must practise it until one succeeds, you see; it should go like this." And he set about playing, but he could only just manage to show us what he was driving at. He had already the grasp of the concerto form.

We no longer possess this springtide sketch of the genre wherein his genius was to bear its finest fruit but there remain several

---

[1] The *concertone* in C for two violins, K.191, is a divertimento rather than a true concerto.
[2] The manuscript, now lost, bore the title: *Concerto per il Clavicembalo.*

adaptations as concertos of sonatas by sundry contemporary harpsichord writers; first, three by John Christian Bach;[1] then, later, movements drawn from works of Schobert, Eckardt, Raupach, Philip Emmanuel Bach and Honauer[2] grouped so as to form concertos, with tuttis inserted in the usual places. These arrangements passed for a long time as original works; MM. de Wyzewa and de Saint-Foix and Dr. Alfred Einstein have restored them to their real authors. They were no doubt exercises undertaken under his father's supervision.

CONCERTO NO. 1 IN D MAJOR FOR HARPSICHORD AND ORCHESTRA (K.175)
December, 1773[3]
    Allegro: C
    Andante ma un poco adagio: 3-4 (in G)
    Allegro: ¢
Orchestra: Strings; two hautboys, two horns, two trumpets, two drums.

This little concerto is full of a vitality that we shall not find again for some years in Mozart's work. It is a final personal outburst before the slumber of the years of *galant* music. Its character is marked enough to distinguish it from all other works of his; that is saying a lot and would not be true of its immediate successors. Its originality would still suffice to earn it a public performance and makes it capable of delighting the pianist who plays it in the intimacy of his home. It is enlivening rather than joyful, very physical, robust and muscular, rather knockabout, without any of the melancholy which pierces through the music of Mozart's Vienna years. No hidden depths, none of the shady and enigmatic nooks which, in later works, charm us and set us dreaming. Its frankness and openness,[4] its athletic vigour, win at once our sympathy; we love this busy and spritely little being as one loves a jovial and easy-going companion; it reveals a side of its creator that we do not often see and we are grateful to it for doing so. It is the counterpart of the Beotian Mozart, the Hanswurst of his letters.

Its brio does not prevent it from taking itself very seriously. The orchestra it opposes to the harpsichord is an ambitious one; no other

---

[1] K.107. [2] K.37, 39, 40, 41.

[3] No. 5 in the *Gesamtausgabe*.

[4] "Aperto" is an indication that Mozart has written at the beginning of several pre-Viennese works, for instance, the flute concerto in D, K.314, the manner of which recalls, with more delicacy, that of this concerto.

concerto of Mozart's before 1782 uses one as large and so many instruments do not become habitual till 1784. As in the classical symphony,[1] the whole nature of the work is indicated by the first theme (ex. 9), a long, wiry, sparkling phrase, given out in three periods and continuing into a little development filled with the same spirit, bounding and skipping in turn. The movement it introduces is, likewise, rather unmelodic; even the second subject is mainly rhythmic and the harpsichord's Alberti basses emphasize the character of a bustling little person, greatly concerned about nothing in particular, which is that of the whole allegro.

The interest lies mainly in the rhythms. Not many works of Mozart, even in his "great" period, have such varied ones. The first

subject affords three, and its codetta introduces a fourth. The second subject in *galant* works is frequently in contrast with the first; a rhythmical and pompous theme is followed by one singing and tender. But here, the difference is not strongly marked. After the harmless tumult of the opening, the pace slackens a little, and nearly two piano bars of tremolo octaves allow us to take breath. The next subject is calmer and more tuneful than its predecessor, but it is not the *cantabile* that John Christian would have given us here and it shows as original a set of rhythms as the first.

It soon lets itself go into *forte*, with amusing alternations of *piano*, and closes the tutti introduction with a last display of fireworks, whose rhythmical outline is still more personal. It quite cuts across

the four-beat rhythm of the movement.

The piano in nowise protests against the example of agitation which the tutti has set and, in its turn, reviews the themes we have just heard, with their dazzling richness of rhythm, expanding them a little but without adding anything new. The orchestra does not let it speak with as much docility as in the next few concertos; it cuts in from time to time to resume leadership, notably towards the end of the exposition when a dominant trill lets us think the harpsichord is tired and about to be silent. It is amusing to see the solo interrupt

---

[1] Except, of course, when a slow introduction precedes them; this, on the contrary, generally contrasts with what follows.

at once, repeating the very phrase the tutti had begun, then be interrupted itself, and finally regain mastery until it has finished its job and rests awhile to let the band conclude the exposition.

The tumult dies down somewhat in the *development* and the harpsichord starts a theme in the minor, the only sentimental passage in the movement; it ceases quickly, however, and the semi-quavers revive the bustle.

The andante belongs to those we called "dreams". It is as individual as the first movement and Mozart's personality, which will be somewhat overlaid by that of his age in the succeeding concertos, still stands out with vigour. It is a *sonata* in three sections whose *development* is but a short transition with an accompaniment characterized by an enchanting murmur of violins and violas. It opens and finishes on a note of languor, but between-whiles the range of feeling is fairly wide; a spritely phrase with dotted quaver rhythm, in particular, contrasts with the softness of the opening and closing themes. The movement is a first expression of the mood which is to inspire the andante of the A major concerto, K.414. Throughout a composer's work, we meet with diverse embodiments of the same thought, reappearances of the same theme transformed, and expressions of the same mood.

The finale is one of the most original in all his concertos. Not the most beautiful, not the deepest, but one of the most original, if only for its form, a *sonata* shot with polyphony, a first sketch of the finales of the G major quartet, the F major concerto, K.459, and the *Jupiter* symphony.[1] Its character is that of the opening allegro: bustle, incessant and aimless restlessness, the frisking of a little dog glad to be taken out for a walk. Its themes are more melodic than those of the first movement, and more numerous; in the thirty-nine bars of the first tutti alone there are four; the first one, a canon; the second, a syncopated figure that recalls one in the finale of the G major quartet; the third, tuneful and light, which resembles another subject in the same movement; and the fourth, a rhythmical concluding theme, given out by violas and basses in unison beneath the repeated semi-quavers of the fiddles.

Polyphony, which had been present at the opening, returns with the harpsichord entry. The canon starts over again and the solo adds a pleasing line of ornament which, from one hand to the other,

---

[1] Sonata form finales occur also, according to Engels, in concertos of J. F. Lang (1724–?94) and Al. Förster (1748–1823).

varies the theme of the strings.   Whimsically, the game stops all of a sudden and a dialogue passage follows, the tutti appearing to want to begin the canon again, the harpsichord interrupting with arpeggios and introducing a fresh subject.   The tutti's two other subjects follow; the solo forges ahead with a bravura passage and the orchestra winds up the exposition with the rhythmical concluding theme.

The *development* is the least interesting section.   At first, the solo dominates it completely; then, after a few new exploits, it makes way for the orchestra which brings back the canonic subject, and the recapitulation opens, almost unchanged.   The most remarkable part of the ending is the passage which leads to the cadenza; generally, this is a pompous succession of chords; here, it is a canon opening in four parts, one last contrapuntal sally which stops as soon as everyone is present.   The cadenza follows, then the rhythmical subject already heard at the end of the two expositions.[1]

The vigorous tone, abundance of ideas and touches of counterpoint of this movement are found also in the finale of the contemporary string quintet in B flat, K.174.

Mozart kept long a warm spot in his heart for this little work. During his travels in 1777 and 1778, he played it in an *Akademie* which his friends the Cannabichs gave at Mannheim; he wrote to his father: "This concerto is much liked."   He took it up again in Vienna in 1782 and 1783 and composed a new finale for it, a series of insipid variations which are a very poor substitute for the beautiful original *sonata*.[2]   Provided with this unfortunate last movement, it was played at an *Akademie* in March, 1783, and Mozart, in a letter to his father, called it "the favourite concerto".[3]

CONCERTO NO. 2 IN B FLAT MAJOR (K.238)
January, 1776.[4]
    Allegro aperto: C
    (Andante un poco adagio): 3-4 (in E flat)
    Rondeau: Allegro C
Orchestra: Strings; two hautboys (two flutes in the andante), two horns.

---

[1] When Mozart returned to this concerto in Vienna in 1782, he wrote a cadenza for each of the first two movements (K.624, I, II; facsimile publication by Mandyczewski).   The andante cadenza is particularly attractive.

[2] K.382.

[3] It was with this new finale that it was published by Boyer in Paris in 1784; the original finale was published only much later.

[4] No. 6 in the *Gesamtausgabe*.

CONCERTO No. 3 IN F MAJOR FOR THREE PIANOS (K.242)
February, 1776[1]
  Allegro: C
  Adagio: C (in B flat)
  Rondeau: Tempo di minuetto: 3-4
Orchestra: Strings; two hautboys, two horns

CONCERTO No. 4 IN C MAJOR (K.246)
April, 1776[2]
  Allegro aperto: C
  Andante: 2-4 (F major)
  Rondeau: Tempo di minuetto: 3-4
Orchestra: Strings, two hautboys, two horns

The three concertos that follow form a homogeneous group. They were written in the space of three months; two years separate them from the first concerto and nine months from the fifth. They represent a "manner" of Mozart's, the *galant* manner of his twentieth year, and if, for that reason, they no longer have for us much intrinsic value, they are still of biographical interest.

The years 1774 and 1775 had gone by without any great event in his life. At the close of 1774, Munich had ordered an *opera buffa* and father and son had stayed in that town early in the new year to supervise the rehearsals. The opera, *La Finta Giardiniera*, had come on in February; it met at first with some success but did not last for more than three performances and all hopes of a settlement at the court of the Elector vanished.

It is during the four years between his return from Italy in 1773 and his departure for Mannheim and Paris in 1777 that Mozart bowed most resolutely to the ideal of the age and made his most determined efforts to assimilate the style of *galanterie* and submit his own expression to the taste of his aristocratic public. He repressed the fire of his Italian works; he refined the native rudeness of his style, which was still apparent in the abrupt rhythms of his D major concerto; he silenced emotions the utterance of which would have surprised or shocked his hearers, and he confined himself to expressing feelings politely commonplace in a form graceful and smooth. The works of this period are as numerous as usual; they comprise the Munich opera, a pastoral drama, *Il Ré Pastore*, masses, motets, litanies, serenades

[1] No. 7 in the *Gesamtausgabe*.
[2] No. 8 in the *Gesamtausgabe*.

and divertimenti, only three symphonies,[1] and finally two well-known groups: the early piano sonatas and the five violin concertos.

The sonatas represent this period at its lowest; there is nothing more mediocre in his whole output, in spite of a few good movements like the andante of the F major, K.280, and it is really a pity that such uncharacteristic works should be so well-known. The violin concertos are better, at least those that are usually played, in G, D and A, but they are far from reaching the level of the great piano ones and it is for non-musical reasons that they are more often performed than these. They fully deserve their survival, however, and on the whole they are the best things that Mozart produced before his journey to Paris.

The violin concertos date from his twentieth year; he was turned twenty when he composed the three concertos we are about to consider. By this time his change of style is complete; no greater contrast can be imagined than that between them and the concerto in D. The fine unity of this work has gone; sentiment has replaced emotion; the themes are separated (or connected), not by significant workings-out but by amiable virtuosity passages; the recurrent motifs that give a movement its unity are lacking. The recapitulations are even less varied than in the first concerto; one single rhythm, established at the opening, is kept up to the end, and it is a commonplace one; the little galant *rondo*, which had been ousted by the grand contrapuntal finale of K.175, reappears for good and banishes in its turn the last traces of polyphony. These three concertos make us realize better the bold originality of the first,

wherein were expressed the fairest dreams of his youth, a joyful assault on life, mingled with a graceful tenderness verging on melancholy.[2]

The transition is fairly well marked in the bassoon concerto of 1774. The tone is already that of *galanterie*; virtuosity has spread; the rhythm is smooth; the *rondo alla menuetto* has taken possession of the finale; but certain witty rejoinders between solo and tutti in the *development* of the first movement recall the living whirlwind of 1773 of which they are a last eddy.

It is therefore with some disappointment that we come to these concertos. Yet they are not without charm. The balance is perfect

---

[1] Abert thinks that the excessively "modern" character of one of them, K.183, in G minor, had displeased the archbishop.

[2] Abert, op. cit., I, 393.

between form and matter. The substance is commonplace but the style is neat and, except in the finale of the F major, one does not meet with those empty passages so common in the sonatas. Without standing out as clearly as the first, each one has its own *nuance*; the B flat, more tender, the F, more playful, the C, more dapper. They deserve that we should linger by them for a few moments.

No. 2 *in B flat.* For depth, there is nothing to choose between these three little works, but in none of the three is the deportment quite the same. This one is the most distinguished of them. More than any other work of Mozart it represents the ideal of the 18th-century gentleman. It is a thing of good taste; the feelings to which it gives utterance could be expressed in the most fastidious drawing-room. At the same time, it is witty and bright and keeps a certain individuality. What is lacking is strong and concentrated emotion, but that was lacking in the very milieu for which it was written. It touches on many subjects and goes deeply into none. This is the ideal of *galant* music; it is the ideal of Mozart's own music during these years and particularly of these concertos, but it is attained in a peculiarly felicitous manner in this one.

The first subject is smooth, amiable and harmless (ex. 10); it has none of the rhythmical audacities of K.175; it replaces them by the alternatives of *piano* and *forte* beloved of all *galant* music and much beloved of Mozart who, later on, made serious use of them, treating them no longer as mere condiments but as a means of expressing deeper feelings. The phrase, like so many of his, unfolds in three sections. A passage in rising thirds follows it and reaches the dominant close which marks the halt before the second subject. This latter, quite Mozartian, is the only distinctive part of the tutti. It is a soft rustle of syncopations, *piano*, like echoing sighs, from first to second violins over held notes of violas and 'cellos. A more commonplace phrase succeeds it, again shifting from loud to soft, then the concluding subject, a mere figure. The solo takes up the first subject, passes to the dominant and inserts a theme of its own, the solo subject which John Christian had been the first to use systematically. All this is graceful and melodic. The strings give out the second subject, but *forte*; the piano takes it from them before they have finished and after two bars strings and solo conclude it in a very charming working-out passage, almost the only one in the concerto, where the rhythms criss-cross with gentle shimmering (ex. 11). This is linked up with the *development* by means of a rising passage which, in the opening tutti, had followed the first subject and of another passage which had separated the second subject from the conclusion; the loose construction allows the composer to assemble, undo and reassemble at will the different elements with which, like a puzzle, he builds up his work. This rearranging of themes and passages is destined later to gain in significance as the cohesion and unity of the whole asserts itself.

Save, perhaps, for the exquisite murmur of the second subject, nothing up to now could not have been signed John Christian. The *development* gives us a glimpse of the true Mozart. In a general way, however important a work of his may be, however commonplace, Mozart keeps back a few personal strains or modulations for his *developments*, especially for just before the reprise. This is so in a number of the *galant* pieces he wrote for the little Salzburg court; it is so here. The piano begins with a harmless phrase in F, twin sister of the solo subject. Then comes a rush in the strings and, suddenly, a little thunder-clap, and we are plunged into C minor by a falling arpeggio on a diminished seventh.[1] The strings are silent; only the acid tone of the hautboy accompanies the momentarily unbridled piano. An agitated and sorrowful tune in D minor breaks forth, crumbling away by degrees in solo runs and modulating to end up in G minor, whence the tutti has no difficulty in driving away the clouds and bringing us back to B flat. The piano, once more at peace, in a bravura passage behind which the composer's true face is again hidden, leads back the first subject whose well-bred, aristocratic good temper makes us forget the passing storm, and the recapitulation unfolds without change.

No more *élan*, no more fire, no more dominating emotion, consequently no more vigorous unity; the work is not disjointed but it holds together mainly by formal means. The little concerto in D, despite its childishness, we felt to be necessary; it answered to a mood of its creator. Not so the B flat, nor the two following concertos. They are well-regulated successions of agreeable sentiments whose order might be different without the work losing anything thereby. The D major concerto was as single, as undissociable, as the G minor symphony of 1773; it is this unbreakable oneness which for the time being goes out of the young Mozart's compositions and which he recaptures fully only after regaining his freedom in Vienna.

From the first concerto's andante to this one, too, it is a far cry.

---

[1] The principle of a *minor* passage after the first part of a movement is, of course, traditional.

The form is that of the *sonata* in two sections, the second of which
repeats the first with a few changes of detail. The orchestra starts
the first phrase and the piano enters at the eighth bar. The character
is that of the first movement—an impersonal sweetness expelled one
instant by the agitation of the second subject in C minor. Here,
too, it is the middle part—the reprise, since there is no *development*
—whose yearning and languor are most truly Mozartian (ex. 12).

The rondo is the most homogeneous movement. It is constantly spritely and gay, with a discreetly plebeian tone not unpleasing to the declining Ancien Régime. In his violin concertos of the preceding year, Mozart had used for his finales the *rondeau* of the contemporary French violin composers. Very different from Rameau's dances *en rondeau*, this form was nearer to the ordinary rondo with its indefinite number of episodes and its inorganic nature. The main difference lay in that it allowed episodes of varying rhythms and beats, whereas the older rondo, or rondeau, usually kept the same *tempo* from one end to the other.[1] Mozart now gives up this heterogeneous model never to return to it. His taste for organic construction leads him to adopt the form of the French dance *en rondeau*,[2] whence he develops the *sonata rondo*, the Mozartian rondo par excellence, one of the richest forms of the classical period. It has been repeated over and over again that the invention of this form is due to Beethoven. This is an injustice to Mozart, and all the more grievous because, in the matter of form, he innovated little, and this rondo is his only important contribution to the growth of structure. Beethoven used it, certainly; but he did not modify it and he left it as he received it from Mozart.

The Mozartian rondo is simple but organic: refrain, first couplet, generally in the dominant or relative major, first return of the refrain, second couplet, moving further away from the tonic, second return of the refrain, followed by a repetition of the first couplet and a last return of the refrain. Originally, the lines of refrain and couplets .vere clear cut. John Christian[3] began to break down their stiffness and, in his concertos, he mixed pianistic passages with the themes and thus softened the hardness of the outlines. But he would pass, abruptly, from couplet to refrain with a double bar followed by a *da capo*, and the segmentation of his couplets was still very marked. Moreover, at least in his concertos, he does not repeat the first couplet after the second return of the refrain. Mozart does, and he also effects transitions between the different parts, so that the plan is no longer so rigid and the unity is greater. The main lines are not yet submerged in the whole as they will be in his Viennese rondos and the

---

[1] Compare for instance the rondo of Bach's E major violin concerto and the finales of Mozart's concertos in G, D and A.

[2] Cf. pp. 49-50.

[3] He used it, not only in his concertos, but in his chamber music and in at least one of his symphonies, op. 18, II, in B flat.

return of the subjects is still regular and predictable, but there is a distinct advance on the simple little rondos of John Christian.

Following French practice, in this concerto Mozart puts his second couplet in a minor key; this is a first likeness to the *development* of sonata form which, at the *galant* period, often opens in the relative minor.[1] The other couplets are, the first in the tonic and dominant, the third, which repeats the first minus one of its four subjects, in the tonic only. This third couplet is a true recapitulation and when, in later works, the second couplet, instead of introducing a new theme, "works out" material already heard, the transformation of the French rondeau into the sonata rondo will be complete.

The themes themselves in this rondo are more interesting than in the allegro and andante. Their popular gait makes the movement more racy. The piano preponderates as it does in the rest of the work; the taste for collaboration with the orchestra, save in a very few bars, has passed with the first concerto and will not return till 1784.

Mozart played this concerto at Munich in 1777 and also, with the two following, at Stein's in Augsburg and Cannabich's in Mannheim the same year. He tried later, apparently without success, to have all three engraved in Paris.

No. 3 in F major for three pianos. The B flat concerto had been composed for himself; the next two were written for others. A sister of Archbishop Colloredo, Countess Lodron, whose husband held a position in his brother-in-law's court, and her two daughters, Louise and Josepha, who were perhaps pupils of Mozart, played the piano —the mother and elder one with ability, if the evidence of the music is to be trusted—and it is for them that he wrote, in February of the same year, a concerto for three pianos.

It is certainly the least interesting of the whole series. The idea of three pianos in one concerto makes us think at once of Bach and the rich contrapuntal effects he drew from this combination. It seems inconceivable to us that one should write for three pianos without utilizing counterpoint, and the ingenuous homophony of this concerto upsets us.

It is obviously unfair to insist on this. The ideal of 1776 was not that of Bach, and Mozart is not responsible for the absence of polyphony in his work, although later, and even in his concertos, he was to give it a generous share. But, once we have granted this, the work is none the less weak. The ideas are commonplace; they have

----

[1] In the *da capo* aria, too, the second part is often in the relative minor.

not even the impersonal charm of the last concerto. No working out; harmonies almost always commonplace and hackneyed; and the advantage he takes of the interplay of three soloists is limited to echoes, a few answers, runs divided between them and relations of theme and accompaniment. The orchestra's part in all this is of the smallest; it is almost completely silent for the greater part of the work.

The first movement has the same plan as in the last concerto; the solo subject appears twice, each time in C major. A new theme, also in C, opens the *development*; it goes quickly into C minor and leads to a sequence of arpeggios alternating between first and second-pianos and recalling the sequences of virtuosity motifs which make up the middle sections in the concertos of John Christian, Haydn, Schobert, Schröter and other contemporaries. It is the only instance of this wearisome device in Mozart's piano concertos; it had occurred the year before in the violin concerto in D, K.218, and he used it later in a violin sonata in D, K.306, composed in 1777.

The rondo has the form of the Mozartian rondo, but its *tempo* is that of a minuet, its themes are colourless, and it has nothing of the wit and vigour of the B flat. In all three movements the third piano part is so reduced that Mozart was able to arrange the work for two pianos without losing anything important. No doubt Josepha was less expert than her mother and sister.

The strictures we have just made do not apply to the adagio. Here indeed the true soul of Mozart is revealed. Generally speaking (we have already mentioned this point), whatever the scope of the rest, his slow movements proceed nearly always from a personal inspiration. His own ideal is fused here with that of his public and inspires movements that are among the purest and most poetic of his youth. One of the most recognizable signs of his genius is the oft-proclaimed superiority of his andantes, for they are the movements that suffer mediocrity least gladly and come off worst at the hands of second-rate composers. It is moderately easy to polish off a dashing scherzo, but only the greatest succeed in their slow movements.

The adagio of this concerto is a *sonata* in three sections, like that of the first one, but here the *development* is more than a mere transition; it is broad and has its own importance. The usual orchestral prelude gives out the two subjects; the pianos enter with the first, then modulate to F. The second piano gives out the *cantabile* solo subject, accompanied by its own left hand and the right hand of the first piano. After a few bars, they exchange sides. This winding theme leads without interruption into the true second subject.

This latter consists in a very simple, almost sketchy theme, syncopated, with a rather peculiar wavy accompaniment which attracts as much notice as the theme itself. It is the first cast of a subject which will return in the F major andante of the great concerto in C, K.503. We have already noted the frequence with which families of themes and even of movements recur in Mozart, and their transformations often bear witness to an interesting growth.

The seven bars of the *development* and the two bars of the cadenza that are derived from it are the finest in the work. Above another rather sketchy subject, one of the pianos outlines in staccato demisemi-quavers the most exquisite accompaniment one can imagine. It is one of Mozart's most captivating examples of impressionism. Leaving aside clear-cut and limpid contours, he seeks for a few bars blurred lines, misty effects, which contrast with the clarity of the rest (ex. 13). Here too we think of a passage in a later work: of the

Ex. 13

Ex. 13—*contd.*

development in the allegro of the quartet in D, K.499. Half-way through, the hautboys enter and cast their biting tone over the rustlings of the pianos. It all ends rather abruptly and resolves into the first subject.

Mozart has left cadenzas for the first two movements. The one for the adagio makes at once for the lovely passage in the *development* and goes over it for two bars before unwinding into commonplace *fioriture*.

No. 4 in C major. The third and last concerto of this group, written for a Countess Lützow, is a trifle more interesting (ex. 14). It has recovered something of the spirit of the D major (that kind of golden age to which one is constantly looking back at this stage of Mozart's life, when *galanterie* seems to have conquered him!), combined with the grace of the B flat, but it still remains somewhat impersonal. Like the two others, it inserts a solo subject between the

first and second ones, and the *development* is in the minor; a new
theme appears in it but has not the sincere note of anguish of the one
which had blossomed forth at this point in the B flat.   The beginning
of the andante is very Mozartian in its yearning, but soon the piano

loses itself in inexpressive meanderings. The finale is again a minuet, rather wittier than that of the three pianos concerto, but this is not saying much.

This concerto would not detain us long were it not for its solo subject. It is the earliest version of a theme which appears twice more in the piano concertos and both times in C major works (ex. 15, a). It is simple and might be by any composer round about 1785. Six years later, the same position, key and association of ideas recall it to Mozart's mind, but enriched (ex. 15, b). Finally, it reappears for the last time four years later, having attained its full stature, both simplified and deepened (ex. 15, c). The origin of this beautiful tune is in the C major Salzburg concerto of 1776, and this is our concerto's main title to remembrance.[1]

Mozart played this concerto at Munich in 1777; he taught it to a pupil at Mannheim where Abbot Vogler played it in January, 1778. He referred to it in a letter to his father of April 10th, 1782, asking to have it sent him in Vienna, which shows that he still took an interest in it at that date.

CONCERTO No. 5 IN E FLAT (K.271)
January, 1777[2]
    Allegro: C
    Andantino: 3-4 (C minor)
    Rondeau: Presto: ¢; Menuetto: Cantabile: 3-4; Presto: ¢
    Orchestra: Strings; two hautboys, two horns.

One has to listen very attentively to these three last concertos to find in each one a distinctive personality under the selfsame court livery which they all wear, whereas from the very first bar of the fifth a sharply marked character proclaims itself. Proud and self-assured,—it curries no favours either by smiling benevolence or by playful amiability; it is just itself and it cares little whether the public

---

[1] Mandyczewski has published in facsimile a manuscript of part of K.246, now in the Mozarteum, which shows how Mozart understood the soloist's part during the tuttis. He did not remain silent as he would to-day, but took his place as a *ripieno* with the other instruments, filling out the bass, unless there was a second piano to fulfil this function. The manuscript shows that the filling out was quite impersonal. The performance of these concertos with large orchestras has rendered this *ripieno* function of the solo part unnecessary.

[2] No. 9 in the *Gesamtausgabe*.

greet it well or ill. The arrogance of its entry is to be somewhat softened later on, but its independent attitude reappears and keeps it clear of the golden chains of *galanterie*. The contrast is as great as between the first concerto and those of 1776.

Only nine months separate this work from its predecessor and these nine months, though well filled, did not see the composition of anything important. Church sonatas, masses, divertimenti and "table music", serenades, arias—nothing of all this affords much interest; nothing of it has survived except the Haffner serenade which figures occasionally on our programmes, one of the few rather mediocre works of Mozart's youth which still keep afloat—one wonders why—when so many of his masterpieces are submerged.

Nothing in all this series would lead one to foresee any change. Yet under the apparently stagnant surface of these years new departures were preparing. Only some external circumstance was needed to set the young musician free from the bonds imposed on him by convention and to enable the hidden workings, of which this concerto was to be the result, to come to light. Such a circumstance occurred in January, 1777. There passed through Salzburg a French pianist of a certain fame, Mlle. Jeunehomme, and Mozart was asked for a concerto. The presence of the foreign virtuosa aroused all his fire; anxious to appear at his best before a more interesting executant than the Countess Lodron and her daughters, he brought to consciousness the labour which, unbeknown to him, had been going on within.

In the 1776 concertos the importance of the public taste was supreme; it determined the tone of the work. Now it is the composer who matters; the audience takes second place. He is much more concerned with "expressing himself" than with timidly nursing his listeners; this alone explains the differences between this concerto and its foregoers. Let us enumerate some of them.

The very personal opening is unique in all Mozart. The themes of the first two movements are characteristic and the middle of the allegro is no longer an episode but a true thematic development. Orchestral and solo interplay is at times very close. The whole andantino bears witness to this independence. It rises far above the slow movements of the earlier concertos and personal expression makes no concession in it to the taste of the day. And even the finale, although it is the most conventional movement of the three, betrays the same originality by the extreme freedom of its construction, its high spirits and the absence of all inexpressive virtuosity.

I. The allegro opens with one of those square-cut unison themes, founded upon the common chord, which occur so often in E flat works of this period. The orchestra starts it but, to our surprise, the solo, instead of waiting patiently for the end of the usual tutti, enters as a usurper and finishes it. The orchestra starts again; the same square-cut, unison, *forte* theme is repeated; the same interruption from the piano finishes it once more. With a change of tactics, the orchestra re-enters, *pianissimo*, with a fresh motif and the piano, apparently put out, keeps silent till the usual hour for its entry (ex. 16).

This appearance of the piano before the customary time is on the whole a rather facile trick which the composer uses to compel attention and Mozart, who always disliked any obvious and forceful device, never returned to it. Beethoven made use of it twice, with a different object; since his time, the solo entry at, or near, the beginning of a concerto has become the rule.

Once the piano has been put in its place the strings continue in a gentler tone. A *cantabile* passage leads to another square-cut motif, which takes us to the second subject through little phrases in which loud and soft alternate sharply. The second subject is a pleasant sinuous theme, entrusted to the first fiddles, which unfolds in two fragments, separated by a horn and woodwind call; in its latter part the second fiddles add a graceful counterpoint. It is followed by a rhythmical passage; then, after a sudden rest, the violins whisper very softly a little hesitant motif which is broken into a moment later by the general fanfare that closes the tutti and ends, according to rule, on a full-close. This time we expect a regular piano entry with the first subject. Fresh surprise! The violins open a rustling theme based on the three notes of the chord, and it is over this, with a dominant trill, that the solo makes its bow. Then, once the strings are silent, it goes on with a new strain whose tone recalls that of several we have just heard. Only then does the first subject come back, shared once again between the orchestra in unison and the piano.

To the accompaniment of discreet held notes on the hautboys, the solo instrument forges ahead and develops the first part of the subject (ex. 16, a) like a serious-minded symphonist. It has modulated to the dominant before it remembers that it is playing a concerto and lets off a few fireworks which bring back a ritornello already heard in the tutti, then the second subject. The piano attacks it alone; the strings add their strength in the fourth bar. The graceful counterpoint which belonged just now to the second violins passes to the first and when the subject is over these repeat it to the piano's

accompaniment. The solo resumes command a few moments later
and the sinuosities of the theme turn little by little into passage
work which leads to the usual trill and close.

Yet we have not reached the end of the exposition. The figure
of the close had concluded the first tutti and it is followed by the same
rest as formerly. But now, it is the piano which enters with the
hesitating phrase whispered just now by the fiddles, and when the
orchestra seeks to crush it with the fanfare that had heralded the first
solo entry it answers back with the very theme, *piano*, with which
the strings had silenced it a minute earlier! A manifest robbery,
accomplished with perfect wit and ease! The orchestra, once again
taken aback, can at first do no more than accompany the victor rather
piteously. But suddenly it changes its mind and, taking advantage
of the piano's arrival on the tonic, trumpets forth in unison the opening
subject. The piano hits back; the orchestra starts afresh; the piano
likewise, an octave higher. Its victory is assured and, just as it did
after its second entry, it sets about working out a fragment of the
subject. The exposition is over.

All this part is more compact and more concise than in the earlier
concertos. The first virtuosity passage is short and no theme is
reserved for the solo. On the contrary, the piano takes a mischievous
delight in sneaking all its subjects from the enemy and using them for
its own ends.

The *development* is quite as thrifty. It is entirely thematic, a
rare thing in Mozart's concertos. We meet in it no subject we do not
already know. The first theme provides most of it; orchestra and
solo throw back its two halves from one to the other and, having
become friends again, play ball with its dislocated limbs. When they
weary of their sport, they wend their way towards the reprise with a
chromatic scale begun by the piano and finished by the orchestra.

The recapitulation is not without a few changes. As soon as it
has replied to the orchestra, the piano launches forth with a new
development of the first subject, modulating from E flat to F minor
and G minor and returning to the tonic in descending semi-tones.
After which it follows more calmly in the track of the exposition.
In the cadenza it asserts itself and carries further with a fiery flight the
rising line of the orchestra which had led up to it and which makes
us think of the G minor quintet.[1] The cadenza is like the other solo

---

[1] It is a characteristically Mozartian motif; we meet it in the most unexpected places; flute and strings quartet in D, K.285, allegro; E flat symphony,
K.543, finale.

developments; no pure virtuosity, but thematic passages based on two subjects, one of which, square-cut, had been heard in the opening tutti and had appeared for an instant at the beginning of the *development*. It is not the superfluous adornment which most cadenzas are, even when they are the composer's own, but just one last working out, entrusted to the solo and forming part of the movement. It is therefore wrong to substitute another one.

The fanfare which had concluded the first tutti closes the cadenza. Have we at last exhausted this little work's bag of tricks? By no means. After the close the fiddles take up again the hesitating theme which occurred before the solo entry. The piano reappears on the scene with the trill with which it had entered originally, and we begin to wonder whether a double bar has not announced a repetition of the movement when the orchestra breaks off and the solo bursts out into a display of rockets, of clearly conclusive character, which from arpeggio to arpeggio, the piano incessantly asserting itself, lead us to the final chord.

II. This hopeful and energetic allegro is succeeded by a very different piece. It is in C minor, the first minor movement we have met in the concertos. For Mozart, as for all his contemporaries, the minor is an exceptional mode. Reserved for the utterance of more individual emotions, it reflects well-characterized and, on the whole, uncommon moods. Even the least interesting composers generally find something touching to say when they turn to it.

We have already spoken of the "tragic" andantes to which this one belongs. This family is well represented in the concertos. Among the movements we have thus grouped together, several of those in C minor are closely related. From 1766 to 1791, and particularly between 1772 and 1784, Mozart composed some twelve andantes or adagios in this key. Three of them are somewhat similar to our concerto; they are those of a C major quartet, K.157, and E flat symphony, K.184, and of the *Sinfonia Concertante*, K.364. Differing in their rhythms, they all begin with themes whose feature is a swing

from tonic to dominant and a little motif of three notes

a sigh or a sob, the presence of which reveals the same mood.[1]

---

[1] It is interesting to observe that these elements are all present in the pathetic C minor andante of an overture of C. F. Abel, op. 7, III, which Mozart had copied out at the age of nine or ten and which passed for a long time as one of his symphonies under the Köchel, no. 18.

It is to the fine andante of the *Sinfonia Concertante* that ours is most closely akin. The same mood has sought utterance in both movements, or rather—since the same mood never recurs completely —two moods as similar as can be. Not only are the themes almost identical but the time signature is the same (ex. 17). Both give vent to that despairing sorrow of the very young, a sorrow that feeds on itself and refuses to admit the least ray of hope. In the *Sinfonia*, it is more concentrated, without any bright moments; in the concerto, it is more outward and its themes more dramatic; and there are some almost peaceful periods; the andantino of the concerto has still something child-like which the other has lost.

At first hearing, what we notice is the recitative-like nature of this movement. Mozart has adopted in it the opera seria style to the extent of stopping some of his phrases on the dominant and concluding them with a full close of the whole orchestra. As Wyzewa and Saint-Foix have remarked, one could almost mistake it for a tragic recitative from some opera of Gluck's and transferred from the voice to the first violins or piano. The strings start, with muted violins, and ni so tranquil a manner that the contrast with what has gone before is most striking. The phrase we have just quoted continues for some time; the wind come in to strengthen the fundamental with held notes or to double the strings, and when the theme stops on a G of the first violins the whole band enters, *forte* and in unison, for the full close (ex. 18).

The piano raises its voice and climbs slowly to the octave. Hardly has it reached it when the strings resume their *melopoeia* to which the solo adds a singing counterpoint, a bird of mourning hovering over the funeral train. Little by little, the *melopoeia* weakens and dies away and we are left with the piano's song which mingles with the recitative (ex. 19). When it is over, the orchestra returns in strength; a quick modulation and we find ourselves suddenly under the serene skies of E flat!

The change is abrupt and characteristic of Mozart. It may well surprise some people. Accustomed as we are to the broad developments of 19th-century symphonists, we tolerate less easily these sharp about-turns carried out almost without warning and justified, it seems, only by the rule which demands at a given moment a passage from minor to major. Yet they are never without emotional significance in Mozart and do not take place just to satisfy a law of form. It is true that we notice them in the places where they are usual in sonata form, but we meet them at many other moments where no rule requires them. They correspond to a fundamental need of his nature. His mercurial temperament, as unstable as an April day, shifts incessantly from one pole to the other; in the midst of the most boisterous laughter a sad thought will come like a cloud to darken his daylight, just as through bitter tears there appear sometimes the sudden rays of a smile. We are not astonished to find this feature of child psychology in a work written at twenty-one by a youth who was in no way precocious and was still as near to childhood as to man's estate.

The part that follows is in E flat. It is a long solo, broken once by the orchestra with a phrase from the first recitative transposed into the major and culminating, like it, in a full close, still in E flat, not without a hint of a *minor* modulation.

A noisy codetta, with syncopated accompaniment, concludes the exposition. The piano enters with the theme of the codetta, according to a custom always dear to Mozart, especially in his concertos, and repeats it with ornaments. The orchestra joins in; both give out the theme a third time and there follows a short *development*, similar to that of a first movement and quite thematic. But it is not much more than a transition and, quickly, two bars of dreamy and shimmering sadness, based on a descending scale of a minor seventh, fall back, discouraged, into the opening *melopoeia*. Their disillusioned grace reminds us of Ernest Hello's definition of Romanticism as "the musical acceptance of organized despair".

All that follows is a repetition of the first part, transposed into the minor. After giving out the first subject, the orchestra modulates as it did just now into E flat and the piano tries to follow it, but after a few bars it yields to weariness and returns to C minor.

What exactly is the transformation that comes over a passage like this when it is transposed from major to minor? Play the part of this andantino between bars 33 and 53 and then pass at once to the corresponding part of the recapitulation (bars 92 to 113). What is the difference? Nothing is changed and yet everything seems different. The outlines, the landscape, the rises and falls are the same; the voices too, and they speak at the same times. But the eye that gazes on this landscape is changed; what it saw in joy it sees again through tears, and details which it overlooked just now appear to it laden with a message of sorrow. It is the same view, with suffering added.

After a moving dialogue between piano and first violins (bars 110–15) the codetta with the syncopated accompaniment leads to the cadenza, a true development like that of the allegro and an integral part of the work. There is first of all a descent enriched by the successive entries of the parts and leading to a pause on a chord of the diminished seventh. Then a fragment of the *melopoeia* gradually emerges which the composer, a few moments later, banishes impatiently, uttering a succession of passionate accents which rise again to the high E flat where he had started. Finally, exhausted, the music falls back on the trill which announces the orchestra's return. The voice of the piano has almost died away; yet, as the orchestra fails to enter, it drags on dejectedly a little longer with a few shreds of a strain, until the violins, now unmuted, and all the other instruments, take up the end of the *melopoeia* at the very place where the cadenza had intruded on it. Then the piano regains courage and leads the *melopoeia* to its conclusion; the orchestra rounds off with a full close and the curtain falls upon this fragment of a nameless tragedy.

III. The brio of the first movement revives with even greater impudence in the rondo. The piano has recovered its strength and it chatters joyfully for close on forty bars before the orchestra appears. The dialogue is more marked than in the other movements and piano and tutti answer each other back with vivacity and good humour. Refrain and couplets, themes and passages run into one another with singlemindedness and there are really no "subjects". The form is that of the Mozartian rondo until the return of the passage which acts as refrain.[1] But then, instead of going on at the same breakneck pace, piano and orchestra start modulating from E flat to F minor, then to G minor and C minor, with a foreboding of some momentous change. A passage based on the beginning of the refrain completes the transition and after a pause on the usual chord of the diminished seventh, rhythm and *tempo* change and the piano opens, *cantabile*, a minuet which makes up the second episode! It is a theme and four variations, in which the piano plays sometimes alone, sometimes with the strings' pizzicati; a coda follows composed of piano arpeggios sustained by tutti chords. The whole leads up to a cadenza—of virtuosity, this time—and we return to the refrain. It is an episode of highly charming fancy. In all the series, for freedom of form, no other finale surpasses this movement, and only one, that of the 1784 E flat, K.449, equals it.[2]

It would be an exaggeration to pretend that Mozart has attained in this delightful work the level of his great compositions of 1784–86. Maturity is wanting here, and even the andantino, however moving, expresses a more youthful, more external sorrow than the "tragic" andantes of the Vienna years. But it is the earliest of his piano concertos which survives to-day on its own merits and, in the history of the young composer's growth, it is an important landmark. We have insisted upon its originality, its independence, even its arrogance, towards its public. It is the first time that Mozart allows himself such freedom, and he will not take it every day. In 1777,

---

[1] This passage announces Monostatos' air in the *Magic Flute*.

[2] Mandyczewski has published in facsimile two *intratas* that Mozart wrote for this finale.

he feels sure of himself, but a short while hence he will be leaving for Mannheim, then for Paris;[1] he will have a fresh public to win, other tastes to conciliate, and once again he will submit to external requirements.   Then, upon his return to Salzburg, he will try once more to please those of whom he had sought in vain to be rid; finally, at Vienna, he will be in the same situation as in France and for some time he will bow to the taste of his new patrons.   Only seven or eight years later, towards 1784, will he recover for good the audacity which the French pianist's visit had given him the opportunity of displaying.

CONCERTO No. 6 IN E FLAT FOR TWO PIANOS (K.365)
1779 or 1780[2]
    Allegro: C
    Andante: 3-4 (in B flat)
    Rondeaux: Allegro: 2-4
Orchestra: Strings; two hautboys, two horns, two bassoons.

Between the sixth concerto and its predecessor there elapsed an interval of eighteen months or two years, an interval filled with important events since Mozart's last journey abroad took place during this time.

A few months after the composition of the fifth concerto, he left to seek fortune away from Salzburg, fortified by the presence of his mother and the counsels of his father.   The departure was sad; the young sister Nannerl was particularly afflicted and wept, says Leopold, all day long; her tears dried up only in the evening, at the hour of piquet.   Mozart and his mother stopped one month in Bavaria: at Munich, where he vainly solicited a post, and at Augsburg, where he made the acquaintance of his cousins and, in particular, of his girl cousin, the celebrated Bäsle, with whom he was to keep up a correspondence the lively tone of which has caused certain commentators to raise their eyebrows.   From Augsburg they went to Mannheim where they spent the winter and where the favourable welcome given them by the Elector Charles Theodore raised a few hopes.   There, Mozart composed some works for flute, some piano and some violin sonatas, and found his first love, Aloisia Weber, whose sister Constance he was later to marry.   Mannheim not producing

---

[1] On the way, at Munich, he played this concerto on October 10th.
[2] No. 10 in the *Gesamtausgabe*.

anything, mother and son wended their way to Paris, where Wolf-gang stayed through the spring and summer of 1778. Three months after their arrival Frau Mozart died and her son was harboured by the Grimm d'Epinay *ménage*. His letters inform us of the desperate attempts he made to win a footing in Paris, all the more frantic for his knowledge that their failure would spell a return to his abhorred native town. He won a certain fame; he found pupils in the nobility, among others the daughter of the Duc de Guines, for whom he wrote the concerto for flute and harp (the father played the flute, the daughter the harp and, moreover, "composed" under the bored guidance of Mozart); the *Concerts Spirituels* gave a symphony he had composed for the occasion in the "Parisian taste"[1] and a *Sinfonia Concertante* for four wind instruments[2]; Noverre, ballet master at the Opera, entrusted him with the music for a ballet which was cut out at the last moment, mislaid, and rediscovered by Victor Wilder in 1874.[3] The narration of these events is accompanied in his letters by recriminations against the country and its inhabitants and ex-pressions of patriotism as interesting for the historian of German national feeling as they are unpleasing to French ears.[4]

The result of all these endeavours was that Grimm advised him to pack up and get home. He left empty-handed but the wiser for his experience of the world, on September 26th, 1778. He passed through Mannheim where friends kept him for another two months, and Munich, where he found Aloisia, now unfaithful, and returned to the fold on January 15th or 16th, 1779.

These eighteen months are of no great interest for the student of his concertos, but for himself they are most important. The artist in him gained from them, by seeing at its source in Mannheim the new instrumental style of which only traces had reached him hitherto, and by entering into contact in Paris with an operatic art other than that of Italy. The influence of these new musical experiences was to be lasting. Moreover, as a man he gained much. During his stays in Bavaria, the Palatinate, France, he learnt to face life alone and to drink deep of disappointments, both amorous and professional.

---

[1] K. 297 in D, called the *Paris*.

[2] Köchel-Einstein 297 b, in E flat; or perhaps another work now lost.

[3] *Les Petits Riens*.

[4] E.g.: "My whole body seems to be on fire and I tremble from head to foot with eagerness to teach the French more thoroughly to know, appreciate and fear the Germans" (letter to his father, July 31st, 1778; tr. E. Anderson, II, 872).

It was in the course of these eighteen months that he emerged for good from childhood. The difference between movements as similar as the andantino of the 1777 concerto and the andante of the *Sinfonia Concertante* of 1780 consists in that the former is the work of an adolescent, the latter the work of a man. There lay the most important result of the journey.

Mozart, therefore, returned to Salzburg to lie down again under the yoke of the archbishop. For the tourist who attends Mozart festivals in his native town, his music, "all grace and smiles", cannot have a more pleasing setting. The position of the city, its perched castle, its baroque churches, its vegetation, its belt of mountains seem to harmonize intimately with the works to which he listens and he feels that Mozart's genius could not have been born and nurtured anywhere but in such a paradise. Without denying the possibility of discovering a superficial relation between Salzburg's charm and the great musician who was born there (of a Bavarian father), it is well to remember that no town in the world was better hated by Mozart than the one where he saw the light of day and where, apart from his travels, he spent the first twenty-five years of his existence. It is to Munich or Mannheim or Prague—to Prague especially, which alone fêted him as he deserved—rather than to Salzburg that he would come back to-day to attend a festival of his works.

His return to Salzburg in January, 1779, was full of painful contrasts. Not that his duties as *Kapellmeister* to Archbishop Colloredo were onerous, but, dazzled and inebriated by his view of a world outside, despite his disappointments in it, he was returning perforce to bury himself, without a future, in a narrow-minded town where no one, except perhaps his father, sympathized with his ambitions or understood to what heights his genius could soar. Here he now saw himself fated to live and die, the servant of a master for whom an artist was an official less important than his chamberlain, art an agreeable but unessential pastime, and from whose taste in music his own was moving further and further. How he must have chafed, and with what despair he must have seen again the baroque domes of the city, as he remembered the vain attempts he had made to free himself!

It is from the spirit in which he speaks of Salzburg in his letters from Munich, Mannheim and Paris that we picture his state of mind, for his correspondence with his father naturally ceased with his homecoming. His only consolation was his music. Even so, it had to please listeners whose ideal was rapidly ceasing to be his. The

difference between what he could compose and what he had to compose can be measured in the two masses, K.317 and 337, which he
wrote at this period, and the *Kyrie* in D minor, K.341, so darkly
splendid, which he wrote at Munich a few months later, away from
the constraint imposed by his Grace's taste.

This does not mean that everything he wrote during this last
stay (January, 1779, to November, 1780) shows constraint. A certain
number of fine works dating from these years are the authentic children
of his untrammelled genius and among them is the concerto for two
pianos. It is a work of joy which he could not have conceived and
fashioned otherwise even if he had neglected completely the reigning
taste.

We do not know its precise date. We only know that it was
written at Salzburg between January 15th or 16th, 1779, the date of
his return, and November 4th or 5th, 1780, the date of his departure
for Munich. Neither do we know the circumstances in which it
was composed but its well-developed virtuosity makes it likely that
he intended to play it with his sister. The agreement between the
two pianos is so perfect, their collaboration so single-hearted, that
one would like to think it was so.

Ex. 22

The tone of the work is one of dignity, worthy of expression in the presence of sovereigns. The impulsive themes of the fifth concerto have no counterparts here save in the rondo where a more "unbuttoned" gaiety, as Beethoven would have said, is always allowable; the composer's personality asserts itself more discreetly and the purely physical go of its predecessor is absent from the first movement. But if it is less full of fun, it is more graceful and of fairer countenance. The less ambitious flight is made up for by a breadth and ampleness in its themes and proportions which was lacking in the restless concerto of 1777. We return to the ideal of the B flat concerto of 1776 with an added ripeness and gravity in the personality. Even to-day, its charm is deeper and it can be taken more seriously than the earlier work.

I. It opens with one of Mozart's most grandiose subjects—a

unison theme based on the common chord, like almost all his E flat first subjects; only, whereas many of them are square and rhythmical, as in K.271, this one is ample and flowing like a wave borne upon a ground swell. It starts on the tonic, falls at once by an octave, rises then along the degrees of the common chord, falls still lower and stops on the dominant. At this point it becomes harmonized and, from *forte* to *piano*, it climbs little by little in a wavy line and, after breaking, draws back gracefully upon the tonic (ex. 20).

The whole orchestra now enters and we continue in a more jovial strain, frolicking with themes in semi-quavers and repeated notes, very different from the opening. We modulate to C minor, A flat and F minor, return to E flat, and land finally on a dominant seventh chord and a pause. Then, under the repeated notes of the fiddles, *pianissimo*, and emphasized by a horn call, we hear violas and 'cellos whisper a rhythmical motif. It is at first just perceptible, like the tramping of a distant army. The strings repeat it, *crescendo*, and the hautboys reinforce them. It comes nearer, asserts itself; we take it to be the second subject. Finally, it invades the whole band and leads triumphantly to the conclusion (bars 30–42).

The two pianos enter gaily with a unison trill, an indication of their mutual relations throughout the work. They repeat the grand first subject whose opening phrase in their hands appears somewhat flounced and frilled, whereas the second strain keeps its austere outline. The first piano gives it out; the second gives another reading of it an octave lower. The nature of their collaboration is clear from the outset. There will be no more counterpoint than there was in the work for three pianos; the soloists will repeat, echo, and accompany each other, but never work equally; each one in turn will be the master. From this conception, admittedly less fruitful than that of Bach, Mozart draws all its possible consequences.

After a short solo founded on the first subject, the tutti re-enters with the figure which had just concluded the introduction. This is a device borrowed from aria form which Mozart has used in three other piano concertos.[1] It gives us the feeling that the past is definitely closed and that the work is turning its prow towards new shores. The concerto derives a certain impetus from it and sets off again more merrily than ever.

Freed from the past, the two pianos seek joyous adventures with a bold theme which skips a tenth at its second note, returns to its

---

[1] K.238, 414, 537.

starting-point, and, once both soloists have given it out, divides
between them in charming ripples, breaking and coming together
until a second melody appears (bars 84–95). This is the second half
of the solo subject and is in B flat. It is entrusted to the second piano,
whilst the ripples continue to flow in the first and accompany the
engaging melody (ex. 21). One bar of tutti (all this time the orchestra
has kept silence or has confined itself to held notes) and the first piano
dives into the true second subject, which is not at all the one we had
spotted in the introduction but a sister theme to ex. 21. It, too,
splits up into two strains; the first belongs to the first piano alone and
comes limpingly forward with a ♪♪↯♪♪↯ rhythm in the right

hand and a ↯♪♪♪↯♪♪♪ rhythm in the left; the other is given to the
second under a trill of the first, and when it is over the first piano
advances again and adds a third strain as a coda (bars 104–20). Few
of Mozart's concertos are so rich in themes; they succeed each other
unceasingly from the solo entry and relieve us of the need for any
bravura passages. The second piano re-enters; the two answer each
other, playing shuttlecock with the arpeggios, and again scales and
trills ripple down, sparkling from one to the other, dazzling with
life, and hint at motifs which melt into runs without ever ceasing
to be expressive. At length, with chromatic scales in thirds, they
swoop down upon the dominant trill which closes the exposition.

The orchestra plays but a sorry part. It has no themes of its own
and now that the coast is momentarily clear all it can do is to rake up
old memories and go back to the codetta which had followed the
"tramping army" subject in the introduction. This is an unlucky
stroke for it calls up at once other memories in the soloists. Hardly
six bars have elapsed since the end of the exposition when the first
piano returns with a theme from the first tutti transposed into G
minor. The other piano follows and the game begins again. We
expect a working-out of this theme like that in K.271, but Mozart
is far too prodigal of his riches to dally with developments. Six
bars later, the first piano enters C minor and the second gives out a
new subject. This one comes before us threateningly, "in shining
armour", with a *tremolando* in the upper register, like a drum roll,
and a menacing semi-quaver triplet in the bass (ex. 22; bars 160–69).
But it is only a cardboard warrior and does not disturb the fun;
we refuse to take it seriously; it passes into the good-humoured key
of B flat and disappears as suddenly as it came. In its place another
theme is outlined—the ninth and last!—as graceful as the foregoing

and so laden with yearning that it cannot express itself completely on the pianos and appeals to the hautboys at what is perhaps the most enchanting moment in the whole movement.[1] In three thoroughly Mozartian bars the woodwind echoes the solo instruments, prolonging and completing the theme (ex. 23). The spirit of this delightful subject persists in a few quiet scales which pass antiphonally from one piano to the other and once again we are in well-known climes when the soloists halt on a dominant seventh chord. A murmur of the violins and we hear afar the "tramping army" subject which had not returned since the first tutti. The pianos take it up and it soon invades the whole band. The *development* has reached its close and through beautiful piano *melismas* we glide back to our starting-point.

We have said that Mozart never varied his recapitulations as much as in his piano concertos. The five first hardly confirmed this statement for their recapitulations reproduced largely their first sections. It is no longer so here. The majestic opening subject reappears and for an instant an air of gravity passes over the face of the work. From grave it becomes sombre as one of the pianos takes up the first fragment of theme in the minor and the other continues, still in the minor, with the second fragment. An almost oppressive atmosphere suddenly reigns over the hitherto serene and light-hearted movement and is rather increased than dispelled when there comes to the fore a little figure of fluttering seconds dear to Mozart and always indicative of heightened stress (ex. 24; bars 212–23). From the first piano this figure passes to the second, in the middle and then in the upper register, then more feebly in the bass, after which it vanishes suddenly and the dark shadows with it.

This excursion into the minor immediately after the reprise is uncommon in Mozart.[2] It appears to have been characteristic of the Viennese school and to go back to Wagenseil who liked to repeat his themes in the minor, not only at the reprise but at other times. It may be from Schobert that Mozart adopted it, for it is frequent with him[3] and his influence on the young Salzburger was still alive in 1779.

---

[1] It is with this theme that the solo violin and viola enter in the first movement of the *Sinfonia Concertante*.

[2] The symphony in C, K.338, contemporary with this concerto, and the Mannheim sonata in C, K.309, offer examples of it.

[3] It is found in his sonatas Op. V, 1 (1st and 3rd movements), Op. VI, 1; Op. VII, 1 (1st and 3rd movements); Op. XVII, 1 (do.); and in his concerto in C, Op. XV.

Mozart admired his music and during his stay in the French capital had taught his sonatas to pupils. The fine A minor sonata, K.310, composed most probably in Paris, contains in its andante an almost literal quotation from Schobert's Op. XVII, 1.[1] Mozart, who assimilated so many and such diverse influences, took from them only what suited his nature, and if this sudden appearance of the minor is a widespread device at this time, it corresponds nevertheless to his unstable temperament which passed without transition from laughter to tears and bordered on sadness at its merriest moments. The angel of sorrow was always watching within, ready to unveil its face.

The rest of the movement recovers the zest which had reigned until the reprise. Only the second of the solo subjects appears here. The true second subject is given out entire and is followed by a felicitous recall of the second fragment of the opening subject, modified in its conclusion and made less grave by a sparkling codetta which scatters itself in wavelets. A bravura passage, the only one in the movement, concludes the pianos' performance; a bridge leads to the cadenza,[2] after which the tutti winds up as it had done in the introduction.

II. The sharp opposition between the allegro and andantino of K.271 does not occur here. On the contrary, the andante, in B flat, sings in more meditative tones of the same happy thoughts and affectionate joy as the first movement. The dark strains that had interrupted, for an instant, the flow of happiness reappear here as fleeting expressions of melancholy. The *development* theme in C minor that feigned ferocity also has its counterpart. The character of the themes is similar, their abundance also; Mozart is as prodigal as ever of his store and there is no thematic working out.

The movement opens with a phrase in broken rhythm—a sigh that dies into a threefold echo. The thought is expressed in fragments but the held note of the hautboys which hovers aloft gives it unity. The pianos enter almost at once with the same motif; the

---

[1] Bars 13-16 after the double bar in the andante of Mozart's sonata in A minor are almost identical with bars 17-21 after the double bar in the andante of Schobert's sonata. The Schobert movement is one of those which Mozart had arranged as a concerto in 1767 at the age of eleven.

[2] There exist in the archives of St. Peter's church in Salzburg cadenzas for the first and third movements, partly autograph, partly in Leopold's hand. They were published by Mandyczewski in 1921, in a facsimile edition. Both are a little perfunctory. That for the allegro makes use of exs. 20, 22 and 23; that for the rondo deals with the refrain and is largely composed of imitative passages between the two pianos. See App. I.

"sighs" devolve on the second, the held note, in the shape of a trill, on the first. The second continues alone with a wavy chromatic theme full of melancholy. The feeling becomes intense when the first piano intervenes to follow the second a third below. But it soon vanishes into arabesques and the soloists attack a vigorous subject to reach a bar of chords of the seventh which they strike together. The mood changes; the pianos are silent and, under more *tenuti* on the hautboys, the strings whisper a figure of trills and repeated notes. The pianos return at the end of two bars but the orchestra, for once, does not withdraw and there follows one of the few dialogues in the concerto. The hautboy *tenuti* turn into a theme which the pianos accompany with broken chords. The passage is repeated with a change of accompaniment; a short intervention of the whole orchestra, with a motif destined to play a more important part at the end of the movement (ex. 25), concludes the first part.

As in the allegro the middle section is a succession of subjects which appear and vanish off-handedly with no thought of development. First come two bars of introduction, in B flat, given to the first piano, and two more, for the second, which repeat them in E flat. Then, abruptly, a new subject is announced in C minor. It would fain be tragic but hardly succeeds, for the first piano takes it up in B flat and it then falls into line with the general tone of the movement. A dialogue is carried on between the soloists and soon a winding figure, more and more split up, brings back the theme in broken rhythm of the beginning. The recapitulation unrolls without important changes until the arrival of the motif (ex. 25) that had closed the first section. When the tutti has finished it, the first piano takes it up, accompanied by the second, in four bars full of charm, to which the orchestra, with a true Mozartian gesture, adds a discreet codetta.

III. The part played by the orchestra, almost inexistent in the first two movements, is more extensive in the rondo. There are also a few thematic developments. A certain kinship can be recognized between the subjects. Passages such as the first and second returns of the refrain, and the beginning of the third couplet, are founded on figures which the pianos work out in various ways, or upon the refrain-theme. In form, therefore, this is the most interesting movement of the three, and while it has recourse to development devices it is as tuneful as the first.

The orchestra opens it. The refrain is a two-step theme which may be based on a French ariette. It has a certain likeness to the refrain of the finale in a divertimento in E flat, K.252, of 1776, and was used again by Mozart with a different rhythm in the last movement of the *Hunt* quartet (ex. 26). It is full of life and, with its silent first beats, not devoid of piquancy.

The tutti takes charge and does not let in the soloists till the refrain is over. The pianos must therefore find something new and the first one springs forward with a subject akin to it but different in rhythm and detail of outline. The second, at first silent, then joins in to

Ex. 28

repeat, an octave lower, what the first has just said. Certain members of the orchestra add their voices and, after the first fragment of the theme, we hear a witty echo from the hautboys (bars 64 and 68). Then all the band returns to the attack with the last bars of the refrain. The pianos seize hold of it forthwith, in unison, and set out for adventure, one armed with its repeated semi-quavers, the other astride its triplets, and for a while there is a desperate struggle between the trot of the first and the gallop of the second (bars 87–98). The galloping triplets win and form a well-characterized melodic accompaniment, whilst a stiff, rhythmic theme appears in the second piano (bar 99). Then the tables are turned and the orchestra adds the richest and most original accompaniment it has devised hitherto, filling out the harmonies and progressing with contrary motion to that of the pianos (ex. 27; bars 113–27). The hour of the return is at hand and we meet, for the first time in the concertos, an example of that art of the reprise which is one of Mozart's charms. The first piano sketches a fragment of melody whose spirit recalls the refrain but which is not derived from it; starting as it does a semi-tone below the tonic, it might be the conclusion of some theme already heard. The second piano repeats it; the first echoes its last notes; the second likewise. Then, with two almost ridiculously simple elements—a scale fragment of five notes and the two thirds of the chord of B flat,[1] Mozart spirits us away into fairyland and we are still marvelling at what has happened when the refrain theme is once again merrily sent upon its way (ex. 28; bars 142–70).

The second couplet conforms to the tradition of the French rondo by opening in the relative minor. The new subject unfolds in the same order as before: subject given out by the second piano and accompanied (in broken octaves) by the first; then reversal of the parts and entry of the strings, which accompany the soloists with a rhythm of their own. A few arpeggios lace themselves from one piano to the other and the orchestra answers with a fragment which also recalls the refrain; we modulate from G minor to F minor, E flat, G minor and C minor. The first part of the subject returns (bar 255) and the band accompanies the second piano, whilst the first supports it with its broken octaves. Then, once more, Mozart prepares us a magical reprise. The C minor theme completed, the

---

[1] A similar but simpler passage, a forerunner of this one, occurs in the finale of the Mannheim sonata in C, K.309, after the last return of the refrain, forty-three bars from the end.

Ex. 29

first piano gives out alone a motif in G minor, which also looks as if it was broken off from something we had already heard; it is characterized by the "fluttering seconds" figure so beloved of Mozart (bar 270).[1] The second piano repeats it, whilst the first adds a counterpoint of trills. Motif and counterpoint pass from one to the other

---

[1] It resembles a passage in Papageno's part in the *Magic Flute*:

"*O wär' ich eine Maus, wie sollt' ich mich verstecken,*
Wär' ich so klein wie Schnecken so kröch ich in mein Haus!"

(Finale of Act I.)

and modulate to G major, whence other chromatic modulations, founded upon two notes of the scale, bring back with masterly economy the key of E flat and the refrain.   In his later concertos, Mozart will write grander rondos, but in his whole work one will not find many passages of greater expressive power than these two reprises, so simple in the means they use (ex. 29; bars 270-96).

The whole refrain is given out by the second piano and repeated by the tutti; it leads suddenly to a pause and concludes briefly in A flat.   Although we are in the recapitulation couplet, Mozart has not yet reached the end of his inventiveness.   Instead of the theme with which the soloists had made their entrance the first time, it is the refrain itself that the first piano picks up, and some thematic working-out follows—a rising sequence founded on the first four bars of the refrain, each piano taking on at the point where the other leaves off. We pass thus from A flat to B flat minor, C minor and F minor; then, we descend on a derivative figure and reach B flat, in which key the tutti enters with another bit of the refrain.   After this escapade, we return to the beaten paths of rondos and the main theme of the first couplet reappears with a slightly different ornamentation and accompaniment.   It concludes on the tonic, and a short tutti bridge, based on the refrain which decidedly dominates this rondo even more than refrains usually do, leads to the cadenza.[1]   The rather long conclusion that follows belongs almost wholly to the soloists; it is a last appearance of the refrain; the orchestra adds only the customary affirmation of the common chord.[2]

These last two concertos are like enough for a comparison to be justified.   Both are more closely akin to each other than to those that come before and after; both belong to the years immediately before Mozart settled in Vienna and during which his genius was beginning to be enriched by contact with a wider world than Salzburg.

Of the first movements of both, it is true to say that each one represents a mood.   One cannot say as much of the 1776 concertos. But, though both be personal, their personalities are different.   The fifth is self-assertive and aggressive; it overrides the *galant* conventions.

---

[1] See note 2, p. 111 and App. I.

[2] In a performance at Vienna with Frl. Aurnhammer, Mozart added two clarinets, two trumpets and two kettledrums in the first and last movements.

One finds only faintly in it the ideal of "society music" reflected by most concertos of the time. It is the expression of a young, inexperienced, unsubtle, rather dogmatic spirit; originality rather than depth is, quite naturally, its principal feature, and its exuberance is not without stiffness. It is athletic, not sentimental; it is an "extrovert" and recalls in this respect the little D major concerto, K.175.

The sixth concerto, on the other hand, though quite as personal, is more tactful. Before his journey to the Palatinate and France, Mozart could put himself at his public's level, but then his work lost proportionally in personality; sometimes, he would assert himself, but then he removed himself from his public and risked offending it. On his return, however, he showed that he possessed already to a high degree that art of satisfying his own aspirations and placating his public which is still to-day one of the reasons for his popularity. To put oneself within reach of one's audience without demeaning oneself: that is what he learnt in 1777-8; that is what he felt strong enough to do in the concerto for two pianos. Its first movement is not less personal than that of K.271, but it emphasizes most that aspect of the composer's personality which is closest to the collective personality of the Salzburg public. Mozart's own personality is richer and riper than it was two years earlier; it has lived more; it sees life less simply.

In the slow movements, the relation between the two works is different. The C minor andantino of K.271 is not only personal but deep; it expresses an intimate sorrow. It is not its personal character which separates it from the allegro; it is that, below the plane on which we are all alike, below that deeper plane on which we differ, it penetrates to a region where the personality of each of us finds again the common foundations of the human soul, where the artist, although he sings of his own sorrow, becomes also the voice of all. This andantino still keeps, nevertheless, the simpleness and immaturity of the first movement; this is what distinguishes it from the andante of the *Sinfonia Concertante* to which in other respects it lies so near.

The andante of the concerto for two pianos remains on a middle plane; its personality is an everyday one. A few bars promised to light up deeper zones; they were but fleeting.

In the rondos, the relationship is appreciably the same as in the first allegros. That of K.271 contains parts, such as the pretty minuet, which are chiefly rococo; that of K.365 sings from end to end the soul of its maker. The latter work is therefore the more homogeneous; whereas K.271 passes from a personal movement, full of exuberant joy, to one deeply sorrowful, ending upon a rondo where the taste of the day is more obvious than the spirit of Mozart, the other keeps throughout its three movements that note of conciliation between audience and composer which it struck at the start.

We have arrived at the end of the group of the first six concertos. A group, strictly speaking, they are not, save for one whom the abundance of material compels to classify. They do not form a group as do the concertos of 1782, and 1784 and 1785-6. Three years part the first from the second, and three years during adolescence is a long time. More than a year separates the fourth from the fifth, and between fifth and sixth comes the great journey. It is only from time to time that Mozart thinks of the genre; after 1773, a few symphonies (the last before Paris), serenades and divertimenti especially, occupy him; then, in 1775, his five violin concertos. Passing occasions call forth in 1776 the composition of three more piano concertos and the visit of Mlle. Jeunehomme produces in 1777 the E flat. Betweenwhiles, serenades and divertimenti continue to pile up. At Mannheim and Paris, nothing brings him back to the genre;[1] the concertos he writes are for other instruments and are ordered from him by amateurs or by the Concerts Spirituels.

There is, then, no succession in the composition of these works and it is natural that they should show no connected growth. It is indeed the first of them that shows most clearly the dramatic conception which is Mozart's great contribution to the form. This conception vanishes altogether with the 1776 concertos which, with all their charm, are pure concertos "für Kenner und Liebhaber," where the orchestra serves only to introduce the solo and fill in the gaps left by its silences. The dramatic conception is more visible in the two first movements of K.271, but less than K.175; as for K.365, though it be no stranger to the idea of the dialogue, it is a dialogue between soloists, not between solo and tutti, that it gives us. If Mozart, after leaving Salzburg, had written no more piano concertos, we might have said that he had half grasped several conceptions of the genre without developing any one of them.

Two years separate Mozart's return to Salzburg from his final departure in October, 1780. These two years are too important in

---

[1] But at Mannheim he sketched the beginning of a *Sinfonia Concertante* for piano and violin, in D, Köchel-Einstein 315 f.

the history of his work, if not of his life, for us to skip them once we have completed the study of the sixth concerto. They are more decisive even than his year at Mannheim and Paris for it was during them that the fruits of his journey, and especially the enrichment of his personality which was its principal result, appear in his compositions.

They are important, above all, for the growth of his musical thought. For that of his style the works written in the Palatinate and in France are more significant, but the *Stilwandlung* of 1777-8 was over by the time he got home; it is the renewal of his inspiration that is shown by his last period in Salzburg and his first months in Vienna.

The half-dozen symphonic works of 1779-81 speak of something new; there are in them strains as yet unheard. We discover, clearly constituted for the first time, some of the fundamental elements of his musical personality as we know it at the period of his maturity. These works are the symphony in C, K.338, the serenade and divertimento in D, K.320 and 334, the woodwind serenades in B flat, E flat and C minor, K.361, 375 and 388, and the *Sinfonia Concertante*, K.364; to these one should add the *Kyrie* in D minor, K.341. The period of his prime begins with them. All of them exceed, both in scale and power of thought, what he had written hitherto, and they are worthy to rank with the best compositions of his Viennese period. There is a world of difference between his most ambitious works written before 1779 and the symphony in C, the *Sinfonia Concertante* and the E flat serenade. Only a single movement, from time to time, like the andante of the violin concerto in G and the andantino of the piano concerto in E flat, K.271, had reached at one bound the heights whither, after 1778, he will arrive almost every time he seeks to write "for himself". They are beautiful, no doubt, but in their promise rather than in their fulfilment; the others attain what the earlier compositions had only half seen. Before 1779, Mozart wrote interesting works; only after then did he produce works of genius.

We would go even further and say that in the orchestral sphere we must wait till the 1784 concertos to find works as fine as the best of the period we are considering. After he settled in Vienna, one recognizes uncertainty, almost timidity, in his symphonic writing; his genius opens out in his chamber music and in his C minor mass, but the three concertos of 1782 and the 1783 symphony (the *Linz*) are less daring than the concertos, symphony and serenades of 1779 to 1781.

Two elements, particularly, in his later Salzburg works, show us by their presence that his musical personality is approaching maturity —two fundamental elements, traces of which can be discerned earlier but which henceforward were always to be present. One is the breadth and majesty that we are wont to call Olympian; the other, the sorrowful restlessness, reaching at times to tragedy, which Heuss many years ago called "*daimonisch*"—a word that has since become a stock part of Mozartian terminology. The alternation of these two moods—of vigorous joy, majesty, sweetness and sorrow is characteristic of Mozart; it is present throughout his work after 1782, and it is in several passages of the works we are considering that, for the first time, with a somewhat primitive brutality, it asserts itself.

The beginning of K.365 is a good example of the Olympian tone; the opening subject is one of Mozart's longest and fullest themes. But beyond this majestic portico the dignity unbends and gives way to graces and smiles. The majesty is more sustained in the C major symphony, a work which begins with a well-known Italian overture motif (ex. 30) common with him and always the expression of a solemn mood. But it is in the allegro of the *Sinfonia Concertante* and the E flat serenade that this feature is most impressively illustrated. Both movements begin with common chords, at first sustained, then repeated with a dotted crotchet rhythm. This too is a favourite form of opening, especially in E flat works; we find it again, condensed and more wiry, in the E flat piano concerto of 1785, K.482. It occurs often with John Christian Bach and the other *galant* composers and appears in the initial chords of the *Emperor* concerto.

In the E flat serenade, solemnity alternates with other feelings; the tutti of the *Sinfonia Concertante*, on the other hand, retains its majesty up to the entry of the soloists. Indeed, there are few works where Mozart keeps up so long an Olympian strain; we have to wait till the concertos of 1785 and 1786 to find an introduction where nobility and serenity of thought are so constantly sustained. This solemn beginning is not just a façade; the whole movement has the same character, though from time to time its serenity is coloured with pathos. The same nobility inspires the slow introduction of the B flat serenade, but the rest of its allegro is playful rather than solemn.

At the other extreme is the anguish which we sometimes perceive, like a sinister undercurrent, in his most joyful works. It is not a new feature but hitherto it had appeared only intermittently. From

1778 onward it comes to stay, and it is in certain movements of these three years that we see it asserting itself for good.

Sometimes it alternates with other emotions, falling into the middle of a quiet passage like a bolt from the blue. In the first movement of the *Sinfonia Concertante* the soloists have hardly come in when they give out a disturbing theme under which the orchestra outlines a plaint-like accompaniment. The mood persists and the anguish heightens till suddenly it disappears as abruptly as it had arisen, with one of those charming emotional about-turns so typical of Mozart.

The intrusion of the threatening *daimon*, the sudden rent that discloses the depths, is still more marked in the E flat serenade. The first movement begins like the *Sinfonia Concertante* with majestic chords, but majesty gives way at once to sweetness; the chords break up and a sensual, caressing theme succeeds, with shimmering clashes of seconds that enhance the woodwind colour. The music progresses for some time in a calm and playful mood, not devoid of vigour, when, abruptly, the second subject dies down in a fluttering of trills. From the ensuing silence arises the desolate voice of the hautboy in a tragic soliloquy. This lament ceases as suddenly as it started (ex. 31). It is heard again, as unexpectedly, in the short *development*, but loses itself in the return of the majestic chords that opened the movement, and does not reappear in the recapitulation. In its place a melody full of hope unfolds on the horn and ends, somewhat ironically, with the same cadence as the lament. The appearance of a new subject in this section, an effective touch, is found again in the C minor serenade and nowhere else in Mozart.

Sometimes it is in short passages like minuet trios that the anguish is poured out and it is perhaps in such places that we meet with the bitterest harmonies in all his work. The D minor trio of the first minuet in the divertimento in D, K.334 (ex. 32), and the B flat minor trio of the second minuet in the B flat serenade concentrate into their sixteen or twenty bars a cruel poignancy. In their stark desolation they make one think of much later periods, of the *Masonic Funeral Music* and the *Magic Flute*.

And sometimes a whole movement is a prey to this tragic mood. We have already spoken of Mozart's *minor* movements and we shall have occasion to return to them. There are four in the last Salzburg works, counting the magnificent fragment, the D minor *Kyrie*. All four have in common a feature of style frequent in Mozart's *minor* andantes: the alternation of tonic and dominant in the first bar of the theme. It is a common feature in the music of the time; one finds it in the Abel symphony already mentioned. The association between a certain mood and a melodic line or an accompaniment figure is very close in Mozart. The likeness in form between the beginning of the andantes of the E flat piano concerto, K.271, the serenade in D, K.320, and the *Sinfonia Concertante* is particularly marked, and so is the kinship of inspiration between the three. They are three phases of the same work in which the thought grows deeper and richer from one to the other. The final shape is in the andante of the *Sinfonia Concertante*, one of Mozart's most moving pieces. The D minor *Kyrie* recalls it, both by its general character and by certain melodic figures. One feels that both movements have arisen, not only on the same plane of consciousness but also at the same hour of the composer's life. The *Kyrie* leaves earlier religious works as far behind it as the *Sinfonia Concertante* and the symphony in C leave the earlier symphonies and concertos. A mass written on its scale would have had the proportions of the C minor and the *Requiem*.

The D minor variations of the divertimento, K. 334, have the same tragic character but with more violence. They, too, are poignant in their starkness, and they too are the first state of a thought which, more fully clothed, more ingratiating, reappears twice, each time more complete: in the andante of the F major violin sonata, K.377, and the finale of the D minor quartet, K.421.

Themes that betoken agitation are therefore common in Mozart's music of this period, and in all his output there are few movements where the alternation between serenity and anguish is as pronounced as in the allegros of the *Sinfonia Concertante* and the E flat serenade. May we not recognize in this the reflection of the young musician's increasing dissatisfaction with the stifling atmosphere of Salzburg? His attempts to escape from the little town and settle elsewhere had failed: he appeared more and more inevitably doomed to the archbishop's service and, as his wings grew, he felt the oppression of the narrow humdrum and the inept company of the Brunettis and Ceccarellis to be more and more unbearable. The anguish called forth by the cleavage between ideal and reality, which lasted into the first months of his stay in Vienna,[1] inspires the sorrowful andante of the *Sinfonia Concertante* and the acid trios of the minuets. This same anguish, enriching his experience with fresh sufferings, made him throw himself body and soul into the subject of *Idomeneo*, where the themes of departure and deliverance are so important; it caused him to show there, not only a more developed technique than in *Lucio Silla* and *Mitridate*, but a feeling for tragedy absent in his earlier operas. *Idomeneo*, the first of his dramatic masterpieces, the occasion of his final departure from Salzburg, closes worthily two years of works full of majesty and restlessness; there, in the overture, in certain arias of Ilia and Electra, in the temple scene, the magnificent farewell quartet and the choruses, we meet in the highest degree the Olympian and the tragic, the serene and the tortured inspiration which characterizes the symphonic works of Mozart's last months in his native town.

---

[1] The E flat and C minor serenades were composed in that city in 1781 and 1782.

2. The Concertos of 1782: K.413 in F; 414 in A; 415 in C

> I am seething with rage! And you, my dearest and most beloved father, are doubtless in the same condition. My patience has been so long tried that at last it has given out. I am no longer so unfortunate as to be in Salzburg service. To-day is a happy day for me. . . . . Please be cheerful, for my good luck is just beginning and I trust that my good luck will be yours also.[1]

THUS wrote Mozart to his father on May 9th, 1781. From this date he was free—free to shape his destiny or think he was shaping it, free to taste the flattery of capitals, free to end in destitution and a pauper's grave.

His letters relate the circumstances that preceded and followed his break with the archbishop. They show only one side of the picture and for a long time no other was apparent. Of recent years, however, the attempt has been made to prove that all the wrongs were not to be ascribed to the prince of the Church. For some time, Mozart had been airing desires for greater independence and been making attempts, displeasing to his master, to set himself free from the obligations of his position. The prelate had granted him, unwillingly, it appears, six weeks absence to allow him to compose and produce his opera *Idomeneo* which the Munich court had ordered for the Carnival of 1781. The six weeks had become four months without the archbishop taking action. But he was determined to hold him henceforward and keep him within the bounds of duty. He summoned Mozart to Vienna, where he was paying his court to the Emperor. The musician would have welcomed a stay in the capital; unfortunately, the archbishop laid down a condition which took away much of its charm. He made him put up in his own house and treated him as a member of the archiepiscopal suite. Mozart found himself confounded with the lackeys, eating with

---

[1] *The letters of Mozart and his family*, tr. by E. Anderson, III, 1081-3.

the two valets, that is, the body and soul attendants of His Worship, the contrôleur, Herr Zetti, the confectioner, the two cooks, Ceccarelli, Brunetti. . . . The two valets sit at the top of the table, but at least I have the honour of being placed above the cooks.[1]

This was not exceptional treatment; the manners of the day allowed of the incorporation of musicians in the domestic staff. But it is easy to realize that his free life at Munich made such an existence unbearable. In point of fact, the archbishop was not treating him otherwise than his peers treated the musicians in their service, except that his payment was more niggardly; but Mozart aspired to be free; advances had been made to him from several quarters and he was convinced he could win both better earnings and more honour by remaining in Vienna. One day in particular, when he had to play without a fee at a concert in the archbishop's house, he was obliged to refuse an invitation from Countess Thun, whose house the Emperor was to visit that very evening. He was "almost heart-broken" over it. The crisis came when the archbishop, without leaving him as much as one day to get ready, ordered him to set out for Salzburg and, in an interview which Mozart has described, punctu-ated his behest with insults. It was as a result of this scene that the young man left his service and wrote to his father a long letter whence are taken the words quoted at the beginning of this chapter.

This revolt has some historic significance. In the person of Mozart, music cast off the golden fetters of official patronage; his gesture on May 9th, 1781, makes the date the 1789 of musicians. It was he and not Beethoven who casued a "revolutionary wind" to blow in the world of composers; it was this twenty-five-year-old, in whom we are so often prone to see the type *par excellence* of the court musician, who first put the dignity of his art above an assured position and, in order to "live his own life", broke with the tradition honoured by Bach, Haydn, and so many others, seeking to be at the service of none but his genius.

A child of the Revolution without knowing it, the young genius was never really happy till he had wrenched himself free, to his father's intense horror, of the feudalism that oppressed him.[2]

It is on May 9th, 1781, that the Viennese period of his life begins. It was to last ten years and seven months and from it dates most of

---

[1] Id., III, 1060.
[2] Warde Fowler: *Stray notes on Mozart and his music.*

the work we know to-day, except the piano sonatas. The first three of these years, those of his setting up in Vienna and of his marriage, are a somewhat confused time for his art. Full of activity, he is still feeling his way, and many genres interest him. We hear in them a few reminders of the past: the serenades in E flat and C minor, representatives of a form which he was to give up almost entirely. To his new life belong his chamber music, to which he returns after nine years, his C minor mass and sundry fugal compositions, and his first German opera, *Die Entführung aus dem Serail.* To them go his affections; in them we must seek the expression of his soul. The symphony and concerto afford only by-products of his work. It is nevertheless as a soloist that he intends conquering the Viennese public; he calls the piano his "speciality" and adds, "Truly, this is the land of the piano!" but his concertos are less significant, during these three years, than his works for piano solo or two pianos: fantasias, fugues, suite and sonatas.

His first year at Vienna was rather unproductive. The most notable works were four violin sonatas, K.376 and 377 in F, 379 in G, and 380 in E flat, three of which are among his finest; the three wind serenades, of which the B flat had perhaps been composed at Munich, and the two pianos sonata, K.448. Of the B flat and E flat serenades we have already spoken; they are associated with his Salzburg life not only by their genre but by their inspiration, which is close to other works of his last days in that town. But the third, the C minor, which dates from the middle of 1782, opens new paths. It is true that this work, which lacks completely the spirit of a serenade, is related to the two others. It has the changeable temper of the E flat, its abrupt passages from night to day, its rhythmical themes based on the common chord. But despite this it differs from all that had gone before since the E minor violin sonata of 1778. The *galant* frippery has been entirely cast off; the composer's soul lies bare. It is the first of a series which will include the great *minor* works of 1783 to 1788.

RONDO (VARIATIONS) IN D (K.382)
March, 1782[1]
   Allegretto grazioso: 2-4
Orchestra: Strings; flute, two hautboys, two horns, two trumpets, two kettledrums.

---

[1] No. 28 in the *Gesamtausgabe.*

At about the same moment as the composition of this stormy serenade, we meet the first work for piano and orchestra written since Mozart's departure from Salzburg. He had played again at Vienna his 1773 concerto and it had met with success. But the finale in sonata form must have sounded old-fashioned and, to rejuvenate the work, he replaced it with a "rondeau varié", in other terms, a series of variations, which seem to us to-day very paltry beside the original finale.

These variations and the C minor serenade are contemporary also with the superb fantasia and fugue in C, concerning which he tells his sister that he transcribed the fugue while he was meditating the prelude, thus emulating the White Knight who, it will be remembered, invented a new pudding while he was consuming the meat-course. The almost simultaneous appearance of three such different works, two of which are compositions of genius and the third mediocre and frivolous, shows clearly how possible it was for him, as indeed for all the older masters up to and including Beethoven and Schubert, to work on several planes at once, according as he laboured "for himself", for a "select public" or for the "general public". Nevertheless, the distressing banality of these variations for piano and orchestra which, when played as they are meant to be as a finale to the first concerto must make a woeful contrast with the sturdy personality of the two other movements, cannot be explained away by the public they aimed at pleasing. After all, the four Parisian sonatas, K. 330-3, too, had been composed for a similar public and, without reaching the level of the fantasia and fugue, they are far worthier than the variations and bear clearly their author's imprint. The same is true of the two pianos sonata of 1781.

The lack of personality in them should no doubt be considered as the result of the uncertainty in which Mozart stood concerning the likes and dislikes of the capital where he had just arrived and where he was anxious to carve out a place for himself. He felt it necessary at first to travel warily and not to scare his audience with too original works. Let him conquer it first and give it stronger meat later on! The important thing was to live, and to achieve recognition by the Viennese public one had to be ready to sacrifice a little boldness. These variations were made to be performed before an audience unfamiliar and incalculable. The fact of substituting a new movement for the splendid finale shows a submissiveness to prevailing taste which vanishes later.

We must not think that Mozart was distressed by this enforced

docility.   His taste appears to have coincided with that of his hearers.
He was pleased with his rondo.

"I beg you to guard it like a jewel. . . ." he writes to his father and
sister.

"I composed it *specially* for myself—and no one else but my dear
sister must play it."[1]

The movement is seldom played to-day although it has been
recorded, and there is no reason why it should be.   It has nothing
to please modern ears and adds nothing to Mozart's glory.   It is
made up of a theme, seven variations and a short coda.   The theme,
in 2-4 time, is undistinguished; it moves almost entirely within the
compass of five tones and trills mark the weak beats in ten out of its
sixteen bars.   The first six variations are entrusted exclusively to
the piano; at distant intervals, the tutti comes in with the first half of
the theme.   The variations themselves are of the most impersonal
galant type; the first, melodic; the second, in triplets; the third, a
repetition of the theme in the right hand with triplet quavers in the
left; the fourth, the least commonplace, is in the minor with octave
passages for the right hand; the fifth is a trill for one hand and a
repetition of the theme for the other; the sixth, the usual irritating
adagio variation.   The seventh and last, opened by the orchestra,
is in 3-8 time, according to a common and not very felicitous practice;
the piano works away with semi-quavers, the two hands in contrary
motion.   It is followed by the cadenza; then the coda returns to the
tempo primo and to the theme which, shortened, winds up the
movement.

Something of this submissiveness to public taste persists in the
three concertos of this same year.   They form, nevertheless, a genial
little group and Mozart characterizes them with acuteness when he
writes to his father on December 28th, 1782, that they

are a happy medium between what is too easy and too difficult; they are
very brilliant, pleasing to the ear, and natural, without being vapid.
There are passages here and there from which connoisseurs alone can
derive satisfaction; but these passages are written in such a way that the
less learned cannot fail to be pleased, though without knowing why.[2]

Nothing is truer than this appreciation.   "A happy medium

---

[1] March 23rd, 1782.
[2] Id., III, 1242.

between too easy and too difficult": the technique, indeed, remains moderately easy, and the passage work is simple. "Brilliant, pleasing to the ear": we would hesitate perhaps to grant the first epithet to those in F and A, but one must bear in mind the resources of the pianos of Mozart's day. "Natural, without being vapid": strong emotion is indeed absent, but, with the exceptions mentioned in the next paragraph, the music never dissolves into formulæ. As for the "satisfaction" offered to connoisseurs, analysis reveals many exquisite features in the structure that rejoice the delicate and those who do not always require their beauties to be on a large scale.

In these few words, Mozart has himself summed up the characters common to all three. The only point to add is the relative importance of the rondo in two of them. In no later concerto save K.449 does the significance of the rondo so nearly equal that of the first movement. The andantes, on the other hand, are less interesting; two of them are as insignificant as a Mozart slow movement can be.

CONCERTO NO. 7 IN F (K.413)
Summer or autumn of 1782[1]
    Allegro: 3-4
    Larghetto: C (in B flat)
    Tempo di menuetto: 3-4
Orchestra: Strings, two hautboys, two horns. (Two bassoons were added later in the larghetto.)

Set between the last Salzburg concertos on one hand and the great works of 1784 to 1786 on the other, the first piano concerto that Mozart composed in Vienna appears a very timid thing. If we do not take care to consider it with the myopic sympathy we recommended for his first attempts, it will seem commonplace and impersonal. More than one fervent Mozartian has been deceived in it and the writer of these lines owns that he has not always done it justice. Its timidity is perhaps only modesty. It is anxious to remain close to the average feelings of its public; it does not wish to provoke emotions other than those which it is permissible to express in polite

---

[1] No. 11 in the *Gesamtausgabe*. The first of these three concertos was ready to appear by the end of December (letter of Mozart to his father of December 28th, 1782). All three were published by Artaria in the first half of 1783. It is possible that the A major was composed first as their order in the series is K.414, 413, 415.

society; its ideal, in a word, is that of a gentleman in a drawing-room. Like K.238, 242 and 246, it is a product of the Ancien Régime, one of the few works of Mozart's prime which can be so styled. Everything in it is measured and well-ordered. Was it not of music such as this, *mutatis mutandis*, that Abbé Goussault was thinking when, at the end of the preceding century, he wrote:

> Music has so close a correspondence to the manners of a gentleman that 'tis no wonder if it please him and he like it. The agreement of voice and instrument which flatters agreeably and charms his ear, is a constant image of what happens in his life; everything there is in accord, no one thing gives the lie to another, and it can be said that his words, his thoughts, his designs and his deeds are the diverse parts of another music which all men hear and which pleases and edifies all.
>
> On the other side, 'tis no wonder if libertines often savour not this innocent pleasure. 'Twould seem to reproach them for having neither measure nor refinement in their way of life; it fits not with their humour, therefore, to be enamoured of a pleasure which would continually accuse them, and they look for others more suitable to their inclinations and their profligacy.[1]

So much for the libertines; let them seek to go no further! Mozart's seventh concerto would be no country for them to traverse!

But this apparent return to the ideal of a John Christian is not a renunciation of his personality. If the heart of the work represents the collective soul of his hearers rather than his own, originality is not lacking in the form. There are delicacies and ingenious traits peculiar to it and it is they which, although noticeable only upon analysis, make the public who listens without studying the score be pleased "without knowing why". One of its most original features is the manner in which the smoothest phrases can be broken up into fragments which return separately, at distant points one from the other, and act as links between the various sections of the movement. Mozart has never carried further than in the rondo of this concerto his practice of "link themes". Here, these themes are not only independent ideas; they are the *disjecta membra*, so to speak, of main themes joining together different parts of the whole and unifying it by the discreetly used means of repetition. This is one of its most interesting characteristics.

It is not the only one. The themes themselves, though none of them is among those rare melodies of which Mozart had at other

---

[1] *Réflexions sur les défauts ordinaires des hommes et sur leurs bonnes qualités,* 1692.

times the secret, are not commonplace, and their dancing grace, slightly mischievous, is truly his.   One cannot realize it better than by playing one after the other the first movements of K.238 and of this one.   What the earlier work stood for at twenty, this one represents at twenty-six; the ideal is the same but differently realized; and the difference shows us the full growth of Mozart's mind since the days when he played at Countess Lodron's at Salzburg.

I. The allegro is one of his few concerto first movements that is in three-time. (The others are those of K.459 and 491.) It begins with a rhythmical theme of four bars, followed by a contrasted melodic one, of seven; the whole forms the first subject (ex. 34). Then come two secondary motifs, both rhymical and very alike; the second, the longer of the two, leads to a dominant chord. All this is quite normal. But then, instead of starting off again in the tonic, according to custom, Mozart introduces his second subject in C major and does not return to F for eight bars, an "irregularity" which recurs in K.449. This second subject bears a first-cousinly likeness to ex. 34; it, too, alternates between rhythm and melody (ex. 35). The strings give it out; then, once it has returned to orthodox ways—that is, to the tonic—the wind joins them. A codetta rounds it off, a passing thought which does not reappear; then two more motifs, consisting mainly of scales, and we reach the conclusion. We expect the customary *ff*, with an operatic close, to finish the tutti and announce noisily that the orchestra is abdicating before the solo. Here comes a fresh surprise. The *forte* dies down to *piano* and we hear a third subject, cousin to the other two. Its mildness is encouraging and its example leads to imitation; the piano, encouraged and imitative, falls shyly into line behind it, without treading on its heels, and before it has finished comes upon the stage with yet another cousin (ex. 36). We have already referred to the originality of Mozart's solo entries; here is surely one of the most graceful and most personal.

The second exposition follows the same general lines as those of the 1776 concertos. After the introductory phrase whose *incipit* we have quoted, the orchestra gives out the rhythmical half of the first subject and the piano repeats the melodic part and follows it up with a short virtuosity passage, very simple, consisting in rising arpeggios and falling broken scales, and modulating from F to C. It attacks next the solo subject which gives us the impression of having been heard before; it resembles less the main subjects than the subsidiary ones. Another virtuosity passage, no longer than the first, satisfies for the nonce the piano's ambitions and the orchestra ushers in the second subject. It gives it out in its entirety and at the point where, in the tutti, the wind had joined in, the piano resumes and substitutes an ending of its own. A third passage, as simple as the foregoing, and a little hesitating chromatic figure lead to the usual trill.

In all this section none of the numerous secondary themes of the tutti has appeared. The orchestra enters now with the last of these and as soon as it is given out the piano opens the *development* with a new subject, the ninth or tenth! This one is different. It is in the minor—C minor—and tries to behave accordingly. It has a would-be passionate air about it which convinces neither us nor the tutti, and the orchestra answers it mockingly. It starts again, this time in G minor, hoping that a change of key may impress us more. As no one interrupts, it grows bolder, modulates to D minor and turns into a charming bravura passage, based on arpeggios, with guileless crossed-hands effects. This passage, the most vigorous in the movement, is longer than the earlier ones, but at length the piano grows weary and, as changeable as a child, and almost without our knowing it, passes from major to minor, from allegro to adagio, and after a few sighs gives way a moment to the tutti which brings in the subject, ex. 36, of the original solo entry.

Only a few changes of detail mark the recapitulation. But, on the very brink of the cadenza, Mozart remembers the abundance of themes he had scattered over the first tutti and quickly sets about rescuing them from oblivion. He places two between the solo's trill and the cadenza and another one after it,[1] and at last we reach, *ff*, the common chord of F. We are getting ready to clap when he pretends to start all over again. *Piano*, the strings murmur ex. 36, but it is only a joke, and just as we await the solo entry, three chords, *forte*, end the game.

II. The larghetto which follows this pleasing allegro is one of the most ordinary movements Mozart wrote during his Viennese years. Almost its only rival in this respect is the andante of the C major concerto of the same year. It is a movement in binary form where the first subject is given out by the tutti and repeated by the piano. Its rhythm of six-beat phrases overlaps agreeably the four-beat rhythm of the bars, but that is its only originality. The whole

---

[1] A very fine cadenza, beginning with an energetic pedal more redolent of the concerto K.459 than of this one, preserved in the archives of St. Peter's in Salzburg, was published in facsimile by Mandyczewski in 1921; we give it in Appendix II, and recommend it earnestly to pianists. The MS. is in Leopold's handwriting.

movement unfolds without any change of tone, with melodic developments of a banal sweetness in the right hand and an unflagging Alberti
bass in the left.   A more personal note is sounded in the lovely
strain which acts as a lead back to the first subject (ex. 37).   One
recognizes in it something of that refined and sensuous dreaminess
peculiar to Mozart, but this passage, which returns just before the
cadenza,[1] is the only one where the composer removes his mask.

III.   The rondo has all the qualities of the first movement and
more; it is not only the finest part of the concerto but also one of
Mozart's pleasantest finales in its melodic development and one of the
most original in its form.   We find in it the same breaking-up of
themes as in the allegro and yet the flow of melody is continuous and
nothing less stiffly articulated could be imagined.   The theme of the
refrain looks as if it had been conceived as a whole and yet it allows
itself to be split up with the best grace in the world and its pieces,
once separate, take on with goodwill the parts allotted to them.
When the refrain itself comes back, it is not content with identity;
at each return there is a change, either in the melodic order or in the
harmonization.

The tutti starts and gives out the refrain, a minuet theme of thirty-
two bars which breaks up into phrases of four bars each.   This regularity pertains to the dance character of the movement and is kept up,
on the whole, to the end.   It is the only time that the refrain is presented entire; at each of its two other returns it is shortened and modified, either by having a different bass or by the addition of a new
motif.   With its indolent treble and its very active bass, it recalls the
rondo of the violin sonata in E flat, K.302, and is one of Mozart's
most lovable refrain themes (ex. 38).

The solo enters with a new motif which is not much more than
a variation of the refrain; there is indeed between the different ideas
of this movement the same cousinship as between those of the first.
This motif, repeated in an octave passage, does not reappear.   It is
followed by a short orchestral interruption, a first instance of the
fragmentation already mentioned.   The fragment with which the
tutti intervenes is drawn from the second half of the refrain (ex. 39).
The piano takes it up again and launches forth into a bravura figure
destined to enjoy much working-out in the second couplet.   The

---

[1] A charming cadenza in Leopold's handwriting, based on this phrase,
has been published by Mandyczewski.   See note on p. 133, and Appendix II.

tutti prepares the return of the refrain by borrowing from it another fragment of its second half (ex. 40) which the piano repeats and varies. Then, with a miniature horn fanfare (still on the piano), the first part of the refrain returns to view.

One regrets sometimes that 18th-century composers, especially those of that part of the century which saw the triumph of the rondo, did not more often vary their refrains, and this regret is called forth by certain works of Mozart himself. There is no cause for it here, and at the first return the piano repeats the refrain with a fine triplet bass, a generous variant of the original falling scale (ex. 41). The second part of the refrain is not repeated; in its stead there appears a new "fragment" which will henceforward take the place of ex. 40, which vanishes for good. The last four bars of the refrain conclude and the second couplet opens with the new strain we have just heard, given out again by the piano.

This second couplet is also the last, for Mozart gives up in this concerto and the next the sonata rondo form in three sections in favour of the binary rondo. This latter, from its very structure, tends to be less homogeneous than the ternary one, but here it is not so, and the close kinship of nearly all the themes and the constant return of fragments of the refrain make it a well-blended whole in which only a close analysis can discover "sections". At a hearing, in spite of the apparent symmetry of the phrases, they melt one into the other without any of the usual clear-cut divisions of many contemporary rondos.

In principle, this second couplet repeats the first, but there are a good many differences. The figure with which the first began is replaced by the new refrain fragment. The virtuosity figure sets off now in F minor and for a few moments the placid minuet catches fire, modulates rapidly through minor keys and dies down in the horn fanfare already heard, which once again announces the refrain's return. With the fragment ex. 39, it is the only element that comes back unchanged.

On the third and last appearance of the refrain, it has a coda-like breadth. Here, the variation consists in attributing the theme to the strings, whilst the piano accompanies with a spacious scale which drops and rises over a compass of three octaves. The latest comer of the fragments leads into one last short bravura passage, after which the main theme returns with a descant, a sort of diminution of the original bass, first in the lower register, then in the treble (ex. 48). A new figure, also related to the earlier ones, serves as coda; the solo adds to it a counterpoint of scales in the right hand and after one last *forte* the concerto dies down to *piano*, a conclusion as original as the plan of the rondo, fitting for the mild temper of the whole work.

CONCERTO No. 8 IN A MAJOR (K.414)
Summer or autumn, 1782[1]
    Allegro: C
    Andante: 3-4 (in D)
    Allegretto: 2-4
Orchestra: Strings; two hautboys, two horns.

I. The general character of this concerto is the same as the last; the two works are close relatives. Both live and breathe in the same temperate climate and avoid not only what might shock but even what might merely astonish their public. Both are perfectly urbane.

But the likeness goes no further. Formally, the A major is less interesting than its predecessor. Its thought, on the other hand, is more personal. Its first four bars not only are true Mozart; they are also the Mozart which we at once hail as unique, whereas the Mozart of K.413 was merely he who said, better than anyone else, what was on everyone's lips. Then, in the tenth bar, the simple held note in the woodwind (one bar late) on the return of the theme raises the work at once to a poetic plane.

The first subject has the graceful and melancholy nonchalance, the melting sweetness, which belong to many an A major composition of the master, which reappear with greater breadth in the concerto of 1786 and rise to serenity (not without remembering their sorrowful starting-point) in the clarinet quintet of 1789 (ex. 43).

It is the sentiment whose development we are tracing here; the form has a different history. The theme belongs to a type fairly common in Mozart. One of its first appearances is in the adagio which opens the finale of the *Haffner* serenade (1776), where its meaning is not the same as here. It reappears in the *Prussian* D major quartet of 1789, where it is closer in significance to our concerto. This dissociation of the outline of a theme from its meaning is curious; the number of outlines is perforce limited but the power of expression is infinite.

Warlike strains in the wind, to which a scale fragment answers in the first violins, are now heard thrice; then the violins bring us

[1] No. 12 in the *Gesamtausgabe*. See note on p. 129.

back, *piano*, to the starting-point and the subject begins again. A new string figure, with a rhythmical opening, resolves itself into a retarded scale succeeded abruptly by the usual noisy close on the dominant. The repetition of several of the most important phrases and the tendency of the melodic line to progress by conjunct degrees or at least by small intervals, characterize the whole allegro; through them are expressed the slow-beating emotion and the melancholy and languishing sweetness with which it is so deeply marked. This passage does not reappear; its place later on will be taken by the solo subject.

The noisy close with its very conventional outline is irritatingly, or humorously, contrasting. We know of no other work of Mozart's prime where so marked a contrast occurs between the substance of the thought and the conventional lines that bound it. In the preceding concerto, which resembles this one in the likeness between all its themes, such operatic closes were absent, and greater unity was the result. Here, it is as if each theme was anxious to keep its independence and remain in its own home. For this purpose, they raise between them these barriers, so stereotyped in design, which come and interrupt, some may think intempestively, the flow of feeling.

The second subject has a march rhythm like many subjects in Mozart's Vienna concertos. It is one of the earliest examples of them. But it is an unexhilarating march, still touched by the wilting nonchalance of the beginning and inclining us to dream rather than to step out. It calls up a cohort of ghostly marionettes crossing a two-dimensional landscape. The tune takes great care to avoid the tonic and to repeat the sharpened passing note, and its main stress falls against the beat (ex. 44). The design is cleverly divided between unison violins and violas. Its outline blurs into a beautiful passage which prolongs it: a bass pedal on which there rises in tiers a scale climbing one tone every bar, marked by short runs, where first and second violins overtake each other in turn. Thanks to the clashing seconds that result, the dream atmosphere of the march is retained till the momentary *ff* of a full close (ex. 45). A third subject, similar to the preceding, comes forward, and the tutti ends with a short scale passage, repeated, and a close on the tonic. All this introduction does not leave the key of A major.

We have already said that, if the inspiration is more personal here than in the concerto in F, the form is more commonplace. There is no original solo entry; the piano simply takes up the first subject and expounds it twice, the first time without accompaniment, the second with held notes in the strings. The tutti then comes in with the

figure of the close just heard and the piano, catching at one of its
motifs, derives from it the solo subject, similar in character to the
others. After a bravura passage, as simple as those of the last concerto, we reach the key of E major and the tutti opens the march;
the solo snatches it away at the end of four bars and, adding a semi-
quaver accompaniment, instils some activity into it. The orchestra
relapses into silence, or almost, and comes out of it only at the end of
the exposition to applaud what the piano has been saying with the
familiar cadential figure.

The movement remains rather prim throughout the *development*
in spite of the usually greater freedom of this part. At first comes a
new theme, entrusted to the piano alone and having also a march
rhythm. Like so many others in this concerto it is given out twice.
We are still in E major. A breath of vigour inspires the solo; after
four bars of arpeggios we are in F sharp minor and piano and violins
engage in a short conversation in which the answers overlap in an
almost dramatic manner. The vigour rises to passion; orchestra
and piano stride quickly over the regions of the tonic and relative
minors, landing finally, with strong emotion, on a succession of trills
and a pause. This is the most exciting passage in the movement and
the most interesting for the interplay of piano and strings. The left
hand and bass strings double; the harmonics are provided by the violins
and violas and right hand arpeggios of the piano an octave higher.

Mozart's reprises are most various and often masterly; this one is
simple and even perfunctory. After a pause a cadenza is indicated,
a falling scale of three octaves; then a silent bar, and the strings take
up the first subject. The idea of filling the hole, as it were, between
the end of the *development* and the beginning of the recapitulation
with a cadenza comes back three years later when he composes
another piano concerto in A: an instance of the fact that not only the
feeling but the technical imagination follow similar paths in identical
keys. This kinship of thought and form between works in the same
key is particularly clear in him; a journey through his music is constantly reminding us of it.

Yet, if kinship exists between keys, it also exists between works
of the same period, and this passage recalls also a resemblance of this
kind. It is only in the concerto in A that Mozart has used the reprise
with a mere cadenza, but the feeling which this device expresses—
the emotional about-turn which consists in passing sharply from one
mood to another very different one—is found again, at the same point,
in each of the 1782 concertos. Here, the cadenza expresses it; in K.413,

a modulation and change of *tempo*; in K.415, a modulation, change of rhythm and short cadenza—three different ways of translating the same experience.

The recapitulation does not repeat the first part unchanged. It condenses the passages that follow the solo subject and second subject; in the last, Mozart repeats a figure from the exposition but wittily inverts it, retaining the same harmonization. The third subject, given out by the strings, taken up by the piano, follows this passage, and the last runs, most of them a mere assertion of the chord of A, prolong it. Only then does the dreamy pedal return (ex. 45); more hurried now, it leads to the cadenza. The collection of cadenzas contains two for this movement;[1] the shorter one of the two, based on the third subject, is by far the more attractive. Then, with a certain flippancy, a codetta ends the movement.

II. The andante is far from having the insignificance of those of the other two concertos of this year. It begins with a solemn theme, almost religious, exceptionally fully harmonized.[2] To hurry it as is sometimes done is to rob it of its meaning and full value should be given to the bass (ex. 46). It is given out by the strings and followed by a second theme whose outline recalls the first subject of the allegro; the repeated notes of the accompaniment give it a lighter step than the first. Then, in the briefest glimpse, we see lands full of poetry through a half-opened door that closes again immediately, leaving us full of wonder and desire (ex. 47).

The piano repeats the first theme, then, before passing to the second, inserts a fresh one reserved for it and which does not return. The second subject appears in A; its melodic line is ornate and it leads to the trill which closes the first solo.

---

[1] The manuscript of the cadenzas for this concerto (K.624, 7–14) has on the back sketches for the other A major concerto, K.488, of 1786; this may help to date them. It is curious that Mozart should have taken up this little A major work again, no doubt for teaching, at the moment when he was thinking of the greater work in the same key.

[2] This theme is taken from the first bars of the second movement (andante grazioso, 3–4, in D) of an overture of John Christian Bach, composed in 1763 for a revival of Galuppi's *La Calamità dei Cuori* (Saint-Foix, III, 323; C. S. Terry, *John Christian Bach*, 272). John Christian had died on January 1st, 1782, and the presence of this theme, surmises Saint-Foix (V.319), may well be an act of homage to the deceased composer whom Mozart always loved and whose death day he called "a sad day for the world of music". See p. 388, note 1.

Again the door is half-opened and our eyes light upon the mysterious region seen just now.   But this time after the two bars, instead of closing, it opens wider and we launch forth into fairyland.   The piano enters it boldly with its very first chord.   We pass from major to minor—a transition seldom without special meaning in Mozart —and suddenly the mystery deepens.   The rustling thirds of the fiddles and violas end one phrase; those of the piano open another.   Already in the major they were crepuscular, but the twilight was that of a beautiful day going to rest; in the minor, it is threatening and bodes of ill to come.   The strings die away to *pp*; the solo re-enters *mf*;[1] there is not only a change of light but also an uprush of energy, a greater strain and a motion towards the unknown.   What does the future hold for us? the piano seems to ask.

It travels on, forsaken by the orchestra, with the air of a solitary rebel.   It repeats the figure an octave higher and adds a stormy commentary, then quietens down somewhat upon the chord of E minor (ex. 48).   The orchestra, conquered, devoid of initiative, can only murmur its theme afresh, *piano*, but still in the minor.   The solo sets off again in an angry climb, punctuated by accents against the beat, and stops in B minor.   Again, the orchestra raises its voice and, still submissive, repeats the same lesson (ex. 49).   A third time the piano returns, but, more at ease, it brings back the major now, though only for an instant, and first the horns, then the hautboys sustain and accompany its steps.   Without leaving the figure, but with a fresh significance at each repetition, it leads it through a threefold assertion to the point where the strings take it up again, in A minor, whilst the piano confines itself to announcing with a trill the end of the exploration (ex. 50).

Mozart is fond of linking up the *development* to the exposition by opening it with the last motif of the latter, especially in concerto first movements where the absence of a double bar makes the device easier than in a symphony or quartet.[2]   But he does it seldom in andantes and yet more seldom does he build the whole *development* upon this motif.   This time, not only does he begin by taking up the theme which had just died down but, held by its beauty, he is unable to tear himself from it.   However, even with new material, he could not have created anything more unlike what had gone before.

---

[1] The *piano* marked in the solo arrangement published by Breitkopf is not in the *Gesamtausgabe*, but is clearly needed by the feeling of the passage.
[2] K.482, 537.

The recapitulation leaves out the solo subject and repeats the others without change. Of the two cadenzas in the collection K.624, the longer is based on the second subject; the other, on the third; this latter is by far the more attractive.

III. If the andante of this concerto is much superior to those of the F and C major, its rondo is less interesting than theirs. Its refrain is a 2-4 theme whose tripping step and decided air contrast with the melting sweetness of the first movement and the solemnity of the second. The rondo keeps this character throughout; there is nevertheless more contrast between its themes than in the minuet-finale of K. 413.

This rondo is also in two parts, the second of which, with a few modifications, repeats the first. The tutti alone gives out the refrain which is composed of three motifs, the second of which is in unison (ex. 51, a, b, c). The first couplet begins with a new theme; then the strings recall the unison motif (b) and the piano takes it up with contrapuntal treatment. The first violins then accost a fresh subject which the piano completes and the two converse for a few bars. The motif (b) reappears in the piano with a triplet accompaniment. The rest of the couplet is concerned with it, repeating it with different harmonization and passing it from piano to orchestra and back again.

Piano, then tutti, repeat the first part of the refrain; the tutti broaches (b) but before finishing it modulates epigrammatically from A to D. The solo opens the second couplet with a new subject; violins and violas converse upon it for a few bars, then the piano concludes. After a moment of energy, passing through B minor and E, we rediscover, in A, a subject of the first couplet. The working-out of (b), transposed from E to A, is taken up again without change and an interesting section of eleven bars—the most interesting in the whole rondo for its orchestration: a contrapuntal development of (b) on a tonic pedal of horns and second fiddles—leads to the cadenza. The *ad libitum* part of the cadenza ends with the subject that had opened the first couplet, but after six bars the piano tires of it; the tutti seeks to complete it but also gives it up; the piano makes one last effort, then, accompanied by the strings, adds a few bars of *cadenza obbligata* and ends up on a dominant seventh chord instead of the usual trill. The movement infringes the conventions still further by giving the last return of the refrain, just after the cadenza, to piano and allowing the orchestra to join in only six bars from the end, with ex. 51 (c).

Apart from the lead to the cadenza, the most interesting moments in this rondo are the rare ones when piano and orchestra interplay. Thus, in the development of (b) which we have mentioned, the violins give out the motif, whilst the piano accompanies with chords on the strong beats, a combination which does not occur elsewhere in Mozart (ex. 52).

RONDO IN A (K.386)
October 19th, 1782
    Allegretto: 2-4
Orchestra: Strings, two hautboys, two horns.

Another source of interest in this rondo lies in its likeness to a second rondo in A for piano and orchestra, entered by Köchel under the number 386. The score of this was not published in Mozart's time and the manuscript, not quite finished, but still almost intact in the last century, seems to have been disleaved at the casual hands of auctioneers.[1]

The date inscribed on the manuscript and noted by André: October 19th, 1782, leads one to think that it was conceived as finale for this concerto. It has the same tone of melancholy nonchalance as the first movement of K.414; possibly Mozart considered that a certain monotony might arise from the likeness of the two movements. He may then have substituted the present finale, whose lively and dapper step is very different from the allegro. It certainly belongs to the same period and may be studied here.

It opens with a tutti of unusual length. Most of Mozart's concerto rondos let the solo give out the subject; some of them, however, make it wait till after a short tutti exposition; but in no other is this exposition as extensive as here. It includes the three sections of the refrain, of which only the first will return each time (ex. 53). The second one is rather insignificant and only eight bars long; the third, fuller, consists in a unison passage, *piano*, then *forte*, and leads to four bars of coda.

Thereupon the piano enters with the first strain, slightly modified.

---

[1] It belonged at one time to Sterndale Bennett. Two leaves have been retrieved of late and from these, as well as from a piano arrangement published by Cipriani Potter for Novello's in the 'forties of the last century, Alfred Einstein has reconstructed the whole movement (Universal, 1936).

Ex. 51

Ex. 52

Ex. 53

Ex. 54

Ex. 55

It leads with three transition bars to the first couplet which opens in E with a favourite Mozartian theme.[1]   The solo then opens out into passages of measured and graceful virtuosity where hand crossings play a part, but comes quickly back to the *cantabile* with a tune which constitutes the movement's second subject (ex. 54).   It is a close relation to the second subject of K.415 (ex. 15 b).   A very short virtuosity passage follows it and ends on an interrupted cadence, after which the tutti concludes the section.   This is the only moment in the rondo, with its repetition later on, where the regular and rather languid rhythm is broken by something harsher.   A lovely dialoguing passage brings back the refrain (ex. 55).

This latter returns first in the solo, then in the orchestra, which adds the octave figure and modulates to F sharp minor, the key in which the second couplet is laid.   It opens with demi-semi-quaver arpeggios on the common chord, which the tutti crosses with an accompaniment in contrary motion, partly indicated in Potter's arrangement.   But the virtuosity soon ends and from the threats of storm there arises ex. 54, transposed into the minor with an altera-tion in the bass which makes these bars the most original passage in the movement (ex. 56).   The melody starts again, modulating by falling degrees to D major, where it halts a moment, to pass next into A minor, E, and thence back to the tonic key and the refrain.

The rest of the movement is made up of the refrain, repeated com-pletely by the tutti and followed by a very short piano passage which leads to the interrupted cadence of the first couplet, after which the beginning of the refrain is given out for the last time; the piano adds bars of runs and the rondo ends in a typical manner with a couple of sharp rejoinders from tutti to piano.

The very moderate virtuosity of this movement and its technical simplicity are its chief external characteristics.   In form it resembles the two-couplet rondos of K.413 and 414.   It modulates less than the last and its rhythm is more uniform.   If Mozart really wrote it for the concerto in A, there is no cause to regret that he replaced it by the present rondo, which is better.   But it is a pleasant little piece and its reconstruction by Alfred Einstein is a work of piety for which all Mozartians are grateful.

---

[1] Based on the third, fourth and fifth degrees of the scale.   See the first movements of the C major concertos K.246, 415 and 503; also the beginning of the *development* in the first movement of the D major quartet, K.575.

CONCERTO NO. 9 IN C (K.415)
Summer or autumn, 1782[1]
   Allegro: C
   Andante: 3-4 (in F)
   Allegro: 6-8; Adagio: 2-4
Orchestra: Strings, two hautboys, two bassoons, two horns, two
   trumpets, two kettledrums.

The first two concertos of this year had kept within moderate
limits of thought, technique and orchestration. If the appreciation
expressed by Mozart which we quoted earlier is true for them, the
epithet "brilliant" is more suitable for the third and its orchestral
part, at least, is proof of a real emancipation. After the prudence of
his beginnings, Mozart grows bolder; he indulges his taste for counterpoint and rich instrumentation. The orchestra is the biggest he has
used till now. Unhappily, the piano part still remains timid and the
counterpoint ceases when the solo comes on the scenes. The result
is an unequal and heterogeneous work where great beauties remain
unknown because they lie side by side with weaknesses and banalities.
After the piano entry, the work loses itself in conventional virtuosity,
smiling and sparkling but empty, and we are reminded of those
ambitious churches which the Middle Ages had left unfinished, where
behind a magnificent Flamboyant façade lies a mean nave, hastily
put up with insufficient funds in later times. Yet, just as there may
exist inside a few pillars from the grander epoch, so the tuttis bring
back something of the opening splendour. But each time the piano
speaks, endless scales and arpeggios drive away the counterpoint
and finish off the work poorly, just as the patched-up supports and
plaster ceiling of a debased period complete the Flamboyant fragment.
   We have said enough to show that the work, although not
perfect, is far from being uninteresting. It is interesting, first of all,
in that it shows the influence of the polyphonic masters upon Mozart.
This influence dates from this very year 1782 and this concerto is the
first of the genre where one notices it. Engrossing while it lasted,
like all those Mozart underwent, it inspired a certain number of fine
works. Two of the best known of these are the first of the six quartets dedicated to Haydn, in G, in the finale of which *fugato* alternates
with homophony, and the first movement of the *Haffner* symphony,
K.385. There are also some attempts in out-of-date forms where

---

[1] No. 13 in the *Gesamtausgabe*.

Mozart's personality has left its imprint: the superb fantasia and fugue in C, K.394, and the fugue in the suite in the style of Handel, K.399, movements full of fire which are in nowise exercises "in imitation of . . ."; a prelude and fugue in A for violin and piano, K.402, unfortunately incomplete,[1] and especially a four-part fugue in C minor, of great beauty but almost as enigmatic as Beethoven's Great Fugue. It is generally known (if indeed it can be said to be known!) in the version for two pianos, but it is more intelligible in the arrangement which Mozart made of it for string quartet; it is illuminated by the harrowing adagio, K.546, which he added to it as a prelude. The crown of these polyphonic works is the choral part of the C minor mass, that masterpiece of sacred music which, after more than a century of neglect, is at last coming into its own. The *Qui tollis*, *Cum sancto spiritu* and *Hosanna* (to quote only the contrapuntal numbers) are summits which lose nothing of their greatness when they are heard in the neighbourhood of Bach's finest choruses.[2] Counterpoint is here as vital a means of expression as harmony and nothing is more unfair than to see in it a pseudo-archæological curiosity. It has that limpid, singing quality which is the charm of Mozartian polyphony and which is found at its highest in the finale of the *Jupiter* symphony.

The first movement of this concerto is interesting also in that it is another example of that Olympian strain that we saw appear in his musical personality towards 1780. The mood to which it corresponds finds several times expression in the key of C major; the concerto, K.503, the quintet and the *Jupiter* symphony are notable instance, of it. Sometimes, Olympian serenity is allied to physical energys and it is so here.

I. The work begins, with a mildness belied by the rest of the movement, on a march rhythm: ♩ ♫♩♩. We have already met this rhythm; henceforward, it will be frequent. It is typical of concertos and Mozart is merely complying with custom in adopting it.[3]

---

[1] The fugue was finished by Stadler. A great many sketches of fugues, for one or two pianos, string trio and quartet, given in the second appendix of the original Köchel, are also proofs of his infatuation at this period with polyphonic composition.

[2] The best pages written on it are in Saint-Foix's third volume and in Henri Gheon's *Promenades avec Mozart*.

[3] This theme, in its outline but not in its rhythm, is a variation of the first bars of the mass in C major, K.337.

The first violins give out this subject alone. For one moment it might be taken for a fugal entry. But when the theme (ex. 57), at the end of two bars, starts again two degrees higher up, the second violins repeat it at its original pitch, doubling the firsts a third below. The fugue is nothing but a canon! Then violas and basses take the place of the seconds while the firsts continue with a counter-subject in broken rhythm in which the other strings, giving up the march, end by joining.

The whole orchestra, hautboys, bassoons, horns, trumpets, drums and strings, thereupon bursts forth *ff* with a fresh subject. Proud and mighty, it climbs with a dignity not devoid of liveliness the eight degrees of the scale; then the basses pick up a new fragment and the violas pursue them in a canon at the octave while the violins emphasize the weak beats with chords: the whole leads to a full close.

The emotional strain has gone on heightening rapidly since the entry of the full orchestra. One would expect the full close to call a halt. But Mozart, instead of stopping and setting off afresh with a new theme, holds on the G, the fundamental of the last chord, with the basses, bassoons and horns, and this note, falling suddenly from *forte* to *piano*, becomes a pedal on which for twelve bars there is built up a dashing contrapuntal development in three parts. It is the most authentically polyphonic part of the whole work. Over this pedal the violas trace a moving figure, whilst the fiddles converse in phrases which resemble each other without being identical and link together in a single discourse (ex. 58). At the end of eight bars, the strain is relaxed; the pedal loses its power through repetition; the counterpoint fades away and in the first violins we hear a new theme— the fourth—of an archaic and Handelian cast.[1] All this passage is highly poetic and intensely vigorous; it is the image of a young god and the idea it gives us of the work is one of splendour. But, alas, it is deceptive! None of its first part—eight bars out of twelve —will come back; the polyphony is not much more than make-believe; it bears little relation to what follows the solo entry.

From the beginning of the pedal, the mark is *piano*. We return to the broad daylight of *forte* with a variant of the first subject which, like it, comes forward with mock fugal gestures and, like it also, breaks its promises. After a brief return to *piano*, the concluding subject brings back the full orchestra, *forte*. All of a piece, it is

---

[1] Beethoven works it hard in his overture *Zur Weihe des Hauses*, itself an archaistic piece.

nevertheless destined later on to break up, like the themes of K.413; the first part, spacious, based on the scale, does not return till after the cadenza; the next, formed by the favourite Italian overture motif (ex. 59), and the third, a mere formula, conclude also both exposition and recapitulation.

Let us cast a glance back at this unorthodox tutti. It is an experiment, and interesting like all that is new. But can it be called successful? It has fifty-nine bars. Now, of these, twenty-three—that is, two-fifths of the whole—will not be heard again, and they comprise some of the finest and most vigorous stuff in the tutti. Out of the thirty-six that return at one time or other, only nine will be utilized by the piano; as for the remainder, seventeen will not be heard till the end of the movement, either before or after the cadenza. There remain the first seven (the march), the last eight (the second and third fragments of the concluding subject) and four towards the middle (the Handelian figure); these are the only ones that we shall meet several times·in the body of the allegro. What conclusion can we draw from this?

First, that few elements are common to tutti and solo; orchestra and piano have each their own themes. This, for a *galant* concerto, is exceptional; we know that the custom is to let both give out most of the subjects, only one or two of them being reserved either for the solo or for the orchestra. One might be tempted to consider Mozart in this respect as a forerunner and this concerto as an ancestor of modern works where each instrument has its motifs, never borrows its neighbour's or lends him its own. We think that it should rather be looked upon as an archaism, a return to the practice of the preceding epoch. In the works of the older concertists, harpsichord and orchestra tend jealously to keep their own themes and nothing, or almost nothing, in the melodic material is common. This is still sometimes the case with Philip Emmanuel Bach, and in the best of Schobert's six concertos, op. 12 in E flat, written only fifteen years earlier than this one, all that the solo keeps of the first subject is the chaconne-like bass. When we remember that nearly everything in the introduction of our concerto has an archaic aspect, it seems clear that Mozart owes this feature to the studies he had been making of the Bach and Handel period.

Only, in his age, the structure of the concerto allegro is no longer the rondo-concerto of an earlier time, in which the main theme came back like a refrain in the tutti between each solo. Mozart's concerto is the sonata-concerto and the sharing of subjects is a condition

Ex. 56

Piano

Ex. 57

Ex. 58

Tutti

Ex. 59

Ex. 60

Piano

Ex. 61

Piano

Quatuor

implied in its very formula. The result is an upsetting of the balance, a heterogeneous character which strengthens the impression we had already and prevents us from classing the movement, in spite of its beauties, among his successful works.

The piano enters with seven bars of new material, of no great originality and rather colourless after what has gone before. Then the strings repeat the first subject as we had it at the beginning; in the middle of the fourth bar, that is, just before the violas' and basses' entry, the piano adds a trill to the counterpoint, then continues alone and finishes its phrase. From this time on to the end of the exposition the orchestra's part is confined to accompanying, or to interposing very short, commonplace figures, mere links between one solo phrase and the next.

There is no solo subject or rather the second subject is itself entirely reserved for the solo. The bravura passage which separates the orchestra's silence (at the end of the first subject) from the second subject is most ordinary; it consists mainly in a one-bar figure repeated seven times on different degrees of the scale of G major. As for the second subject, it belongs to the family of those we find in two other C major concertos, K.246 and 503, and in the rondo K.386. These four subjects are at bottom merely transformations of the same idea, whose fullest realization is reached in the great K.503 of 1786. (Exs. 15 and 54.)   The piano expounds it twice; the second time, the soloist should vary it; it is meaningless to play it again exactly as it is written. Then another virtuosity passage brings something more original; the Handelian theme from the introduction, given out first in the right hand, in double counterpoint with a semi-quaver running figure. The usual trill which one expects to close the exposition does not check the piano's volubility; it pursues uninterruptedly with the second fragment of the conclusion (ex. 59) and only after a new display of high spirits and a series of scales does it come to the end of its race.

The tutti's intervention, generally important at this stage, is short. It consists in a reassertion of the first subject in unison in violas, basses and bassoons, under the repeated notes of the fiddles, followed by the third fragment of the concluding theme.

The *development* is, after the opening tutti, the most interesting part of the movement. The piano starts off with a vigorous and contrasted theme, in minims and semi-breves followed by semi-quavers, treated in imitation, and for four bars we plunge again into the polyphonic atmosphere of the beginning (ex. 60). Two bars of tutti take us from G to C (the whole movement modulates extremely little; we hardly leave the tonic or its dominant), and the vigorous figure is repeated. It lands us in E minor and here the orchestra tries timidly to join in. But of all its riches at the beginning the poor thing has preserved only the first subject, and it keeps on going over it as if it was reciting a lesson. Moreover, only the first fiddles know it; the other strings and the hautboys just sustain and accompany them. For six bars the first member of the subject passes from key to key, rising from A minor to C, from C to E minor. But the piano does not remain aloof. To each repetition of the theme it adds a graceful counterpoint (ex. 61), a figure formed of a falling scale and a held note, and itself of polyphonic origin. This is one of the loveliest moments in the concerto and the only one in the movement where there is interplay between piano and orchestra. At last, at the end of the sixth bar, the piano gets rid of its feeble antagonist and forges joyously ahead, borne on a characterless arpeggio figure which it repeats half a dozen times in different keys, and comes quickly back to C major. Naïve, and not highly original!

But now, after this effervescing of carefree virtuosity, a change of one note (from E to E flat) carries us suddenly into the minor. Mozart pulls up abruptly, almost tragically, and drops in a broken scale to the tenor regions, where he lingers a while with his favourite and touching figure of fluttering seconds, before coming back, via a cadenza, to the first subject. He is like a child at play whose brow is suddenly overcast and who cuts short its game, assumes for an instant a serious look, then throws it off and returns to its former occupation.

To the end of the solo, the exposition is followed except for insignificant changes and without, of course, leaving the key of C major. Few of Mozart's concertos reproduce the first section so slavishly. After the last trill, the orchestra comes in with the "proud and mighty" subject which had followed the first theme in the opening tutti. It ends again with the little canon between basses and violas, then we stop on the dominant chord for the cadenza. Mozart has left a most vigorous cadenza for this movement. It sets off with fiery flight in the canon that has just stopped, each hand playing in octaves. Then comes a recall of the second subject and finally the Handelian theme, treated as in the solo part. To conclude, the orchestra gives out the whole of the final subject and the allegro finishes, note for note, like the first tutti.

II. The andante is a ternary movement: A—B—A—Coda. We

have already alluded to its complete insignificance. It has not even momentary glimmers of personality, like that of K.413; its common-placeness is constant from end to end. It is, moreover, afflicted with repetition mania; thus, the uninteresting first subject is heard six times in all! Mozart had at first thought of a movement in C minor, four and a half bars of which he wrote and then crossed out; the mood this movement would have expressed is no doubt that of the C minor interlude in the finale.

III. The rondo is the best movement. By its construction and the ingenious use it makes of its material, it ranks among Mozart's most original finales. During his first years in Vienna, he amused himself with composing rondos that follow no fixed model, where the refrain comes back unexpectedly and mingles with the episodes. This one and the finale of K.449 are the most whimsical of them. To its agreeably irregular structure, it adds changes of movement, twice interposing an adagio in the minor, 2-4, whereas the rest is a 6-8 allegro.

Its character is different from that of the first allegro (as far as one can speak of a general character in that heterogeneous movement); the Olympian sereneness, the "young god" vigour of the finest bars in the opening do not appear. The unexpectedness of the form reflects that of the thought; its spriteliness, vivacity, whimsicality and ingenuousness, and its constant Mozartian changes of temper, make it one of the master's most lovable, if not his deepest, pieces.

The piano opens the game with a 6-8 motif (ex. 62). Though reminiscent of a jig, its rhythm is not really that of any set dance form. It makes one think of a solo performed by a rustic who has an elf among his forebears and who adds to the yokeldom of his confrères a light, mischievous touch inherited from his distant ancestors. It appears simple and, at first, inoffensive, but it has plenty of tricks up its sleeve. Let us call it A.

The tutti repeats it and adds a second motif, less characterized, which we will call B, after which a codetta with a syncopated rhythm, of the same stock as A but more roguish, leads us to a dominant seventh close (ex. 63). We start again with a third motif (ex. 64), C, which also ends with a codetta based on A (ex. 65), and only after this long introduction which ends on the common chord of G does the piano speak again.

This opening corresponds by its position to the refrain of a rondo, but by its content it is more like the first tutti of an allegro. It is composed of five elements which we have rather arbitrarily

distinguished one from another; such riches is not the rule in a mere
refrain.   Moreover, except for the adagio which follows it and which
is a parenthesis, all the movement is built upon the material of this
beginning.   No new tune appears in the rest.   It is more than one

can say even of many allegro tuttis, including especially the one we have just been studying; these are often content to present us with a selection of the main themes.   Here, the whole cast files past us.   One hesitates, therefore, to call such an introduction a refrain; but, whatever name we give it, it is truly one of Mozart's most felicitous finale openings.

Very different is the plaint exhaled by the piano on its return. We had stopped on the chord of G; we start again in C minor.   Since the E flat concerto of 1777 we had not heard so desolate a lament.   For some fifteen bars there unfolds one of those "tragic" andantes like those of that concerto and of the *Sinfonia Concertante*, like that which will be heard a few years hence in the great E flat concerto of 1785 (ex. 66).   All this interlude has a recitative-like tone; it is a lonely voice, singing of suffering, which rises in the midst of the communal joy.   The orchestra, startled by the intrusion of this unknown being, is at first almost silenced; then, at the conclusion of the first strain, violins, hautboys and bassoons echo it (ex. 4).   They repeat the same fragment a bar later and finally, when the close is reached, the whole orchestra joins in perfect accord with the piano and corroborates its declaration.   And once again we stop on the chord of G, as before the beginning of the interlude.   The return to the same point emphasizes the parenthetic nature of these fifteen bars, a mere insertion which one could skip without the logic of the movement suffering thereby.

A pause, which should not be curtailed, and theme A comes back, first in the piano, then in the tutti, exactly as if nothing had happened. But what follows is different.   We compared the first part of this rondo, up to the adagio, to a first movement introduction; that which now opens is like a *development*.   It unfolds entirely in the key of the dominant and bases itself only on B and C and one of the two codettas of the refrain.   When the tutti has done with A, the piano goes on with B and, supported by the strings which supply the intermediate parts, enters on a bravura passage (ex. 67).   But virtuosity finds little place in this movement and after ten bars it ceases and the syncopated codetta ex. 63 leads us back to C, given out first by the tutti then, an octave higher, by the piano.   Another solo passage, rather longer, and again there appears the syncopated rhythm, but inverted (ex. 68).   A cadenza prolongs it[1] and the return of A marks the end of the second part of the rondo.

---

[1] K. 624, 17; printed also in the piano part in the *Breitkopf* edition.

In the sonata-rondo form, which Mozart has used in half his concertos, the third couplet is a recapitulation. But this movement has nothing regular about it. And the third part which opens here is certainly not a recapitulation. Indeed, it is rather a continuation of the *development*. Now it is that the innocent motif A opens its bag of tricks. Hitherto, it has quietly kept its place, appearing when it was needed, in the piano or the orchestra, with as reserved a mien as its elfin boorishness allowed. Henceforward, it unmasks itself and all this is changed. Hardly has the tutti stopped on the chord of C major when, without any preparation, and *ff*, it attacks that of E minor and passes, after three confirmatory bars, to *piano* and the key of A minor. And then open the most bewitching pages of the concerto.

For a moment which one would wish to be longer, strings and piano engage in a fairies' game with two bits of this theme (cf. ex. 62): the first bar and the "fluttering seconds" which end each half. The movements of the players lead them through the keys of A minor, D minor, C, A minor and G. The fragments play the part of accompaniment, while the solo's right hand performs arpeggio and scale passages, unless one considers these as accompaniment and the thematic fragments as the chief thing, which is quite defensible.

To begin with, the first fragment comes forward in the fiddles, playing in thirds, then in the violas and 'cellos; next, the "fluttering seconds" travel quivering from top to bottom of the orchestra (ex. 69), and this time violins on one hand, violas and 'cellos on the other, play in sixths and thirds. Like a rustle of wings, the game is carried on to a fresh return of the first fragment. Then the piano overcomes its reserve and lets itself be drawn into the sport; the infectious seconds invade it and appear in its right hand. The theme crumbles away more and more; reduced to its first three notes, it alternates with the fragment (ii). It sways between C minor and G, flitting from fiddles to piano, from piano to fiddles. The horns support it, the other instruments are silent. One feels that the end of the exquisite entertainment and the return to business are at hand. The first codetta of the refrain, again inverted, and theme C bring us back to familiar ground. But this rondo does not desert so easily the paths of fancy; theme C itself sets about modulating and passes into C minor when the strings take it up. The wandering lasts only a moment, however; we get back to the tonic and a bravura passage already heard, concluded by the refrain's second codetta. And the past seems to be deleted and the movement to start all over again when this codetta, as of yore, stops on the chord of G and the "tragic" andante raises its lamentation. We were far from it and the reappearance of this mournful ghost is weird in the highest degree.

> At the hour of greatest joy, a kind of bottomless gulf opens suddenly, then closes up,

says Joseph Baruzi with deep understanding of the master and, if one

Ex. 68

Ex. 69

had to say what distinguishes Mozart from his peers more than aught else, "opening a gulf", precisely, between them and him, one would reply: the bringing together in his work of two infinities. . . .

The adagio unfolds with very little change and vanishes as suddenly as the first time. And then begins the coda, as wonderful as all that precedes it. After a last hearing of theme A, regular and complete, the piano, which had been expounding it, instead of stopping to allow the orchestra to repeat it, as had happened hitherto, pushes on at once with fragment (ii) and keeps it going in both hands, in unison, whilst violins and wind whisper a variant of fragment (i) and add a new conclusion. Then the parts are reversed. The quivering goes over to the violins and violas and fragment (i) falls to the piano, where the parts are doubled; this device, which strengthens the tone and becomes regular in the 19th century, is uncommon in Mozart. Little by little, the rustle of wings of fragment (ii) spreads, from fiddles to violas, from violas to 'cellos and basses, at the same time as *piano* drops to *pianissimo*. To the very end, the solo keeps up its version of theme A; it adds two final bars, and shimmer of strings, piano chords and woodwind *tenuti* die away in a concluding *pp*, like the hum of the countryside at the end of a beautiful day.

We have already pointed out the characters which are common to these three concertos: their moderate technical difficulty, the "average" level of their emotion, the peculiarity that all three pass from *development* to recapitulation by means of a cadenza, or a change of *tempo*. Moreover, in two of them, K.413 and 415, the preponderance of rondo over andante helps to distinguish the group from the concertos that precede and follow it.

What can these concertos mean for us to-day? No more than the first six can they hope for great popularity; they will never be the possession of more than a small number of hearers and performers. Moreover, the inequalities of the C major risk causing its undeniable beauties to go unnoticed.[1] But those in F and A (as well as K.271) deserve a place in the repertory of amateur societies whom the technical difficulties of more famous works discourage. Both are perfectly homogeneous pieces, graceful without pettiness, genial without banality; moreover, the A major awakens deeper feelings by the smiling wistfulness of its allegro and the gravity of its andante. We earnestly recommend amateur orchestras and soloists to revive these lovely things, for it is in the intimacy of a small group rather than on large platforms that this art, still so close to chamber music, most fully exerts its charm.

Let us now put back the group we have been considering in the work of its composer as a whole, whence, for the purposes of study, we isolated it.

Compared with the earlier examples of its genre, can we say that it registers a development? Its ideal is still the *galant* ideal which

---

[1] It is precisely the existence of these beauties that make a recording of this concerto desirable, since it deserves better than the complete burial it suffers at present.

inspired the Salzburg concertos; the languor of the second, the Olympian carriage of a few bars in the third are its chief expressions of
personality.   But personal strains had also been heard in the Salzburg
works; there is nothing new in this.   As regards form, we have
noted the freedom of the rondos in the F and C major.   But the
finales of the two E flats also showed freedom and that of the two
pianos concerto had, moreover, organic unity.   Such unity, it is true,
is even greater in the 1782 works; there is some progress here, but of
a secondary kind.

On the whole, we must own that Mozart, at the end of this year,
is no nearer the great concertos of his maturity than he was on leaving
Salzburg.   These three works are not distinguishable in any essential
from those that went before them.   The orchestra is not "emancipated", save for a few bars here and there; the wind instruments, far
from being the soloists they will become later, are not even the
strings' equals.   In vain does Mozart increase his band for the C
major; it remains in essence a string orchestra and the wind has merely
ad libitum parts.[1]   If Mozart had written no more concertos after
his ninth, he would have left charming pages to which we could still
listen with pleasure, but he would not have been the "father" of the
modern concerto.

And if we compare this group with the principal works of the
same year, its importance does not appear any greater.   We have
said that the concerto, as well as the symphony, in 1781, 1782 and 1783,
interests him much less and draws much less upon his deepest forces
than chamber music, opera and polyphonic writing.   The two
great wind serenades in E flat and C minor belong to the first eighteen
months of his life in Vienna and three of the four violin sonatas he
wrote in 1781 are among his grandest.   Already in the summer of
1781 he was working at *Die Entführung* and the idea of composing
operas, which was never far from him, continued to absorb his
attention till 1783, since the unfinished *Oca del Cairo* and *Sposo deluso*
date from that year.   The C minor mass must have been begun about
the time he was composing the three concertos.

And finally, it is in 1782 that, after eight years of neglect, he takes
up again string-quartet writing.   Here, in the G major quartet, the
first of the six dedicated to Haydn, far more than in the piano concerto,
must we seek the complete Mozart of this period.   There had been
works as sincere and moving before it, but none as full.   The C minor

---

[1] He says so himself in a letter to his father of April 26th, 1783.

serenade, deeply personal as it was, had uttered but two opposing, complementary sentiments; sorrow and serenity.   But in the quartet it is impossible to isolate one single dominating emotion; its affective life is as rich as that of the soul itself and the various facets of his sensibility are lighted up in turn.   The emotional quality of this work is particularly hard to sum up.   It may be that the minuet does not mark any progress, in this respect, over the magnificent minuet in canon of the serenade, but the three other movements are all richer and fuller than their predecessors; through the whole work there flows the sap of a vigorous spring.

His chamber music, then, is ahead of his orchestral work.   The gain had been marked since the last year at Salzburg and the B flat serenade.   The significance of the *Haffner* and *Linz* symphonies and of the 1782 concertos is slight beside that of the C minor serenade, this quartet and the D minor which comes a few months later.   Only in 1786 and, especially, in 1788 will the symphony catch up; the concerto will do so sooner, in 1784 and 1785, in those twelve great works to the threshold of which our study has at length brought us.

PART III

1. The Tenth Concerto: K.449 in E flat

CONCERTO NO. 10 IN E FLAT (K.449)[1]
February 9th, 1784
  Allegro vivace: 3-4
  Andantino: 2-4 (in B flat)
  Allegro ma non troppo: ¢
Orchestra: Strings, two hautboys and two horns *ad libitum*.

MOZART had married early in August, 1782, the summer in which he composed the concertos we have just been considering. His wife was Constance von Weber, the daughter of a music copyist and stage prompter, who had died several years earlier. She lived with her mother and three sisters.[2] They had once dwelt in Mannheim and Mozart had made their acquaintance when he stayed in that city; he had then fallen deeply in love with one of the sisters, Aloisia, and she is often mentioned in his letters to his father. On his return from Paris, he passed through Munich, whither the Webers had moved, but Aloisia had forgotten him and he felt the blow keenly. When he met the family again in Vienna she was married and he then noticed Constance, of whom no mention had been made three years earlier. He married her after a long struggle with his father, who, possessed of sounder judgement than his son in practical matters, was much averse to the union. Outwardly, he ended by yielding, but he was never reconciled to the idea of seeing Wolfgang married to "a Weber" and he was not wrong. Constance was not a bad soul, but to be a helpmeet to Mozart she should have had two qualities she lacked: enough vision to appreciate her husband's genius, enough practical common sense to compensate for the almost total absence of it in him. Without deep understanding, without practical qualities, she was a burden rather than a help. They remained united, nevertheless, during the eight and a half years of their

---

[1] No. 14 in the *Gesamtausgabe*.

[2] She was the first cousin of Carl Maria von Weber who was some fifteen years younger.

married life, and if there were domestic quarrels they were not serious.

These first years in Vienna were happy. Mozart won a certain success, modest perhaps compared with that of more fashionable *artistes*, but enough to make him comfortably off. Lessons came in abundance; *Akademien* or concerts, where he played as soloist, performing his works or those of others, succeeded one another with some frequency.

> Altogether I have so much to do that often I do not know whether I am on my head or my heels. I spend the whole forenoon giving lessons until two o'clock, when we have lunch. After this meal I must give my poor stomach an hour for digestion. The evening is therefore the only time I have for composing and of that I can never be sure, as I am often asked to perform at concerts.[1]

Thus does he describe a typical day in a letter to his father of December 28th, 1782. His letters are expressive of happiness; he relates complacently the success with which he has played a concerto—his or another's, he does not say—in an *Akademie* given by his sister-in-law Frau Lange.

> The theatre was very full and I was received again by the Viennese public so cordially that I really ought to feel delighted. I had already left the platform but the audience would not stop clapping and so I had to repeat the rondo; upon which there was a regular torrent of applause. It is a good advertisement for my concert which I am giving on Sunday, March 23rd. I added my symphony which I composed for the Concert Spirituel. My sister-in-law sang the aria *Non so d'onde viene*. Gluck had a box beside the Langes, in which my wife was sitting. He was loud in his praises of the symphony and the aria and invited us all four to lunch with him next Sunday.[2]

In the same letter, dated March 12th, 1783, he announces that he is himself to give an *Akademie* on the 29th of the month and the next letter, written on the evening of the concert, speaks of its success and, what interests us more, enumerates the items played; it shows that the patience and musical appetites of a hundred and fifty years ago were more extensive and capacious than ours.

> I need not tell you very much about the success of my concert, for no doubt you have already heard of it. Suffice it to say that the theatre could not have been more crowded and that every box was full. But what pleased me most of all was that His Majesty the Emperor was present and,

---

[1] Trans. E. Anderson, III, 1242.
[2] Id., III, 1254–5.

goodness, how delighted he was and how he applauded me! It is his custom to send the money to the box-office before going to the theatre; otherwise I should have been fully justified in counting on a larger sum, for really his delight was beyond all bounds. He sent twenty-five ducats. Our programme was as follows:

(1) The new *Haffner* symphony (K.385).

(2) Madame Lange sang the aria "*Se il padre perdei*" from my Munich opera (*Idomeneo*) accompanied by four instruments.

(3) I played the third of my subscription concertos (K.415).

(4) Adamberger sang the scena which I composed for Countess Baumgarten (K.369).

(5) The short *concertante Symphonie* from my last *Finalmusik* (K.320).

(6) I played my concerto in D major (K.175), which is such a favourite here, and of which I sent you the rondo with variations (K.382).

(7) Mlle Teiber sang the scena "*Parto, m' affretto*" out of my last Milan opera (*Lucio Silla*).

(8) I played alone a short fugue (because the Emperor was present) and then variations on an air from an opera called *Die Philosopheen*, which were encored. So I played variations on the air "*Unser dummer Pöbel meint*" from Gluck's *Pilgrimme von Mekka* (K.398 and 455).

(9) Madame Lange sang my new rondo (K.416).

(10) The last movement of the first symphony (K.385).[1]

The success of *Die Entführung aus dem Serail*, of which we hear frequent and satisfied echoes in his letters, kindled his desire to write other operas, and more than once he alludes to some libretto or other, German or Italian, which had attracted his notice. In 1783 he undertook another Turkish opera, but in Italian this time, on a libretto of Abbate Varesco, the Salzburg chaplain who had put together *Idomeneo*; this work, *L'Oca del Cairo*, was given up after the first act had been completed. Either from ill-will or from incapacity, the librettist did not comply with the composer's requirements. The same year, he began another Italian opera, *Lo Sposo deluso*, but abandoned it even more quickly. Only three years later did he meet the ideal partner, the Abbate Lorenzo da Ponte, from his collaboration with whom arose his greatest *opere buffe*, *Le Nozze di Figaro*, *Don Giovanni* and *Cosi fan tutte*.

His letters home follow at the rate on an average of three a month. As they have all been kept for the period we have reached, they provide us with fairly copious information on his life. From the beginning of the year, they had been announcing his visit and that of his

[1] Id., III, 1256-7.

wife to Salzburg, a visit which was delayed, now by the fear that the Archbishop might keep him there, now by his wife's pregnancy and the impossibility for her (according to Mozart) to be delivered in Salzburg, now merely by "the weather and circumstances". This reconciliation visit finally took place in the summer and the young couple, accompanied by the little Raymund Leopold, born in June, stayed three months with Leopold and Nannerl. This was Wolfgang's last visit to his native city, that city which absence never made dear to him.

> I have no desire whatever to see Salzburg or the Archbishop. . . . It would never enter my head voluntarily to make a journey thither, were it not that you and my sister lived there.[1]

External civilities were observed but cordiality does not seem to have been established between Constance and her new family, and Mozart returned to Vienna disappointed. On his way back he stopped a few days at Linz, where he gave a concert of his works. A symphony was apparently indispensable; as there was no time to send for parts from Vienna, he composed one in four days, that in C. K.425, known as the Linz, the first he had written since he had settled in the capital.

The concertos K.413, 414 and 415 were composed, it is thought, during the summer of 1782. Between that moment and February, 1784, no piano concerto came from him. The most significant works of these fifteen or sixteen months belong to choral, dramatic and chamber music. He had vowed to have a new mass performed in Salzburg if he succeeded in leading Constance thither as his wife. This vow won for us the great C minor mass. If God held to the letter of the vow, He may have reproached His votary with defaulting, for the mass is unfinished; but it is probable that the exceeding loveliness of what was written has made up in His eyes for two thirds of the Creed and all the Agnus Dei, which are missing; the work, unfinished though it be, is worth all Mozart's completed masses together, and much more! During the second half of the year, the young man worked at L'Oca del Cairo and his letters are full of remarks and complaints on the progress of the work and the difficulties arising from his collaboration with Varesco. His only orchestral composition was the Linz symphony which still keeps a place in the repertory but had neither the power nor the variety of the C major symphony of 1779, and of the four great works of 1786 and 1788. Finally, he

---

[1] Id., III, 1276.

continued at leisure the series of quartets he had begun and by the end of the year had added two more to that in G—those in D minor and E flat. The D minor was written out, we are told, during the night which preceded his child's birth; he went from his table to his wife's bedside, and back to his table, without this constant shifting interrupting the continuity of the music. It is probable that he was not composing but merely writing out the music which had already been worked out in his brain. A prodigious memory enabled him to do without written notes; he could rig up his constructions and modify their details in his mind, as less talented beings draw up their plans and make their erasures on paper.[1]

Such is the list of the important works of the year. There is another group to which no masterpiece belongs but of which we must say a few words, for it touches closely the piano concertos. It is that of the concertos for horn.

These four works are the only concertos he wrote for an instrument other than the piano after leaving Salzburg, with the exception of the E flat work for violin[2] and the clarinet concerto. Some of them owe their existence to his friendship with Ignaz Leutgeb, an old Salzburg acquaintance settled in Vienna. Leutgeb, who had been a horn player at Salzburg, had set up in the capital where he supported the cult of music with the earnings of trade, and had a little cheese shop in the suburbs—"the size of a snail's shell", said Leopold[3]—prosecuting the while the practice of the horn. He seems to have been a good soul, with an excellent temper, patient and simple. He allowed himself to serve as a butt for Mozart's Beotian humour, the exuberant overflow of which was poured out on him. For him were written at least two concertos and a quintet for horn and strings, works themselves conceived as playthings, and the conditions Mozart laid down for their composition show that he did not take them seriously. Thus, at one time he compelled Leutgeb to pick up on his hands and knees a number of orchestral parts he had thrown on the floor. Another time, the virtuoso cheesemonger had to remain kneeling behind the stove whilst Mozart began a concerto. The musician perpetuated on the scores the pitiless fun he made of him; the dedication of the second concerto, K.417, runs:

---

[1] We have been told that a contemporary composer, Frédéric d'Erlanger, worked in the same manner.

[2] Saint-Foix thinks that this work was written in 1786.

[3] Letter to Wolfgang of December 1st, 1777.

Wolfgang Amadeus Mozart took pity on Leutgeb, donkey, ox and fool, at Vienna, March 27th, 1783.

The fourth is written with red, black, blue and green ink; one page is adorned with a drawing showing the horn player in action; one movement is headed allegro in the orchestra and adagio in the solo; another is annotated with a whole humorous commentary upon the performer's execution:

A lei Signor Asino—Animo—presto—sú via—da bravo—Coraggio—e finisci già—bestia ... ajuto—respira un poco!—avanti,—avanti! questo poi va al meglio ... ah! trillo di pecore—finisci—grazie al ciel! basta, basta!

One would expect works conceived in such a mood to belong to the class of "musical jokes", an agreeable specimen of which Mozart composed a few years later. Not at all. Without boasting either the scope or the variety of his piano concertos, they are authentic Mozart pieces, the shavings of his workshop, the small change of his genius, and all four can be listened to with pleasure. As all four by their structure and style are analogous to the more ambitious concertos that precede and follow them, we shall not be straying from our path if we cast a rapid glance at them.

The allegro of the first was dated by André 1782, but its finale was not completed till 1787.[1] The second bears the burlesque dedication and the date we have quoted (March, 1783); the third is not dated and Saint-Foix suggests that it is later than the others; the fourth dates from 1786. The first is in D and has only two movements; the three others are in E flat and have the habitual three movements. The allegros of all four are in that concerto-sonata form which Mozart never gave up; the andantes or larghettos are *romances* with one or two couplets; the finales are rondos, also in two or three couplets. The orchestra consists of strings with either hautboys or clarinets; in addition, the first and third have bassoons, the second and fourth have horns.

Generally speaking, the first movements, which are the most interesting, reproduce on a miniature scale the design of the piano concertos. The main formal dissimilarities come from the difference in the problems to be solved by the composer in the two sorts of concerto. From its very nature, the horn is less independent than the piano; it cannot play alone and its power of expression is limited. It will therefore be less the orchestra's adversary than its collaborator and will from time to time fall back into the bosom of the tutti.

---

[1] It is not by any means certain that the two movements belong together; their orchestration is not identical.

Like all solo instruments other than piano, harp and organ, it is *primus inter pares* and not one of a different order. The tutti's share will be therefore much more important than in the piano concerto and the places where the solo takes an inner part and subordinates itself to the other instruments more numerous. Moreover, as its means of virtuosity are limited (for the valve horn had not yet been invented), the development passages will fall mainly to the strings. And as, for the same reason, the easiest manner for the horn to play as a soloist is to sing, the melodic richness of the works will be relatively much greater than in the piano concertos. The composer scatters treasures of melody throughout these trifles with a profusion which seems to us to border on waste, and *cantabile* subjects, compared with developments and bravura passages, are even more important than in Mozart's other works.

In the three concertos in E flat, riper and more daring works than the first, Mozart's ingenuity, the field of which is restricted by the nature of his solo instrument, bears mainly on the setting forth of the various tunes. He has taken a delight in dividing and reuniting them, in upsetting their order, in the three sections of the first movement, so that the terms, second subject, mock second subject, solo subject, have no meaning, and even the first subjects are not always the same in tuttis and solos. In this respect, the formal study of these concertos is fascinating and offers, so to speak, microscopic examples of the master's infinitely fruitful imagination and of the care he lavished on even the humblest tasks when his heart was involved. There is nothing like it in the great piano concertos; this aspect of his genius can be studied only here.

The first, K.412 in D, is a trial work. Its structure is not different from that of the piano concertos; it has only three main subjects, one of which, as in K.365, is a mock second subject, and its rather hesitant *development* does not stray far from the first subject. The horn part is more timid than in the other concertos. Mozart had no doubt underestimated the good Leutgeb's capacities. As if to inspire him with confidence, he gives the first violins an important, almost a *concertante* part, so that the work is not far from being a *Sinfonia Concertante* for violins and horn.

The second, K.417, is the most broadly-planned of the four. The spacious tunes, their number and their expressive power strike one at first hearing and the work deserves to be performed more often in our concert halls.[1] It is all melody; the linking figures and codettas

---

[1] As its andante is weak, in performance the beautiful *romance* of the fourth, K.495, could be substituted.

are almost entirely absent.   The game of disintegrating and changing
round subjects is carried here to its highest point.

The third, K.447, is less attractive at first sight and treats the
soloist less bountifully, but it is the most interesting for the orchestra,

Ex. 70

Ex. 71

Ex. 72

whose part is considerable.   The tutti repeats each time the second
half of the first subject after the solo, and each time, too, it gives out
the second subject.   But it is in the *development* that it breaks loose.
This section, short as it is, is one of the most remarkable symphonic
passages in all Mozart.   It starts with a new tune, given out by the
solo in D flat, which stops abruptly after ten bars.   The horn then

sounds a G flat which it holds for two bars. At first it is alone; then the strings begin again, but in D major, and the G flat, which was the subdominant, pivoting upon itself in a daring enharmonic modulation, becomes F sharp, the third of the new key. There follow eight profoundly Mozartish bars (ex. 70) of weird modulations. The horn is reduced to holding semibreves while the orchestra, repeating a restless motif, rises from D major to D minor, E flat minor, G major, C minor and back again to G major, where it stops, engages in a conversation with the horn, and whence it passes to G minor and finally to E flat for the reprise. This is one of the earliest examples in Mozart of those *fantasia developments* which characterize the great concertos of 1784 to 1786.[1]

The fourth and last concerto, K.495, displays no such audacity. By the time it was written, Mozart had composed nearly all his greatest piano works and was no doubt growing tired of the concerto game. It is as fruitful in tunes as the others but is on an even smaller scale. Its most remarkable features are its *development* subject, a well-known theme in Bach and Beethoven[2] (ex. 71) and its concluding subject, the accompaniment of which affords a masterly instance of the poetic manner in which Mozart can use the "fluttering seconds" figure (ex. 72).[3]

The andantes are less interesting. The best is the *romance* of K.495 which makes use, with a slight difference of rhythm, of the same theme as the andante of the exactly contemporary sonata for piano duet in F, K.497. The *romance* of K.447, in A flat, is a rondo, the frequent returns of whose refrain—five in all, one-half of the movement!—and the insignificance of whose episodes relate it to the rondos of Philip Emmanuel Bach; with that in D, K.485, for piano, it is the only one of the kind in Mozart. Its theme reappears in an episode of the finale.

The four finales are much alike. They differ less than the first movements from their counterparts in the piano concertos. The most lively is that of K.412 which was completed in 1787. The orchestra

---

[1] The manuscript of this concerto bears none of the jokes for Leutgeb's edification which adorn the others, and Saint-Foix surmises that it may have been written for a professional horn player.

[2] St. John Passion, B minor aria for alto, no. 31; 'cello sonata in A, op. 69, middle of first movement; A flat piano sonata, op. 110, in the *arioso* which breaks in upon the fugue.

[3] A whole study could be carried out on the use he makes of this figure; it appears often in his work and nearly always with an unmistakably passionate meaning.

is treated with a sure and experienced hand. We meet again the little "seconds" figure of the K.415 finale (ex. 62, II and 69); it appears likewise towards the end of the movement and ends by taking possession of the whole orchestra (73 a and b). Of all these horn works, it is this rondo, through its coda, which resembles most the group of piano concertos which we were studying in the last chapter.

On February 9th, 1784, Mozart completed his tenth piano concerto.[1] Between this date and December 4th, 1786, that is, in two years and ten months, a dozen concertos for his instrument were to flow from the fruitful store of his genius. The date is important; henceforward Mozart, who had been hitherto a composer amongst whose works were counted a few concertos, as many for string and wind instruments as for piano, becomes a piano concerto writer *par excellence*. The genre predominates absolutely in his compositions for the next three years. The nine earlier concertos were but preliminaries; it is in February, 1784, that the story of his piano concertos really begins. The importance of the genre in his work is due to its importance during these three years. The twelve masterpieces which extend between these dates constitute the true canon of the concerto.

It is enough just to glance at the list of his compositions during these thirty-four months to recognize this predominance. If we neglect the lesser forms—arias, variations, dances, lieder, cantatas—and confine ourselves to the operas and works in sonata form, we find from twenty-five to thirty items. The operas are the curtain-raiser, *Der Schauspieldirektor*, and *Le Nozze di Figaro*. The *sonatas* comprise ten trios, quartets and quintets,[2] five sonatas and fantasias, one horn concerto and one symphonic movement, the *Masonic Funeral Music*. By extending the period for two days we bring into it a symphony, the *Prague*, composed at the same time as the last concerto of the series. The preponderance of the piano concerto is obvious. Only chamber music can rival it, and even there, works with a piano part number six out of ten. Every winter, throughout this period,

---

[1] It is the first entry in the catalogue of his works which he kept from that date till his death.

[2] One quintet, three trios, two quartets with piano, four string quartets.

concertos succeed each other at the rate of almost one a month, in February, March and April, 1784 (two, even, in March!), in September and December, 1784, and February and March, 1785, in December, 1785, and February and March, 1786; the last one arrives all alone in December of the same year.

We crave forgiveness for these dates and figures; they enable us to see at a glance the numerical importance of concertos in the master's activity at the period on whose threshold we stand. The musical importance of each one of them is no less. Neither among the foregoing concertos, nor among the earlier symphonies or *sonatas* are there works into which Mozart's thought and soul entered so deeply and which he undertook in so serious a mood. The only exceptions to this generalization are to be found in *Idomeneo*, the *Sinfonia Concertante* for violin and viola and the first quartets dedicated to Haydn, and of these the quartets antedate by only a few months the concertos we are about to study.

The reason for this preponderance is clear; it is Mozart's success as a pianist. From 1784 to 1786, he is a fashionable virtuoso, perhaps not the most fashionable, but certainly one of those who received abundantly of the public's inconstant favours. At that time the virtuoso-composer had not yet become the almost extinct species he is to-day, when we wonder at, even more than we admire, a Dohnanyi or a Rachmaninov playing his own music, and Wolfgang's success as pianist called for a more abundant output of works. It was natural that the quality as well as the number of such works should gain by his rise to fame.

What differences are there between these Viennese concertos of 1784-6 and the nine compositions of Salzburg and Vienna which cover the twelve preceding years? They can be summed up in the words: elaboration of form and deepening of thought.

It is not so much that the movements are longer and the themes more numerous, though this is true in most cases. It is especially that the structure is more complex and more daring; that the relations between solo and orchestra, which hitherto had been almost rudimentary, become closer and more diverse; that the orchestration grows richer and draws on more resources. Most of them are more richly scored than the first nine and, apart from actual number of instruments, Mozart gets much more out of his orchestra.

The emotional scope of these twelve concertos surpasses indisputably that of the earlier ones. Not only each one has its own personality, but the personality is vaster and richer and the elaboration of form is but the manifestation of this growth. Whereas in five out of the six Salzburg concertos and in those of 1782 Mozart, for fear of scaring his public, has held back the more essential part of himself, henceforward he gives himself whole-heartedly to his work and throws himself into it completely, so thoroughly in fact that he ends by getting ahead of his audience and, after barely three years finds himself forsaken by it. The dramatic and individual character of his themes is emphasized; the passages which reveal an inner life return more often and no compositions, whatever they be, are more authentically, more exclusively, more fully his own than these twelve concertos. Had he been a more conscious creator he could have said, like Jean Cartan:

I have won for music new parts of myself which had hitherto stood apart from my work. Now they are coming in and taking part of their own accord without the slightest effort.

The result of this expanded form and deepened thought and feeling is seen in movements more ambitious, more charged with meaning than anything he had written hitherto for piano and orchestra and even, with the few exceptions already mentioned, for any combination whatsoever.

In his well-known book, *Beethoven et ses trois styles*, Lenz said that the study of Mozart's music showed that the artist, but not the man, had changed with time, that the latter had remained the same from beginning to end of his career, whereas with Beethoven the man as much as the artist had developed. This view is most unfair to Mozart. If one takes into account the fact that he lived twenty years less than Beethoven, one must admit that the importance of the "man's" development, with all that this word implies of inward and elemental forces, was no less great in him than in the later musician. He died at the age when Beethoven had written his three first symphonies and his op. 18 quartets, when he was, that is, at the beginning of his "second manner". Now, if it is a far cry from Beethoven's first compositions to the *Eroica*, it is quite as far from the *galant* baubles that Mozart was writing in 1775 and 1776 (and we forbear from going back further, though at that time thirteen years of composing reached away behind him!) to the *Magic Flute* and the *Requiem*.

Ex. 73ª

Ex. 73b

Ex. 74

Ex. 75

As Mozart took care to tell his father,[1] the first of the four concertos written for the Lent[2] of 1784 requires but a small band: strings, hautboys and horns—in which the wind parts are *ad libitum*. It is best, however, to retain these latter; not only does their colour relieve the greyish hues of the strings, but also here and there they add important elements to the score.[3]

I. The first movement is, in the series of the twenty-three concertos, one of the few in three-time. The others are those of the F major, K.413, and the C minor, K.491, and its closest relationship is with the latter. The instability which this time-signature connotes and which one expects in a *minor* work is surprising in the usually serene key of E flat. But it is unmistakable. The whole movement is born of an unstable, restless mood, sometimes petulant and irascible, uncommon in Mozart, and this makes the concerto something exceptional in his work, something which, by its climate if not by its form, reminds one of Philip Emmanuel Bach.

The first four bars betray this mood (ex. 74); the key is affirmed by the first, doubted by the second (are we in the relative minor?) and gainsaid by the third and fourth (we are in the dominant). Such an entry, neither major nor minor, neither tonic nor dominant, is unique in Mozart; its closest analogy in classical music is with the opening of Schubert's G major quartet.

The four remaining bars of the first subject bring back the tonic

---

[1] Letters of May 15th and 16th, 1784. This concerto and that in G were written for Babette Ployer, one of his pupils, the daughter of the archbishop's agent in Vienna and niece of the Abt Max Stadler. It was for her that he set the composition exercises preserved in the National Library in Vienna. Her autograph album, which came into the Mozarteum collection some years ago, contains a funeral march by him, signed "*Del Sigr. Maestro Contrapunto*" (Köchel-Einstein, no. 453 a).

[2] See note at beginning of next chapter.

[3] This is so in the first tutti, bars 51-2, for the little hautboy phrases echoed by the violins; in the andantino, bars 41-4, 70-3 and 118-22; and in the finale, bars 213-18, 238-42 and 262-6, where the hautboy and hord *tenuti* add not only to the *timbre* but also the harmony of the whole.

key and this is confirmed by the codetta of seven bars. But then comes a fresh surprise! Plunging and rearing there rushes up in unison a fiery little theme which stampedes into C minor and adds ferocity to instability (ex. 75). Against the incessant agitation of the second violins and violas, it renews itself on different degrees of the scale, then, just touching on E flat major, bivouacks an instant in B flat and camps in F where the frenzy of its semi-quavers is somewhat quietened. But F major is only a stage; it is as dominant of B flat and not for its own sake that it is sought out and our motif does not tarry in it. We return to B flat, in which key the second subject unfolds. This theme, harmonized in sixths and thirds, full of yearning and still glowing with ill-quenched fire, is broken up by a commentary of dotted quavers and finishes as it began, on the chord of B flat (ex. 7).

The appearance of the second subject in the dominant instead of the tonic is exceptional in an opening tutti.[1] Already Mozart's concerto in F, K.413, had allowed itself this violation of the rules but only for a moment, and the subject, born outside the fold of the tonic, had quickly entered it. Here, the excursion into the dominant dates from before birth and only after expounding the whole of it does the movement resume the high road of E flat. Besides, what was just a formal and non-significant irregularity in K.413 is here yet another symptom of the feverish mobility and restlessness which have reigned since the beginning and which, though a little quietened after the solo entry, persist to the end.

The charming link theme which leads us, on a B flat pedal and through rustling harmonies where seconds preponderate, towards the conclusion, is one of those passing thoughts which Mozart sometimes sprinkles so bountifully in his concertos. We have already noted in three of them characteristic and interesting subjects playing their part in opening tuttis and then returning no more.[2] We shall find another in K.459. As the composer progresses towards compression and unity, this waste ceases.

At length, the concluding subject affirms with the four times repeated common chord the key of E flat, so neglected hitherto, which had risked becoming a mere man of straw, lending its title to a work full of wandering modulations. The subject is rhythmic and manly and contrasts with the sometimes passionate, sometimes tender

---

[1] It occurs in two of John Christian's concertos, op. XII, 5 and 6, in G and E flat, but both times the subject concludes in the tonic. In Beethoven's C minor concerto, the second subject is given out wholly in the relative major.

[2] K.365, 413 and 415.

but always uncertain strains heard hitherto.   The conclusion is rather
long and ends with a trilling figure which will be important in the
development.

Let us glance back over this tutti.   Its instability struck us at first
sight; the restless subjects and the frequent modulations are the clearest
mark of this mood.   Almost one half is spent outside the main key:
in the relative minor, the dominant and the "ultra-dominant".
But there is more to it.   Even in the E flat parts accidentals are abundant enough to undermine the feeling of the key.   Now an A
natural threatens us with a sally into B flat (bar 3); now a D flat
hints at an escape into A flat (bars 65-6); now a B natural carries us
past the dusky fringes of C minor (bar 71).   Thus, at no time, till
the final codetta of four bars closes the tutti, are we safe from the
quicksands of modulation or the threat of them, and this is the expression of a most exceptional state in our composer.

The great majority of his other tuttis keep within the tonic or,
if they modulate, do so only for a few bars and generally into closely
related keys.   (The E flat major swooping suddenly into the G major
of K.453 is unique.)   Generally, these tuttis modulate little or not
at all, with three exceptions, two of which we know, this work and
K.413; the third is the great C major concerto of 1786, K.503.

Sir Donald Tovey has often insisted on the importance of Mozart's
concertos and, in particular, of the relations between their opening
tutti and the rest of the allegro.

> The most important aspect of classical concerto-form is . . . the relation
> between the opening orchestral ritornello, with its procession of themes,
> to the solo exposition which works out these and other themes in sonata-
> form.   No two ritornellos of Mozart repeat each other in all points of
> this relation, and in every concerto there is some unique feature which is
> no minute detail, but a matter affecting large areas. [1]

Here, the unique feature is the modulation which covers such a
large part of the introduction, and especially the giving out of the
second subject in the dominant.   Should one consider this departure
from the rule to be happy innovation?   Is there not rather in it the
danger that a tutti thus treated may, as Tovey says, resemble a symphonic exposition so closely that the arrival of the solo will be merely
an unjustified surprise?   The beginning of Beethoven's C minor
concerto is not free from this peril, but there, between the subjects,
there is change of mode as well as of key.   Moreover, the size of the

---

[1] *Essays in Musical Analysis*, III, 42.

movement gives it almost the dimensions of a symphonic exposition. Not so here. It is true that the keys are somewhat diverse at the start, but the brevity and speed of the work are such that we do not linger in any of them, not even in B flat; the concluding theme comes back to the tonic and dwells on it long enough for the subordination of all the others to appear indisputable. On the whole, these secondary keys do not open up independent paths that stray far from the main road; they are rather loops or short cuts which run near it and culminate in the end at the same point.

The piano's entry exerts a calming influence. From now on, nerves are less on edge and there is not so much restlessness. It is as if the piano had the advantage of experience and years over the orchestra. It has in any case more muscle; its entry is the most vigorous and most direct in all Mozart. Not only is there no introduction but also the first subject, which in the orchestra was merely wiry, has brawn added to it by the piano which fills it out with all the notes in the scale and clothes its spareness in sinuous outlines (ex. 76).

Typical of this change of mood is the non-appearance of ex. 75. In its place we have a short but interesting development of the first subject with collaboration between solo and strings. After twelve bars of solo, the notice of the strings is attracted to a little element of three rising notes (bar 7 of ex. 76, marked ⌐¬) which plays a discreet but important part in the first subject. They seize hold of it and repeat it murmuringly whilst the piano carries down into the bass the figure which ends this same subject (bar 11, marked [ ]). The solo continues with a scale motif, related to the subject just given out, though not derived from it, and the strings go on whispering their now falling three-note theme.[1] Then, after eight bars, the adversaries exchange weapons; first violins and violas take the scale and the piano the three-note motif which it decorates with an arpeggio line. Having calmed the orchestra's fever with this game of battledore and shuttlecock, it attacks almost alone the solo subject. It begins in C minor in a questioning strain, repeats the question in B flat and finds the answer in F with the figure which, in the opening tutti, had concluded ex. 75 and introduced the second subject (ex. 7). This latter has nothing new to say and it says it, as before, in B flat, dividing itself between piano (harmonized part) and first violins (answer in dotted quavers). For the pedal point in the introduction

---

[1] The harmonization of this passage is characterized by Mozart's mannerism of the flattened leading note.

Ex. 76

Ex. 77

Ex. 78a

Ex. 78b

Ex. 79

the piano substitutes a few bravura bars, the first and almost the only ones in this concerto, which is one of the least virtuosi; and the whole orchestra concludes in B flat with the rhythmical and manly subject already noted.

The second half of this subject includes an element of repeated quavers in the treble and a chain of trills in the bass (ex. 77), trinkets with which orchestra and piano amuse themselves during the *development*.[1] The piano repeats at first the end of the exposition,

[1] Mozart is fond of building the first parts of his *developments* on elements drawn from the concluding subject of the exposition; cf. K.482 and 537.

modulating; upon its return to B flat strings and hautboys again give out
the trill, in unison; the piano interrupts them with an arpeggio figure;
the orchestra starts afresh, this time in C minor, the piano does
likewise; and this innocent manœuvring is reiterated, with modulations, three times.   Combination now succeeds alternation; the
piano gives out the trill and the strings the quaver figure, passing
through sundry keys to end the game in A flat (ex. 78).   All this
passage is in a thoroughly Mozartish delicate vein of humour.

What follows is different.   As in the last concerto so here, just
before the reprise, a cloud passes over the face of the work.   The
change of mood is much less abrupt than in K.415; it is less joy yielding
to sadness than playfulness giving way before earnestness.   The
change is marked in the disappearance of the trill figure and the slowing
down of the strings, whose quavers turn into crotchets.   The new
passage, a short one, carries on the interplay; it is based on arpeggios,
quavers in the piano, crotchets in the strings, balancing and crossing
each other gravely, yet reminding one of a game of ball (ex. 79).
The earnestness deepens as the orchestra passes to held notes, then
contents itself with punctuating the strong beats with quavers, and
finally, is silent.   In the piano, the emotional stress that so often precedes Mozart's reprises heightens, yet without reaching the uncertainty of the opening; then, just as it is on the point of turning to
anguish, it breaks on a dominant close and four bars of simple and
profoundly quiet music bring us back to the beginning of the story
(ex. 80).   Are we not reminded here of the three sister bars, quieter
and profounder still, which close a moment of much more emphatic
restlessness, in the corresponding part of the great E flat symphony
of 1788?   Thus, from masterpiece to masterpiece, moving thoughts
foreshadow and recall one another like memories and premonitions
throughout a life.

The orchestra comes in with the first subject; the piano takes it
up at the ninth bar and engages with it the same conversation as before,
with a few slight alterations, and passing through the key of B flat
minor.   The solo subject begins in F minor and closes in B flat,
whence the codetta carries us back to E flat and the second subject.
The recapitulation follows the same track as the exposition but the
bravura passage is twice as long.

Drawing to its close the movement remembers its stormy origins
and lets loose the fierce little ex. 75.   Its innings is brief and after ten
bars it is cut short by the pause for the cadenza.   But its message is
taken up again at once by this latter, which starts with the same figure

of dotted crotchets and arpeggios. Written no doubt for Babette
Ployer (since Mozart extemporized his own), it is more curt than
most; it reflects admirably the spirit of the concerto. The only other
theme brought in is precisely (with ex. 86) the most vigorous of all:
the upstanding concluding subject. And the allegro ends with the
nineteen bars which had concluded the first tutti, repeated unchanged.

II. The andantino[1] has none of the agitation and vigour of the
first movement. It is a *cantilena* in two strains, guileless and calm,
neither deep nor complex. Its chief interest, although it still uses
only the strings with woodwind *ad libitum*, lies in its scoring.

It consists in two alternating themes, preceded by a tutti introduction which contains only the first of them. After the piano entry,
each theme is given out thrice and the movement breaks up therefore
into a short introduction and three stanzas.

Introduction:	A	(1st half only)			
			Orchestra	22 bars	B flat
1st stanza:	A	(whole)	Piano	18 bars	,,
	B		Piano, accompanied	11 bars	F
2nd stanza:	A	(whole)	Orchestra, then		
			piano, accompanied	18 bars	A flat
	B		Piano, accompanied	10 bars	E flat
3rd stanza:	A	(whole)	Orchestra, then		
			piano, accompanied	18 bars	B flat
	B		Orchestra accom-		
			panied by the piano;		
			then alternating tutti		
			and solo	21 bars	,,
Coda:			Orchestra and solo	6 bars	,,

Exs. 81–3 give the *incipits* of the main themes.

The most interesting details are the following:

The flowing accompaniment of ex. 83 which returns in the third
stanza beneath the piano *canto*.

The string answers in A, stanzas 1 and 2; on them is based the
charming little coda.

The Alberti bass accompaniment of B; it is carried out by the

---

[1] Mozart asks his father, in his letter of May 9th, 1784, to note that in none
of the four concertos (nos. 10 to 13) is there an adagio.

Ex. 84

Ex. 85

Ex. 86

violas the first two times; the third time, the piano uses it to accompany the violins and hautboys.

The first two stanzas are alike; the second confines itself to repeating the first in the new key of A flat (the "double-subdominant"). The third is more of a variation; the theme B is treated with great felicity (ex. 84).

The presence of four-note chords should be noted in this movement; Mozart seldom uses such dynamic effects and when he does he means them. The pianist should therefore play them with full strength, here and at the beginning of the solo in the allegro and, generally, wherever he meets them in Mozart.

III. The gait of the finale is neither that of a gallop, nor of a race, nor even of a dance, but just of a swinging walk, swift and regular, and the virtue of its refrain, with its sketchy outline and its "sillabato" diction, as the Italians would say, rests in its rhythm rather than in its melody. It is one of Mozart's few rondo refrains which are not tuneful and the movement obeys no strong emotional impulse. But the grace of the ornamentation with which piano and fiddles clothe the bareness of its outline; the way in which the movement keeps up its pace, hardly ever taking breath; the wonderful fruitfulness with which it renews itself unceasingly, even though it is for ever coming back to the same point; its mixture of rondo and variation; all make this finale one of the most lovable in all Mozart and, as regards its form, the most fascinating in all his concertos.

It is usually possible to divide Mozart's rondos into two, three or four sections, separated by returns of the refrain. The stanzas are easily recognized and the mind is not obliged, for the needs of analysis, to see divisions and sections where the composer himself has not placed any. But this one is different. From the moment the piano is first heard, in the thirty-second bar, it is almost a *moto perpetuo*, without even a quaver rest and almost without a full close. The greater part of its progress, carried out at a brisk pace but never breathless, is founded upon a single theme, taken up, adorned, varied, developed, with a bewitching diversity, seconded from time to time by another, less well characterized, subject, whose part is inconspicuous. Here it is, as we see it at the outset (ex. 85). The orchestra expounds it and follows it up at once with the other subject (ex. 86), concluded by a codetta in E flat.

The piano repeats the beginning of the refrain, embroidering it; then, half-way through, guided by the first fiddles that outline the theme, throws itself into a variation (ex. 87), which leads to a full close in E flat. Here one might see the start of the first couplet if one wanted to divide this strongly unified finale into the usual sections.

Picking up a figure of the variation (marked: I in ex. 87), through a short contrapuntal passage provided by another figure of the same example the solo reaches the second subject of the refrain which it gives out, somewhat modified, in the dominant. But this is not what interests it. It leaves it a few bars later and, after a *fantasia* passage where crossed hands play a part[1] and strings collaborate in echoes, the violins bring back ex. 85. Whilst the strings banter with a little three-part canon entry, the piano joins them with a fresh variation of the theme, derived from ex. 87, I. Then it monopolizes the game: the strings are again reduced to accompanying whilst it plays with contrapuntal runs, of which that in the right hand has grown out of the same figure I (ex. 88). But there is more than that in the run, and we recognize with some astonishment a theme destined to reappear six years later in the clarinet quintet.[2] The counterpoint soon ceases and the solo forges ahead with a volubility that makes us think of the irrepressible and garrulous finale of K.271. Then the rhythm slackens an instant; minims mingle with the quavers; finally, we set off again with a new rhythm ♪♫𝄾♪♫𝄾♪♫ and in this disguise the refrain reappears, with its skeleton outline still sketched out by the violins (ex. 89). All the strings take it up, and now they too decorate it and borrow figure I from the piano.

The refrain closes abruptly and, without any mention of ex. 87, the piano, roughly, lets loose a new subject. (Note again here the thick chord, to be sounded with due strength.) It is in C minor, a kind of hasty homage which the rondo pays to its ancestral form where the second stanza is in the minor. It is but a gesture; Mozart is far too good-tempered and too much at peace with the world to penetrate into the profundities of the minor mode and after four bars, neither more nor less, he again comes back to sunny keys. Without pulling up, the piano pursues its course which, thanks to triplets, becomes a gallop, breaking ground with new themes. But the main subject is on the watch; the movement belongs to it and never escapes it for long. In the midst of the triplets, here it is, first in C minor, then, quickly changing its mind, in A flat and, eventually, in sundry major keys. The piano, recalled to order, adorns it with a scion of figure I, with which the triplets intermingle. Still irresistible, neither breathless nor dishevelled, piano and strings pursue their exploration through what one might almost call the rondo's second couplet until a passage already heard (the crossed hands and echoing strings) summon all

---

[1] Crossed hands are not common in Mozart's concertos and their presence here is a likeness with the finale of the little E flat concerto, K.271. There is, moreover, a certain kinship of climate between the two movements; this one is a more sober reincarnation of the other.

[2] And also a phrase from the *Magic Flute*, in the second trio of the second act: "*Soll ich dich, Teurer*," at the words: "*Der Götter Wille mag geschehen*".

Ex. 87

Ex. 88

Ex. 89

Ex. 90

together. And then, without loss of speed, the mood becomes dreamier and we dive under the sparkling surface of the waters. With a spaciousness seldom surpassed by him, Mozart makes ready for the return of the refrain. It has, in fact, so often shouted: Wolf, wolf! in season and out of season, that our credulity is exhausted and has to be restored. A sudden return would leave us unconvinced. It must therefore proceed with some ceremony and, in an extended transition, make us believe once again in the necessity of its appearance.

This transition takes up nineteen bars—two more than the main part of the refrain. It consists in a B flat pedal point held at first by the strings, then by the wind whilst the strings murmur in unison Mozart's beloved "fluttering seconds" figure. The piano part is exceptionally rich, almost constantly in three-part harmony, and the Mediterranean softness of the sixths tempers the feverishness of the broken chords (ex. 90).

The return of the refrain does not spell rest for the piano. As before, the violins outline the skeleton and the solo clothes it, this time in broken octaves, thus prolonging into the refrain the rhythm of the end of the couplet—one of the many devices[1] thanks to which the unity of this rondo is so perfect.

The impetus of the movement is nevertheless beginning to wear out. There is indeed a third couplet but it is quite perfunctory; it confines itself to recalling the *minore* of the second (but in the major), and passes straight on to a passage from the first, to stop on the dominant seventh chord which introduces the cadenza. Its vitality is not extinguished, however, and in the middle of this passage it slows down and, dreaming, soars away into the distant realms of D flat where it muses a while before returning to earth. In so hard-working a finale, this is even more unexpected than the pedal point we heard just now (ex. 91).

After the cadenza, the conclusion is in 6-8 time, a common practice of the period which Mozart has followed more than once.[2] Here, it is hardly felicitous. The threefold rhythm appears lopsided and halting after the spritely gait of the rest. The refrain returns one last time and after we have heard it so often, upright with the crotchets, flowing with the quavers, but always assured, it seems enervated in its new shape. Yet it is not at the end of its tricks and its

---

[1] Not invented by Mozart, of course; there is an expressive instance of it in Rameau's *La Villageoise*.

[2] K.382, 491; K.451 ends in 3-8 time; K.459 goes into triplets which have the effect of 6-8.

last bars, based on a three-note figure which announces the main theme of the E flat string quintet, hold a delightful surprise in store (ex. 92).

Despite all the affection we feel for the first movement of this concerto, we tend to think that the main interest of the work lies in its finale, a judgement we should not express concerning any other concerto except K.365, 415, 459 and perhaps 450. It is indeed a masterpiece, the equal of the superb finales of the F major in that same year, of the D minor and A major in the following ones. Its distinctive quality is its oneness, by which it differs from the ordinary Mozartian last movement. When, score in hand, one notes each return of the first subject, in its entirety and in the tonic, it is possible to pick out the four expositions of the refrain and the three couplets of the Mozartian rondo; but on hearing it one's impression is that the refrain never leaves the stage and that the whole piece is built up on its variations and their derivatives. And this is so. Our short analysis will have given an idea of the many shapes in which it unceasingly presents and re-presents itself; a study of the score or of the piano arrangement can alone reveal all its exquisite detail. To this unity in multiformity must be added the unity of rhythm, broken just enough to prevent monotony, and the breadth and gradualness of the linking passages which spare us the clear-cut divisions occurring between the sections in some rondos. Especially noteworthy are discreet devices like that, already mentioned, which consists in introducing the new rhythm with which the refrain is to return some little time before its actual reappearance, so that this reappearance seems to be the unbroken sequence of what has gone before. Also the distinctions between solos and tuttis are less hard and fast than usual and the collaboration between piano and orchestra is almost continuous. Such formal unity, we repeat, is unmatched in Mozart's concertos and, in his other work, one has to reach the last rondos of his chamber music, those of the B flat *Prussian* quartet, K.589, and of the E flat string quintet, K.614, to find parallels to it.

Despite its small dimensions and the exiguousness of its orchestra, this composition is therefore most individual. It opens worthily the era of the greater concertos. Yet it is not closely related to any of these. In reality, it is isolated in Mozart's work; its first and last movements fall in with no group of his compositions and do not bear clearly the mark of any period in his life. Mozartian they certainly are, but not in the narrow sense in which this word is sometimes used; they do not clearly recall anything else in him; their originality was long taken for queerness and they have been treated as one usually treats originals and eccentrics: they have been left to themselves. Performances are however now more frequent and the work has been recorded; a wider public has thus been introduced to the rather rough beauties of the first movement, the wavy lines of the andantino and the passion for unity of the finale. It is now more fully realized that if its size may cause it to be classed as a minor work, in its deep sincerity, in the strength and concentrated nature of its feeling, it belongs truly to the race of the twelve masterpieces at the beginning of which it stands in date.

2. *The Eleventh Concerto: K.450 in B flat*

CONCERTO NO. 11 IN B FLAT, K.450[1]
Finished March 15th, 1784
    Allegro: C
    (Andante): 3-8 (in E flat)
    Allegro: 6-8
Orchestra: Strings, flute (in the finale only), two hautboys, two horns, two bassoons.

ON March 15th, rather more than a month after finishing his tenth concerto, Mozart completed another. As a third was to follow on March 22nd and a fourth on April 12th, the creative activity of the young master, then twenty-eight years old, must have been as intense during this Lent of 1784[2] as in the summer months of 1788 which saw the appearance of his three great symphonies.

The tenth and eleventh concertos are as different in nature as they are close in time. The three other concertos of this winter show strong kinship, but between these two there is only the vague family likeness which is present in most works of any one artist. In all respects, the eleventh is at the opposite pole to its predecessor. This latter had been written for a small orchestra where the wind parts were optional; the other demands a larger orchestra where the wind play as important a part as the strings. K.449 united in continuous collaboration piano and orchestral instruments; K.450, in its first movement at any rate, combines them seldom. K.449 was unstable and unpredictable; K.450 is urbanity and good temper personified. The ideal of the one was individual; that of the other is social . . . and one could contrast them in several other respects.

In these early months of 1784 Mozart attained a degree of

---

[1] *Gesamtausgabe* No. 15.

[2] In Lent the opera was in abeyance and concerts became more frequent. The celebrated *Concerts Spirituels* in Paris, founded in 1725, owed their inception to the need felt by the musical public to fill the gap left by the cessation of operas.

popularity which he was never to exceed. He was the fashionable
virtuoso. A letter of March 3rd to his father gives a list of
Akademien or subscription concerts where he is to play: twenty-
two between February 26th and April 23rd. "Have I not enough
to do?" he adds. "I do not think I can get rusty at this rate."

He says that the pianist Richter has organized six concerts but that
the nobility who have subscribed declare that "they will not enjoy
them if he is not to play". He announces with satisfaction that, at
his first private concert, on March 17th, "the room was full to over-
flowing and the new concerto I played had an extraordinary success.
Everywhere I go, I hear its praises".[1]

The legitimate pride he feels resounds in this concerto and the
next, both of them written for himself. In the six composed this year,
there is a difference of character between the three he wrote for his
own performance and the three written for Babette Ployer and Marie
Theresia Paradis.[2] The first, through their pride of bearing, their
outward splendour, their assurance of success, express sumptuously
the personality of an artist who, filled with the favours of the public,
knows that he is master of his audience and savours his triumph. The
others carry less state and their thought is more delicate; nothing in
them competes with the more individual feeling of the composer.

To use Abert's distinction, the eleventh concerto, and the twelfth
and fifteenth which are like it, were written partly for himself and
partly for his public. They mark a return towards the worldly ideal
of society music. But it is with triumph and no longer with sub-
mission that Mozart now embodies this ideal. He does not subordinate his innermost spirit to it; he transforms it and makes something
personal of it. His Apollinian genius, in which are blended grace
and power, shines in it as brightly as in the more original works of the
following years.

> It is (H. Abert says with truth) as if Mozart had wished to test in his
> concertos to what point the spirit of society music could be united with
> the personal feeling of the artist. He still stands, to a great extent, upon
> the ground of the Ancien Régime, with its joy in life and its nimble wit.
> These concertos have become true models of art in which both artist and
> public take a share. Social impressions and genuine æsthetic experiences
> interplay continually in them.[3]

---

[1] Probably this one or K.449. (Letter of March 20th.)

[2] But see pages 258, 259.

[3] Op. cit., p. 214.

The three 1784 concertos written for himself achieve with mar-
vellous art this balance between personal and social ideals. The
Salzburg concertos and the first of the 1782 group insisted most on
the latter; the 1785 and 1786 works will dwell more and more on the
former; those of 1784 succeed with incredible skill in mirroring the
soul of their creator while yet giving utterance to that of their public.
So classical an achievement could be obtained only during the very
brief moment when a perfect concord of feeling and thought, a perfect community of culture and civilization existed between the deeper
nature of the musician and the collective soul of his listeners. The
rather rapid growth of Mozart's personality in the years that follow
dissolves this unity and carries him away from the Viennese public's
elegant but restricted conception of beauty.

I. If one reached this concerto after having run through the ten
preceding ones and without knowing those that follow, one would be
surprised in its very first bars by its originality. Not by its originality
of theme or rhythm or harmony, nor by any uncertainty of key, as
in K.449, but by its orchestration. Nothing like it had occurred hitherto
in any of Mozart's concertos (ex. 93). Anyone who heard the
beginning of this movement without knowing it was a concerto
might fancy he was listening to a woodwind serenade or divertimento.

Then, when he heard the elegantly balanced answer of the strings
(ex. 94), he might think it was a *concertante* serenade for strings and
woodwind. And the continuation of this opening, with its repeated
alternations between the two groups, would confirm his impression,
until the complete blending of both in the *forte* of the fourteenth bar
enlightened him as to the symphonic nature of the work.

Such an introduction is indeed quite new in Mozart. And its
charm is equal to its novelty. There is no stiffness in the antiphonal
treatment of the two groups and the repeats are not literal. See
how the notes with which the wind concludes are minims the first
time and the second time have the value of a minim and a crotchet,
and how the strings, which the first time began after the third beat,
start the second time after the first. And admire how delicately the
blending in the fourteenth bar is prepared. After the sharp opposition
of the beginning, the distinction between wind parts and string parts
becomes gradually less clear cut (ex. 95), and, in the three bars before
the *forte*, wind and strings, whilst keeping their individuality, play
together (ex. 96).

Considered thematically, these thirteen bars exhibit equally delicate

details. The second strain, instead of being brutally contrasted with
the first, resembles it in that the interval of a second predominates
in its outline; the wind call in bars 8–10 (ex. 95) is derived from this
same strain, the first notes of which it reproduces, and when in the
eleventh bar wind and strings unite without blending, each sketch the
same figure, one lot ascending, in quavers, the other descending, in
semi-quavers (ex. 96).

A proud and stalwart passage follows this discreet beginning,
according to a formula common in the *galant* style which returns
more than once in Mozart's concertos, and we stop on a loud close
in F major. This concerto is a well-bred gentleman; it does not
wander off into the eccentric paths of K.449 and keeps to the key of
B flat prescribed by the code of musical good manners. It is therefore
without change of key that a new subject comes forward, an occasion
for wind and strings again to disclose their separatist tendencies
(ex. 97). So skeletal a silhouette predestines it to variation; it demands such treatment as imperiously as the rondo theme of K.449;
and as soon as it has been given out, the woodwind reiterate it whilst
the violins trace above it a decoration strangely recalling the outline of
ex. 87, I, in K.449. We say, strangely, because these two concertos
are in truth, of the whole series, the two between which one would
least expect to find a likeness, and this is indeed the only one.[1]

The rest of the tutti is taken up with a rising passage on a pedal
of repeated quavers, or *Trommelbass*, straight from Italian opera, and
with the concluding subject which comes perhaps from the well-
known French song:

> Il a passé par ici,
> Le furet du bois joli.

In giving out this latter, wind and strings divide at first, then come
together, as in the opening theme (ex. 98).

Their last notes coincide with the first of the piano. The solo does
not tackle the first subject straight away. In Mozart's concertos, solos
which start at once with the first subject are about equal in number to
those which prefix a few introductory bars. In 1784, however, he
prefers the simpler method and this concerto is the only one in the
year where the piano makes its bow with a passage of its own. It is a
cadenza obbligata of some ten bars, accompanied by the strings,
leading us to a trill on the tonic.

----

[1] It also recalls the clarinet quintet; cf. p. 188.

The piano entry drives the orchestra into the background. With his return to the *galant* ideal Mozart appears also to have returned to the virtuoso conception of the concerto where the orchestra is neither collaborator nor adversary but just accompanist. After their assertive intioduction, strings and wind keep their peace or at the most interject a few modest comments, a few punctuation marks. The piano monopolizes almost entirely the subject which had been so gracefully distributed between fiddles, hautboys and bassoons; only the little figure (a) of ex. 95 remains to the wind. The solo subject follows at once (ex. 99); it begins in G minor, a key unsympathetic to the mood of the movement, quickly escapes from it and modulates into F. After a rather long bravura passage, consisting in broken scales and octaves, the piano expounds the true second subject (ex. 100),[1] which had not yet been heard. We are still in the exposition which, in the classical concerto, is in two parts; the first and second do not always utilize completely identical material; it is enough if most of what is presented in one or other of them reappears somewhere in the course of the movement.

In the virtuosity passage that follows, the strings intervene shyly, seeking, maybe, to collaborate on equal terms, but only succeeding, so purely rhythmic is their contribution, in stiffening slightly the line of pianistic ripples (ex. 101). The piano does not even notice their presence and continues along its royal road, once they are silent, with undiminished splendour.

The trill on the chord of F at length sets the orchestra free or rather transfers the piano's vitality to it for an instant, and it enters in full force with the "stalwart" theme of the first tutti. This time it does not lead to a close but loses itself in the concluding subject, scored as before. The piano, as if remembering the trick which had come off so well in the last concerto, picks up its last notes, puts semi-quavers in the place of quavers, and sails off afresh with a joyousness undimmed by the key of F minor. Right hand, then left, then right again run over the keyboard in passages derived from the conclusion. For the nonce, the orchestra is silent and one hand accompanies the other, but, in the greater part of what follows till the reprise, both hands play in tenths or octaves and the instruments complete the harmonies, sometimes following, sometimes opposing the piano line with sketchy figures. All take part; woodwind echo strings, strings echo woodwind; groups divide up, bassoons against hautboys, 'cello and basses

---

[1] It is almost the same as that of the E flat quintet for piano and woodwind (first movement), composed one month later.

against fiddles and violas (ex. 102)! The song of joy which grows
out of this lofty game, although it is confined to the piano and violins,
is a kind of idealized horn fanfare. But everything has an end and
beneath the trill, in which the piano at last finds peace, whispering
violins call up the shadow of the first subject. Little by little its
chromatic outline is defined and illumined; the piano's decisive tone
gives it precision and, ere the solo instrument reaches the end of its
run, hautboys and bassoons are giving it out as at the opening of the
movement.

The *development* which is just over is, as is befitting, the part of
the movement where fancy plays most freely. In true *developments*,
the composer is expected to build up elements already "exposed" in
the first section and to make a new whole out of familiar themes.
Such *developments* are the rule in the greater part of the chamber
music and symphonies of Mozart's Viennese period, but exceptional
in his concertos. Instead, we find those which have been called
fantasia developments, the type which before Mozart is found in
the sonatas of Schobert[1] and in at least one sonata of John Christian
Bach,[2] actually one of those that Mozart, as a child, had arranged as
a harpsichord concerto. In this kind of development, says Abert,

> what matters is the continuous flow of harmony which drives the same
> ideas, with few changes, through the most diverse keys. No goal is sought;
> the motion is itself the essential; the figures carried on it, first of all based
> on simple chords, then, in the later works, thematic, serve only to strengthen
> the harmonic structure; there is no question of a development in the strict
> sense. Around this harmonic erection, built mainly on progressions in
> the bass, the solo, here at the climax of its virtuosity, weaves a rich design
> of figures and passages, romantic adventures, bold flights towards an
> unknown, always hidden goal; only at the beginning and end, as often
> in Schobert, smaller phrases arise, melodic and harmonic, like bridgeheads.[3]

It is in his concertos, we have said, that Mozart varied his recapitulations most. Yet the ten concertos we have studied hitherto have only
partly borne us out. The work which showed greatest freedom in
its recapitulation was the concerto for two pianos. Even K.449, in
other respects more emancipated than its predecessors, had been
content to repeat the main outlines with a few changes of detail.
The concerto we are studying is the first to break sharply with this
unenterprising practice and open new paths in its last section.

---

[1] Op. II, 1; IV, 1; XIV, 3, 5.
[2] Op. V, 4, in E flat.
[3] Op. cit., p. 207

It does it from the very reprise. The chromatic subject, ex. 93, formerly monopolized by the piano, is now shared between it and the wind, the piano appropriating the part taken earlier by the strings. In the first exposition, the "stalwart" passage succeeded the first subject; in the second, the solo gave out almost at once its special subject. Now, the recapitulation has to recall the main features of the first two parts. How is Mozart to manage this? He recalls, to begin with, the "stalwart" passage which unfolds for several bars. But this is a mistake; the passage has been heard twice already; that should suffice. The movement changes its mind, stops on a broken cadence with a brusquerie unwonted in so courteous a work, and calls on the solo subject. This latter, however, does not return in person but is represented by a variation, in C minor. The bravura passage which followed it in the exposition, the second subject (in B flat) and the runs that concluded it, ex. 101, are brought back with no changes save those of key and of a few details in the figuration.

Before the piano has finished its last run, the violins broach one of the two members of the cast of themes that have not yet been heard again: the mock second subject so gracefully shared and commented upon by them and by the woodwind in the first tutti, ex. 97. They start it beneath a trill into which the whole life of the piano is concentrated for the time being. The woodwind repeat their earlier part and it is now the piano's turn to decorate the theme with a variation. After this interlude, it comes back to the passage which concluded the exposition, reproduces it with slight changes and leads to its final trill. There is still one theme to return, the *Trommelbass* passage after ex. 97 in the opening tutti. Here it is, first of all *pp*, then raising its voice and heralding the solo cadenza. The cadenza which Mozart wrote for a pupil, K.624, 19, reviews the concluding subject, ex. 98, the solo's last passage and the mock subject; it is commendably brief. The piano does not speak again and the end belongs to the orchestra which repeats unchanged the last bars of the introduction. Only, when we think we have reached the end of our course, a prank, already played at a similar moment in K.271 and 413, calls back the motif which the violins had used to accompany the solo entry and the allegro ends up, so to speak, like a whiting at dinner, with its tail in its mouth.

This recapitulation is therefore far from being a facsimile of the first solo, with the tonic key instead of the dominant. Nevertheless, it is rather by reshuffling its materials than by transforming any of

them that it renews itself. We have described elsewhere[1] the means
Mozart uses to carry out this reshuffling, here and in his other concertos. In this work, he calls up two themes from the introduction
which had been missed out in the second exposition; the passage
which followed the first subject in the opening tutti comes next time
at the end of the solo, before the conclusion, and, in the recapitulation,
retrieves its place in the wake of the first subject; the solo subject is
repeated in the shape of a variation; and finally, twice over, the piano
replaces the strings in a dialogue with the woodwind.

II. Associations which are foreign to the mind of the artist but
present in our own are sometimes in danger of making us see in his
inspiration elements which are absent from it. The influence of
19th-century Church music may incline many a modern listener to
find a religious inspiration in the andante of this concerto. The
theme has the bearing of a hymn (ex. 104). Yet it is doubtful whether
its pious character is more than accidental. It is unlikely that Mozart
intended a religious piece here; neither the fashionable public for
whom the concerto was written, nor the composer, proud and careful
of his popularity, who was playing it, would have thought this the
place for such an emotion. But this will not hinder some concert-
goers from finding its theme devotional and recognizing in it "Sunday
echoes in weekday hours".

This movement, of which Mozart is careful to tell his father[2] that
it is an andante and not an adagio, has the form of a theme with two
variations and a short coda. Even if we banish the epithet "devotional" we cannot deny that its tone is solemn, yet at the same time
simple and almost naïve. It is Mozart at his best,[3] peaceful with
the peace of passionate natures, deeper and richer than the negative
tranquillity of merely placid souls. It is the counterpart in Mozartian
language of the theme of the Kreutzer sonata variations. The movement has also in common with the andante of the celebrated sonata
that almost all its interest consists in the theme and that the variations
themselves please us mainly because they allow us to hear more than
once a well-loved tune.

The variations are double, that is to say, each half is given out

---

[1] Part I, Chap. 2.

[2] Letter of June 9th, 1784.

[3] Several bars of this theme were radically rewritten after a part of the
movement had been composed (cf. Köchel-Einstein, p. 570).

twice. The theme and each variation comprise therefore four parts.
The interest resides, we have said, in the loveliness of the theme;
the variations themselves are decorative and embellish it rather than
transform or throw changing light upon it, and their greatest charm
is in their orchestration.

Ex. 106

Ex. 107

Ex. 108

Ex. 109

Each half of the theme is given out by the strings and repeated, with slight decorations, by the piano. The first variation also belongs to the piano and strings. These latter repeat the first half with slight changes in the harmony, and above them the piano weaves a beautiful design of demi-semi-quaver arpeggios (ex. 105). Then the instruments are silent and the right hand goes over the theme again, richly harmonized with chords,[1] whilst the bass embroiders a design similar to that of the right hand in ex. 105. The second half of the theme is treated likewise.

The piano starts on the second variation alone. It is a slightly modified repetition of ex. 104, except that the rhythm is syncopated; in the fourth bar, the strings take hold of it and treat the theme a little more freely and the right hand superimposes a flowing figure of embroidery in demi-semi-quavers. The woodwind, which had hitherto kept out of the picture, take up the tune in their turn; the piano reproduces it in arpeggio sextuplets and the string pizzicati punctuate it with a variation in semi-quavers; this is the fullest passage in the movement (ex. 106). The second half follows the same plan, but the sextuplets are replaced by double semi-quavers. The end of this variation is prolonged by a few bars where the piano chords repeat those of the wind one bar late. The coda, as simple and moving as the theme, is treated antiphonally by the solo and the whole orchestra, after which the melody, escorted by hautboys and horns, dies out in the upper register of the piano (ex. 107).

III. The finale is a rondo in 6-8, a time which is used by Mozart in three out of his four piano concertos in B flat, but elsewhere much less commonly than 2-4.[2] Its refrain, given out by the piano and repeated by the tutti, which adds a long ritornello, is one of his most pleasing rondo themes (ex. 108), both fiery and graceful, and perfectly illustrative of the union of these two qualities which characterize Mozart's genius. With what power and ease it sails down from the fifth degree of the scale to the second while appearing to be rising ever higher, creating its illusion thanks to the fact that the ear is more struck by the three degrees climbed by three consecutive notes (bars 1, 3, 5) than by the leap downwards of a sixth (bars, 2, 4, 6)! The

---

[1] We have already said that it is important to give Mozart's comparatively infrequent chords their full weight.

[2] About two-thirds of his finales after his return from Paris in 1778 are in 2-4 time and most of the others in 6-8. 6-8 is unusual in first movements, where he prefers C, or, less often, ¢.

very outline of the tune, apart from its rhythm, calls up a galloping horse, and the three repeated notes at the beginning of each fragment (a similarity with the finales of K.456 and 482) is like a horn call.

The rondo it draws after it and which at times, so to speak, it carries upwards on its wings, is a sonata rondo, one of the few in Mozart which are quite regular. We have spoken at length of this form elsewhere.[1]

Among Mozart's numerous rondos of his Viennese period which adopt it only a dozen are "regular" in that they use in the second couplet elements already presented in the first. The majority bring in at this point completely new material. But nearly all treat the third couplet as a recapitulation. A few leave out the refrain between the second and third couplets; the rondo then assumes the appearance of a binary movement, especially when the *development* section is abridged. All these varieties are found among the piano concertos.

The exposition couplet in this rondo begins after the ritornello with a subject in the piano, closely related to the refrain itself in outline and rhythm. Having given it out twice, the piano passes on; it is a fugitive thought that does not return. It is followed by a solo passage where the strings accompany the piano and which, after a short tutti intervention, leads to what may be termed the second subject. This is really a whole section, in elaborating which first the piano and strings take part, then the flute,[2] and lastly the hautboys. It consists in the spinning out of a six-note figure which winds upward from the low B of the fiddles to the high C of the flute. In the piano, the figure is wreathed round with arpeggios in a particularly tricky crossing of hands which proves fatal when one is sight-reading the work (ex. 109). The end of its climb settles us into the key of F, sheltered from further modulations, and a third theme, *cantabile*, unfolds in the solo, then in the flute with a piano arpeggio accompaniment; the orchestra, and particularly the woodwind, emboldened perhaps by its importance in the andante, no longer confines itself to an intermittent part, as in the first allegro (ex. 110).

After a pause for which Mozart has left an *intrata*,[3] the piano gives out the refrain, accompanied as at the outset by the strings and the held notes of the bassoons. The orchestra takes it up vigorously

---

[1] Cf. pp. 49 *seq.*

[2] Present for the first time in these concertos, save for the andante of K.238 and the variations K.382.

[3] K.624, no. 21.

Ex. 110

Ex. III

Ex. 112

Ex. 113

Ex. 119

and engages in a dialogue in imitation, a kind of irregular canon, between basses and trebles. After a close on the chord of D minor, we await the traditional *minor* episode when another modulation flings us wittily into the air and catches us again in E flat (ex. 111).

The *development* couplet which opens now is the most interesting of the three. Like many first-movement *developments* in Mozart, it begins with a new theme, made up of a rhythmic first part and a singing second part, a close relative of ex. 109; it belongs to the piano, supported now and again by the fiddles. The very last bars of the passage, which finishes on E flat, are solo, but ere the piano is silent the hautboys, very softly and still in E flat, begin recalling the refrain motif in a slightly varied form and there opens the most ingenious and enchanting section, not only of the rondo, but of the whole concerto.

For some forty bars, until the end of the *development*, everyone —flute, violins, violas, 'cellos and basses, but especially piano and hautboys—together or in turn, expound wholly or in part the refrain theme which seems truly to carry the movement into the air like a winged steed.

The hautboys opens the game by giving out twice, in E flat, the first four bars of the theme, but starting one degree higher up the second time and modifying the last descending interval which becomes a seventh instead of a sixth. The piano continues, beginning one degree higher still, turning the last interval into a fifth, and leaving us in F minor where the sport is resumed two degrees lower down with the hautboy the first two times and the piano the third. We are now in G minor (ex. 112). (The quotation shows the first ascent of three degrees and the beginning of the second.) Having climbed up, we must now come down, but it would be unadventurous to do so in the same manner and by the same steps. So the hautboys remain silent and now all the strings in unison, doubled by the piano bass, undertake the operation, whilst the piano's right hand accompanies them with a new element, a swiftly flowing motif. Not content with varying the scoring, Mozart modifies also the melodic line and the third time, instead of giving out (a) entire, he represents it by a kind of abridgment (ex. 113), which allows him to come down four degrees instead of three. We are now on D, one degree lower than when we started. The next bars pursue the same "working-out" of (a) but entrust it to the piano's right hand, whilst the florid accompaniment passes to the left. The hautboys and flute sustain; the strings are silent.

As a sign that the entertainment is over and that we are going on to other things, Mozart interposes here a flowing passage where the strings have the theme and the right hand doubles them, *arpeggiando* the two highest parts; this passage interrupts the constant modulating and asserts for a moment the key of D minor.

But here comes again a reminder of the refrain.

Ex. 114

says the piano, and the hautboy follows suit. Then, with a mischievous alteration of one degree, the piano says (ex. 115) , but this time the hautboy also allows itself an alteration (ex. 116) The piano now says (ex. 117) . A third thief joins in and the flute echoes; and for the last three bars of the *development* the three instruments carry on a witty chirping with ex. 117. The flute has not finished its last (ex. 118) when the piano starts on the refrain, this time for good and in the tonic key.

This *development* has consisted in three things:

The repetition, on different degrees, with modulations and slight modifications, of the first bars of the theme;

The addition to it of an accompaniment whose outline recalls that of the theme itself;

The repetition on different parts of the scale, but without either modulation or modification, of a fragment of the "developed" figure.

It is clear that the last of these is what is most like a Beethovenian "working-out"; it is also the one which is least frequent in Mozart, except in a few works like the E flat quintet. The Mozartian "working-out" is most often a mingling of variation, modulation and instrumental dialoguing and the lesson taught by this passage is borne out by the study of his symphonies and chamber music.

There is no need to dwell on the rest of the movement. After the repetition of ex. 108 by the orchestra, the piano omits the solo subject which had opened the exposition and passes on at once to the solo that preceded the second subject (ex. 109). This latter follows, in B flat, and after one last bravura passage, the tutti prepare for the cadenza with a part of their first ritornello. The cadenza written by

Mozart[1] is a fragment of the *development*. It begins with the theme in the right hand and the florid accompaniment in the left. After recalling the subject with which the *development* had opened it introduces ex. 108 in the bass, again travels down three consecutive degrees, and this time the right hand accompanies it with a passage where arpeggios alternate with scale fragments. Then the arpeggios infect the bass; ex. 108 vanishes and the customary flourishes lead us promptly to the final trill. The refrain is heard one last time, followed now by its second half that we had not met since the beginning; and the work gives itself up with rapture to the *strepitoso arcistrepitoso, strepitosissimo*, with which, according to Da Ponte, every opera buffa finale should conclude, and few passages in Mozart's concertos show more indisputably the kinship between their genre and opera. The *strepitoso* is cleverly managed and Mozart keeps his full force in reserve. The whole ascent of ten bars in *pp*, and only when the movement has but four more bars to run does he let loose all his artillery. The passage is an amplifying of the common chord; a B flat pedal in the strings, emphasized by a violin gruppetto on the strong beats and a bass uprush of three notes before every other bar; arpeggios in the piano; fanfare on the horns, then on the flute and hautboys, and finally on the bassoons. Once everyone has fallen in, the orchestra throws itself into its last *ff*. There are more significant codas in Mozart's concertos; there are noisier ones, or ones that are noisier for a longer time; none is conceived on a larger scale and in none are the physical effects more astutely prepared (ex. 119).[2]

In opening this chapter, we said that this concerto was very different from the one composed a month earlier. This latter was unstable and, at times, stormy; the one we have just been studying is sunny and serene. K.449 had a passionate and introspective nature, at least in its first movement; K.450 is a fair, unreflective athlete, troubled by no problems. Not a cloud crosses its brow; not a bar in any of its three movements betrays sadness or doubt.

The difference is quite as noticeable in the relations between piano and orchestra in the opening allegros. K.449's orchestra was small but it behaved towards the piano like an equal. K.450 marks a step backward in this respect. Its first movement reverts to the stage of the Salzburg and 1782 concertos; the orchestra is silent when the piano

---

[1] K.624, no. 22.

[2] Eight bars in this part of the movement were added afterwards and are written on the back of the MS. (Cf. Köchel-Einstein, p. 570.)

speaks, or raises but a humble voice to accompany; gone are the collaboration and dialoguing which had enriched the earlier concerto. No more symphonic passages between orchestra and solo; no more sharing of themes; not only the solo subject but even the second subject never fall to the tutti. It is true that the andante and especially the finale, with its splendid second couplet, regain some of the ground lost; on the whole, nevertheless, K.449 is in advance of its successor, not only in the depth of its emotional life but also in its symphonic development.

It is as if the composer (and this is quite understandable) had not been able to keep up his progress all along the line. For progress there is, but not here. Not in the dealings of piano with orchestra but in the orchestral parts themselves, in the relations between the various groups of instruments, is there a step forward. It consists above all in the independence of the wind. In this respect, the leap forward, from the earlier works to this one, is truly gigantic. In none of his earlier symphonies or concertos[1] had the wind separated themselves to such an extent from the strings nor been entrusted with parts so original and so expressive of their nature. It is not only that they enjoy the right of expounding the chief themes as fully as the strings. They have indeed this right, but they have also themes of their own. The chromatic opening of the first subject, for instance, is given out by them in the first place, by the piano in the second, and again, in the recapitulation, by the wind. It is true that violins and violas murmur the rising scale that leads to its return, but that is an announcement of the subject and not the subject itself; when it comes back, it is reserved to the hautboys and bassoons. The same is true of the first, *arpeggiato* part of the conclusion, ex. 98. In the *development*, where the accompaniment is most interesting, the wind group stands out against the strings and formulates alternately with it the figure that sustains the piano triplets and semi-quavers, ex. 102. In the slow movement its part is less striking and in the second variation, it is only when piano and strings have each given out the theme, that it sings it in its turn. But in the finale, one of its members, the flute, risen late to eminence, represents the whole orchestra in the third subject, ex. 110, and we have seen with what expressive originality

---

[1] We must underline *symphonies* and *concertos*, for his chamber music comprised already several works for woodwind, culminating in the magnificent serenades in B flat, E flat and C minor. And in *Idomeneo* the wind had been treated with as much freedom as in this concerto and had shown itself in all respects the equal of the strings.

the hautboys behave in the *development*. In a word, though this concerto be poor in interplay between solo and tutti (and even that is true only of the first movement), in the importance given to the wind it opens a path along which are to travel most of its successors, several of which have been called: wind concertos with piano obbligato.

The piano part is harder than in K.449, by all the distance that separated Babette Ployer's talent from Mozart's. More difficult, and also more "modern". The use of thirds is fairly frequent in the first movement and owes perhaps something to the technical progress made by Clementi since 1772, but the harmonizing in thirds of the first subject, in the solo part, has quite the appearance of an imitation by the piano of a woodwind effect. There is another orchestral effect, already well-established at this period, in the right hand of a bravura passage which appears twice (bars 119–21 and 264–5).

We discuss later on the character of the key of B flat in Mozart's work; it is enough to say now that K.450 is far from being as isolated in his productions as its predecessor was. Among other compositions in the same key, the fine violin sonata of the same year, K.454, and the celebrated quartet called (but not by Mozart) *The Hunt*, K.458, also of 1784, sound the same hymn of joy under the same sunlit sky; an equally dazzling light fills them, and their first and last movements, at any rate, are equally free from even passing cloud. The kinship is emotional, not formal; their themes are not alike and their construction is as different as their genres; but the identity of the inspiration is unmistakable, and the B flat trio of 1786, K.502, belongs to the same race. Such kinship, on the other hand, is much less close between this concerto and that in B flat of the end of the year, K.456.

But if there be kinship between works in the same key, there is also kinship between works of the same period. The description: "fair athlete", fits the next concerto as well as this one. There is in it the same assurance, pride, lack of hesitancy and disquiet; it shows an almost identical aspect of the fashionable young virtuoso; and this holds good also of the F major concerto of the end of the year. K.450 is as representative of a period in its author's life as K.449 was unique, and it will be followed by works which form with it one single family full of life and joy.

3. The Twelfth Concerto: K.451 in D

CONCERTO No. 12 IN D (K.451)[1]
Finished March 22nd, 1784
   Allegro assai: C
   (Andante): ¢ (in G)
   Allegro di molto: 2-4
Orchestra: Strings, flute, two hautboys, two bassoons, two horns, two trumpets, two kettledrums.

HARDLY had Mozart completed his B flat concerto—perhaps even he had not quite completed it—when, in this miraculous winter of 1784, he started on another, the third in one month and a half! He finished it on March 22nd, one week after the last! By the letter to his sister where he tells how he had composed his C major fantasia while writing out the fugue we know that he could keep going several works at the same time, and he may well have been meditating the concerto in D before he had finished writing out the B flat. On the other hand, the fact, attested by a letter to his father of October 31st, 1783, that he composed his *Linz* symphony in four days, makes the composition of the present work in one week appear quite likely. The dates of some of his works, vouched for by his catalogue, as well as revelations like that about the *Linz* symphony, prove that he could compose at high speed. If one finds it difficult to believe what one reads about this, one should remember the feat performed by Paul Hindemith in January, 1936. He was to have played a viola concerto in London. The death of the king happened a few days before the concert and obliged the organizers to change the programme at the last moment. Hindemith thereupon offered to shut himself up for four hours and write on the spot a funeral piece to the memory of the deceased sovereign. The offer was accepted and the work performed. It was a composition which lasted some twenty minutes and had the scope of the first movement of a symphony. This contemporary example makes more credible the feats that anecdotalists tell us of Mozart.

---

[1] *Gesamtausgabe*, no. 16.

One feels here that at any rate the first movement was composed at one stroke. The pride and the joy of knowing oneself to be at the height of one's powers which inspired the last concerto quicken also this one; but these sentiments are raised now to the intensity of passion. And, with this growth in the degree and breadth of emotion, the form becomes richer. The first movement is the most powerful and most complex that Mozart has written hitherto, and one of the most powerful and complex in all his orchestral work. The only criticism that can be made of it is that it throws the two others somewhat into the shade. It is no longer in the finale that orchestra and solo collaborate most but in the first allegro, which contains the most splendid instances in all Mozart of interplay between the protagonists. It is a masterpiece of that brilliant art, sincere in spite of its display, radiating satisfaction, confidence and power, which was Mozart's in 1784. Among the six concertos of the year which express the ideal of the fashionable young virtuoso, it holds the place held by the great C major concerto, K.503, in the six that are to follow.

I. The allegro is not only the movement in which we grasp for the first time, in all its breadth, the symphonic conception of the concerto which Mozart had reached, but one of those where we grasp it best. Here is probably one of those works which fulfil so wholly the ideal of the genre that people have seen in them, as Spohr did, "symphonies with piano" rather than concertos for piano and orchestra—a false interpretation of the Mozartian concerto but one which has the advantage of reminding us of the supreme importance of the orchestra, the "emancipation" of which others, equally falsely, have attributed to Beethoven.

The orchestra is bigger than in K.450. Mozart retains the flute which had appeared in the rondo of this latter and adds trumpets and kettledrums. This is the largest band he has used hitherto in his concertos though all these instruments had already appeared in some work or other, the flute in the andante of K.238 and the rondo of K.450, the trumpets and drums in K.175, 382 and 415.

The movement opens to the same march rhythm as K.415, a rhythm we meet again in the three concertos that follow. But whereas in these works the march tune is first given out *pp*, by the first fiddles or woodwind only, here it starts *forte* and with the whole orchestra, dropping, however, to *piano* in the second bar. The first subject is a scale of D major which in the course of ten bars rises two octaves. Its line is indicated by the flute and first violins; bassoons

Ex. 121

Ex. 122

Ex. 123

and basses sound a tonic pedal with repeated quavers, and every two bars the *piano* is broken by a *forte* where hautboys, horns, trumpets and drums reinforce the rest of the orchestra. Moreover, each of these *fortes* marks a halt in the rhythm, so that this first octave gives the impression of a majestic stairway climbed with vigorous strides (ex. 121). After the first octave the pace quickens at the same time as a *crescendo* leads to *forte*, and the phrase ends on the tonic, two octaves higher than it began.

This first phrase is succeeded by a second, *ff*, consisting also in D major scales, but descending ones, with dotted quaver rhythm, and divided in imitation between the upper parts and the violas and basses (ex. 122). It leads to the dominant chord which is followed by an upper pedal, in semi-quavers, given to the second fiddles. A subsidiary theme is given out by the hautboys, horns and trumpets, and we fall back to *piano*, but, as at the opening, the other instruments burst in every other bar with explosive *fortes* (ex. 123). The *forte* ends by staying for good and with it the fragment (a) (in ex. 123) with which first violins and flute had interrupted the wind's *piano*; on it is built the dominant close which concludes this first section.

These twenty-five bars form in reality one single strain and they give the whole movement its character. The quivering power, scarcely subdued, bursting forth in *fortes* which are dynamic and not just *galant* "surprises", the pedals whose action is both to hold back the passion and intensify it, and the importance of scales in the melodic outline, are present all through this allegro.

The principle of contrast reigns in it but this principle, so dear to *galant* composers, is no longer a mere game. Mozart's genius gives it the significance of a struggle between two aspects of his own nature. Passion and gentleness strive here for mastery as, indeed, they do throughout the movement. Gentleness demands a calm and well-ordered bearing; it imposes the scale figure and the *piano* in the first and third sections of this passage. But it cannot restrain the impetuous rush of passion which breaks through constantly in the *fortes* that interrupt these sections and triumphs in the dotted quaver part and in the close. We are, of course, in a classical period and the struggle is stylized; the rhythm is regular and the outbursts of passion occur at equal intervals; the twofold nature is none the less evident. But, as the adversaries are after all but two aspects of the same soul, it has to be shown that, though foes, they are brothers; the underlying unity has to be expressed. This unity is safeguarded by the pedals, the lower one of which ties down the rising scale by its feet, as it were,

Ex. 124

Ex. 125

Ex. 126

Ex. 127   Ex. 128

and prevents it from losing touch with earth. The study of the rest of the movement in which *fortes* and *piano* alternate sharply, where subjects built on scales or common chord arpeggios predominate, where pedals are frequent, will show that this interpretation holds good, not only for the first twenty-five bars but also for what follows.

A less significant movement would stop after the close before starting off again with the second subject. But the concern for unity in duality which characterizes this allegro forbids such a procedure.

After the close, instead of the expected halt, the bass continues un-interruptedly with a fresh dominant pedal, a link with the preceding passage, and over it flutters the fascinating transition section, nine bars long, which leads to the second subject.[1] Its rhythm recalls the fragment (a) (ex. 123) of the close. Here, passion is quiet and the charming dialogue between violins, flute and hautboy unfolds with idyllic gentleness (ex. 124). There is not in all Mozart a more en-chanting instance of the expressive power with which he combines wind and strings.

This last fragment is also built upon the scale of D. The second subject is composed of the arpeggio of the common chord, divided into two parts, the first of which belongs to the hautboys and horns, the second to the violins and flute. Like nearly all Mozart's concerto second subjects, it appears only to make its bow and then withdraws without entering into the history of the work. Still *piano*, there opens a modulating passage with a syncopated rhythm, dark and mysterious, different from what has gone before (ex. 125). Just before the end, we suddenly rise to *forte* (ex. 126).

One of those surprises which Mozart loves to keep back for the end of his developments separates us from the conclusion. We expect the *forte* to end upon a full close. Not at all; it leads to an interrupted cadence. At once we drop to *piano* and the tutti appears about to finish with a commonplace little phrase which Mozart has used hundreds of times (ex. 127). Then the interrupted cadence is taken up again, with a truly Mozartian change of harmony, and after it the commonplace phrase once more, and only then, but without any break, does the other little phrase, hardly less commonplace, which is to serve as a conclusion, link on to it. Like the second subject, it consists in a fragment of the common chord and its kinship with its predecessors is recognizable in that it rests on a pedal, gaining thereby more dignity and .poise than its levity would otherwise allow it to enjoy.[2] A conventional but assertive figure of four bars completes the introduction.

This first tutti is to an eminent degree the *argument* of what is to follow. This is of course true of all opening tuttis, but in varying degree. That of K.415 was hardly an *argument* at all, incorporating as it did only a small part of what was to enter into the substance of

---

[1] In the first concerto, also in D, the second subject had been likewise ushered in by a dominant pedal.

[2] It recalls a concluding strain in the finale of the G minor quartet, K.478.

the movement and comprising a development which did not reappear. That of K.450 left out almost all the material of the first solo, including the second subject; K.482 will do likewise. Here, on the contrary, we have almost all the elements with which the rest of the movement is built up. The only absent ones are the unimportant solo subject (ex. 129) and the *fantasia* part of the *development*. Even the bravura passages, which at first sight seem so important in this concerto, derive from this tutti. The movement, then, is highly organized and unified —the most organic first allegro we have hitherto met. To find a movement comparable to it among the concertos already dealt with, we should have to look among the rondos, and even so we should hardly find one before K.449. These concertos of the beginning of 1784 register in truth the first great step forward that Mozart has made for a long time towards organization and unity.

The piano tackles the first subject with the abruptness of K.449. It tackles it alone and the orchestra lays down its weapons while the solo scales the two octaves. Compelled to compensate with brilliance of display for the relative weakness of its tone, it decorates the line of scales with embroidery.[1] No mark of any kind is indicated, but it is clear that it, too, alternates between *forte* and *piano*, and the noisy outbursts are rendered here by minim chords in the right hand and upward drives in the left. These nine bars of unaccompanied solo are exceptional in this concerto where close and continuous collaboration between piano and orchestra is the order of the day.

The tutti returns with the descending dotted quaver scale, ex. 122, given to the strings alone, and the piano accompanies it with a decoration of rising scales and arpeggios in semi-quavers, now in the bass, now in the treble (ex. 128). A solo passage, doubled by the strings, on a dominant pedal, leads to the key of F sharp minor and the solo subject (ex. 129), which is repeated one degree lower, in E, and ends in a short, pretty passage of interplay, where wind and strings toss backwards and forwards a little trilling motif, as if they were alone in the world, appearing quite to ignore the solo who seeks vainly to attract their notice by emphasizing each wind repartee with a run (ex. 130). All this episode is new.

We meet the opening tutti again with the exposition of the second subject, rescored. In the preparation passage, the upper pedal is now

---

[1] This opening is interesting as a piano rendering of an orchestral passage. It is Mozart transcribing Mozart; the equivalent of Bach transcribing Vivaldi and Liszt or Busoni transcribing Bach.

given to the right hand of the piano and the figure to the strings and flute; the fragment (a) seesaws between flute and piano. The fluttering figure is, if possible, even lovelier than in the introduction, for the piano's presence enriches the landscape with an additional hue. The whisperings of this figure so loved of Mozart and which he never uses without clear intent, circle now between flute, hautboy and piano; the former have the figure itself and the piano the echo (in the recapitulation it will be the other way round).

The second subject is given out by the flute, doubled at first by the first hautboy, then by the first violins; the solo—an indication of the band's uppish attitude towards it in this concerto—takes hold of it only when it is repeated and even then does not enjoy it alone, for the first violins continue to double it an octave lower. One would expect here a bravura passage; instead, falling suddenly into the minor with true Mozartish sensibility, the piano engages a short conversation with the wind; then follow three bars of *arpeggiato* chords (a resounding but brief return for its former subjection), a fragment of a downward scale in the wind, with piano *gruppetti*, and the strings' re-entry with ex. 125 which they reproduce without changing anything but the key, and which closes, still in A, with the *forte* of ex. 126. During these fifteen bars, the piano is not silent, but its part is merely that of a commentator, if not of an accompanist. After two bars of silence, it comes in and strengthens the lower parts with an Alberti bass in the left hand; then, growing bolder, it decorates with arpeggios the violin line; finally, in the *forte*, diatonic and chromatic scales, in one hand after the other, dart through the barrage of repeated notes and join up the top and bottom of the octaves which limit the leaps of the strings (ex. 131). Only then can it launch forth in a song of triumphant bravura, and even so it is still kept in sight by the held notes of the wind and the staccato of the strings which follow it until the expected arrival of the trill announces the end of the exposition.

As if to mark the oneness of the movement, the orchestra re-enters at this point with neither a new subject nor ex. 128, but with the downward scale figure in dotted quavers, ex. 122. It links up with the last bars of ex. 126, as one had heard it in the beginning, and joins on to the interrupted cadence and the little commonplace phrase, ex. 127. The interrupted cadence is repeated, as in the first tutti, then, instead of the little phrase, it resumes where it had stopped, one third higher, and finally, once again, yet another third higher. We are far from A major; far, too, from what has gone before, and thus, with silken tread, the *development* steals upon us (ex. 132).

Passion united with strength, complete self-assurance raised to the pitch of pride have reigned hitherto; more mysterious strains came to disturb them only momentarily in the modulating and syncopated subject, ex. 125. And now, in a twinkling, the boundaries set up by this superb certainty have vanished, and we awaken on unknown seas. When we realize it, we are already far from land. What has been needed to delete one world and call up another one so different? Four bars of modulation, the piano re-entry, a break in the rhythm, which cause the same figure, thrice repeated, to end by corresponding to a different personality.

In an instant, the interrupted cadence motif has led us to new shores. It is the piano which launches us upon the waters with an arpeggio of the diminished seventh chord of the super-tonic, one of the most suggestive of chords. When figure (b) returns, we are in E minor. It is just a port of call. The voyage starts afresh and, passing through the same modulations, the piano arpeggios land us in B minor (ex. 133).

The flight towards infinity of these sixteen bars is the greatest moment in this fine allegro. We have met nothing like it hitherto in these concertos. Formally, it is a *fantasia development*,[1] the immediate forebears of which are in Schobert and John Christian Bach. But the distance between them and it is immeasurable. There is even a great distance between it and the *fantasia development* of K.450. And yet, outwardly, the two are similar. Here as well as there, the second solo begins with the repetition by the piano of the last orchestral phrase, but what was just a bit of mischief in K.449 and 450 is now full of meaning. Here as well as there, the piano passages were a *fantasia*, but whereas in K. 450 we never lost our foothold, here, suddenly, we are possessed by a sense of depth and Mozart takes off into the unknown. If we look back, we must not stop at immediate predecessors ; to breathe the same air, we have to go as far as John Sebastian's D minor concerto and the great pedal point of its first movement. And, for even closer kinship, we must turn to the next concerto and to Beethoven—to his work in C minor and still more his violin concerto, with the "voyage on uncharted seas" at the beginning of its *development*.

Arriving in B minor, the *fantasia* continues, but a more square-cut rhythm marks a return to familiar regions and emotions. Through the rising arpeggios and the falling scale fragments there is outlined a misty theme, implied in the piano's right hand and traced by the

---

[1] Cf. p. 200.

fiddles. The dreamy mood of the opening of the *development* gives way to a passion which grows and reaches its climax, as so often happens, on the eve of the reprise.[1] As the moment draws nigh, the piano predominates and the accompaniment thins away, as though the satellites of the solo instrument felt it seemly to let it traverse alone the valley of tears that separates it from the triumphal return. At the moment of greatest tension, a succession of chords of the seventh on the super-tonic comes crashing down on to a pedal (ex. 134). Anchored for an instant on the chord of A major, the spirit of the work, which its twofold nature and its wealth of passion have shaken but not overwhelmed, gathers itself together in a unison ascent, made easier by stages, and, once victory is assured, the orchestra, which had forsaken it in the hour of its greatest distress, returns, but *piano*, with its tail between its legs, to beg a share in its glory.

The adventure of these thirty-four bars of *development* is magnificent, but how brief! Hardly one tenth of the whole movement! The shortness of his *developments* is the most constant formal feature in all Mozart, from his childhood's earliest compositions to those of his last year. And, in a general way, his most original, his most significant are precisely his shortest.

The recapitulation unites again piano and orchestra. At the beginning of the movement, the orchestra had been master of the first subject; in the second exposition, the piano; now, both combine. The march rhythm of the first bar and the soft scales belong to the orchestra; the forceful outbursts are punctuated by piano runs (ex. 135). The secondary subject, ex. 128, is treated as in the first solo, except that the piano adornments now take the shape of arpeggios in triplets. The solo subject does not reappear and ex. 128 leads straight on to ex. 123. The pretty figure with "fluttering seconds" which prepares the way for the second subject returns with no change save one of scoring (ex. 6) and of key. The same is true of the second subject, the syncopated passage, ex 125, and the *forte* which follows it, ex. 126, and we reach again the interrupted cadence and the little commonplace phrase along which we had formerly slipped into the unknown. Now, its business is to conclude and, instead of unexpected modulations, Mozart inserts here the final bravura passage, the sole one, in fact, only ten bars long and entirely organic, since it is but the assertion of the tonic key without which no classical symphonic movement is complete.

The dotted quaver figure, ex. 122, which had concluded the first

---

[1] Cf. p. 32.

solo, returns now and the codetta of ex. 123 leads to the cadenza. The
one which Mozart has left[1] consists almost entirely of quotations
from the main themes and a passage of crossing of hands, all the more
remarkable because that species of virtuosity is absent from the concerto. In the hitherto excessively uncommon event of a pianist
playing this work in public, we recommend the use of this cadenza,
tuneful and full of go and, most important, moderate in length.

The movement concludes with ex. 128 and its conventional
codetta.

This allegro, far superior to the andante and rondo, is one of the
peaks of Mozart's concertos. Its most obvious character is its architectural strength and beauty. It is monumental in the highest degree,
but less by its dimensions than by its robustness. We have already
insisted upon the oneness of its first tutti. This quality persists
throughout the rest of the movement which is derived from its opening
tutti more completely even than in other concertos. One has the
impression that Mozart the orchestral composer felt in its creation
even more delight than Mozart the pianist, so thoroughly orchestral
is it. This is so true—and the same holds good of many of his other
concertos—that a satisfactory performance of the work depends even
more on the orchestra than on the pianist. A performance where the
band is excellent and the pianist passable will be nearer to the ideal
than one where the contrary obtains. In theory, orchestra and piano
are equally responsible, but in practice the orchestra influences most
the nature of the performance.

Reading these lines, anyone who had never heard this concerto
would think that the piano plays but a subordinate part in it. This is
not so. Although its part, according to Mozart himself, is easier
than in the preceding one,[2] it is still brilliant. Mozart combines here,
with a skill he has equalled only in K.503, the lustre of the band with
the splendour of the piano. He satisfies the claims of both, so that
neither seems sacrificed to the other. How does he manage this?
The best answer to this question will be a brief study of the relations
of piano and orchestra. This question is at heart the central problem
of the concerto and we hope to be forgiven if, within a narrower
horizon, we go over ground already covered.[3]

---

[1] In the *Breitkopf* collection, K.624, it figures by mistake under the *Coronation*
concerto, K.537 (no. 32).

[2] Letter to his father of May 26th, 1784.

[3] Cf. I, 3.

One of two things must happen: either the piano plays alone or it must play with the orchestra. The passages of complete solo, so long in the last concerto, are uncommon and short here. The longest is the exposition of the first subject, which is interesting in that Mozart, instead of giving the theme unaltered to the piano, as he often does, or of dividing it between piano and orchestra, modifies it so that he makes the piano as far as possible the equivalent of the orchestra. In the four bars of chords that follow the second subject and where the piano plays alone, he seeks to contrast sonorities; chording being uncommon in his piano writing, his intention is unmistakable.

One sees therefore that the piano's independence is almost nil. It is significant of the importance Mozart gives to his orchestra that even the solo subject is accompanied by a held note on the hautboys, representing the other instruments, that the orchestra leads off in the second subject and that, when the piano takes up, it is doubled by the fiddles. There are only two bravura passages: those that assert the keys of the dominant at the close of the exposition and of the tonic at the end of the allegro, and here, though supported by the wind, the piano is temporarily master; but its virtuosity remains within the framework of the movement and never spreads itself in irrelevance.

All this does not amount to much. Most of the time the piano builds on the foundations of the first tutti. Thus, to ex. 122 it adds first its semi-quaver scales, ex. 128, then its arpeggio triplets; it adorns slightly the second subject by breaking up minims into quavers; it strengthens the bass of ex. 125 and sets off ex. 126 with its scales, and, at the reprise, other scales, spurting upwards like rockets, punctuate the orchestral *fortes*. In every case, its part is superimposed on that of the orchestra and is not indispensable to it.

But it is just as much based upon the opening tutti when it inserts itself into the orchestral score and takes over the part of one of the instruments. It does so in the complex of passages and figures which makes up the second subject. It gives itself the upper pedal which had at first fallen to the violins, takes from them fragment (a) and excludes them from the dialogue with the wind in the "fluttering seconds" passage, ex. 6.

Finally, in the few sections which do not derive from the opening tutti, its part sometimes consists in decorating the orchestral framework (bars 110–12, after the solo subject), sometimes is that of an interlocutor (bars 186–200, at the beginning of the *development*); now and again it combines so closely with the orchestra that there is no longer subordination of one to the other and its mass blends with

that of the strings and wind in one symphonic whole, as in the part
of the *development* which begins in B minor where piano and violins,
beneath the held notes of the flute and hautboy, give us a glimpse of
a new tune (bars 200 and foll.).

We see, therefore, that the unity of the work depends as much on
the extremely close collaboration of solo with band as on the various
devices we have been analyzing. Is it necessary to add that this unity
is far from being merely formal? Mozart lavishes so much care on
his work's architecture precisely because the thought which inspires
it is itself of architectural stature, a thought powerful and serene which
can express itself only in a well-builded whole. There is here no
opposition between matter and manner; if he attends to one, he does
not neglect the other; the thought is as important as the frame; the
inspiration, less tormented though quite as passionate as in K.449,
deeper and more original than in K.450, is worthy of the splendid
form in which it is embodied.

We have already characterized this thought. There are two aspects
of thought in a work of art: the revealing of the creator's deeper
nature, to which every work of value, whether the artist will it or not,
contributes something, and the expression of the mood reigning in
him at the moment the work was created. K.451 makes manifest, like
so many other compositions, this interplay, this blending of strength
and tenderness, of passion and quiet, of sun and shadow, which—as
far as it is possible to shut up a spirit in the nutshell of a formula—
is the central principle of Mozart's soul. But it manifests them at a
moment of happiness, in the joy brought by success and the recognition of his talent as composer and executant. Transpose this manifestation into a moment of conflict and trial and you will have the
concertos in D minor and C minor. There, we have struggle; here,
merely possibility of struggle. The difference is between one who is
capable of fighting and one immersed in the fight, between happy and
triumphant passion and a suffering passion at grips with disharmony.

The deeply personal stamp of this work is therefore indisputable.
And yet it falls into a long line which comprises not only other compositions of Mozart but also those of many other musicians: that
of the operatic aria. This is obviously true of all *galant* concertos
which owe to the aria a great many of the differences which separate
them from the concerto of the previous age. But whereas this kinship
is only formal and hardly recognizable in concertos like K.449 or
the D minor, it is here both deeper and more general. D major is
with Mozart the key *par excellence* of virtuosity blended with pride

and power. It is that of the passionate and haughty aria where a possibility of tragedy exists but which is not itself tragic. To realize this, the reader should turn to one of the grandest of these serious and passionate, but not tragic, D major arias: that of the king in *Idomeneo*: "*Fuor del mar ho un mar in seno.*" Mozart has often used the key of D major for works where virtuosity was to shine, but it is in this aria that he comes nearest to the spirit of our concerto and in it one grasps best the kinship between the two genres. The main formal differences are, naturally, the subordination of the orchestra to the voice in the aria, and the much greater breadth of themes and bridge passages in the concerto. In this latter respect, in fact, K.451 is remarkable. It has a sweep and a grandeur which are found again, in Mozart, only in a few other concertos and the string quintet in C, and of which even the quartets and symphonies know nothing. Remember the breadth of ex. 124, the link between first and second subject. In such a movement, one feels the accuracy of the judgement which says that if Mozart did what everyone else was doing, he did it very much better. And if, in the past, it points to the *Idomeneo* aria, in the future it shows the way towards the *Prague* symphony, also in D, also a work of power and passion without tragedy; also a work where, as Saint-Foix says justly, "there blend elements of drama and joy"; where, in "brusque and almost lashing rhythms . . . one divines the presence of more struggle and forceful impetus than real happiness"[1] —an appreciation which suits admirably the movement we have just been analyzing.

II. In the andante the trumpets, one hautboy, and one bassoon are silent. A yearning, sensuous melody opens the movement, entwining itself round the fiddles like a creeper, then drawing the flute and bassoon into its coils. How far we have come from the vigorous allegro! And yet the pedal which holds down the creeper by the roots warns us that this languishing and seductive figure is of the same lineage as the resounding themes whose echoes have just died away. Its chromaticisms, too, are close to the first movement, and its dusky charm has already been felt in the syncopated motif, ex. 125. Its weariness, full of longing, is all Mozart's own; yet it would be difficult to find another page in him where it is expressed with such Chopin-like intensity! One does not know at what to wonder most: its formal likeness with the allegro, in the pedal and chromaticisms, or

---

[1] *Les symphonies de Mozart*, p. 139.

the absolute contrast which its enervated state affords with the power of the opening movement (ex. 136). As the whole theme is repeated and both halves contain the sinuous figure, this is heard four times, and each time the scoring throws a different light on it. First, *piano*, in the strings, with bass and horn pedal; then, *forte*, in the fiddles, haut-boy and flute, with the same; a third time in the solo, unaccompanied, *piano*, and lastly in the woodwind, with a piano trill. The sym-phonist, master of orchestration and lover of woodwind, which the virtuoso composer has become, here displays with zest all the resources of his imagination.

The movement—an andante and not an adagio, as Mozart is careful to remind us[1]—is a rondo in two couplets. The first one is in D and consists in a succession of short, breathless phrases, given out by the piano, to which the beloved woodwind answers with a kind of echo (ex. 137). The "concerto with woodwind obbligato" character grows still more pronounced and we next have a long phrase, as sinuous and nostalgic as the refrain, which passes without a break from hautboys and bassoons to piano. The pedal, of course, is not absent; it is even doubled, in basses and flute, and its fixity redeems the instability and waviness of the middle parts. Thus, throughout the whole movement, Mozart makes up for the indecisiveness of his melodies with the firmness of his pedal points (ex. 138).

The sinuous figure winds through the strings with a piano descant; then through the piano itself, in half a dozen more bars where the supple lines intertwine and come asunder in turn with affectionate ease and heady charm—six bars which are a masterly instance of solo and orchestral collaboration (ex. 2). And so, rising and falling, then lifting up in one last effort and led from above by the airy sighs of the woodwind, the tune subsides on the tonic of D whence flute, hautboy and bassoons bring it back in two bars to the key of G. And how indeed, save by means of a pedal point, grounded in the basses and reinforced, then decorated, by a piano trill (ex. 139)? The refrain is repeated unchanged by the solo, then by the tutti, and the piano opens abruptly the second couplet on the chord of E minor.

This one is composed of two distinct parts. The first has the same character as what went before, with its plaintive accent, its panting phrases, its woodwind echoes and wavy lines; the strings are com-pletely silent. Then, a rise of the woodwind on the chord of E minor,

---

[1] Letter to his father of June 9th, 1784.

a flattering of the leading note, a trill on B and suddenly the landscape changes: we are in the white light of C major.

The next section shows a very bare picture in the score. Here are its first three bars (ex. 140). The uninformed executant (and how many are informed, even among the great soloists?) who plays what he sees written and nothing more, is shocked by the insignificance of the passage. "Mozart is sometimes very empty," he says, and without going any further closes the volume and seeks out in the works of Liszt or Tchaikovsky the concerto he will play at his next "appearance". He is wrong. Far from being empty, Mozart leaves him here a fine opportunity of showing off his talent as extemporizer within the confines of a skeleton melody. The few notes, whose leanness on the staves disgusts our virtuoso, are but a canvas upon which the pianist is to build his own part, keeping, however, the outline sketched by the composer.

> In the same way as the singer (says Sigmund Lebert in his edition of the concertos published in 1880 by Cotta) performed his aria on the stage or in the concert-room, so the solo player on the pianoforte gave his *cantilena*, only with richer ornamentation, as he had to compensate for the poverty of tone with a greater quantity of notes. . . . Have we not heard in our younger days reliable men, who had themselves heard Mozart play, speak of the richness of improvised ornamentation and modulation, with which he embellished his performance? At that period ornamentation was an important element in pianoforte playing, so that a composer who did not want it had to mark specially: *senza ornamenti*.

This fashion survived the 18th century and in the Romantic period degenerated into an abuse; already the variants with which Hummel overlaid his master's concertos in his edition published by Litolff are no longer in Mozart's style. It is none the less true that some passages in the andantes of Mozart's concertos are but sketches and require completion, either by the soloist's own talent or rather, alas! by the science of the editor. Such was already the case with the *cantilena* of the first couplet. Here, the completion is indispensable.

To excuse the modern pianist who thinks he sees Mozart's complete and final idea in the score, it must be said that the composer's very sister asked for explanations about these bars, for in Wolfgang's letter to his father of June 9th, 1784, he wrote: "Tell her from me that, in the andante of the D major concerto, in the solo in C in question, yes, most certainly, something is missing. . . . I will send it her as soon as possible, with the cadenzas."

The additional bars sent to Nannerl escaped the notice of editors

Ex. 142

Ex. 143

Ex. 144

for a hundred and fifty years and only came to light when Alfred Einstein published his revised Köchel in 1936. They figure in it as no. 626a, M. on page 824. Saint-Foix identified them as belonging to this movement and Einstein confirmed the identification in 1941[1] (ex. 141).

The task of completing *cantabiles* was, therefore, not always left to the executant, even in Mozart's time. What Mozart did for his sister the modern editor must do for the pianist of to-day. Lebert, with Cotta, and Reinecke,[2] with Brietkopf, realized this, and one cannot urge too often pianists who play these concertos in public to follow their indications in passages like this—that is to say, wherever a theme in long notes demands more singing power from the instrument than it can give.

In the last part of this solo, the ascending echoes of the woodwind which we have already heard twice (ex. 137) answer the piano and a pedal point in the basses and horns warns us of the coming reprise. But here two bars are not enough to lead us back to the refrain and the tonic key. The breadth of the transition is worthy of the movement. Upon the pedal of D (as dominant of G minor), a variant of ex. 136 wreathes itself in imitations in the strings, and for a short instant counterpoint, much to its surprise, finds itself enlisted to sing nostalgia and desire; then everything is lost in the great pedal, whilst from the heavenly regions flutes, hautboys and bassoons sail down to join the cohort of strings, the first two in a straight line, but breaking step, the bassoons in graceful and expressive windings (ex. 142).[3]

At its last appearance the refrain belongs to the piano, then to the orchestra as a whole, with the difference that the wind vary its final bars. The coda is fairly long; it is made up of the same wavy and languishing phrases as the rest, given out by the piano, repeated by the wind with solo accompaniment (merely sketched). The strings enter only right at the end and even then their part is subsidiary. Till its last bar, this andante keeps its character of a dialogue between piano and wind; till its last bar, the soft rhythms and lines rest upon, and are supported by, the firm ground of a pedal point (ex. 143).

This movement has not the grandness of the former; its world is

---

[1] *Music Review*, vol. 2 (1941), p. 242.

[2] Reinecke not always, and notably in this concerto.

[3] Here too the piano part is but a sketch. Clearly the D of the right hand, held for five beats, then repeated as a minim an octave higher, is meaningless. These two bars must be filled out with scales, simple or ornate, and trills.

narrower and its thought affects a smaller part of us.   But it is sincere and original; longing and nostalgia are feelings that have often inspired Mozart's music, but seldom as intensely and as continuously as in this andante, where there is scarcely anything else.   It is one of the most moving as well as one of the last examples of his "dream andantes".

Rondo form is often used by Mozart in slow movements, but generally with the *romance* variety: ABA—C—ABA—Coda.   Here, the plan is simpler: A—B—A—C—A—Coda.   There are eight or ten examples of this plan in his work, nearly all of which date from the year of this concerto and the two following ones.   They are to be found in trios and sonatas, in a serenade and in a horn concerto; there are no others in the piano concertos.

III.   It is usual to consider Mozart as a pure songster whose works are a succession of enchanting and expressive melodies.   He is contrasted (in this, as in so many other ways) with Beethoven, who is thought to have possessed to a lesser degree the gift of melody, but to a far higher one that of organization.   Whereas Mozart was content with opening the flood-gates to his torrent of tunes, Beethoven, with apparently unpromising themes, built up vast architectural ensembles.

Very incomplete concerning Beethoven, such a judgement is quite untrue of Mozart.   There are, of course, many melodies in his music and many expressive ones, but they are far from making up the substance of his chief works and in many movements they are insignificant. Such is the case in the finale of this concerto.   Analysis can discover in it three or four themes, undistinguished melodically and more remarkable for their rhythm than for their outline, and it is with them, and with pianistic passages which derive more or less directly from them, that the whole movement is built up.   There is no trace of those successions of tunes of which we hear.

This rondo has not the melodic interest of the two other movements, neither has it the triumphant power of the first or the sensuous charm of the second.   But it has the broad build and spaciousness of the allegro, something of which had reappeared in the transitions of the andante.   Despite its insignificant themes, it is one of the most monumental examples of that sonata rondo which was Mozart's main contribution to the growth of musical form.

We have spoken at length of the sonata rondo in an earlier chapter.[1]

---

[1] J, 2.

Let us say here, once again, that, deriving from the French dances
en rondeau, it is treated with such breadth by Mozart, especially
in his concertos, that he is practically its creator.   And yet, one may
still read in modern works that Mozart's rondo has the form: A B A
C A, that is to say, a two-couplet rondo, and that Beethoven enlarged
this form and made it more organic by adding a third couplet repeating
the first, in the manner of a recapitulation, and thus produced a masterly
cross between the sonata and the rondo.   The number of Mozart's
sonata rondos is so great and many are movements of such scope and
conclude such important works that assertions like this are both in-
excusable and deplorable.   Of course, Beethoven left large-scale
sonata rondos, like that of the Waldstein sonata, but they differ from
Mozart's in their greater size and not in their more organic structure
or stricter unity.

We have given elsewhere[1] a schematic analysis of this finale.
The refrain (ex. 144) is given out by strings and flute and the piano
enters only after the tutti has begun the first couplet.   Such an entry
after the beginning is original; the solo's usual behaviour is to make its
appearance coincide with the opening of the couplet.   The new
subject, like those of the refrain, has in common with several themes
of the first movement the fact that it is built on the common chord.
The couplet's second subject, in A, is limited to four degrees of
the scale; it hesitates coyly on its first note, then rushes forward
at full speed to the end of its miniature course.   It recalls the rondo
refrain in the flute quartet in D and shows once again what close
kinship of manner and matter unites Mozart's works in the same
key (ex. 145).

The refrain is repeated at first by the piano, which varies its second
part, then, unchanged, by the orchestra; thereupon a *minor* subject,
given out by the solo, opens the second couplet.

Hitherto the tutti's share has been less extensive than in the opening
allegro.   It is true that it gave out the second subject before the piano,
but it has been content mostly to support the solo in its swift progress
and accompany it with slight figures.   In this second couplet which
corresponds to the *development* of the sonata, its relations with the
solo are more like what they were in the first movement.

The couplet begins with a theme in B minor.   The piano gives it
out twice, then no more is said about it.   Now comes the most interesting moment.   Still in B minor, the strings recall ex. 145 and the

---

[1] Pp. 51, 52.

Ex. 145

Ex. 146

Ex. 147

piano does at once likewise. This theme does not appeal to the protagonists either. They end by finding what they are seeking in the
refrain subject and start a game with it. But first the pitch has to be
settled. B minor being too much in the shade they enter G major

and the flute repeats in it the first four bars of the refrain.   But, with
an abruptness which calls up for an instant the opening of the finale of
the ninth symphony transposed on to the comic plane, the piano dis-
agrees and, in two arpeggio bars, carries the business into E minor.
This time, the hautboy is cut short by the piano and the bassoon repeats
the same bars in C major.   The new pitch pleases everyone and the game
can continue.   Now reduced to its first four bars, our subject finds
itself tossed from hautboy to flute, from flute to hautboy, rebounding
like a ball from the jaunty sarcasm of the one to the canting suavity of
the other.   The players do not remain stationary but each time work
a little higher up the field—that is, the scale—ending up where they
were a minute ago, in E minor.   The strings are but onlookers,
following the players by the side of the pitch, but the piano accompanies them with a brilliant commentary of arpeggios of, alternately,
the common chord and the dominant ninth, and so voluble that it
silences them for a moment (ex. 146).

And now we have to get home.   Each one does its best.   Hautboys, flute, piano, fiddles, each time draw a little nearer the goal,
which is finally reached by the fiddles after several attempts; whereupon strings and piano repeat together the complete text of the refrain
(ex. 147).

All this passage is worthy of the rondo *development* in the previous
concerto and of the finest bars of solo and tutti collaboration in the
two other movements of this one.

The third couplet, the recapitulation, repeats the first without
important change.   The cadenza, which begins like the first solo,
consists in a passage of broken chords with crossings of hands and an
imitative development of ex. 145 ; it is brief and shapely.   The refrain's
last appearance and the rather long coda are in 3-8, and this beat, even
weaker and more skipping than the 6-8 of K.449, is kept up to the
end.   The coda brings in the second subject again and the rondo
concludes with a unison strain of the whole orchestra based on the
common chord.

Prolonged contact with this concerto has convinced us of its greatness.   The first allegro is one of the most imposing movements, not
only in the concertos but in the whole symphonic work of Mozart.
It shows in him the great architect who can erect spacious, well-knit
wholes, inspired by one lofty idea.   Earlier in this century, almost all
the concertos of the father of the modern concerto were unknown.
The years between the wars saw a good many of them issue forth
from the *Gesamtausgabe* and recover life in the orchestra, and by now

all have been recorded, some of them several times. Mozart is much
better known to-day than he was forty years ago but revival has been
irregular and not wholly in relation with the importance of the compositions revived. A number of first-rate works, among them this
concerto, still await a discovery and a recognition which, let us hope,
will not be long delayed.

4. The Thirteenth Concerto: K.453 in G

CONCERTO No. 13 IN G (K.453)[1]
Finished April 12th, 1784
    Allegro: C
    Andante: 3-4 (in C)
    Allegretto: Presto: ¢—2-4
Orchestra: Strings; flute, two hautboys, two horns, two bassoons.

AMONGST the friends and patrons whose names recur in Wolf-gang's letters to Leopold was a family called Ployer, hailing from Salzburg. The father was the archbishop's agent in Vienna; the daughter, Babette, an accomplished pianist, was one of the young composer's pupils.[2] He had written for her the concerto in E flat, K.449; for her also he wrote the concerto in G.

In this wonderful Lent of 1784, for the concerts of which he had already produced three masterpieces one after the other, his fruitful-ness was not yet exhausted. Other years will know a more abundant flowering; 1784 is the one in which he composed the greatest number of first-rate works. Between February and May and between September and December in this year, six concertos, two sonatas, a quartet and a quintet followed close one upon the other—all of them authentic masterpieces.

The twelfth concerto was finished on March 22nd. Mozart then turned to a quintet for piano and wind instruments. This work,[3] whose inspiration is close to that of many other of his E flat composi-tions, has also the self-assurance and grace of the concerto in B flat, K.450; it is a piece of "society music", written "half for his public, half for himself", and in a composite style related to the concertos its contemporaries in its piano part and, in its wind writing, to the great serenades of earlier years. As a whole, it has a *concertante* character; the protagonists come to the fore each one in turn and pass their themes from one to the other with a generosity that reminds us more of the divertimento for string trio, K.563, than of the severer style of the quartets. The presence of a theme from K.450 in its first movement and, in the rondo, of an *obbligata* cadenza in which everyone

---

[1] *Gesamtausgabe*, no. 17. [2] See p. 178, note 1.
[3] K.452.

takes part shows how near the work is to the concertos; at this moment, Mozart is so much the "fashionable virtuoso" and is so full of his public that, even when he composes chamber music, he still thinks in terms of his favourite genre. The same influence will also be visible in the andante of the C minor sonata, in the autumn. The composer was well pleased with his quintet.

> For my part, I consider it the best thing I have written as yet in all my life (he wrote to his father on April 10th). It has met with extraordinary success.

The quintet finished, he began at once another concerto. It is characteristic of his generous nature that two out of the four concertos written this season should have been composed for others. In spite of their difference in personality from those he wrote for himself, they are certainly not inferior. Into the works composed for his young pupil, Mozart poured as much of himself as into those which were written to show off his own gifts.

The concerto in G is as much a masterpiece as those in B flat, D and F, but the great differences between them and it bear witness to the diversity and richness of his genius. Expansiveness, joyous and confident splendour reign here no longer; the inspiration is more intimate and more subtle. It is impossible to sum it up in a word, as can be done, at a pinch, with the concertos in D and F; with its mixture of the sad and the happy, the feeling that animates it is more indeterminate and also comes closer to that of everyday existence. Not every day do we feel "proud", like the concerto in D, or "festive", like that in F; but the more complex strands of the work in G enter into most moments of our life. It is one of Mozart's most ethereal concertos, with a pastoral strain—pastoral like the fields on the Delectable Mountains—and it takes us close to the most ethereal of Beethoven's concertos and the loveliest of his violin sonatas, both of them in G (ops. 58 and 96).[1] We welcome it, not at those times when one single thought absorbs and masters us, but at those much more

---

[1] One wonders whether Beethoven's choice of G major for the expression of this inspiration is not due to this concerto, where the same inspiration is unmistakably present. We would go further and see in Beethoven's work a spiritual offspring of Mozart's. The filiation between his C minor concerto and Mozart's is a commonplace of musical criticism; only the neglect of K.453 has prevented musicians from noticing its kinship with Beethoven's Op. 58. Prof. Sidney Newman has pointed out to me the likeness between bars 65-8 of Mozart's work and bars 60-2 of Beethoven's (first movements). In both cases the strains belong to the conclusion of the opening tutti. Beethoven's is a variation of Mozart's.

frequent moments when our mood is an ever-changing compound of diverse elements, equal in force, which come forward, rise, fall back, without any variation in the emotional pitch of the whole.

I.   Here, again the first movement opens with a march rhythm, but how different from the massive strength of K.451! It is no longer the army itself but merely its shadow of which we catch a glimpse in the fifteen bars of the first subject. The body of the troops, represented by the first violins, are but ghosts; ghosts, too, the "drums" of the second violins and violas; ghosts again, but rather more substantial, the fifes of the flute and hautboys which finish off each fragment of the theme, according to an exquisite formula of Mozart's.[1] The subject grows ever so slightly livelier and more emphatic, repeats its last notes and finally draws in and closes on the tonic (ex. 148).

The favourite *galant* formula of a mysterious opening followed by a *fortissimo* then appears complete. The whole orchestra outlines a linking figure (ex. 149) with a codetta of scales, and we await the customary noisy dominant close.   But Mozart is as much concerned here with formal unity as he was in the last concerto and the rigid, impersonal barriers of Italian opera style no longer satisfy him. Instead of a close, the orchestra repeats the codetta in a slightly different version, and the woodwind, omitting the semi-quaver scales, add an arpeggio theme (ex. 150), destined to provide later on a pleasing interplay between solo and orchestra (ex. 158).   After pretending to stop on a cadence, this new theme follows on by throwing a bridge across to the second subject.

This latter comes forward, breathless and limping. Is it to be minor or major? It does not know at first; then it plumps for major. Reserved for the strings, it hesitates, like much of this movement, between laughter and tears. The wind take it up and the strings echo them (ex. 151). It is a reincarnation of ex. 148 and one of the most interesting instances of that kinship between various themes of the same work which, in Mozart as in Haydn, in Clementi and, later, in Beethoven, tends to replace the more rudimentary and less organic principle of contrast. Bars like these sum up the essence of Mozart's genius and, more clearly than any explanations, express its charm and reveal its secret. They are the best answer to the question: What did Mozart create that no one else created?

---

[1] The same woodwind flutterings, this time with mocking intent, occur at the end of Guglielmo's aria:"*Non siate ritrosi*",also in G, in the first act of *Così fan tutte.*

What follows is also very Mozartish.   From G major we dive into
E flat, with an abruptness worthy of K.449.   This sudden change and
the explosive *forte* after the first bar reveal a subterranean force ever
ready to burst forth from under a polite and graceful exterior (ex. 152).
The clamour dies down quickly and then at once begins a tonic pedal,
over which for an instant the strings brood meditatively (ex. 153 a).   The
pedal starts again an octave lower, the violins return to their meditation
and a counterpoint of the woodwind in unison discloses for a flash a
vision of immensity (ex. 153 b).   In the limits of a few bars Mozart,
without grandiloquence, with simplest harmonic means, brings us to the
edge of space and lets us see the heavens open; an instant later, a bright,
sociable theme capped by a conventional figure concludes the tutti.

One cannot insist too much on the lack of uniformity in the concertos of his "great" period.   Far from falling into line, one after
the other, in the same formation, nearly all progress along different
paths.   Thus, K.450 gives out in its opening tutti only a part of the
movement's materials, and in the solo after it the piano expounds
almost entirely new subjects and passages, whilst the orchestra keeps
silent.   K.451, on the other hand, pours forth straight away nearly
the whole contents of the allegro, and the solo, without omitting anything but also hardly adding anything, does but embroider what is
given, in continuous collaboration with the orchestra.   This concerto,
finally, combines both methods.   As in K.451, the solo exposition
repeats the greater part of the tutti whilst instruments and piano
collaborate unceasingly, but it is like K.450 in that it introduces
significant new passages.

The piano prefixes a rising scale to the first subject: the simplest
form of the solo introduction.   It gives out the subject, decorating it
and lengthening it slightly; the wind answer as they did just now.
The strings start ex. 149 and the solo superimposes a decoration which
extends into a bravura passage.   Its own subject, in D, is more important than in the last concerto.   Long and winding, it remains on
the whole within the limits of five degrees and returns continually to
its starting-point like a *moto perpetuo*.   It is repeated and its latter
half spreads out into a dialogue with the woodwind (ex. 154).

Over this happy landscape there suddenly passes a cloud; the
figure (a) of ex. 154 opens out and, tossed from flute to hautboys,
wanders through minor keys whilst the bassoon adds a counterpoint
and the piano accompanies it with downward arpeggios.   It is a
charming Mozartian development where the free and aimless motion
of the harmony matters more than the melodic line (ex. 155).   Its

Ex. 153 (a)

Ex. 154

Ex. 155

ethereal, unemphatic melancholy, so "pre-Romantic", is as fugitive as the other moods that pass over the face of this concerto, a mezzo-tint work demanding delicate sensibility and subtle understanding rather than technical skill. It survives an instant in the hesitations of the second subject (ex. 151), then fades away in the self-assured conclusion. The second subject itself is given out twice, first by the piano alone, then by the wind an octave higher; the strings accompany them as in the first tutti and the piano takes over the echo (ex. 3).

The progress of the inspiration is now broken and virtuosity speaks alone. A mild virtuosity, indeed; the work is for a pupil and Mozart keeps for himself the "difficult" concertos. But its intrusion is none the less noticeable. The end of the exposition is one of the recognized places where it is given free rein and often it arises without effort from the substance of the music. K.451 showed admirably how a bravura passage could continue and develop what went before, not only without interrupting it but even making it clearer. Here, these few pianistic bars are an insertion foreign to the spirit of the movement which does not require virtuosity. Its delicate nature, full of shades, is expressed in gentleness and hesitation; the interplay of solo and tutti in passages like ex. 151 and 155 render it perfectly. Displays of skill are contrary to it and the arrival of these broken scales, a petty ornamentation in which the concerto sacrifices to convention, intrudes into the flow of its thought.

The transition theme ex. 149, abridged, links up with the closing figure and we met again the Mozart of *fantasia developments*.[1] The expected cadence remains hanging in the air on a sub-dominant chord, the strings whisper a little mock-innocent motif; then, without preparation (we are in D major), strike the chord of B flat. The piano enters again and suddenly we are sailing in mid-sky, far from all landmarks. For some twenty bars, the solo rises and falls in arpeggios of three octaves, whilst flute, hautboys and bassoons follow it in turn like shadows. Through the most diverse keys, constantly modulating, like a wandering spirit, now here, now there, its beautiful restless soul pursues its course. Neither motif nor outline: it is pure motion, itself its own aim, its own *raison d'être*. It seems to say: "I climb up into heaven, I go down to hell, I take the wings of the morning and remain in the uttermost parts of the sea."

The most formal of musicians is here the freest. His music has indeed fixed points by which it passes, but between them it soars upward with a fancy no Romantic has surpassed (ex. 156).

In the course of the cruise, we put in at B major and the mass of the orchestra, delegating its powers to horns and hautboys, rests while the piano performs a run in two parts through which there shimmers a melody, a passage recalling the episode in the same place in K.451, to the *development* of which concerto this one is closely

---

[1] See p. 200.

akin. A modulation of genius, one of the most striking in all Mozart
(ex. 157), brings in the piano once more, in C minor. Thereupon the
solo starts a game with a little five-note motif, in which the strings
play a discreet part.

We have said elsewhere[1] that Mozart seeks constantly to vary the
recapitulations of his concertos. This one combines elements from
the first tutti and the first solo and also brings in new material. A
transitional figure, ex. 150, which had served to introduce the second
subject, behaves now as if it were a main theme and appears three
times in the course of the recapitulation under different shapes. It
introduces the second subject, as it is entitled to do; but it seems to
be quite as indispensable to the solo subject, which it also heralds; and
finally, in the last bars, when we stop on the tonic, it returns and insists
on having the last word so that we shall remember the movement
by it. These are not mere repetitions. The second of these appearances is a fresh development, a dialogue in canon between flute, bassoon and piano (ex. 158).

In other respects, this third solo differs from the first mainly in the
greater length of its orchestral passages. But, just as the piano finishes
its trill, a surprise awaits us. Instead of closing on the tonic, it stops
on the chord of E flat and the orchestra repeats the "dive" of the
first tutti, ex. 152, which leads to a 6-4 chord and the cadenza.[2] The
movement concludes with two of its most characteristic themes, the
mysterious pedal of ex. 153, followed by the original concluding
subject, and ex. 150, promoted to the rank of a main theme and clearly
determined to leave us the final impression of the movement.

II.   Andante, and not Adagio, says Mozart.[3]   In most of the earlier
concertos dissimilarity rather than relationship existed between the
first two movements; moreover, in the three concertos of this winter,
K.449, 450 and 451, the inspiration was slighter in the andantes, and
they contrasted with the allegros in feeling and importance. But
here the andante is, in these respects, the allegro's equal—perhaps its
superior. Far from contrasting with it, this second movement carries
on its thought, emphasizing it and bringing out its essential elements.

---

[1] P. 23.

[2] Neither of the cadenzas written by Mozart for this movement is interesting. We recommend soloists to extemporize their own, remaining within
the limits of Mozart's own and, above all, ending up *piano* to link up with
the soft orchestral entry.

[3] Letter to his father of June 9th, 1784.

The mingling of serenity and sadness is more marked; the lights are higher, the shadows deeper. The neighbourhood of smiles and tears, in the music as in life, is closer, and their common origin in the depths of the composer's soul more visible.

The theme with which it opens is one of the most expressive, the most pictorial even, in all Mozart. Through its position at the head of the movement, its different returns, its transformation at the end, it presides over the whole andante. Yet it is not what a refrain is to a rondo for we are not led back to it; it is the theme itself that comes forward from time to time to remind us of its presence (ex. 159). Is it a lament? is it a meditation? A question it certainly is, and incomplete; a lonely voice rising in a desert and, later, when it is given to the flute, a forsaken faun in the light of a sun-bathed, empty "afternoon". It sums up the movement like an inscription carved over a portal and repeated at intervals inside the building. It is one of the few themes in Mozart which seem to need the help of literature to be complete, and to call for words.[1]

What follows expands rather than answers the query. It is a long, unbroken effusion, beginning with the voice of the hautboy, like a solitary reedpipe in the depths of marshes; then the flute joins it and finally the bassoon, and the three engage in a conversation whence the strings are excluded. The two upper parts intermingle and interlace with ease and suppleness. They commune in apparent calm; only the sharpened *appoggiatura* in the rising line of the bassoon and hautboy introduces a slight quiver. But calm in Mozart is often deceptive or fugitive. Passion lies deep with him, and even in moments as idyllic as this one we feel that it is at hand (ex. 160).

The strings interrupt this meditation with a call supported by the horns; the woodwind maintain their attitude and answer back with sinuous, caressing strains. The game begins afresh and the wind look as if they would have the last word. Suddenly the sky clouds over—the idyll becomes a lament and passion rises from the depths to over; whelm everything. The violins breathe out a plaint in C minor in which bassoon, hautboy and flute join in—not just a sigh of melancholy, but a lament rising from the bottom of the heart. As in the first movement (ex. 153), the depths close at once and order is restored (ex. 161).

And now the piano puts the question. It does so without changing

---

[1] Perhaps those of the fine aria: *Bella mia fiamma, addio!* K.528, of 1787, the 3-4 part of which shows kinship with our andante and where the pathetic ending of ex. 159 is set to the words: "*Resta, o cara!*"

Ex. 160

the text. But how different is the commentary it adds! After the pause it plunges into G minor and then rears up in wrath (ex. 162). The exceptional violence of the emotion is proved by the presence of a chord, to which the executant should give its full weight. But this violence, like all emotion in this movement, is but passing; it dies down quickly and loses itself in the all-pervading tranquillity of ex. 160.[1] The piano pursues with (a), alone, and reaches the chord of G major. Once more the clouds pile up; ex. 161 comes into sight with a new casting of parts (ex. 163), and the solo adds an ornate coda, in triplets, which weakens its pathos and intensity. The piano once more silent, we expect a new theme; instead, the flute puts again the same question, ex. 159, supported only by the hautboys and bassoons. Thus orchestrated, the strain reminds us more than ever of an *Après-midi d'un faune* in 18th-century idiom.

What answer will the piano give this time? It finds it far away, in a work dating from six years earlier, the "Paris" sonata in C, K.330. It is the theme (F minor in the sonata, D minor here) which opens the interlude in the middle of the andante (ex. 164). It proclaims itself with concentrated vigour, but this new spurt of energy has no morrow and crumbles away in sinuous, broken phrases. Its continuation consists in short questions in the woodwind to which the piano replies in phrases with free rhythms as thickly decorated with chromaticisms as the calls of the woodwind are bare. Modulations into distant keys heighten the sense of anguish. The whole passage is in reality a single theme, divided between piano and orchestra (ex. 8), where the thought wanders fancy-free. Whenever the motion appears to slacken, flute and hautboys spur it on afresh. We halt finally in C sharp minor and the strings, whose part in all this passage has been almost nil, busy themselves with carrying us back as fast as possible to the tonic.

To the question, put for the fourth time, the piano answers with a variant of ex. 162. Then the opening tutti is repeated with the addition of the piano in ex. 160 and, after the usual trill, we stop for the cadenza on a 6-4 chord, led up to softly by the woodwind. This is the last time Mozart inserts a cadenza in an andante. He has left two; the better one is a short meditation, pungent in its conciseness, upon the first notes of ex. 163.

The closing bars are among the finest in the movement. For the

---

[1] The leaps of a twelfth towards the end of the solo are but a sketch which the pianist must fill out himself; it is nonsense to play these two bars as they are written; cf. pp. 229 and 232.

fifth time we hear the opening strain, sung by the flute and the haut-boy, but it is no longer a question (ex. 165). It has at last found its answer and this is no other (we might have guessed it, so natural does it now seem!) than the sombre strain of the conclusion ex. 161. In it the question dies away, trusting and peaceful (ex. 166).

This andante, on which analysis takes little hold, is the most closely knit we have met hitherto. Within its four divisions, marked off by the returns of the questioning theme, the thought is continuous and the substance intimately unified; the beginning of each division (exs. 162, 164) is characterized, but its sharp outline becomes blurred in what grows out of it and the only other independent theme is ex. 161. The inspiration flows unbroken, like a river, under changing skies, now clear, now overcast, but always full of colour. The wood-wind preponderance gives the whole movement bright and melancholy hues and a flavour of reeds and rushes that vanishes in the piano arrangement. Except for the opening bars, a few forte bars a little after ex. 160, some collaboration in ex. 161 and the end of the develop-ment, the strings are kept down to accompanying, either supporting the woodwind with a rocking figure (bars 6 to 11, 42 to 46, 102 to 104), or punctuating the angry strains of the piano (ex. 162). Once again we are listening to a concerto with obbligati wind parts!

No concerto andante of Mozart's had reached hitherto such full-ness. There had been pathetic ones, even tragic ones;[1] none had pene-trated into the soul with such breadth and depth. What is admirable is not only the quality of the inspiration but its variety.

> Here (says Abert in his fine study of the concertos) here is the point where the fire of his genius has freed the traditional type most completely from the dross of fashion and period. All trace of the *galant*, such as we find it in John Christian and, much less, in Philip Emmanuel, is weeded out of these movements. True; in many of them Mozart still holds to the older conception, which presented here an idyll or an elegy, but the working out is personal and all conventionality is gone. On the other hand, there passes through most of these movements, as in the andantes of his piano music which are related to them, a strain of meditation and dreaming, which, together with an irresistible charm of sonority and melody, leads straight to a well-characterized type within Mozart's work.[2]

III. In spite of his unpractical nature, Mozart had certain orderly habits. Thus, he kept a thematic list of his compositions where he noted

---

[1] The *Sinfonia Concertante* for violin and viola, K.364.

[2] Abert: *Mozart*, II, 209.

down the day on which they were finished, from February, 1784, to
a short time before his death, and for one whole year he kept his
daily accounts in a notebook which contains also English exercises
and translations of letters into English.   So it happened that, on May
27th, 1784, he entered in it: "*Vogel Stahrl*"[1] 34 kr., and opposite:

adding: "*Das war schön!*"

The notes attempted by the starling are the beginning of the finale
of this concerto.   It was its song, no doubt, that endeared the bird to
Mozart and made him buy it.   When it died, he gave it a grave in his
garden with an inscription in verse.   This concerto is therefore placed,
as it were, under the patronage of those feathered folk of whom
Mozart was so fond.

For the first time since his trial work, eleven years ago, Mozart
gives up the rondo form in a piano concerto finale.   Instead, he writes
a theme and five variations, followed by a long coda.   The theme has
the tone of a German folksong and reminds us of Papageno's first air
(ex. 167).   It has repeats; the first variation also; the others are double
variations.

The first variation belongs almost entirely to the solo.

The second is shared between solo and tutti; the theme is given
out by the wind to a brilliant triplet accompaniment in the right hand;
then by the piano's right hand, doubled by the fiddles, while the left
hand performs a similar accompaniment.   The interest bears on the
accompaniment and the scoring for the theme itself is unvaried.

The third is a true variation.   The expositions are given to the
wind which present the theme in a new form, now separately, now
together.   The strings are silent or accompany with repeated notes.
The piano performs a slightly different version of it with an Alberti
bass in the left hand and a rhythmic accompaniment figure in the
violins.   The second half contains a charming passage in free imitation
for the woodwind (ex. 168).

The fourth is in the minor.   Even in his most insignificant *airs
variés*, Mozart always gives us something of himself when he comes
to the *minore*, and this variation is the most interesting of the five.
The orchestral part is remarkable for the bareness and archaic character
of its melody and the even more archaic character of the writing, in
three and four parts, and of the scoring.   Wind and strings are not
separated and the former double the violins.   The effect is strikingly

---

[1] Starling.

austere (ex. 169). The syncopations occur again in the piano, whose melodic line is a little more ornate; Mozart also makes use of contrast between the registers.

All impressions of sadness or inwardness are banished by the vigorous variation that follows, with downward rushes of five notes in the wind and piano trill in the first half, and rising semi-quaver scales in the orchestra in the second. The solo is quieter in the second half and instead of concluding it breaks off abruptly, whereupon strings and piano join in an original transitional passage where the solo instrument overlays the syncopated downward progress of the strings[1] with fragmentary chromatic scales in octaves (ex. 170). A long pause announces the sixth variation or coda.

This is pompously preceded by a double bar and headed: Presto: finale, an allusion to opera buffa. And, true enough, this coda, unique in Mozart's instrumental work, has quite the style of comedy. Its length is about one third of the movement. Mozart rejuvenates his theme by retrieving it after starting far away from it, by recalling it several times, always incomplete or varied, and by inserting between these recalls a development on a figure derived from it. The beginning of the presto, with its mock mystery, its horn calls, its quick, dry oppositions between wind and strings, between short fragmentary figures, and its sudden forte, plunges us straight into opera buffa. It is repeated with the addition of the piano and reaches a state of great excitement. After a noisy close and a pause, it falls again to piano and starts "developing" a figure derived from the theme. This is the most interesting part. To the semibreves of the strings, flute and hautboys oppose this figure, and the piano links up the two with the fireworks of its scales (ex. 171).[2] This performance is gone through thrice. Piano and wind combine, still discussing the same motif, and ascend the scale over a tonic pedal of basses and horns (ex. 173). The growing excitement breaks out in a forte, then loses itself in a chain of spluttering gruppetti in the piano which ends by retrieving the theme, one half of which it gives out, accompanied by the strings. The wind do likewise; a loud and long close brings us back to our starting-point (ex. 171) and the game begins once more with some reshuffling in the teams. Then piano, hautboys and bassoons imitate one another with another fragment (ex. 172) and,

---

[1] Compare with the duet "La mia Dorabella", also in G, in Così fan tutte (bars 41-9).

[2] Compare with Despina's and Don Alfonso's "Secondate! per effetto di bontate", in the finale of the first act of Così fan tutte.

after a dazzling succession of closes and alternating *fortes* and *pianos*, the whole orchestra stops to allow one last return of the theme. But the patience of the players is exhausted; the woodwind mockingly prevent the piano from getting beyond its fourth bar, and the concerto finishes abruptly, in the highest of spirits, after hacking up beyond all hope of repair the unfortunate theme, the last shreds of which, as the curtain falls, woodwind and piano are merrily throwing to and fro.

Certain formal likenesses connect this concerto with that in D composed a few weeks earlier. The long themes, the spacious transitions and, especially in the allegro, the general breadth of plan, which reaches its highest point in the development, are features common to both. But this one is less architectural; it does not move forward, like the other, in great, evenly balanced masses; the sections are not opposed, but derive one from the other and are related instead of being contrasted, especially in the andante which is a veritable stream, full of changing hues of emotion rather than themes. And the movements, too, are nearer to each other than in K.451. We have noted the kinship between allegro and andante. Their relationship with the finale is at first sight less evident; yet the opening of the variation theme is similar in form, if not in feeling, to the first subject of the allegro. And in the presto, we find something of the breadth of the two other movements: large-scale workings-out, themes inseparable from their developments and, between the returns of the opera buffa cadences, an uninterrupted flow of thought.

As in the last concerto the orchestra's part is important and there is frequent interplay. Conventional accompaniment figures are rare; the woodwind answer the solo or converse with it, or add characteristic accompaniments (ex. 156); the orchestra repeats passages from the first tutti and the piano adds a fresh part (ex. 166) or replaces one of the instruments (ex. 163). There are many fine passages where the piano combines intimately with the body of instruments, especially in the first movement (exs. 154, 155, 158) and variations; in the final presto, piano and orchestra play together symphonically for many bars (exs. 170, 171, 172). This concerto ranks with those in D, K.451, and C, K.503, in the forefront of the whole series for the interest in the relations of solo and orchestra.

The first two movements, we said, are more alike than in earlier concertos. They both have the same quiet temper, the same delicate sensibility, the same moderation. Both proceed by allusions rather than direct statements: allusions to passion (ex. 152), depth of feeling (ex. 153), mirth (end of the solo subject), power (ex. 149), melancholy (ex. 156); only the flight of fancy ex. 156 is completely realized, and for this reason the *development*, although it is non-thematic and contains nothing but fresh material, is not a digression but the moment in which the movement attains its full significance.   The andante, it is true, has deeper shades, but on the whole moderation, too, reigns in it; it passes close to idyll, elegy, tragedy; but none of these succeeds in mastering it.   And if, at times, it recalls Debussy, the delicate and restrained playfulness of the first movement, the reserve with which it hints at greater things without insisting, brings to mind the art of Watteau and the comedy of Marivaux.

Mozart has left a certain number of works in G major but only three or four times has he chosen the key for important ones.[1]   It is therefore hard to say that it shows definite characteristics with him and Lüthy[2] is right in pointing out that keys with few accidentals, such as G and F, are those in which the emotion is least clearly characterized.

Though our concerto does not belong to a family of works in the same key, two of its movements come from the same source as parts of other works in G major.   The andante is a close relative, both in its sentiment and in its themes, now dark and meditative, now ornate, of the andante of the quartet, K.387—another 3-4 movement in C whose themes also alternate between austerity and ornamentation. And is not the "moderate" tone of the allegro, half-sunshine, half-shadow, that of those two lovely rondos in G major—in the first duet for violin and viola, K.423, and the first quartet for piano and strings, K.478—two works approximately contemporary with our concerto?[3] In these three movements we find a clear utterance of one same mood.

---

[1] Violin concerto, K.216; string quartet, K.387; this concerto; and a violin sonata, K.379, which one hesitates to include, for its most characteristic movement, the allegro, is in G minor.

[2] *Mozart und die Tonartencharakteristik,* Strasbourg, 1931.   He notes also that joy, which Mozart expressed by G major in his youth, finds its outlet rather in D and A in his maturer years.

[3] 1783 and 1785.

5. The Fourteenth Concerto: K.456 in B flat

Concerto No. 14 in B flat (K.456)[1]
Finished September 30th, 1784
  Allegro vivace: C
  Andante un poco sostenuto: 2-4 (in G minor)
  Allegro vivace: 6-8
Orchestra: Strings; flute, two hautboys, two horns, two bassoons.

> We now have here the famous Strinasacchi from Mantua, a very good violinist. She has a great deal of taste and feeling in her playing. I am this moment composing a sonata which we are going to play together on Thursday at her concert in the theatre.[2]

THE "famous" Mantuan is known to-day, if at all, only by the sonata which Mozart composed for her and the "extraordinary" story concerning it, one of the more trustworthy of the many tales of the kind related about him.

As usual, Mozart had made up the whole work in his head, but had negligently put off transcribing it to the last moment. As time was pressing, he contented himself with writing down the violin part and played his own from memory, to the astonishment of the Emperor who followed the performance from his box with opera glasses and saw on the piano, instead of a score, a sheet with merely the violin part and a few scanty indications.

Like the quintet K.452, the sonata[3] betrays in its style the proximity of the concertos. Each part is *concertante* in turn, and as the work was written for a violinist the fiddle part is the equal of the piano. There is no longer any trace here of the piano sonata with violin accompaniment, a type to which some of Mozart's other sonatas still belong. Its inspiration is close to that of the B flat concerto, K.450; it reflects the same self-assurance and the same joyous sense of power and success; but in the magnificent andante, the starting-point of

---

[1] *Gesamtausgabe*, no. 18.
[2] Letter to his father, April 24th, 1784; E. Anderson's translation, III, 1304.
[3] K.454; no. 15 in Peters' edition.

which is the same as the concerto's, the inspiration is much deeper. His genius may have been stimulated by the charm and talent of the twenty-year old virtuosa, for Leopold Mozart who heard her at Salzburg a year later declared that "no one can play adagios with more feeling than she; she puts her whole heart and soul into the melody she is rendering and her tone is as beautiful as it is strong".

This sonata is the last of the masterpieces composed by Mozart since the beginning of February.   Six great works in three months! Such wonders are so well known in his case and his biographers have thrown such light on his periods of intense production that we readily imagine him to have spent all his short life working at the same rate. As a matter of fact, these prodigious periods are exceptional; not more than four can be counted in the eleven years of his life in Vienna. This one, and the summer of 1788 when he composed his three last symphonies in six weeks, are the most extraordinary.   Usually, his activity was far more normal and sometimes he would write nothing for months at a time.   The Mozart who wrote untiringly and poured forth without rest or effort his treasures of melody is just a myth.

Between the end of April and September, 1784, composing stopped almost completely.   The concert season was over; the nobility and gentry had scattered; if Mozart composed at all, it was for himself and nothing went down on paper.   He does not seem to have left Vienna, even for his sister's wedding in August; he wrote to promise her a visit the following spring, a promise he was never to fulfil.   At this point the letters to his father which are one of our main sources of information concerning his life come to an end. The correspondence between parent and son did not stop, but, with one exception, no letters after this date have been preserved.   It has been supposed that those destroyed contained allusions to Freemasonry, into which Mozart had been initiated a short time earlier and to which Leopold himself was soon to belong.

After a rather grave illness, which was probably responsible for his not attending his sister's wedding, work was resumed in September with a new piano concerto.   For whom this work, at a time when concerts had not yet started again?   On February the 14th of the following year, Leopold Mozart was staying with Wolfgang and wrote to his daughter: "Sunday" (the 12th) "your brother played a magnificent concerto which he had written for Paradis in Paris" (*nach Paris*).[1]

---

[1] "*Dein Bruder spielte ein herrliches Konzert, das er für die Paradis nach Paris gemacht hatte.*"

Maria Theresia Paradis was a blind pianist and a friend of the Mozarts who had formerly stayed in Salzburg and was planning a tour in Paris.[1] It has generally been assumed that the reference in this letter is to the concerto in B flat, K.456. The "magnificent concerto" cannot be any of the previous ones, for Mozart speaks of all of these several times in his letters and never says that they were written for anyone but Babette Ployer or himself. On the other hand, the D minor is mentioned separately by Leopold in the same letter; there remain the F major, K.459, of December, 1784, and this one. But the F major has the self-assured, proudly joyous and rather external character of those in B flat and D, K.450 and 451, which we know to have been written for himself, whereas the more intimate feeling of K.456, its less showy piano part, connect it with those in E flat and G, K.449 and 453, both of them composed for someone else.

There are, however, objections to accepting it as the concerto mentioned by Leopold, and these apply equally to K.459.

Maria Theresia's stay in Paris had taken place in the first half of the year. She played fourteen times there between April 1st and June 10th. The programmes of her concerts given by the *Journal de Paris* contain works by Kozeluch, Gervais and Haydn, but say nothing of any by Mozart.

The word *nach* is ambiguous. If it means: For Maria Theresia Paradis to take with her *nach Paris*,—Leopold's remark can be explained only if we suppose that Wolfgang had promised a concerto for her tour and that K.456 was a belated carrying out of this promise, nearly four months after she had left France, or that she had planned a second visit which never came off, and for which Wolfgang wrote this concerto.[2]

If the *nach* can be understood as meaning: After her stay in Paris— the remark is intelligible. Maria Theresia Paradis, having returned to Austria, had asked him for a concerto, which he completed in September. But there are difficulties in the way of accepting *nach* in this sense. The identity of the *herrliches Konzert* must therefore remain doubtful.[3]

I. The orchestra is as large as in the G major but the scope of the

---

[1] Haydn composed his concerto in G for her.

[2] Perhaps for the *Concerts Spirituels* in Advent.

[3] Cf. H. Ullrich: *Marie-Therese Paradis and Mozart* (Music and Letters, October, 1946).

Ex. 175

Ex. 176

Ex. 180

Ex. 177

Ex. 178

Ex. 179

work is smaller, its aim less ambitious. Very Mozartish, this concerto is nevertheless far from containing all Mozart. In the E flat, K.449, the musician had displayed the variety and instability of his moods; in the B flat, his joy in success; in the D major, his pride and strength; and his joy in covering much ground in little space in the G major. Here, he draws in and exhibits but a small part of his riches.

The tutti which opens the allegro contains nearly all the important elements of the movement; the only one absent is the piano's special theme. Its personality breathes mildness. No abrupt modulations, like the dive into E flat in the concerto in G; a mainly smooth rhythm, where one recognizes the march of the three last concertos, firm but supple, without roughness or haste, and a readiness to slacken and pass from crotchets and quavers to minims and semibreves (ex. 179). Instead of the vigorous repeated notes of K.451 and 453, the gentle undulations of broken thirds, fourths or fifths preponderate in the accompaniment and give the movement its velvety softness.

The themes themselves have this soft, reticent character. They all show a strong family likeness.[1] Three of them contain the same figure (ex. 175 a). Four give prominence to repeated notes and in three cases the note repeated is the tonic. They tend to return to the tonic and rest on it. The figure of the falling and rising scale (ex. 175 b) is common to two of them; all avoid wide intervals and move usually in conjunct, or at least proximate, degrees. Quiet, rather lyrical, their outlines are not clear-cut. There is in them neither drama nor eloquence, and they are melodically undistinguished.

And yet this tutti is not monotonous. Twice over, without ceasing to be mild, it introduces variety; once at the opening of the second subject; once before the concluding theme. In both passages, the rhythm slows down and the emotion concentrates into chords. The first is perhaps the finest moment in the allegro; a silence marks it off from what precedes; uncanny progressions lead it into B flat minor, and at the end, when one expects to hear the second subject enter in the minor, it rediscovers the major with arresting simplicity (ex. 177). The subject itself (ex. 178) would pass unnoticed but for what went before it; admirably enhanced by this preparation, by the great circuit which Mozart makes to bring it in, its innocence is almost dramatic. By seeking afar what he had at hand, Mozart makes us

---

[1] The first subject occurs in a concerto of John Christian Bach, op. 13, IV (bars 5-6 of the first movement); it had already been used by Mozart in the andante of his violin sonata in B flat, K. 378.

believe that he sets great store by it.   Seldom does he set off his themes
by delaying them so long; seldom does he appear to consider them so
important.

On the brink of his conclusion he uses a device which had succeeded
in the G major (ex. 153 a and b).   Over a *cantus* given out by the
strings he superimposes when repeating it a woodwind descant (ex.
179).

In its dynamic marks, the movement shows a favourite *galant* practice, frequent in these concertos: the *piano* exposition of the first
subject, followed without transition by a *forte* passage;[1] the second
subject and its long preparation given out softly; and a concluding
forte.

As in the three last concertos, the scoring gives as much weight to
wind as to strings: one wonders even whether the wind is not favoured.
The two groups are opposed, mass against mass, in the first subject,
as in K.450, and they mingle in the *forte* transition theme (ex. 176)
which follows.   The fine modulating preparation of the second subject combines both, but leaves each one its individuality; questions
and answers succeed quickly but the parts remain distinct.   The second
subject itself belongs to the wind and at first the strings accompany
them with repeated thirds; in the codetta the wind play alone.   There
is the same opposition of groups in the concluding subject (ex. 180).
Simpler than its immediate predecessors in key progression, rhythm
and melody, this concerto is their equal in orchestration.

The solo exposition follows the same paths as the tutti.   It neglects
none of the contents of the latter and adds two fresh passages: the
first, before the second subject—the solo theme; the other, before
the conclusion.   Its innovations are therefore insertions; in other
respects it goes over, almost bar by bar, the opening tutti, modulating
to the dominant at the beginning of the solo subject and decorating
and enriching the orchestration with the piano part.   The chief
interest lies in this intervention of the solo.   Thus, piano and wind
fill in the silence which, in ex. 175, marked off the different parts of
the theme; in the repeat of the transitional subject, ex. 176, the right
hand accompanies the hautboys and flute with a figure of repeated
broken octaves which plays an important part in the andante.   The
wind descant, ex. 179, is replaced by a piano flourish, and hautboy,
flute and bassoon merely double the strings.   As in the tutti, the

---

[1] With variations of detail, we meet it in more than half of Mozart's Vienna
concertos: K.414, 415, 450, 453, 456, 459, 466, 467, 488, 491, 537.

moment of greatest loveliness is the announcement of the second subject; when the rest is forgotten, one remembers still the way in which the piano filigrees play round the austere lines of the orchestra and soften their harshness with their wavering contours and shimmering chromaticisms (ex. 181 a and b; cf. with ex. 177).

The solo subject has the same character as the others; we find in it the repeated notes, the falling and rising scale and the accompaniment of undulating thirds and fourths.   On the whole, the piano part is much less brilliant than in the concertos which we know to have been written for Mozart himself.   The writing recalls that of the G major, but chords are more frequent, both in the piano transposition of the orchestral theme, ex. 179, and in the solo passages, repeated at a few bars interval, which follow it (ex. 182).   This is a somewhat uncommon feature in Mozart, whose style, in this respect, lags behind that of some of his contemporaries.

As in the two previous concertos, the orchestra is well occupied; the strings, discreet but indispensable, take part even in the solo theme.   The second subject is given out by the wind and the piano takes it up as it is repeated.   Seldom does the solo have a completely free hand; even in the great virtuosity passage at the end, the wind add an accompaniment figure of an individual nature.

The *development* is neither a *fantasia* nor a thematic working-out but a mixture of the two.   The beginning and end comprise new elements, *cantabile* passages given to the piano.[1]   But the middle is a series of repetitions in the orchestra of ex. 180, the martial, square-cut rhythm of which carries scale passages in the piano; scales and figure progress in fourths through various keys, from D minor to B flat. The presence of this figure gives the *development* a certain thematic character, whilst the incessant modulation and the nature of the solo part assimilate it to the *fantasias* of the previous concertos.   But it is far from soaring like them; it is the least attractive part of the movement and one of the least interesting *developments* in Mozart's greater concertos.

The reprise takes place with the mildness that characterizes the whole movement.   There is no rise in the emotional pitch at the end of the *development*; just a short obligatory piano cadenza, accompanied, and *in tempo*; then, three bars of transition in the woodwind, in long notes, rising from soft to loud, bring back the first subject, on whose arrival everything drops again to *piano*.

The recapitulation has few surprises for us.   Sometimes, after omitting in the solo exposition themes given out in the first tutti, Mozart retrieves them in the last section.   Here, he has not allowed

---

[1] The first of these constitutes a new subject.   The introduction of a new subject at the beginning of the *development*, the invention of which practice Torrefranca attributes to Sammartini, is fairly frequent in Mozart's chamber music (cf. K.458, 478, 575), but rare in his concertos (cf. K.414).

himself the chance of doing so and the recapitulation reproduces in its main lines the solo exposition, keeping, of course, to the key of B flat. The main changes are in the decoration which the piano adds to the first subject. Even the bravura passages are faithfully repeated; nevertheless, at the last moment, as if such literalness had ended by annoying him, Mozart introduces in midmost solo two astonishing bars of woodwind, highly personal in their chromaticisms (ex. 183: they follow what corresponds, in the recapitulation, to ex. 182), the only true "surprise" in this, the best behaved and most conventional first movement in all Mozart's Vienna concertos.[1] Right at the end of the solo the return of ex. 180, accompanied by piano scales, is a felicitous recall of the beginning of the *development*. The more pleasing of the two cadenzas written by the composer for this concerto, the first, contains a noteworthy chord passage based on ex. 179, which itself returns in the last tutti, with its flute descant.

Every work of art worthy of the name creates a world of its own. It induces in those who approach it a particular mood, perhaps not identical with that in which the artist found himself when he conceived and carried it out, and liable to vary from observer to observer, but the existence of which is undeniable. Our awareness of this mood, different with each work, constitutes what we may call its *world*.

The differences between such *worlds* are infinite; no two great works induce the same mood. Nevertheless, generally speaking, the world into which a work leads us belongs to one of two sorts, according as it is contained in time or is outside it. This is independent of its medium. A work belonging to an art whose formal exigencies require duration, like poetry or music, may nevertheless be outside time; whilst a picture may, in the sense we intend, imply its presence. For it is not by its form that art participates in time; it is by the conditions obtaining in the mind of the artist at the moment he conceives his creation.

There are *crisis* works, whose whole existence arises from an experience in time, having, like a drama, beginning, middle and end. Their world, when one enters it, has but a limited duration; they have a conflict to resolve, a course to run; this task once completed, their world vanishes. Everything in it is movement and becoming; instinctively, we identify ourselves with these works and call them *dramatic*. This is independent of the medium; although it occurs more seldom in painting, sculpture, architecture, than in literature and

---

[1] Cf. a comparable outburst at a similar point in the allegro of K.537.

music, there too the work may have the qualities of a drama and imply the existence of a precise and supremely important moment. Such an element is recognizable, for instance, in sculpture like the tympanum of Autun cathedral, in the painting of Van Gogh, in many a Flamboyant or Baroque piece of architecture.

Other works, on the contrary, belong to a universe in which time has no part. They are born outside it, outside a precise moment in their author's life, and their world is unchanging. It is the same in all its parts. It seems to have existed from all eternity; we go into it in our turn, we experience its domination, we bathe in its atmosphere; but we do not identify ourselves with it, as we did the drama of the *crisis* works; it will go on living when we leave it. All forms of art can call forth this world, as well as the other, but none as fully as music and architecture. We *enter* a motet of Byrd or Palestrina, or a fugue of Bach, as we enter Westminster Abbey, and we leave it similarly. You can go into the cathedral by any door you please; you can begin many fugues (not all, of course, for some fugues are dramatic) at different points; no doubt the composer intended them to be played from beginning to end, but you can nevertheless begin at one or other entry without the work becoming thereby nonsensical. Its world, like the cathedral's, is accessible through several doors. And when we leave the cathedral, we know that its world will persist, that we can enter it again as often as we like, that we shall find it again every time we cross its threshold. The world of the fugue and motet, likewise, which predates our hearing of the music, will endure, unchanged, when the notes have ceased sounding. We enter and leave it at will.

What a difference with *crisis* works! These bear witness to a moment in the artist's life; they have an historic or at least a biographical significance; like a drama, they unfold in a time sequence and any disarrangement in it makes them unintelligible. Their episodes follow each other as inevitably as those of the conflict whence they spring; you cannot make your way in where you choose; you must go through the door and there is only one. Their world lasts only as long as the recital of the conflict; once this is over, it scatters and will not live again till you choose yourself to live through the drama once more.

The world of the movement we have just quitted does not belong to this category. In it, everything is description, not drama; environment, not crisis; being, not becoming; rest, not action; stability, not change. No experience, bounded in time, unfolding like a drama— even like a happy drama—stands behind this still music, one of the few completely still allegros that Mozart has left us. Its world is without boundaries or frontiers; we enter it where we will, by the gate of our choosing; the obligation to follow the movement in the order of the notes is a purely formal one. The only reason that prevents us from stopping at the end of the exposition or beginning at the *development*, or from repeating this or that section, is that we should upset the order of key sequence: a valid reason, no doubt, but a formal one, not affecting in any way the meaning of the work. It would be much less serious to change the order of the different sections and the tonic-dominant-tonic sequence than to intervert two of the variations in the andante that follows it, although all of them, save one, are in the same key, for it is a dramatic movement and its episodes succeed each other in an order prescribed, not by rules, but the law of its own emotion. The allegro, on the other hand, is comparable to the cathedral whose world has neither beginning nor end in time, or to a landscape with quiet outlines and indefinite horizons, which we can approach from all sides, where we can sojourn as long as we like.

We would not dare to say this of the other concertos of this year. K.449 is to a high degree the experience of a moment; K.451 is a work of passion, expressive, it is true, of happiness and triumph, but passionate notwithstanding. And if the word passion appears too violent for K.450 and 453, there too, nevertheless, the first movements are narratives and not descriptions. It would not be hard to show, by means of a purely formal analysis, to what extent this dramatic element is lacking in K.456; that its themes, with their soft outlines, are hardly distinguishable one from the other and mingle their personalities; and especially that Mozart, by laying almost all his cards on the table at the first stroke and repeating in his first solo all the elements of the tutti, deprives himself of the possibility of causing us surprises, without which there can be no dramatic interest. But that is touching merely outward signs; the static, non-dramatic quality of the movement resides in the thought which inspires it.

Therefore let us not reproach it with its absence of surprises and contrasts and its lack of variation in emotional pitch. Let us wander without effort in these peaceful vales; let us yield without reserve to their pervasive influence; they cannot exert it if we persist in seeking to receive from them strong impressions which they do not desire to impart.

II. The andante consists in variations, an uncommon form in the important works of Mozart, who generally treats the *air varié* as a trifle.

It is the first concerto andante in a minor key since the *Sinfonia Concertante*, K.364, and, in the piano concertos, since the E flat, K.271, of 1777. There seems to be some relation in Mozart's andantes between the variation form and sadness, for most of those which adopt it, in important works of his maturity, express a feeling of melancholy.[1]

There is no need to say that a movement in G minor forms a complete contrast with the allegro. Mozart is not, of course, the only musician to put side by side the reverse and obverse of the medal, mildness and passion; but the opposition between two moods is particularly sharp in him, not only from one movement to another but also between different sections of the same movement. The transitions, which sometimes take the shape of conflicts, by which a Beethoven or a Franck passes from darkness to light are very rare with him; he prefers to turn the picture round suddenly and show one face after the other.[2]

The variation, we said, is a form he uses seldom in his serious work. But it happens that in 1784 and 1785 he has recourse to it several times: in three of his concertos and in his string quartet in A.[3] These four movements, with the finales of the serenade and concerto in C minor and the andantino of the divertimento for string trio, K.563, are the most interesting examples he has left of this form.

When he introduces variations into an unimportant work, he expends his ingenuity, like other *galant* composers, on decorating the melodic line of the air varied. He brings in a few superficial changes of rhythm, but the harmonies remain much the same from one variation to the next. Music-lovers of the end of the 18th century, who made a Gargantuan consumption of *airs variés*, liked to hear their favourite theme as often as possible, and the composer's task was to present it to them with just enough variety to avoid monotony.

Such is, on the whole, the goal in the variations of the B flat concerto, K.450, where the changes bear mainly on the accompaniment.[4] But the three other examples of the year aim higher. Those of the G major concerto, nos. 4 and 5, bring forward new versions of the

---

[1] The D minor variations of the divertimento in D, K.334; those, in D minor also and akin to them, of the violin sonata in F, K.377; the C minor andante of the piano concerto in E flat, K.482, whose form is a cross between variations and rondo.

[2] See the discussion of this point in IV, 1, pp. 327–9.

[3] Without counting an *air varié*, K.455.

[4] Including under this term the piano ornamentation.

theme, and in the presto decompose it and reconstitute it again. The coda of the variations of the A major quartet goes further and launches out into a grandiose development, surpassing in scope all the rest of the movement.

The andante of our concerto is worthy of the neighbourhood of these two movements. Formally, it is less ambitious than they, but it surpasses them in strength and depth of feeling. It consists in a theme and five variations followed by a coda which corresponds in length to a sixth one. The theme, in which the rhythm ♫ ♩ predominates, is divided into two parts; the first has eight bars grouped two by two; the second breaks the symmetry with a codetta which prolongs it to thirteen.[1] The first variation has repeats, like the theme; the second, third and fourth are double; that is, the repeats are themselves varied, so that the subject is varied in reality twice within each variation; the fifth is single and flows into the coda.

Except in the *major* variation, the harmonic basis remains the same; the most important alterations are in the third, which is also the most daring in rhythmic and melodic changes. The outline of the theme remains intact in those variations (nos. 2 and 5) where the *cantus* belongs to the tutti and the decorations to the piano; in the third, where piano and tutti are contrasted, and the fourth, where it is so much altered that it is practically a new subject, it undergoes notable changes. The original rhythm is altered only in the third variation.

Except, again, in the *major* variation, the changes consist in breakings up and diminutions of the melody by the piano (nos. 1 and 3); in decorations of the theme with demi-semi-quavers (nos. 2 and 5); in differences of scoring; and in a renewal of the melody and especially of the rhythm (no. 3, the only *minor* variation where the orchestra is entrusted with the task of varying).

The piano never expounds the theme in its original state. In the first variation it decorates it with sobriety. In the repeats of no. 3 it does likewise, but here its alterations are less purely decorative and affect also the significance. In the *major* variation it is content with repeating, with very little ornamentation, the theme in the new form in which the wind have just given it out. The decoration it adds in the second and fifth variations consists in arpeggios and scale fragments in one case and in repeated broken octaves in the other; these latter give it a certain impressionistic character; the style is rather different

---

[1] Except in the *major* variation, where the second part is eight bars long like the first.

from Mozart's usual piano writing, where misty effects are uncommon. In the coda, a dialogue arises between the solo and the orchestra and decoration gives way to the mere repetition of thematic fragments.

We said that the order of these variations revealed a dramatic inspiration. They are indeed the story of an emotional experience full of anguish, of that dramatic anguish which will fill the G minor quintet and which, in this same concerto, reappears most unexpectedly for an instant in the finale. The theme, which resembles a French *ariette* rather than a German or Italian song, expresses despair carried almost to a point of physical suffering, but without agitation, without a hint of rebellion. We are at a later stage than that of revolt, at the last moments of a tragedy. It is an expression of that complete hopelessness, that utter disillusion, accepted without attitudes or eloquence and all the more poignant, which 18th-century music renders with an intensity seldom equalled by the passionate and feverish cries of Romanticism (ex. 184).[1]

The piano repeats this lament with ever so slight a touch of dreaming or meditation; by diminishing the note values it holds the movement back and likens it to recitative; it is as if it recoiled upon its own emotion and took delight in it (var. 1; ex. 185). The wind give it out again in its primitive shape (var. 2); then, in the repeat, strings and piano combine. The theme is expounded by the first violins, still unchanged, and the piano surrounds it with expressive embroidery where arpeggios predominate (ex. 186). The second half is treated likewise. The stress increases slightly; the nature of the feeling remains unaltered.

The orchestra then breaks out in a *sforzando*, after which everything drops again to *piano* except the violas and basses which rush to the attack with scales of demi-semi-quavers (ex. 187). They end by carrying the other strings with them and giving them a series of jerks (a) to which correspond repeated chords in the wind. The piano resists this fury and returns, dreamier than ever, to the mood of the first variation (ex. 188). The impatience and irritation of the orchestra at the sight of such disdainful aloofness hardly leave it time to finish and when it reaches its conclusion the raging scales again surge upwards. This time they infect all instruments and follow each other with dramatic imitations. After two bars of truce, the vigorous figure (a) resounds throughout the orchestra and we finish with a return of the scales. This time, the piano reply betrays a little more

---

[1] The example gives only the upper parts.

agitation, but on the whole it maintains its own position against the orchestra and the opposition between them makes this variation the most stirring in the andante.

After this outburst of wrath, the only one in the movement, mildness prevails again. In the exquisite *major* variation, the theme, transformed, is given to the hautboys, and the flute answers with a free canon at the octave (ex. 189). The piano repeats it in a new form. Is it peace, and has the vanishing of the hopeless mood suddenly opened the heavens to us? The return to G minor proves that it was but a respite of calm, a night of happy dreams amid successive days of suffering.

The violins take up the theme for the last time and the piano's commentary transforms it. The embroidery line in the bass and the repeated broken octaves in the right hand add a restrained quivering, all the more impressive for its being *piano* (ex. 190). There is no repeat and in the second half the subject is divided between strings and wind and the accompaniment confines itself mostly to the quivering treble octaves. The motion does not stop this time with the end of the theme but, with light *sforzandos* against the beat in the hautboys and basses, and rising passion, climbs to a dominant close, the climax, after which the coda, calmer but not less despairing, unfolds itself. Like warriors recalling the episodes in the struggle on the evening of a battle, woodwind and piano converse upon the first notes of the theme, against the ever-darkening background of strings, and the movement dies down with the violins humming in feverish throbs (ex. 191).

III. The finale is in 6–8 time, like those of Mozart's two other Vienna concertos in B flat. This is the only feature which its refrain has in common with theirs. It is, on the other hand, strangely like the theme of the andante (ex. 192). But the likeness is one of those which strike the eye and not the ear. It would be wrong to think it intentional. It is not meaningless, however; it arises because Mozart, in composing this concerto, and in spite of the difference between its

movements, was haunted by the figure and themes

with repeated notes, prominent in all three. His choice of themes betrays this perhaps unconscious obsession.[1]

It is a sonata rondo like most of the finales in his Vienna concertos, but its plan differs greatly from those of the sonata rondos we have studied hitherto. The piano starts it but gives out only a small part of the refrain (ex. 192). The orchestra repeats it and in the course of some fifty bars pours out a flow of melody which appears to form one single idea but which later on breaks up and provides four or five motifs, destined to come back separately and to act as links between the main sections. This structural device is peculiar to his rondos

---

[1] A Kozeluch trio in G minor, "op. 24 or 27" (sic), affords a curious coincidence with exs. 184 and 192 and, more curiously still, recalls for the ear as well as for the eye these two themes which, when we hear them, do not recall each other (ex. 193)! The melody recalls the andante and the rhythm the rondo. The refrain of the rondo is also met with in an unfinished string quintet in E flat, reproduced by Jahn and Abert (App. II; Einstein-Köchel, no. 613 a).

and we noticed it in the first and third movements of K.413.[1]   We
quote three of these motifs (exs. 194, 195, 196).

This long prelude, which corresponds to a first-movement tutti,
since nearly all its elements are made use of in the course of the rondo,
finishes up in the tonic.   The first couplet or episode which starts
at this moment has the form of a sonata exposition.   The first subject
(ex. 197) is given out by the piano and followed by a fairly long solo
into which its first notes intrude from time to time to remind us of
our starting-point.   The orchestra has little to say; at distant intervals,
a bar of woodwind links up the different solo strains.   We modulate
quickly through E flat, C minor and G minor, and land in F.

The second subject then displays its lopsided mass; it advances
with the nimble haste of a cripple, one of whose crutches has been
stolen, and who pursues the thief brandishing the other.[2]   The woodwind mock it (ex. 198) and, when it changes places and gives itself to
the hautboy and bassoon, the piano jeers at it too.   After another solo
in which the orchestra is a little less reticent, a fragment of the refrain
is heard, ex. 195; the woodwind give it out, then, while they repeat
it, ﹒the piano answers with a variant of ex. 194 (ex. 199).   After a
third fragment, ex. 196, we halt in B flat upon a dominant seventh
chord, whence an extempore solo cadenza brings us back to the
refrain.

If the *development* of the allegro disappointed us after the *fantasia
developments* of the previous concertos, what comes now may console
us.   After the repetition of the refrain, the orchestra rapidly rids itself
of the bonds that tied it to the B flat-F alternation and to the mild
and festive world of the first couplet; it traverses with rising audacity
and passion the keys of E flat and C minor and, without changing its
figure—a fragment of the refrain—proclaims the key of B minor,
whose dusky reign spreads over the middle section of the rondo.

A silence; then the piano confirms the proclamation.   And now,
each one with a different rhythm with impressive singleness of notes
and purpose, bassoon, violins and solo emphasize the new key.   The
flute and the hautboy alone have held notes; the violins crackle furiously; the bassoon moves in great strides against the stormy sky across
which zigzag the piano arpeggios (ex. 200).[3]   All this, however

---

[1] Cf. pp. 130 and 134.
[2] Cf. the refrain of the rondo in the G minor quintet, K.516.
[3] The bassoon and violin parts are not accompaniments and should be
played prominently to equal the strength of the piano; the nature of the
passage is not expressed if the piano arpeggios preponderate like a solo.

Ex. 191

Ex. 192

Ex. 193

Ex. 194

Ex. 195

Ex. 196

Ex. 197

Ex. 198

Ex. 199

Ex. 200

Ex. 201

dramatic, is but preparation; the stage is set, the world called up; the voice has now to speak.

Bassoon, hautboy and flute are silent; the strings start an accompaniment of repeated chords and against this restless background the piano gives out a tragic recitative (ex. 201). It has a familiar sound and is laden with associations, even for us who know but by hearsay the music tragedies of the 18th century; even we are reminded of at least one masterpiece of the century, the contralto aria in the St. John Passion, and the years which have elapsed since then have enriched it with Beethoven's 'cello sonata in A and his op. 110.[1]

The voice ceases and the storm, momentarily arrested, resumes its angry course. It travels through the skies of minor keys, from B to E, to D and B flat, proclaiming each time the furious assertions of ex. 200 which the message of the recitative has exasperated instead of appeased. Then the intensity drops to *piano*, the storm moves off; minor turns into major; while the recall of a passage which had preceded ex. 198 in the first couplet announces the disappearance of one world and the return to another.

This episode, only some thirty bars long, is the most stirring part of the rondo and perhaps of the whole concerto. With its harmless opening, this movement puts side by side in rash propinquity the mild, durationless world of the allegro and the world of conflict of the variations. No example could light up more clearly the distinction we made between the two. Bold though it be, it is not without precedent, for it falls into the tradition of the *minor* couplets of French rondos whose unrecognizable prodigy-offspring it is.

In a regular sonata rondo we should now hear the refrain once more. But the tornado we have come through carries us beyond that stage and the appearance of ex. 192, carefree and skipping, would jar painfully on our quivering nerves. So the movement passes straight away to the third couplet with ex. 197, whose more reserved merriment does not offend us with an indecent contrast.

The sonata rondo in which the second return of the refrain is missing and the second couplet joins on without a break to the recapitulation appears some ten times in Mozart, thrice in his piano concertos.[2]

[1] Middle of the first movement; *arioso dolente*. Mozart was to remember it two years later in another work as remote from tragedy as this one, the fourth horn concerto, K.495.

[2] K. 456, 459 and 488. Among other instances of this form are the rondos of the sonata for two pianos, the quintet for piano and wind instruments, the two quartets for piano and strings and the divertimento for string trio.

The omission of the refrain is not always as dramatically significant as it is here. In some of them, the second couplet itself is much reduced and the form comes near to that of the rondo in two couplets, where the second repeats the first and the last traces of the *development* are a few bars of modulation, after the first return of the refrain.[1]

The third couplet or recapitulation follows the lines of the first, except that it does not modulate to F. The few differences are in the figuring of the piano runs and in a witty insertion of three bars at the end of the last solo, where hautboy and second horn forestall the tutti entry by punctuating the piano passages with the first bars of the refrain. Ex. 194 leads to the pause for which Mozart has left a short cadenza which incorporates bits of the refrain, of exs. 198 and 201 and of a run from the last solo. The final return of the refrain is divided between orchestra and piano which relieve each other with gusto every two or three bars. The exs. 199 and 196 conclude the movement.

This concerto has a twin most unlike it, the fiery piano sonata in C minor, completed four days later. Several times in his life Mozart wrote two important works in quick succession and in most cases there was between them a contrast of inspiration as complete as between the first and second movements of this concerto or between the concerto as a whole and this sonata. The concertos in D minor and C, K.466 and 467, in 1785, the quintets in C and G minor in 1787, the symphonies in G minor and C in 1788 are illustrious examples of this coupling of two opposites.[2] The quick succession of two such different works is but another manifestation of his tendency to pass without transition from one aspect of reality to another, to show abruptly the other side of the medal. Obviously, the variations and the dramatic episode in the rondo of the concerto could form a link with the sonata; but, in spite of the likeness between all Mozart's *minor* compositions, it is a far cry from the melodious and dramatic sorrow of the first to the burning passion of the second, whose allegro

---

[1] As in the quintets in C and G minor and the *Coronation* concerto, K.537.

[2] Here are some others: the quartets in D minor and E flat (June-July, 1783); the concertos in A and C minor (March, 1786); and, without emotional contrast, the quartets in A and C (January, 1785); the concerto in C, K.503, and the *Pragne* symphony (December 4th and 6th, 1786); the quartets in B flat and F (May-June, 1790).

flies up as straight as a tongue of flame and whose expressive power is concentrated more in rhythm than in melody.

Five weeks after the concerto Mozart entered in the list of his compositions another B flat work, the quartet known as the *Hunt.* Here, we are nearer the world of K.456. Compared with the three previous quartets of the "Haydn" series, it appears somewhat superficial. Has the habit of the platform led Mozart to produce a more fashionable work? In any case, it belongs truly enough to the lineage of the concertos and the Strinasacchi sonata. In the andante, we hear an echo of the anguish which inspired the variations of K.456; on the other hand, the sunny counterpoint in the finale announces the concerto in F.

6. The Fifteenth Concerto: K.459 in F

CONCERTO No. 15 IN F (K.459)[1]
Finished December 11th, 1784
    Allegro: ¢
    Allegretto: 6-8 (in C)
    Allegro assai: 2-4
Orchestra: Strings; flute, two hautboys, two horns, two bassoons.

THE works of the autumn of 1784 succeeded each other at less prodigious speed than those of the winter and spring. From October to January they spread out at the rate of one a month: the C minor sonata on October 4th, the B flat quartet on November 9th, this concerto on December 11th, the quartet in A on January 10th. And, with one exception, this was the rate at which they were to appear throughout the following twelvemonth.

The new concerto is of the same race as its five predecessors. Composed almost certainly for Mozart himself,[2] its inspiration is near to that of the B flat and D major, K.450 and 451. It sings the same confidence and happiness, the same triumph of the composer and executant, master of his talent and his public. It sings them in the highest degree and never more in his work shall we hear so whole-hearted a joy so ingenuously expressed. Not a cloud comes to darken, even for an instant, the brilliant sky of the allegro and rondo, and the appearance of the minor in the allegretto, however pathetic, is but passing and exerts no influence over the rest of the movement.

I. If the emotion of the work puts it close to the other concertos of the year, its first movement contains nevertheless a number of elements peculiar to it which distinguish it as clearly from the works that precede it as from those that follow.

What Mozart aims at is clear.

On one hand he wants a movement with numerous and well-marked themes. The first tutti is a succession of somewhat *cantabile*

---

[1] *Gesamtausgabe*, no. 19.

[2] See p. 259.

subjects whose strains are all of much the same length. It is one of his most varied and most loosely knit first tuttis. Moreover, after the first subject, nothing preponderates; the other themes are all of equal importance and none of them turns out to be the second subject, not even a mock second subject (as in K.450 and some concertos of the years to come). From this multiplicity of themes arises the divergence between the tutti and the solo exposition. Only one half of the former and one third of the latter comprise elements common to both.

On the other hand he wants this rather rhapsodical diversity of the opening to be compensated by the predominance of the first subject throughout the rest of the movement. It predominates through its rhythm, almost always present, even in the solo passages, and through its melody, reminders of which are frequent. The presence of one same accompaniment figure in the piano part is also an element of unity, and the absence of exceptional modulations is perhaps due to this same concern for singleness.

Finally he wants a movement which returns to the ideal of K.451 and where the orchestra shall be as important as the solo. In no other concerto are the bars where the orchestra predominates and where the solo confines itself to accompanying or decorating its part so numerous. And, as in four earlier concertos of this year, the wind have parts as personal as those of the strings.

Throughout the movement, whether the orchestra or the piano be to the fore, square-cut phrases of two or four bars preponderate; in the uniformity of its rhythm, this concerto is unique.

All this converges towards one object: the expression of a single feeling which infuses the whole movement, to an even higher degree than in the last concerto.

Let us look more closely at some of these points.

There is no need to indicate in more detail the multiplicity of themes in the opening tutti. Six can be counted after the first subject. The first of them is a bird of passage which does not return; the next two figure fairly prominently in the solo exposition and recapitulation; the other three in the recapitulation only. They have distinct personalities: all those that make their first appearance in the solo exposition, on the other hand, derive from the first subject. It is as if Mozart, once the end of the tutti reached, had been frightened at his wastefulness and felt he must economize.

Let us make the acquaintance of this first subject and follow it through the movement. Here it is, as it comes forward at the beginning, *piano*, given out by the typically Mozartian combination of

Ex. 202

Ex. 203

Ex. 204

Ex. 205

Ex. 206

violins and flute (ex. 202). We recognize the march rhythm with which the three last concertos had also begun. It is repeated, *forte*, in the wind doubled by the violins—a fresh example of the *galant* formula of a soft opening followed by a *forte*. Its strophic character

and its division into four-bar sections are obvious.   Its second part is
similar (ex. 203).   We meet it again at the beginning of the solo
exposition, first in the piano only, then in the hautboys and bassoons,
accompanied by the solo (ex. 204).[1]   After the short and rather insignificant solo subject, with which the movement concerns itself no
further, the wind, instead of letting the piano perform its bravura
passage without interruption, recall in imitation the opening notes of
the theme (ex. 205) and it is to its rhythm, with its triplet accompaniment which now becomes an integral part of the subject, and partly
with its very notes, that the piano throws itself into its first solo (ex.
206).   But at the end of nine bars, the flute and then the bassoon
return with the fragment (a) of ex. 202 which ends by being
not only the title but also the matter and the signature of the
movement, and the piano meekly resumes its accompaniment
triplets (ex. 207).

The second subject's entry dethrones the dotted rhythm and the
triplets for an instant, but not the two and four-bar phrases; as soon as
tutti and piano have given it out, however, march rhythm in the
orchestra and triplets in the piano begin again and after a few bars of
virtuosity lead up once more to ex. 202, the last three bars of which
are repeated by the wind in C minor, whilst the piano supports them
with its untiring triplets.   The end of the solo contains at first elements
from the first tutti, but as soon as the usual trill sounds the end of the
exposition, the whole band starts a fine working-out with (a).   Beginning *forte* and in the treble, it sweeps grandly down to the bass, whence,
after two bars of minims and semibreves, it climbs back to the treble
and modulates to A minor, the key in which the piano re-enters for
the *development* (ex. 229).

The middle part has the free and easy ways of a *fantasia development* but even here the dotted rhythm does not slumber and, in the
wind parts, it punctuates the piano's two-bar phrases and ends by
spreading to the right hand.   The triplets, of course, are not
inactive, and except for the explosive chord, struck twice over,[2]
which opens the section, they do not cease for a single beat in one
hand or the other.   And when the solo stops on the dominant
chord of D minor, it is still to the rhythm of (a) that, with one of

---

[1] In performance, the wind should stand out and the impression should
not be given that the piano triplets are the chief thing.

[2] Cf. p. 300 for the likeness between this passage and the andante of the
D minor concerto.

those short cuts customary in Mozart at such points, we reach the recapitulation—we cannot say, return to the first subject, for we have never left it (ex. 208).

Its mastery is almost undisputed throughout the recapitulation. The second subject is episodic, as it was earlier—a mere interlude, like so many second subjects in these concertos, whose presence does not affect in any way, it seems, the course of the movement. After it, the same dotted rhythm calls, the same triplet passages and the same echoes of (a) continue.

It is still to the tune of the first subject that the orchestra announces the cadenza. This, one of the finest that Mozart has left, strides up the keyboard in triplet arpeggios and starts off for a brief adventure on the stilts of (a) before condescending to the neglected second subject, and closes with a return to the triplets.

But in the conclusion—a tardy revenge by all that is neither march rhythm nor triplets!—the movement discards them completely. The orchestra repeats unchanged the last twenty bars of the tutti that had not been heard since the solo entry and the movement finishes without alluding again to the obsessive ex. 202.

Such concern with one rhythm, one theme, one accompaniment figure, is unparalleled in these concertos and is the chief originality of this movement. But this feature which is peculiar to it is not more attractive than another which it shares with its predecessor in D, to wit, the equality of orchestra and solo and the practice on the piano's part of repeating orchestral passages, accompanying or decorating them the while. These passages, less continuous than in the D major, are four in number. The first occurs in the second half of the first subject (ex. 203); the left hand displaces the violas and basses and the right hand adds a decorative counterpoint (ex. 209). The second is in a passage in minims of the first tutti to which the piano contributes a brilliant arpeggio decoration (ex. 210). In the other two the novelty consists in the substitution of piano for violins in the repeat of a strings and wind dialogue in the first tutti, and of a passage from the end of the exposition where the seconds accompanied the enunciation of the first subject by the wind (ex. 211; towards the end of the last solo).

This concerto is no more dramatic than the last. It has no story to tell and no action to reproduce; it is content with radiating a mood of youthful happiness, irresistibly cordial. The symmetrical cut of its phrases and the springing step of its accompaniments make it a kind of dance; despite its rhythm, its texture is too light and too

diaphanous for it to be a march.   It is a relaxation and a game, every
movement of which is carried out to a ballet step.

For some people, says Tovey, all Mozart's concertos are alike . . .
just as, for some, all Chinamen appear alike.   But a superficial
acquaintance with the works of 1784 at any rate is enough to make
us capable of distinguishing them.   At second sight, one cannot confuse the restlessness of the E flat, the confidence and grace of the first
B flat, K.450, like a girl who is pretty and knows it, the "soldierly"
pride of the D major, the mixture of tears and smiles, the "middle
course" of that in G, the mildness of the second B flat, K.456, and
finally the carefree but self-assured joy of this one.   So many works,
so many different moods, so many worlds!

In form, and confining ourselves to first movements, the differences are as great.   Let us review quickly the main points of comparison between this concerto and its predecessors.

It is like the first B flat in the placing of its themes and the absence
of the second subject from the opening tutti.   It is like the D major
in that it repeats passages already given out by the orchestra and adds
to them, or inserts in them, a piano part, and in that it treats the
orchestra as the solo's equal.   It resembles both, and also the second
B flat, in the absence of modulations in the opening tutti and, generally,
throughout the movement.   Finally, it is like all the others except the
E flat (where the wind parts are optional) in the importance it gives to
flute, hautboys and bassoons.

It is unlike all, except the first B flat, in that its first tutti is an introduction rather than an *argument* of what follows and in that the solo
exposition, instead of going over its traces, departs from them.   And its
lack of modulations distinguishes it from the G major and especially
the E flat, the most modulating of all the concertos.

It is unique, finally, in that its first tutti, amongst its many motifs,
contains neither second subject nor mock second subject, in that it
departs so little from the rhythm and melody of the first subject, and
in the uniform design of its phrases, where two and four-bar divisions
predominate.

This comparative analysis confirms the impression we had already,
that it is closest to the two concertos which, like it, were written for
Mozart himself—the B flat, K.450, and the D—and farthest from the
three composed for others—the E flat, G and B flat, K.456.[1]

.   .   .   .   .

---

[1] With the reservations made on p. 259.

II. The second movement is a 6–8 allegretto which has somewhat the nature of a Brahms intermezzo. The absence of a slow movement is characteristic of this work, whose joyous high spirits are so foreign to meditation. An andante or an adagio, after such a first movement,

Ex. 211

Ex. 212

Ex. 213

Ex. 214

Ex. 215

Ex. 216

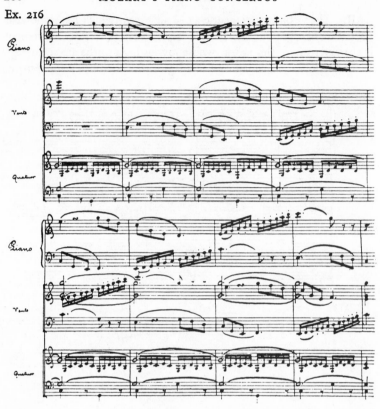

would be a contrast, and Mozart, returning to the ideal of homogeneity which had inspired the G major, avoids contrasts.[1]

---

[1] It may be that Mozart had thought at first of a movement in a more
usual *tempo*. Among the concerto fragments in the Mozarteum there is
the beginning of an andante in C, Köchel-Einstein 466 a, the scoring of which
suits this concerto perfectly, despite the third edition of Köchel which says
by mistake "trumpets" instead of "bassoons" and which, basing itself on this
erroneous datum, connects the movement with the concerto in D minor.
However, key and scoring fit equally well the concerto in G.   The spirit of
the thirty-seven bars of the fragment (twenty-five of tutti, eight of solo, four
of tutti, followed by a sketchily indicated fresh solo entry) is akin to the
andante of K.453 of which it might be a first sketch, inferior to the final
realization; this may be an argument for connecting it with this work.   One
might say quite as well, however, that Mozart, having begun it for the concerto
in F, found that it merely repeated less felicitously what had already been said
in the G major and decided thereupon to compose a completely fresh movement; whence the present allegretto.   The only clear conclusion is that it was
probably destined for one of the two concertos.

To the light-heartedness and serenity of the allegro this allegretto adds an easy grace, capricious and, at times, melancholy. In a more moderate *tempo*, it is quite the counterpart of the first movement. It has the binary form common to several of Mozart's andantes and adagios.[1] Preceded by a tutti, it consists in two identical halves, each of which is made up of a main subject, given out first of all in the tutti, of a plaintive theme, in G minor the first time, C minor the second, and of a little conclusion. The movement ends with a coda built on the first subject. It is therefore a *sonata* without a *development*, a form which must have been all the more acceptable to Mozart that the *development* is always the shortest section of the three with him.

The tutti is more than an introduction; it is almost an independent section prefixed to the movement. After the first subject (ex. 212), fiddles and hautboys bring in a sinuous, climbing figure with a taste for modulation, which tarries a moment in F minor and foreshadows the sombre-hued second subject before disappearing for good and all. The modulations by which it returns to C major recall the transition to the second subject in the first movement of K. 456 (cf. ex. 177).

The piano expounds the first subject in its turn and adds a gruppetto which gives it an unexpected likeness with a theme of Brahms's sextet in G (ex. 213).[2] It is about to repeat, but at the second bar flute and hautboy stop it by echoing the same motif a sixth above; the solo answers back, a third below; hautboy and bassoon reply yet a third lower, which lands us in D minor, whence a modulating piano passage leads to a close on the dominant of G major.

Here, a "regular" movement would bring in its second subject. But our concerto is much too original to be regular; moreover, this movement shares with the other two a liking for single subjects. Instead of presenting us with a new one, it entrusts the flute with re-expounding the opening of the first theme (ex. 212) in its upper register, and the first violins accompany it with an Alberti bass figure destined to become almost as prominent as the famous triplets in the allegro. Flute and bassoon start a canon on the first subject; the piano

---

[1] Piano concerto in C, K.503; quintets in C and G minor; string quartets in G, B flat (*Hunt*), and C and B flat (K.589); piano quartet in G minor; and others.

[2] This sextet contains another figure common to Brahms and Mozart, the

of its first movement, an important element in the andante

of the *Prague* symphony, K.504.

takes it from them almost at once and the violins continue with their
seesaw figure. This passage returns, much extended, in the second
half.

The piano pursues with a new codetta and ends up in G major.
Thereupon the second hautboy and second bassoon sound repeatedly
the chord of G major which it has just struck. Then, after one bar,
they flatten the third and at the same time the first hautboy, then the
flute, put forth a moving lament, far removed from everything we
have heard hitherto in this concerto, except for the few F minor bars
in the prelude.[1] The piano repeats it, embellishing it slightly (ex. 214).
The wind give out the second half, just a downward scale, full of
hesitation with its halts of three beats at each stage. This time, the
strings take it up with a slight reshuffling of the parts, and the piano
unfolds at the same time a winding variation (ex. 215).

This sorrow, so simple and straightforward in its expression, is
quickly allayed and the major mode comes back as suddenly as it had
departed. Two short fragments, which afford piano and wind a game
of ball, conclude the exposition and a solo transition brings back the
tonic key and the first subject.

The second half reproduces the first with a few changes of figuring in the piano part, until it reaches the passages which modulated to
G. This time we do not leave C major. The first subject returns as
formerly, inclined to consider itself as a canon. Piano, hautboy and
bassoon ask for nothing better and the game starts again on a broader
basis. A rising scale tacked on to the subject for the occasion is a
particularly useful participant, and its straight path makes a graceful
contrast with the windings of the rest (ex. 216).[2]

The second subject steps forward in C minor and is followed by
the same fragments and codetta as in the exposition. They bring
back the first subject, upon which the coda is founded. The conclusion of the first tutti is repeated, a reminder by piano and orchestra
of the theme's first bars. The coda itself is a four-bar pedal on which
upward scales are built; the piano comes in last. A short series of
gruppetti is like one last regret for the first subject; then the scales
begin again and the movement, borne aloft on the wings of the flute,
loses itself sky-high (ex. 217).

---

[1] It recalls a theme of the finale of the F major piano sonata, K.332 (bars
50 and foll.).

[2] There is at this point some likeness with the andante in C of the string
quartet in G, K.387.

By its *tempo*, this movement is unique in Mozart's concertos. But it has more than originality in its favour. It is one of his pieces where apparent simplicity is most closely allied to subtlety. What delights us in it are the curves and counter-curves of its melodic lines, the presence of a certain contrast to which the allegro had made us grow unaccustomed, and diversity of rhythm. Gone, the phrases of two and four bars; here, the themes and their fragments, often quite short, are of very various lengths. The graceful irregularity, the charming wilfulness of its first and main subject (ex. 212) are qualities that belong to the whole allegretto, and, though it does not embody an experience of any poignancy or depth, it calls up a world of harmonious and changing shapes, where sadness speaks but to make us enjoy the better the serene air in which we move.

III. However original the allegro and allegretto, however infectious the spirits of the first and harmonious the motion of the second, the strongest part of this concerto is the finale. There lies its centre of gravity; when we think of the work, it is what represents it in our memory.

A formal analysis, of the kind which boils down the most complex works to the state of

> Theme A—1st subject—23 bars.
> Theme B—2nd subject—15 bars, etc.

might present this finale as a sonata rondo with omission of the refrain after the second couplet, similar in design to those of K.456 and 466, and within the narrow field of truth assigned to it, such an analysis would not be wrong. But a glance thrown on the score presents a different and more essential picture. The first page and several of those that follow have a neat, regular appearance; notes of equal value, rests, pauses, line the leaves from top to bottom, one correctly above the other in vertical construction. Twice, however, this symmetry is broken by the intrusion of a different texture, where lines, long and short, straight and winding, wander in all directions, but rather from side to side than from top to bottom: a polyphonic texture.

The juxtaposition of homophony and counterpoint is the fundamental character of the movement—that, and not its irregular sonata rondo plan. We have here one of those pieces where exist "essentially academic elements and light, even popular or bantering tunes",[1] the best known instance of which in Mozart is the finale of the quartet in

---

[1] G. de Saint-Foix: *Les symphonies de Mozart*, p. 233.

Ex. 217

Ex. 218a

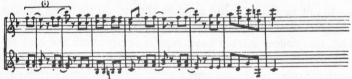

Ex. 218b

Ex. 219

G, but to which belongs also in the last resort the finale of the *Jupiter*. Saint-Foix reminds us that "the predominant use of *fugato* in a symphony finale has precedents"[1] and that examples can be found in Austrian composers, some of whom like Dittersdorf and Michael Haydn were elder contemporaries of Mozart. (We are not speaking of the finale in fugue form, such as Joseph Haydn had written in some of his op. 20 quartets and Mozart in those he composed at Vienna in 1773, but of the alternation of the two styles.) To the three movements just mentioned should be added the finale of the E flat string quintet, his last instrumental work,[2] where twice over a five-part *fugato* comes to give zest to the adventures of a most un-solemn 2-4 tune.

The presence of limpid homophony and strict counterpoint within the framework of the same movement, a manifestation of the principle of contrast in unity, gives this finale a rich, strong organism. We shall see that there is not really juxtaposition, even in the masterly manner of the quartet in G, but union, and that the matter of the harmonic part occurs in the *fugatos*. It is largely with the same motifs that the movement passes from homophony to counterpoint and comes back to homophony. The sharing of themes is not as complete as in the finales of the *Jupiter* and the quintet; in this respect, the concerto stands half-way between the quartet in G and them.

Although analysis reveals a certain number of themes, at bottom there are only two subjects: one, rhythmical, belonging in the first place to the harmonic parts; the other, melodic, belonging to the *fugatos*. The first one is the refrain. Each of its two halves is given out in turn by piano and orchestra (ex. 218 a and b). (The fragment marked (i) and the alternations in the parts at the beginning of (b) play an important part later on.)

Once that is done, instead of the orchestra continuing with the usual ritornello, the basses strike up at once a fugal entry on a new motif (ex. 219). There follows the exposition of a four-part fugue, in close counterpoint, with the answer treading on the heels of the subject two bars behind it, followed by a miniature *stretto* which reduces the distance between them to one bar; then polyphony gives way to harmony. The race continues with frenzy; violins and violas break out in *tremolandos*; and, after opening the gates of D minor, B flat and G minor and shutting them immediately, it stops clamorously on the

[1] G. de Saint-Foix: *Les symphonies de Mozart*, p. 233.

[2] With the partial exception of the clarinet concerto, a good deal of which is an any case earlier.

chord of the dominant.   The horns sound a C, the beginning of a
long pedal, and, *piano*, the fragment (i) of the refrain is whispered by
the basses, gains the upper regions, starts twice, extends to the whole
orchestra, and finally breaks forth, *ff* and alternating, in wind and
basses, whilst violins and violas return joyously to their *tremolandos*.
With vicissitudes of *piano* and *forte*, the fragment (i) or its rhythm and
the *tremolandos* lead us by degrees towards a full close, after which,
upon a tonic pedal in the basses, the concluding theme, entirely homo-
phonous, scampers up and down; it is one of the most unblushing
borrowings the concerto makes from opera buffa, a regular comic
finale, chattering, busy about nothing, quite brainless (ex. 220), but
scored and eked out with irresistible wit.

    This tutti is so long—almost one fifth of the movement—and so
important, that only its loyalty to the key of F prevents us from
forgetting we have a concerto, for a symphony would have modulated
by now.   The piano's entry gives us the feeling of a lost child found
again; it appears a little lustreless after this scintillating introduction.
The solo comes forward in the company of a rather undistinguished
theme which remains inconclusive and loses itself in the virtuosity
that follows it (ex. 221).   That follows it, or rather that would follow
it if only the irrepressible woodwind allowed.   For, hardly does the
piano return to the tonic than they disturb the peace with drum taps of
(i).   The piano tries to start off again, and again they interrupt it;
this happens several times until the unescapable victory of the piano
silences them.   Even so, once its rockets have carried us into the key
of the dominant, the rhythm of (i) begins again, this time in the strings,
beneath a solo trill; its infectiousness conquers the piano and only
when everyone, solo, strings and wind, has surrendered to it is it
possible to get rid of the obsession; whereupon the piano forges ahead,
sole master, in a passage of descending scales.

    The second subject is launched by the strings and quickly taken up
by the wind (ex. 222); the piano repeats it, decorates it and at once
forgets it to surrender to virtuosity.   But the orchestra has a better
memory.   Whilst the solo runs up and down in scales, wind and
strings answer each other with the fragment (ii) of ex. 222 (ex. 223);
then arises in the bass the polyphonic figure (cf. ex. 219), lengthened
and broadened, whose appearance marks the first union between the
two elements in this rondo (ex. 224).   And in it, as in the bravura
runs of the right hand, there triumphs the figure of the descending
scale, so prominent in this movement.

    After a pause on a dominant seventh and a cadenza, the piano

Ex. 220

Ex. 221

Ex. 222

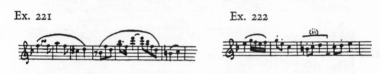

Ex. 223

Ex. 224

Ex. 225

Ex. 226

Ex. 227

Ex. 228

resumes the refrain. It gives out each half alone, then decorates it while the orchestra repeats it. Whereupon, with the same suddenness as the basses just now, first fiddles, flute and hautboy dive into a *fugato*. The subject is the same (ex. 219), but this time it is underlined by a counter-subject, the little rhythmic figure (i) from the refrain (ex. 225). The counterpoint is as closely knit as at first but richer, for a certain independence in the second hautboy and second bassoon raises at times the number of parts to six. Moreover, the entry is not in F major but in the dusky key of D minor, and this, as well as the presence of the counter-subject, gives the passage extreme vigour. The whole power of action of this concerto is condensed into these thirty-five bars. Their swing is irresistible; they are no longer a regular fugal exposition, calling its parts on parade in turn in the same key; they are a series of inroads, at varying intervals and in diverse keys: D minor, A minor, G minor, C minor and, in the last place, B flat major, of ex. 225, which its transposition into the minor has made ferocious, and of its counter-subject with its feverish rhythm. When, in comparative silence, violas and first bassoon make a last entry in B flat, the atmosphere clears without the flight losing any of its strength; at this moment, the mark drops to *piano* and the solo instrument adds its part to the orchestra.

But at the same time it breaks up the game; it will not subordinate itself to the contrapuntal discipline and insists on playing as a soloist. The fiery flight continues none the less; in double phrases, where tumbling arpeggios in the right hand answer sinuous, climbing octaves in the bass, we rise one degree at a time, whilst the ♩♩ ♪ᵞ♩♩ ♪ᵞ of the strings are there to protest against this expropriation and to keep alive the threat of the expropriated (ex. 226). Nevertheless, the piano's return to D minor and the substitution of the polyphonic subject for these drum taps brings the enemies closer, all the more as the piano, giving up its arpeggios-versus-octaves, consents to follow the line of the subject, embellishing it with a sweeping gesture (ex. 227). Little by little, its fierceness is tamed, the landscape becomes familiar, and without a shock, almost without noticing it, we are back at the piano trill, accompanied by (i) of the first couplet. The recapitulation is at work and already half over; the lightning course of dramatic counterpoint has swept the rondo out of its boundaries and made it skip the first subject, ex. 221, and land at the beginning of the solo passage before ex. 222.

After this, the third couplet reproduces fairly accurately the first, keeping of course to the tonic. We recognize the second subject, ex. 222, and the return in the bass of the polyphonic figure, quieter, and in F major; then, to prepare the *strepitoso* which is to usher in the cadenza, Mozart introduces a superb passage on a tonic pedal, the grandest moment, after the *fugatos*, in the rondo. Its elements are a two-bar figure in the piano, rising degree by degree, a syncopated motion in the strings, a divided figure, derived from (i), shared between hautboys and bassoons, and a strengthening of the pedal in the treble by the flute (ex. 228). The mighty wave swells, breaks, and its crest crumbles into falling arpeggios, still urged on by the alternating

♩♩ ♪ ↻ of the orchestra. The piano is silent and a short preparatory passage brings in the cadenza (K. 624, no. 30). It is worthy of the rest. Ex. 224 opens it, but instead of keeping within the two octaves of the original, with a magnificent sweep it drops three and a half and climbs up again a part of them; then, starting high up, the right hand travels down four and a half octaves and reascends in broken sevenths. Then it is the turn of the other subject, figure (i); only its rhythm survives, and there arises out of it a quivering passage based on an upper tonic pedal, which is more like the preparation than the conclusion of a cadenza; with its cluckings in every other bar, it reminds one of a cackling hen, one of those imitations of nature beloved of French harpsichord composers. The cadenza ends on a trill in the right hand and a recall of (i) in the left hand, a reminder of a passage in the first and third couplets.

The conclusion of the rondo consists in a last return of the refrain with a triplet accompaniment which makes it limp comically—the equivalent of the change to 6-8 which sometimes closes 2-4 rondos[1]— and in a much lengthened version of the opera buffa motif, ex. 220, the chatterings of which make this end sound like a council of magpies.

In this very fine rondo, with a conjuror's skill, Mozart, from a subject with dry outlines and a skimpy rhythm, has drawn a broadly wrought movement, with powerful curves, ample, generous contours, a great variety of rhythm and a single, well-sustained inspiration. The allegro was contained, on the whole, in the first bars of the solo; the main elements of the movement were there, a dotted march rhythm and a triplet accompaniment. But no one, on hearing the refrain of the finale, would divine the splendour that is to follow.

---

[1] Cf. K.449, 451, 491.

And yet, the bustling three-quaver rhythm which characterizes it belongs to almost the whole movement; the first *fugato* is the only important section whence it is absent, and the subject itself, whole or in part, provides not only the refrain but also a fugal counter-subject and accompaniment figures.

The fieriness of its motion sweeps the virtuosity along with it. There is not a single bar of idle passage work. Not once do we mark time while the piano performs its flourishes; scales, arpeggios, broken octaves advance, always making for a goal; everything moves forward and one never goes round in circles as one does sometimes in concertos, even Mozart's. We are borne along by a hurricane of undeniable strength.

This strength is not that of passion and the movement's heat is not the heat of the soul. Big and strong though it be, this rondo is not a deep movement. The heat it radiates springs from the speed of its progress, from the distances it covers at one go from top to bottom of the keyboard, the incessant clashes between the fragments of the refrain, the speed of the counterpoint, too, and its closely knit texture. Though it does not avoid *fortissimos*, it is not through noise that it seeks to make our blood tingle but through the use of a rhythm productive of a sure and immediate response—that muscular rhythm of three strokes followed by a rest, one of the most Dionysiac. It is the piling up and the simultaneous attack of all these siege batteries that makes the second *fugato* so breathless and so apparently dramatic a moment—this, and not the presentation of any inner conflict. For in no movement of this concerto is there conflict. Though at times its goal seems to coincide with that of music that is truly passionate, though its effect on us appears to be the same, its starting-point is far from that of passion. It is but acting, and we recognized on our way formal details taken from comedy; it mimics anger and ferocity, and successfully, but this is only a game and it leaves no disturbance or bitterness in its wake.

This is a game, we say; and such a judgement is indeed true of the whole work, even of the touching minor theme in the allegretto, an imitation and not the expression of a melancholy mood. But it is so near in its *tempo* and its form to its stormy successor that we wonder whether the game is not being played "on a volcano". This apparently passionate movement of the rondo Mozart was to rediscover two months later, strangely similar, but under the sway of true passion.

For the concerto in F, so springlike and so carefree, coincides more

than once with that in D minor.   The choice of the key is itself a
sign of kinship and one should perhaps not be surprised if here and
there a melodic line or a harmonic progression in the first recalls the
second, for the space of a flash, to the listener who knows both of them.
But it is impossible to think of a merely fortuitous encounter when
one hears the *development* of the first movement open with the same
chord and the same piano passage as the fiery presto which interrupts
the andante of the D minor.   The only notable difference between
the two passages is that of the key: A minor in one, G minor in the
other (ex. 229; allegro of K.459).   It is just a moment of physical
excitement, one may say, in the concerto in F, and a traditional minor
modulation at the beginning of the second solo; but to one who
knows the D minor, these few bars appear pregnant with foreboding.
They are the warning of the storm, the loosing of which will be re-
counted two months later.

And over the finale, too, the work that is to come casts at times
its shadow.   There is nothing remarkable, no doubt, in that the *tempo*,
2-4, is the same in both rondos.   But a premonitory spirit of the
D minor passes undeniably over the second *fugato*; these thirty-five
bars would not be out of place in its finale; one feels it instinctively
and a closer glance shows us that a subject in the D minor, ex. 247,
is but the inversion of the *fugato* theme, ex. 225.   In spite of the absolutely contrary characters of the two works, somewhere in the depths
of Mozart's soul they draw from a common spring and beneath their
contrasts a kinship unites them.   We have linked up the concerto in
F with the "fashionable virtuoso" concertos of 1784 and it does
indeed wear their livery and walk with their gait; yet one wonders
at times whether it has not something in common with its austere
successor?

This fifteenth concerto is the third and last of those Mozart wrote
in F.   The first was the trifling concerto for three pianos, where the
composer's personality counted for little; the second, the graceful,
shy work of 1782 which had tried before all to be acceptable to the
Viennese public to which it was introducing its author.   The third
alone is representative.

The key of F, in Mozart, like that of G, is one of those whose
character is least distinctive.   The composer does not often have
recourse to it for important works.   Only four other compositions
in F are comparable to this concerto: a violin sonata, K.377; a piano
duet sonata, K.497; a piano (two hands) sonata without a finale,

K.533[1] and his last string quartet, K.590. One might add to this list the first fantasia for mechanical organ, K.594, consisting in an F major allegro between two F minor adagios. It is not enough for one to speak of a "family" of F major works. In this key such important compositions are exceptional, for F major is the key of trifles —divertimentos, light sonatas and sonatinas, *Musical Jokes*.[2]

It is nevertheless possible to single out likenesses between our concerto and each of these works. With the duet sonata and the fantasia, there is indeed no formal similarity, but both unfold with the same vigour and spirit. The frequent triplets in the accompaniment and the important counterpoint in the allegro of K.533 connect it with the first and third movements of the concerto, and in the quartet we recognize, not only (in the finale) the spirits and the vigour and also the use of counterpoint, but also (in the allegro) a similar theme.[3]

The only one of these movements which shows a true analogy in form and inspiration with our concerto is the allegro of the violin sonata. There, as in the first movement of the concerto, triplets preponderate; starting as the simple accompaniment of a bare, wiry theme, they end by clothing its nakedness as ivy adorns and blurs the outlines of a leafless tree. There too, in the main subject, we meet again the motif of the downward scale and the silhouette of ex. 219. The allegro of the sonata, like that of the concerto, has really only one subject whose rhythm and melodic line, fostered by the accompanying triplets, pervade the whole movement. In it, also, a certain detachment with, in addition, a touch of austerity and dryness foreign to the concerto, is expressed with a lively, muscular rhythm, and both movements keep constantly on the go. That of the sonata is a true *moto perpetuo* and recalls the finale as well as the allegro of the concerto. The sonata is the elder by three years; its allegro is, as it were, a first version of the concerto's and has something of the stiffness and severity of first versions; three years later, when the same inspiration

---

[1] It has always been published (except in the *Gesamtausgabe*) with the rondo, K.494, as finale, a movement which it is best to omit for it is unworthy of the other two and has no connexion with them. A counsel of laziness may have urged Mozart to allow them to be published together, if perchance he be responsible for it.

[2] This is not so with the most interesting and strongly characterized group of the F major andantes, in 3-4 or 6-8 time, of works in C major; it comprises a dozen movements, some of which are among the finest in Mozart; by its beat and its inspiration, the *Recordare* of the *Requiem* also belongs to it.

[3] Solo subject in the allegro of the concerto; second subject in the quartet.

revisits Mozart, it puts on more flesh, rounds itself off, and adds good temper and freedom from care to its original liveliness and strength.

The few warning signs of the concerto in D minor we fancied we found in this concerto would not justify our skipping two important compositions of the beginning of 1785 as we passed from one work to the next.   They are the quartets in A and C, the last born of the six dedicated to Haydn.

After the effervescence of 1784, the quiet and inward nature of the quartet in A indicates a withdrawal into himself on the part of the young master.   It is planned on a broad scale; in his chamber music, its dimensions are equalled only by the quintets in C and G minor. Its *developments* are true workings-out and not *fantasias*; its finale is a climax and not a relaxation.   Its andante, a theme and variations, ends with a fine coda which, instead of winding up the movement, rises above it, meditating on what goes before and interpreting it in a detached spirit worthy of the epilogues of Beethoven.   The writing is closer than in the other quartets and the bravura passages for the first violin, turning up regularly towards the end of the exposition and recapitulation as in a concerto, are absent.

The winding, chromatic themes of the allegro and the finale corres-pond to a state of calm after suffering, almost of resignation, of which we caught a glimpse in the concerto and rondo K.414 and 386, and which will be henceforward the character of his works in A.   This after-taste of suffering is somewhat saddening but, after the works of the previous year, what an answer this quartet gives to those who maintain that Mozart has only one string to his lyre!

The inspiration of the quartet in C is less original.   A certain vivacity appears to connect it with the compositions of 1784, but it belongs rather to the same family as the C major concerto which follows it two months later.   It is the earliest and least imposing of the series of works in C which includes the two concertos, K.467 and 503, the quintet and the *Jupiter* symphony.   Next to the over-cele-brated introduction, its most notable features are the threatening shadows that return several times in the first movement and in the trio of the minuet.

These quartets open a fresh page.   The period of the "fashionable virtuoso" is closed; let us attempt to sum it up.   Surface qualities of brilliance, attractiveness, colour, sparkle, proud bearing, predominate over intimacy and inwardness of feeling.   This does not prevent these works, in contrast to his former *galant* compositions, from being highly personal; only, they reveal Mozart's personality at a moment when it does not draw in upon itself, when it expresses itself, on the contrary, most fully by spreading its gifts lavishly on all sides. This "revelation" reaches its highest point in the *Hunt* quartet and the concerto in F, works which speak of joy and strength.

Side by side with this, however, the deeper life goes on. We catch a glimpse of it in the andantes of some concertos, of the sonata and quartet in B flat; but the veil is completely torn aside only in the C minor sonata.

Two strains of thought thus run through the works of these ten months—one, brilliant and external; the other, intimate, sometimes restless, subordinate to the first, but ready to reveal itself unmistakably. One speaks to the actual public; the other turns away from it, or dreams of an ideal one.

PART IV

1. *The Sixteenth Concerto: K.466 in D minor*

CONCERTO NO. 16 IN D MINOR (K.466)[1]
Finished February 10th, 1785
  Allegro: C
  Romanza: ¢ (in B flat)
  Rondo (Allegro assai): ¢
Orchestra: Strings; flute, two hautboys, two bassoons, two horns, two
  trumpets, two kettledrums.

WHEN, in our childhood, we asked to have the same stories
told us again and again till we knew every detail of them by
heart, no familiarity could ever dull the poignancy of certain moments
and their power to stir us. As they drew nearer, our hearts beat
faster; we held our breath and wished we might stay the march of
time, so as to derive thereby a more prolonged savour from the
expectations of their coming.

In as well-known a story as that of Mozart's music, the coming of
the D minor concerto is such a moment. Just as we approached with
emotion the awaited episode in the childish story, so, when we turn
the corner of 1784 and come into sight of this concerto, our excitement
rises. Despite the grand spectacle of the year that is just past, our
emotion increases, the story becomes more stirring and more full of
colour, and there enters into it a sense of adventure and heroism,
hitherto unexperienced.

For the birth of the D minor is one of the great stages in its author's
musical journey and, at the time he reaches it, the work is one of
his newest, one of those that confound most thoroughly those people
who still imagine that Mozart was all his life content with following
beaten paths. It refutes those who have it that his celebrated "beauty
of style", his "perfect form" are but the deftness of the craftsman repeating day after day the same gestures, of the runner who, by dint
of always following the same course, knows every inch of it, never
stumbles and can find blindfolded the shortest way from one point to
the next.

---

[1] *Gesamtausgabe*, no. 20.

At the end of the last chapter, we said that two currents of thought flowed through his works in 1784: one, sparkling and shallow, the other, deeper and more intimate.   This second current triumphs over the former in the concertos of 1785 and 1786, not by cutting it out but by absorbing it.   How could we characterize it more precisely?   We found easily enough the appropriate epithets for the group of the 1784 concertos; these latter had a marked family likeness; but it is much harder to describe in one word the great concertos of which the D minor is the eldest.   When we say: intimacy, depth, introspection, we exhaust the words equally applicable to all of them.   For in addition to the general difference there is another difference between the concertos of 1785-6 and those of the previous year.   Not only was the thought of the latter less inward, but each one of them was less unlike the others.   Here, however, between the six of the next two years, diversity is far wider.   From the D minor to the C major, the E flat, the A, the distances covered are much greater than between the 1784 concertos.   Generally speaking, then, the thought grows deeper and the works have more sharply defined personalities.   It was still possible to speak of a series in connexion with the previous concertos; it is not so with these.

Such considerations make us place these works at the summit of Mozart's concertos.   One cannot make a selection, even a small one, of what is most valuable and most characteristic in his production, of what is most living and most his own, without bringing in every concerto of these two years.   With as much right as his three great symphonies, his finest quartets and quintets, his best operas, his C minor and *Requiem* masses, the concerto in D minor and the five that follow it may claim to represent him at his highest point of creative power.

On February 10th, 1785, wrote Leopold Mozart to his daughter, there was performed in the Mehlgrube an "excellent piano concerto by Wolfgang . . .   When we arrived, the copyist was still copying it out and your brother had not yet had time to play the rondo because he had to revise the copies".[1]   The concerto in question is the D minor.

Whatever differences we may have noticed between one concerto and another, never was the contrast as brutal as between the F major work and this one which was separated from it by only two months.

---

[1] Letter of February 14th, 1785.

We leap at one bound from one world to another totally different. There is no longer any trace of those march or dance rhythms, those opera buffa closes, those good-humouredly symmetrical strains which made up the framework of the F major concerto; had we to discover, in the year that is just past, a counterpart to the new work, it is in the D major that we should find the obsession, insistence, straining, the pursuit of a single idea, which strike us in the opening bars as strongly as the unconcern of the previous concerto had done. But the kinship would remain distant and the D minor contains too much that is foreign to the D major for us to bring them together.

I. It is generally imagined that the opening tuttis of classical concertos are all alike in their general lines, all fulfil exactly the same functions with regard to the rest of the movement and show only minor differences from one to the other. To give out the main themes and outline the main paths along which the rest of the allegro is to pass: such would appear to be the task of all first tuttis.

This simplifies the matter too much. Far from all of them being alike, in Mozart alone two types can be clearly distinguished. The first one—the type which the usual description of a tutti suits best —gives out the chief themes on which the movement is built, in the order in which they are to return later. It is the summary, the *argument* of what one is about to hear. The concerto in D, K.451, is a perfect example of this kind; those of the E flat, G and B flat, K.449, 453 and 456, are also *arguments*, but rather less complete.

In the second type, on the other hand, the tutti is a mere introduction. It gives out the first subject, then busies itself mainly with secondary elements which either do not reappear or prove to be subordinated to other subjects not included in it. The beginning of the concerto in C, K.415, is an extreme example of the introduction tutti; those of the concertos in B flat and F, K.450 and 459, belong to the same category but stand less aloof from what follows. This second type is less organic and ushers in a movement of looser form; the *argument* tutti precedes a more unified movement.

The fine tutti which opens the D minor concerto is an *argument*. It lets us hear all the themes of the movement save the solo introduction and the second part of the second subject. Not only does what follows not add anything essential; the very character of the whole movement is expressed in the first fifteen bars. This, the most personal concerto we have met hitherto, proclaims its originality in the first subject itself. None of the singing themes here, with well-marked

rhythms and clean articulations, with which *galant* concertos habitually begin, including most of Mozart's, but one same note throbbing
against the beat, whilst, under its monotonous pulsation, a menacing
bass emphasizes each bar with an uprush of three little notes—a
formula usually expressive of passion and threatening. Repeated
notes, piano, with a syncopated rhythm, and the formula of the
rising triplet: with these two elements common to all the music of
the time is built up this opening, one of the most personal and the
most powerful in Mozart.

Out of this misty background a melodic outline arises and is at
once swallowed up; after a further bar of repeated notes the figure
begins again one degree higher (ex. 230; bars 1 to 5).   Then, cutting
out the melodic motif, with heightening stress, thrusting home ever
more swiftly and more truly, whilst the woodwind from horns to
flute one after another add their colour to that of the strings, and still
piano, the phrase rises, degree by degree, to the octave, where the
strain is relaxed somewhat and whence we climb down again to the
starting-point (bars 5 to 15).[1]

The *fortissimo* then breaks loose.

On analysis, one recognizes the old *galant* formula of the soft
beginning followed by the sudden *forte* which opens so many of
Mozart's concertos, but renewed with genius.   For here, instead of
driving ahead with a fresh subject,[2] the movement retraces its steps.[3]
The syncopated murmur breaks out into a *tremolando* of semi-quavers;
the rumbling triplets turn into flashes of lightning and rend the instrumental web, springing from bass to treble with gathering speed;[4]
woodwind and horns plunge into the midst of the tumult, through
which one perceives, punctuating each first beat, the metallic note of
the trumpets, like armour glinting through the depths of a forest.
The working out unfolds with alternating violence and pathos, without ever abating its intensity, and concludes with a five-bar close on
the dominant, another conventional gesture into which Mozart infuses
life by making it expressive of passion (bars 16 to 32).

---

[1] As this concerto is so well known we give fewer quotations of it than
of the others and we confine ourselves as a rule to referring the reader to the
bar numbers.

[2] Cf. K.414, 415, 450, 453, 537.

[3] The concertos, K.456, 459, 467 and 491 also repeat the first bars forte
after a soft opening.

[4] The kinship of these bars with those that open the Queen of Night's
second aria in the *Magic Flute* will be recognized.

The second subject, in the relative major, is shared by hautboys and flute, supported by bassoons and fiddles; it opens with a series of questions and answers, in contrasted rhythms (ex. 231; bars 33 to 34), rising each time by one degree, then breaks into a chain of short sighs which the fiddles send backwards and forwards beneath the held notes of the hautboys (ex. 232; bars 39 to 40); these bring us back into D minor.

Again passion proclaims itself. The powerful, agitated passage that follows (bars 44 to 71) is based on a rising figure of great strength (ex. 233; bars 44 to 45) and on a wailing one (ex. 234; bars 49 to 50), against which beat falling arpeggios (ex. 235; bars 48 to 49). The general line is that of rise and fall which characterized the first bars of the allegro; the forces rush to the attack, withdraw and start afresh, with alternating *fortes* and *pianos*. The music surges with the frenzy of a soul driven on by irresistible passion. Then, suddenly, on a suspended cadence, the rhythm breaks off, the mark falls to *piano* and a few sighs in the violins conclude the fiery passage and announce the closing subject.

This speaks of peace—a peace of desolation, almost of despair. Flexuous and caressing, its rhythm is freer than usual with Mozart; it unfolds in three fragments with one same movement of rise and fall, over a most graceful and expressive counterpoint (ex. 236; bars 71 to 74).

For many who write on Mozart, there appears to be no greater compliment than the word "Beethovenian". When a critic is at a loss for terms to express his admiration for a passage he declares it "worthy" or, more often, "*almost* worthy of Beethoven". Even Abert scatters his pages with, "fast Beethovensche" which would lead one to believe that the Bonn master is the sole paragon and that perfection can be attained only inasmuch as one resembles him.

This doubtful compliment, which sees in our composer an inferior variety of Beethoven, is seldom deserved. If "fast Beethovensche" pages abound in Haydn and Clementi, they are rare in Mozart. Many pages, likewise, of the young Beethoven recall Clementi and Haydn; very few recall Mozart and these are precisely the least Beethovenian ones. At distant intervals, a detail in one may make us think of the other, and we have ourselves occasionally used the word "Beethovenian" when speaking of Mozart. But they are only passing moments. Here, nevertheless, we have a whole movement over which there passes unmistakably a breath that heralds Beethoven.[1]

---

[1] At a time when Beethoven's glory eclipsed Mozart's, this concerto was the only one of its composer's which was commonly performed.

What is like Beethoven and is uncommon in Mozart is the persistence of the strife and passion. Usually, with him, a passionate outburst is followed by relaxation and a softened, sentimental answer, the alternation of passion and sentiment, of tension and relaxation, is typical and frequent;[1] it is thus, and not in a continuous flow, that the feeling progresses in his passionate movements. With Beethoven, on the contrary, the struggle is carried on relentlessly; no rest, no intrusion of another mood comes to interrupt it; no appeasement comes to break the effort until it has achieved victory.

Now, we find precisely this in the D minor concerto. The easing off in the fifteenth bar was a return to the beginning rather than a break or a slackening in the strain; the silence which parted the fiery close from the second subject was dramatic and brought no relief. And from bar 44 (ex. 233) to bar 68, the urge is constant and the passion advances, not in a series of forward and backward movements, but in an unbroken flood of increasing power, in a way unparalleled in Mozart outside this concerto but representative of Beethoven. The only truly Mozartian feature is the sudden drop in the sixty-ninth bar and the despairing gentleness of the conclusion (ex. 236). Relentless struggle, a piling and speeding up instead of alternation in the progress of the passion make this allegro a work of Mozart's which may rightly be termed Beethovenian.[2]

One awaits the solo entry with some anxiety. What does it hold in store? So dramatic a work cannot belie its promises to the point of returning to its start and repeating the beginning of the tutti as if nothing had happened since, as if its world was as serene and timeless as that of K.456. How will it incorporate the new element into the substance of the drama? In what shape will it bring back the first subject? Our expectation is great.

We are not disappointed. With the corresponding passages in the C minor and C major, K.503, the piano's first words constitute the most moving solo entry in all Mozart's concertos. The piano's appearance gives us the feeling, not of an instrument added to many others, but of a personality substituting itself for the anonymous orchestral mass; it fills us with the same awe as a human voice rising

---

[1] Openings of K.457 (i), 550 (iv), 388 (i), etc.

[2] Even the piano writing has two features uncommon in Mozart and typical of Beethoven: much use of the lowest registers and wide spacing. In our opinion, despite the absence of formal likenesses, there is kinship between this allegro and the first movement of Beethoven's D minor sonata, op. 31, II.

suddenly from a body of instruments. Taking up the thread of the discourse where the tutti had broken off, the piano gives out a theme similar in feeling to the last but even freer and more wandering. Though written out in bars it has a recitative character which the performance should retain; to play it too strictly is to empty it of its soul. Three times it climbs and falls back, with increasing languor; it rises one last time, breaks up completely and streams away in semi-quavers to a woodwind accompaniment (bars 77 to 78, and 88; ex. 237).[1]

Its impetus once exhausted, the strings take up again the throbbing of the first bars and the piano almost at once adds the excitement of its semi-quavers. It quickly leaves behind the rumblings of the orchestra and, shortening the exposition, reaches with one leap the cadence preceding the second subject (bars 91 to 114) and this subject itself (ex. 231).

Making use of a favourite device, Mozart now casts his parts differently, giving the piano what had formerly belonged to the flute. A short passage introduces the key of the relative major and leads to a fresh subject distinguished from the rest of the movement by its singing and almost blithe nature (ex. 238). Expounded by the piano with a witty addition of the strings, it is repeated by the wind whilst the piano decorates it with a scale (bars 127 to 143).

In the key of F major the air clears but the movement loses none of its vigour. The thirty solo bars which follow let loose a torrent of passion and energy, and the tension is no less than before, even though the struggle and anguish are less apparent. The piano speaks almost alone. With the scales, arpeggios and broken octaves which are the usual elements of its speech, it mingles memories of its fiery ascent, ex. 233. Twice its course leads to the trill of F major; twice it starts afresh, with increased impetus, as if carried away despite itself beyond all appointed bounds. The section is longer than the usual bravura passages which close first solos, but never savours of padding; there is no vain display of skill; the piano, in its turn and to the best of its ability, carries on the work started by the orchestra.

After so long a silence the force with which the tutti enters again appears even greater than usual. It repeats and transposes into F the

---

[1] There is a great likeness of mood between this movement and Philip Emmanuel Bach's magnificent D minor concerto (Wotquenne, no. 17; unpublished) which also opens with a stormy tutti, even more raging than this one, followed by a cembalo entry in a quiet, elegiac tone, with a new rhythm.

passage which, in the first tutti, preceded the vigorous close,[1] then, leaving out the close itself, skips to ex. 236, a subject which Mozart considers particularly important, for he seldom gives out his concluding themes at the end of a first solo (bars 174-93).

A glance back over this exposition justifies our calling the first tutti an *argument*. The piano has expanded its message; it has made the intention clearer; but, apart from the first strain and the singing theme in F major, it has brought nothing new. As for the orchestra, each time it had to speak alone, it just repeated its first words; moreover, its part was smaller than in the previous concertos; as if it felt that after its first tutti it had nothing further to say, it drew aside and let the piano go over in its own way the paths already opened.

The dramatic temper of the work was obvious at the start, but hitherto there has been the announcement of a drama rather than a drama itself. Now we penetrate into the heart of the conflict.

To the concluding subject there joins on quite naturally the solo recitative, ex. 237. This return to the beginning of the exposition is a feint.[2] The times, indeed, are changed. The solo will no longer speak alone and in the short struggle about to open the parts will be shared out equally between piano and orchestra. The latter will have the threatening subject, ex. 230; the former, the strain with which it made its bow, ex. 237, and virtuosity.

Twice does the piano raise its wandering song, first in F major, the key where the tutti had stopped, then in G minor, and each time with changes which alter its meaning. Twice do the instruments answer it with the rumbling theme from the opening, as if they were seeking to lead it towards a fuller utterance (bars 192-220).

The second time, they land in E flat and in this optimistic key the piano re-enters with a third variation of its theme. But the triumph of this subject is short-lived. Hardly is it finished when the piano sweeps down into the bass and forsakes it completely. Three times

---

[1] Mozart remembered this entry (bars 175-8) in Fiordiligi's aria in the first act of *Così fan tutti*; the words of the passage are an expression of constancy in a tone of indignation:

"E potría la morte sola
Far che cangi affetto il cor."

The key is the same in both passages and the notes almost identical.

[2] The plan of starting the *development* with the solo introduction of the exposition and of omitting this introduction in the recapitulation occurs again in Mozart only in his other minor concerto, K.491; it is used by Beethoven in his violin concerto.

over (subjects in three strains or repeating themselves three times are among Mozart's most authentic signatures) the solo scales the keyboard in arpeggios of the common chord and comes tumbling down it in diminished sevenths, rising from E flat to F minor, from F minor to G minor, while in the sky rent with lightning the full body of strings re-echo the wild triplets of the first subject (ex. 239)—a most dramatic reduction of it to its simplest shape.[1] The piano forges ahead, with hands widely spaced; then, in one last torrent of fire, the flood streams from top to bottom and gathers in the bass (bars 247–50), whence, with momentarily weakened but still unbroken spirit (the sudden *forte* of the last bar before the reprise bears witness to this), regains the starting-point of the movement by the shortest road and with the simplest means (ex. 240).

The second subject, ex. 231, appears unchanged[2] but the singing theme, ex. 238, is now given out in D minor, a key we shall leave no more. The long solo that follows it (bars 318–55) corresponds in the main to that of the exposition; we meet again the threefold trill and ex. 233, but the change of mode is enough to infuse it with a very different spirit and the figuring of the runs is also new. All this part has a vigorous, striving quality which persists with growing intensity till the end, but not the angry nature of the development; it is indeed the issue of the movement, but an issue of despair; the fight continues, but we know now there can be no triumph. The ray of hope in the singing theme, ex. 238, has died out with the theme's return in the minor, and it is to win exhaustion, not victory, that the struggle goes on. These thirty bars and those of the *development* are amongst the finest instances of expressive virtuosity that the music of the genre affords; Mozart attains perfect formal beauty thanks to the very might of his passion.[3]

Mozart has left no cadenzas for this concerto which he composed, as well as those that follow, for himself and which he no doubt never taught to pupils. But there is one by the young Beethoven

---

[1] Cf. the *più allegro* of the C minor fantasia, K.375. It is tempting to play all this with a shattering *fortissimo*. But Mozart, contrary to what our taste would expect, has marked bars 232–52 *piano*, at least in the tutti.

[2] This is the only example in Mozart of a second subject appearing all three times in the same key.

[3] "The most permanently satisfying art is that which arrives at formal beauty as a consequence of intense preoccupation with something else, as impassioned speech tends to be metrical, rather than by deliberate organization" (*Times Lit. Supp.*, article on Raphael, January 27th, 1927).

which is a shrewd commentary on the movement and which, both Beethovenian and Mozartian in character, corroborates with unexpected emphasis what we said just now on the nature of the work. One would like to hear it more often and one regrets that in the recording by His Master's Voice the soloist should have inserted instead of it a cadenza full of commonplace virtuosity which, far from throwing light upon the movement or summing it up, is just an intrusion.

The end has not the perfunctory brevity of certain conclusions of first allegros, where one feels that after the executant's display all has been said. Some thirty bars long, it repeats more tersely the fiery passage (bars 44–71) which, in the initial tutti, followed the second subject; relieved of the repetitions which had emphasized its energy, its wiry vigour is admirably suited to an epilogue. It is followed by the concluding subject, ex. 236, whose languidness, after this last spurt, sounds even more desolate. It has already closed two sections; it cannot suffice to close the whole movement, so, in a short coda, under the weary, drooping lines of the upper parts, Mozart calls up in the bass one last echo of the "menacing" triplets which thus run through the movement from end to end.[1]

Thought is so closely united to form in this allegro that there is little to add about the latter. The concentrated and passionate inspiration imposes on the movement a strict unity. The first tutti contains only important elements and it contains nearly all of them. The *development* links up with the tradition of thematic *developments*, not after the fashion of movements which play with secondary figures[2] or bring in new motifs, but like those that are concerned with only primary elements.[3] It is a summary, expressing the soul of the work at its purest, not by freeing it from the shackles of form like certain *fantasia developments*, but by confining itself to the use of significant material.

In the recapitulation, Mozart is confronted with the problem which confronts all concertos whose opening tuttis are *arguments*: how to make it more than the repetition of the first solo. Here, the compulsory return to the minor is itself a transforming feature; moreover,

---

[1] Note in these last bars the Mozartian "fluttering seconds" figure. Its presence gives this ending a certain likeness with a movement whose inspiration is close to that of this concerto: the adagio for piano in B minor, K.540.

[2] K.449, 537.

[3] K.271, 491, 503, 595.

the great bravura passage at the end is remodelled and the coda adds novelty to the conclusion.

The roles of solo and tutti are well differentiated. On the whole, alternation or opposition preponderates over collaboration. The message of the movement is imparted first of all by the tutti, then repeated in its own tongue by the solo. The *development*, after a passage of contrasts, affords a few bars of interplay, then the solo again acts alone. In the last part, the solo predominates till the cadenza, and the eloquent conclusion falls to the orchestra. Save for the *development*, the only moments of interplay are in the second and third subjects, exs. 231 and 238, and especially the fine passages where the piano joins the orchestra to sustain or stimulate it in the main subject (bars 95–104, 261–7). And indeed, does not opposition rather than collaboration become the expression of a conflict?

II. In Mozart's works in minor keys, some contrast between allegro and andante is almost *de rigueur*.[1] Here, the contrast is complete. If anything in music depicts the moment when after a storm the sun shows its face and drives away the last shreds of cloud, the theme which opens this concerto's second movement does it. Nothing more fragrant and more springlike exists in all Mozart. There still abides in the air a slight humidity left by the storm and the face of the sky, though calm once more, is glimpsed through a hanging veil of moisture. Everything has taken on a brighter hue; everything revives after the tempest (ex. 241).

The movement which it ushers in has no *tempo* mark but is clearly andante. It is headed: *Romanza*, a term which does not connote any precise form and is given to any slow movement, rondo or variations, the character of whose chief theme recalls the "romance" of vocal music. This one is a spacious rondo. Like all concerto romances, it begins with the solo, and this gives it a personal and lyrical character, as if the composer himself was before us and was baring his heart. A summary will show its plan clearly.

Refrain: Main subject—tonic—piano, then tutti (1–16).
            Subsidiary subject, followed by the second half of the
                main subject—piano, then tutti (17–36).
            Codetta—tutti (36–9).

---

[1] The adagio non troppo of the G minor quintet is an exception.

1st couplet: Tonic, then dominant; return to tonic—piano, with
           tutti accompaniment (40–63).

           Codetta of the refrain and transition—piano (63–7).

Refrain: In a shortened form—piano, then tutti (68–83).

2nd couplet: Piano, with important wind accompaniment.

           1st subject—double bar and repeat (84–91)—relative
           minor.

           2nd subject, with return to the 1st (92–107)—tonic,
           then relative minor.

           Long transition (108–18)—return to the tonic.

Refrain: Main subject—piano (119–26).

           Subsidiary subject, as above (127–41).

           Codetta (142–6).

Coda: Tutti, then piano, with accompaniment (146–62).

The key is B flat, the sub-dominant of the relative major of D minor.

In the refrain and first couplet the strings do more work than the wind; the latter intervene only in order to double the strings in the *fortes*. Moreover, when the orchestra plays with the piano, it is confined to accompanying. In the main theme of the refrain (ex. 241) we recognize Mozart's "fluttering seconds" and, in the codetta which closes the refrain and first couplet, the threefold division of a phrase which is so characteristic of his rhythmical scheme.[1]

The opening of the second couplet affords an astoundingly brutal contrast with what precedes it. Hitherto, nothing had belied the smiles of the limpid, ingenuous song with which the romance had begun. The rest of the refrain and the first couplet had led us through a sunny and well-watered countryside and we had at length come back to the refrain. The first half of it is over and has ended, *piano*, in B flat, when suddenly a *fortissimo* breaks out in strings and solo, on the chord of G minor; the andante turns into a presto[2] and the solo sets off with breathless triplets in search of Heaven knows what wild fancy. Full of anguish and fury, it pursues its quest in treble and bass, with frequent crossings of the hands, whilst the wind, roused brusquely from their torpor, follow it and trace out in quavers or crotchets the

---

[1] The solo in the first couplet, especially in bars 48–55, is but an outline; the pianist must fill it out. (We suggest one of many ways of doing so: ex. 242.) He must also fill in the chords of the bass in bars 56–67.

[2] No *tempo* mark; the proof of the change is in the note value.

melodic lines implied in its semi-quavers (ex. 243). How deceptive was the peace of the romance and how superficial! Calm in Mozart is neither deep nor lasting. We are plunged again without warning into the mood of the allegro's most feverish moments.[1]

After the double bar, the scoring is more subtle. Now the bassoon doubles the piano treble, now the hautboy doubles its bass, while the other wind sustain. Then, the episode goes back to its beginning (bar 100) and we finish as we had started, on the chord of G minor (bar 108).

A transition of great breadth links up this section with the refrain. Its task is to bring the movement back to its former state of mildness. The piano shows itself at first disinclined to be peaceful; it still pushes on with dishevelled triplets, then travels rapidly from top to bottom of the keyboard, both hands in unison, whilst strings and wind mark the beats; but at length it loses its impetus in a succession of grand bars where the wind and it move up and down in contrary motion from one end of the register to the other, the wind in quavers, the piano in semi-quavers, then in triplet quavers, finally in simple quavers—a transition whose masterly rhythm reminds us of a horseman reining in his steed from gallop to trot, from trot to walk, bridling it without hurting it and without the slightest jerk in its progress (ex. 244).

The piano writing has the same Beethovenian features as in the first movement. The G minor episode covers all registers of the keyboard. In the fine pedal point which constitutes the coda, the hands are well spaced and, as happens sometimes with Beethoven, the intermediate parts are given to the tutti (ex. 245). On the other hand, the Mozartian device of decorating a tutti passage by the piano on its second appearance is used only once (bars 142–5; repeat of bars 32–5).

The presence of the tempestuous episode in the middle of a peaceful romance makes this movement unique. The episode itself is but an extension of the *minore* of French rondos and there is another example in Mozart of a rondo romance broken by a *minor* allegro,[2] but so violent a contrast within a slow movement is unparalleled in his work.

·   ·   ·   ·   ·   ·

---

[1] We have already pointed out (p. 300) the likeness between the beginning of this episode and that of the *development* in the allegro of K.459. Leopold wrote to Nannerl that this part was "astonishingly difficult". He added (letter of January 14th, 1786) that it should be played "as swiftly as the possibility of bringing out the tune clearly allows".

[2] In the B flat serenade for wind instruments, K.361.

Ex. 244

Ex. 245

Ex. 246

Ex. 247

Ex. 248

Ex. 249

Ex. 250

Ex. 251

III. The finale is one of his few minor key rondos.[1] It is sometimes quoted as a noteworthy example of an irregular rondo. Irregular rondos are indeed not uncommon with him, but this finale is not one of them. It is a sonata rondo very similar in plan to that of the last concerto, where the second couplet—a true *development*—joins on directly to the third without a return of the refrain or of the first subject. Its chief formal distinction is its long coda in the major which follows the last appearance of the refrain.

This is shown by analysis. A general glance, however, gives rather the impression, as in the F major concerto, of a movement in two sections, each of them opening with an important orchestral

---

[1] The others are those of the piano sonatas in A minor and C minor and of the violin sonata in E minor. An earlier sketch of this rondo, thirty-seven bars long, is published in the André edition of Mozart's works. Cf. Köchel-Einstein, no. 466.

passage, and followed by a coda. The first of these sections modulates into the relative major; the second traverses several keys, then returns half-way through to the tonic.

As in the concerto in F, the piano gives out the theme, then withdraws and leaves the place free for a long orchestral development. The theme is one of the finest refrains in Mozart. It has nothing that we associate with a rondo. Its fieriness brings it into line with the mood of the first movement[1] but its passion is more external and more ardent. Twice over it gathers impetus; then, with some difficulty, breaking away in the treble from the tonic, it starts its last strain three times over (ex. 246).

Thereupon opens a magnificent passage. There is nothing more fiery in all Mozart, not, even the finale of the G minor symphony (bars 14–63). The violins lead off with the initial climbing strain of the refrain, but in the fifth bar an E flat proclaims that the music intends modulating. Then, violins, violas and basses throw from one to the other the first fragment of the theme; we pass through, without stopping, the key of the relative major and we land on a dominant close where the quaver motion settles in for good. Without a break (bar 31), second fiddles, then firsts, strike and hold in quavers a dominant pedal which throbs and quivers against the background of woodwind and horns. From this mass a rising movement carries us degree by degree to the tonic where the pedal starts afresh, this time in the basses. One thinks of a swarm of bees whence now one, now another, emerges and re-enters it instantly. The game begins again in the opposite direction, then a theme in long notes, with wide leaps, is heard in the first violins. Finally, a short codetta, just a descending scale, closes the whole thing sharply in the tonic. A part of these riches will not return or will return so altered and in so fugitive a guise that one hardly recognizes it.

The piano begins the first couplet with a subject in a panting rhythm (ex. 247), already used in the *Domine Deus* of the C minor mass. It is a shortened version of ex. 237. It vanishes immediately before an aggressive return of the refrain to which is linked a run which modulates into the relative major (bars 74–92). But the hour for the major mode has not yet struck. The piano discovers another subject (ex. 248), in F minor this time (bars 93–8), dry and incisive, unaccompanied like the preceding one. The wind repeat it, *piano*,

----

[1] It recalls also a rondo for harpsichord in C minor of Philip Emmanuel Bach, Wotquenne 59, no. 4.

and the solo decorates it (bars 99–102). A few bars of virtuosity lead us into F major (103–11), and then, suddenly seized with a fit of loquacity, the piano launches out into a succession of lengthy runs in which the vitality of the fine flight in the earlier bars is scattered and lost (bars 112–39). We end by stopping—for the second time—on the expected trill and the wind give out a fresh theme.

This one is as different from the rest as was ex. 238 from the other themes in the allegro; in its way, one of Mozart's most typical and most exquisite tunes. It has nothing any longer of what we have experienced hitherto: fire, strife, impetus (ex. 249). The piano takes it up without a change and adds a short passage which closes the first episode. Then it unceremoniously turns its back upon the theme and in three bounds reaches a pause; after which it gives out the refrain.

As in the concerto in F, the second couplet begins with an orchestral passage, based on the first notes of the refrain and transitional in character; it soon stops on the dominant chord of A minor. We enter then the *development* of the sonata rondo, entirely thematic and divided between tutti and piano. Its opening bars recall those of the first couplet: the main subject, ex. 247, is expounded by the piano and followed by an angry reminder of the refrain. Then, starting in the piano and spreading contagiously to the flute and bassoon, the first two bars of the refrain travel in haste through the most various keys, stopping at last in G minor, whilst the piano ravels their course with a figure in broken thirds which climbs up and down with a rhythm independent of theirs (bars 211–29).

And now comes the turn of ex. 247, hitherto so much kept in the background. The piano sounds it in G minor, then, with the flute and hautboy, proceeds to dismember it (bars 241–6), after which appears a rather insignificant fragment (ex. 250), close relation of the seventh and ninth bars of the last subject. This fragment is quickly followed by another, an echo of the bar 240, and the same trio, supported by the bassoon, play about with them for some time, driving them through sundry keys and registers, through which themes and instruments pass like roulette balls through the coloured strips of the croupier's circle. A chance stroke having made them pass into D minor, the game is up, and the piano hastens to make the return to the tonic key definitive (bars 247–71).

Here, a regular rondo would allow us to hear the refrain. But we have met it so often that Mozart leaves it out, as well as ex. 247, which we have just quitted, and begins the third couplet or recapitulation with ex. 248 in D minor, a key from which we shall stir no more till the cadenza. In its main lines this couplet reproduces the end of the first one, but the passage which follows ex. 248 is much shortened. Ex. 249, transposed into D minor, now shows us its once sunny landscape under cloudy skies; its spritely gait contrasts ironically with the sadness of the minor mode. A vigorous set of runs leads to the final trill. This is a signal for the orchestra, which rediscovers its initial fire after this long interval and lets loose the "long notes" theme, with wide spacings, which had concluded the first tutti (bars 339-46). It is but a transition and, like other fiery themes in these concertos,[1] announces the cadenza.[2]

From now onward we enter new paths; everything is transformed and the rondo becomes as original as it was at the outset. The cadenza concludes without orchestral intervention. The pianist follows it up with the refrain, but in the seventh bar breaks off and casts it from him with a few angry chords (bars 247-54). One bar of silence,[3] then the horns sound their bass A, a pedal upon which the basses outline an accompanying figure. The hautboys give out the "happy" theme, ex. 249, in D major, and the piano follows suit. The whole band bursts forth with a *ff*, the quaver movement of which (bars 371-6 and 383-8) recalls a passage in the first tutti (bars 33-51); the piano hits back with flourishes (bars 377-82, 389-94). Then, the mark having again dropped to *piano*, over an Alberti bass of the solo's the woodwind repeat a modified, more winged version of ex. 249, and the brass round it off with a fanfare (ex. 251). No louder, the fanfare re-echoes from brass to woodwind, the piano opposes it with scale thrusts, and after a further pedal of seven bars, still soft, the strings rush upward, *ff*, in a joyful scale; and two sudden chords end the movement.

Such is this rondo of very mixed merits.

Through its general build and its thematic unity (two main themes, exs. 246 and 249; two subsidiary, exs. 247 and 248), it is a near relative of the rondo in the last concerto. But it differs radically from it by its feeling and in some respects is inferior to its predecessor.

In works of the *galant* period in minor keys, custom allowed the composer to end his first and last movements on a bright note by passing into the major just where, in the exposition, he had entered

---

[1] For instance, in the allegro of K.449.

[2] Beethoven's cadenza for this movement is less successful than that for the allegro.

[3] It must be given its full value.

the key of the relative major. Haydn often acts thus,[1] especially in his finales; Beethoven also.[2] Mozart, however, seldom takes advantage of this facility, and never in his first movements. Twice, a finale of his is entirely in the major,[3] and twice, too, a finale steps into the major in its last bars.[4]

The incentive to such a modulation into the major is emotional rather than formal. It is indeed possible to conclude in several ways a work which begins with a conflict like that which inspired the first movement of this concerto and which is at the origin of many minor key works of the *galant* period—a period, let us remember, when the minor mode is an exception and corresponds to well characterized moods.

The conflict can be brought to an end by triumph, as in Beethoven's C minor symphony and post-Beethovenian works like Brahms's first symphony or that of César Franck.

It may "triumph over sorrow by distraction" (Saint-Foix). As if the composer had hitherto described suffering rather than felt it, he turns his back on it abruptly and sings of a contrary mood. Haydn often appears to do this; Beethoven himself did it at least once, in his F minor quartet, where the intrusion of a coda in the major after a rondo full of anguish is puzzling. The major conclusion of the variations in the C minor serenade is perhaps a parallel instance in Mozart, and his G minor quartet for piano and strings avoids in its finale any allusion to the uneasiness of the allegro; everything has been said on the score of sorrow and the time has come to speak of other matters.[5]

---

[1] C minor symphony; several sonatas and quartets.

[2] Fifth and ninth symphonies; F minor quartet, etc.

[3] G minor quartet; G minor quintet.

[4] C minor serenade and this concerto. In the B minor adagio for piano the change to the major takes place in the last two bars.

[5] The finale of the G minor quintet is one of Mozart's movements about which opinions differ most. Some find it admirable; others condemn it absolutely as trivial and unworthy of the other three, "an unworthy finishing of an unfinishable work" (Dunhill).

It is hard to share such extreme opinions. It does not occupy among Mozart's finales the place of honour which the allegro occupies among his first movements, but neither does it deserve the hard things said of it. Some may prefer a pessimistic conclusion; Mozart himself has left enough such for us to take him seriously when, for once, he concludes a pathetic work on a joyful note. The movement is not a sham ending and it is clearly related to what goes before. There is no more "distraction" than in the concerto.

Continued on p. 328

We have just quoted what Saint-Foix says of Mozart. We ourselves prefer to say that the composer usually has recourse to defeat
or resignation after a work inspired by suffering. Of the chief minor
compositions of his maturity, more than two thirds close on a note
of sorrow or passion or, at most, find peace, formal rather than
emotional, in a major modulation in the last bar.[1] In these examples,
the finale either confirms the feeling of the beginning, with additional
passion,[2] or else comes back to such feeling with weary resignation.[3]

The case is at first sight less clear in the D minor concerto. Is
there just an about-turn here, a purely formal juxtaposition of a major
ending to a work in the minor? Or is there struggle and triumph?
Is the serenity of the end attained by "distraction" or by conquering?

Continued from p. 327

It is true that none of the first three movements announced so soaring a flight;
at the end of the adagio ma non troppo the mood was as sorrow-laden as at
the beginning of the allegro. But the adagio bars which prefaced the finale
prepared us for a change. In the very first, the rhythm spoke of motion
towards something new. Nothing is less static than this introduction, despite
its slowness. The atmosphere is dark but we do not abide in it. We feel
we are passing through a thick wood, or are living the cold, dark hours that
come before dawn. Towards the thirtieth bar we begin to glimpse the light,
when the first violin replaces the falling lament with a questioning and almost
hopeful rising figure. The branches thin out, the spaces of sky grow broader;
and with the refrain of the rondo, to which not only the outline of its theme
but also the rhythm of its accompaniment seem to give wings, we emerge
into open country and rise up into the air. The transition is quick and in
some ten bars we pass from deepest depression to perfect serenity, but a transition there unmistakably is. Mozart knows that neither struggle nor flight
are the only escape from suffering; it sometimes suffices to let time go by, to
pass through sorrow as we pass through a wood and reach the happy meadows
that stretch beyond it.

"Souffre un moment encor; tout n'est que changement.
L'axe tourne, mon coeur; souffre encore un moment" (Chénier).

Granted, withal, that the movement is on the long side; but that is not generally
the object of the criticisms made of it.

One might add that its kinship with the allegro is attested by the likeness
of certain themes in the two movements (bars 30 of the allegro and 66-8 of
the finale, for instance).

A sheet of sketches sold in 1928 shows that Mozart had originally thought
of a finale in the minor. Its refrain, in 6-8, with the same rhythm as the present
one, was a forerunner, in its melody, of the opening bars of the G minor
symphony.

[1] D minor quartet, K.421, finale; adagio in B minor, K.540.

[2] C minor sonata; G minor symphony.

[3] C minor concerto; first organ fantasia in F minor, K.594.

One's first impulse is to answer: by "distraction". The passage from minor to major is sudden; there is no transition. If the cadenza came immediately before ex. 250 the task of preparing the change might have fallen to the soloist, but this is impossible, for the few bars of the refrain which follow the cadenza oblige him to end in D minor. The appearance of ex. 249 in the major gives therefore the impression of a change of front like those in the C minor serenade, Beethoven's F minor quartet or many a work of Haydn.

But might not the change have been prepared by earlier moments? Have we not heard signs of struggle? Was not the great first tutti (bars 14–63) the result of a conflict even more savage than that which inspired the first movement? Surely; and if such a state of stress had been kept up throughout the rondo, we should not have been tempted to speak of "distraction". But there was no growth in the conflict. On the other hand, the spirit of strife had exhausted itself in bravura runs (bars 111–39). The return of the energetic refrain might have revived it, but the rather finicky interludes combined by piano and orchestra on ex. 247 and on the refrain itself carry us away from it again. The exs. 246, 247 and 248 wore a passionate air, but there was nothing inevitable or dramatic in the order of their appearance.

This was not the case, however, with the contrast between their group and the major subject, ex. 249. Between these there was not only difference but opposition; the first time, the contrast was really dramatic. It was less so when, in the recapitulation, ex. 249 reappeared in D minor, but became dramatic again in the coda. The use here of the only element which is opposed to the general spirit of the movement cannot be due to chance or to a purely formal need of ending the work in the major; one is compelled to see dramatic meaning in it, to look upon it as a climax, a victory of serenity over the tumultuous anxiety of earlier moments. With the significant emergence of the "happy" theme, cutting the refrain short after the cadenza, it is impossible to think of mere "escape"; there is conflict and triumph here, and though the progress of the battle is traced less continuously and less consistently than in Beethoven, this feature, unique in a Mozart finale, should nevertheless be added to the list of Beethovenian traits already noticed in this concerto.

There is no need to repeat how unique a place this work occupies in Mozart's concertos. It is further from the "entertainment" ideal than any of the earlier ones, even the most personal. It is an account of a poignant experience, a "crisis work" if ever there was one, and

any performance which neglects this fact will be bad.   Nowhere are
just graceful playing, "perfect phrasing" and an optimistic interpretation more unseasonable than here; soloist and conductor must agree
to see in Mozart something more than "a charming blend of Susanna
and Cherubino"[1] and to give full value to the stormy accents in the
work.[2]

Through its depth and significance, the D minor concerto registers
a great step forward.   Its form, in its first and third movements, is
less original; we saw that the latter followed the same lines as the
finale of the concerto in F.   In interplay between the protagonists, it
loses the ground gained by several works of 1784: those in E flat, D,
G and F afforded more numerous and more varied instances of collaboration.   Besides, the passages in the rondo where piano and orchestra
combine are the least convincing in the movement and stand aside
from its emotional progress.   It is in the concertos of 1786 that Mozart
regains the ground lost here.

The D minor concerto is an isolated piece, not only in Mozart's
concertos[3] but in all his work.   Its key has been little used by him.
Besides this concerto, the two string quartets, K.173 and 421, are his
only instrumental compositions in it.   He had recourse to it from time
to time for slow movements: the andantino of the serenade in D,
K.320, the variations of the divertimento in D, K.334, and of the violin
sonata in F, K.377, the adagio of the hautboy quartet and the first
part of the little piano fantasia, K.397.   The meaning which the choice
of this key gives to all these works is made clear by the family of
choral and dramatic compositions in D minor: the interludes and
choruses of *King Thamos*;[4] the fine *Kyrie* of 1780, K.341; Electra's
first aria and the chorus "Corriamo, fuggiamo", in *Idomeneo*; the
Domine Deus of the C minor mass and, especially, the banquet scene
in *Don Giovanni*, and the *Requiem*.   D minor is associated in Mozart
with a dusky, foreboding, inward, unlyrical emotion, a passion of
struggle rather than of laments and cries, expressive of threatening fate.

---

[1] Ernest Newman.

[2] "There are dark spiritual depths in the first movement of this concerto
that merely dainty orchestral and piano playing is incompetent to reveal"
(Ernest Newman).

[3] Amongst his unfinished works are six bars of a piano movement in D
minor, perhaps intended for K.537 (Köchel-Einstein 537 b).

[4] Dating from 1774, but extraordinarily close to our concerto at times.

It speaks of danger, physical and moral: the danger of the storm which annihilates the wicked Pheres in *King Thamos*, that with which Electra threatens Idamante and Ilia, that of the monster from whom flee the terror-stricken throng of Cretans, that of the Last Judgement (*Requiem*) and of damnation (*Don Giovanni*). This inspiration, half felt in some parts of both quartets in D minor, so completely expressed in the *Kyrie*, *Don Giovanni* and the *Requiem*, is rendered fully, in all Mozart's instrumental work, only by this concerto.

2. The Seventeenth Concerto: K.467 in C

CONCERTO NO. 17 IN C (K.467)[1]
Finished March 9th, 1785
   (Allegro maestoso): C
   Andante: C (in F)
   Allegro vivace assai: 2-4
Orchestra: Strings; flute, two hautboys, two bassoons, two horns, two
   trumpets, two kettledrums.

THIS concerto followed the last at four weeks interval. Between
the two there is absolute contrast. On one hand, passion, conflict,
storm of the spirit; on the other, calm and majesty. We have already
noted[2] how, more than once, Mozart produces, one after the other,
two first-rate works of highly contrasted inspiration: the autumn
before, with the concerto in B flat, K.456, and the sonata in C minor;
in 1786, with the concertos in A and C minor; and again in 1787
and 1788 with the quintets and symphonies in G minor and C. We
said that it was but one manifestation of his very mobile nature, ready
to leap without transition from one aspect of reality to another, from
one mood to its opposite. Sometimes the sorrowful work precedes
the joyful one; sometimes the contrary. In February and March,
1785, the order is optimistic: the song of peace comes after the tempest;
the luminous C major exorcizes the sombre and *daimonisch* D minor.
Nevertheless, the concerto in C is not a blithe work; it is powerful
and motionless rather than joyful, and in its immobility we recognize,
albeit frozen, the billows of the D minor.

I. The first movement is headed *maestoso*,[3] a mark which should be
observed and not replaced in practice by *brillante*, as is done by
some musicians who consider they know what Mozart wanted better
than Mozart himself. But the first subject, as we hear it in the first
eleven bars, belies this indication. It is a march like so many first

---

[1] *Gesamtausgabe*, no. 21.
[2] See p. 278.
[3] Not, it is true, in the autograph, but in all editions.

subjects in concertos of the period,[1] but a tiptoed march, in stocking feet, and even when woodwind, brass and drums interrupt the strings, it does not rise above *piano* (ex. 252). It is almost a comedy motif and we should not be surprised to see Leporello emerge from it.

But this impression is soon rectified. Conforming to the plan of the quiet beginning followed by a *forte*,[2] Mozart repeats the theme with all the resources of his orchestra, modulates at once with unusual freedom and, passing quickly through A minor and C minor, settles a while in G major on a tonic pedal. We are baulked of our expectation of meeting a new subject in this key and return to the tonic, whose domination has been strengthened rather than undermined by this excursion into the dominant. The work shows at its very outset a grip and an intensity worthy of the D minor.

The expected new theme is not the second subject; it is a rather more than fugitive idea, one of those we have called mock second subjects, and it plays no part in the body of the movement; we shall not hear it again till the end. It is shared out among the woodwind and the colour of its scoring enriches it with associations. Its horn and trumpet call makes it almost a Romantic, whilst the bareness of the answer, drawn and quartered between hautboys and flutes in their upper register and violas and basses, awakens the memory of the trial by fire and water in the *Magic Flute* (bars 28–35; ex. 253).

After giving out these two themes, it would seem that the tutti had but to conclude and admit the solo. But this concerto does not act like its predecessors. Instead of a closing figure, the march, ex. 252, begins again, first in imitations in the strings, *piano*, then, when all the orchestra has joined in, *forte*, and the music launches forth into a working-out whose progress, led with a steady step and insistent in its regularity, reminds us of the straining and pitiless vigour of the D minor (bars 36–63). There is no modulating; everything comes down, in the last resort, to rises and falls of one octave, repeated several times, without haste, now with the whole orchestra, now antiphonally, with strings and woodwind (ex. 254). Such calm perseverance is irresistible; its strength is in its mass, not in its fire or speed;[3] the music looks neither right nor left; its progress is due to singleness

---

[1] Cf. K.414, 415, 451, 453, 456, 459, 537.

[2] See pp. 262, 283, 310.

[3] On condition, once again, that the movement is taken at a moderate speed and even heavily, *maestoso*, and not *brillante*. Played swiftly and lightly, this passage becomes a kind of breathless race that keeps on coming back to its starting-point, which is nonsense.

Ex. 252

Ex. 253

Ex. 254

Ex. 255

Ex. 256

Ex. 257

Ex. 258

Ex. 259

of will. No passage demonstrates better than this both the kinship and the contrast which unite and separate the twin concertos; in one, vehemence and wrath; in the other, self-assurance; in both, a will firm and inexorable.

The *piano* of all the last part of this section has but heightened its calm implacability. We suddenly return to *forte* with the third appearance of the march which, cut down to its first bar and repeated by the whole band, acts as concluding subject[1] (bars 64–8).

The orchestra lands on its full close with such finality that the solo dares not tread the stage without being invited. Three times over, a member of the woodwind family beckons it on, in three phrases which are the clearest revelation of Mozart's dramatic genius expressing itself in a symphonic idiom. Though the style owes nothing to that of opera, they are like three graceful maidens holding out their hands to the bewildered and fearful piano, three Ladies introducing Tamino into a new world. Admire their expressive gradation and the way in which chromaticisms give the third an almost suppliant tone (ex. 255; bars 68–74).

The solo's first bars show the effect of this shyness and the piano makes its bow with a delicate coloratura which certainly has nothing of the tutti's massive self-confidence. Strings and wind continue to beckon it on and support it; finally it plucks up courage on a pause where the soloist should improvise a short cadenza (bars 74–9).

The strings start the march and the piano adorns it with a trill, but in the fifth bar the solo takes it from them and advances alone. The last part of the theme, however, with transparent scoring, is shared as in the tutti between strings and wind, whilst the piano superimposes a decorative counterpoint (bars 80–91).

Instead of the development of bars 12–26, the piano sets out alone with an undulating theme in three strains (ex. 256; bars 91–4), recalling that with which the solo had entered in the last concerto, ex. 237. Like this latter, it is almost a recitative and should be played accordingly. This caressing tune, so different from what we have heard hitherto, quickens and melts into a virtuosity passage which modulates to G major. Two tutti bars assert the new key and the piano gives out the solo subject, which has no connexion with what has gone before; its half aggressive, half elegiac air brings back the world of the D minor and at the same time announces the panting tones with

---

[1] The return of the first subject in the conclusion is a device of the North German school, often used by Haydn in his quartets and already favoured by Mozart in 1773.

which the G minor symphony opens (ex. 257; bars 109–21). But violence and sorrow are both out of season; Mozart casts them quickly aside and in their place installs the sunny carelessness of the second subject (ex. 257), crossroads where meet the paths of piano and orchestra which seldom come near each other elsewhere in this concerto (bars 128–42).

The reader will remember that at the beginning of the solo, the piano had avoided sounding the first notes of the march theme, ex. 252, and later on had sought to distinguish itself from the tutti. It overcomes nevertheless for an instant its loathing to repeat what the orchestra has said, and, following the latter's example in the first tutti, it outlines imitatively the first fragment. But it quickly gives it up, for the strings recognize the passage and catch on to the imitation, and it hovers above them for a moment, motionless, with fluttering broken octaves (bars 143–7). This concerto, however, is not one of those which go over the lines of the first tutti with the docile collaboration of the solo. This recall of the first exposition was but transitory and the strings' imitation, undertaken beneath the piano's presiding octaves, grows into a splendid passage of pure virtuosity, the amplest and most powerful we have met hitherto.[1] The march goes on haunting us with the ghost of its first notes which it moves from register to register, with a progression from subdominant to subdominant which we meet again later on in the movement. The piano comes down from its lofty immobility, and, with both hands, throws itself into the thickest scrub of arpeggios and broken octaves that Mozart has ever set up before his executants. It is a rich and splendid passage, revelling unreservedly in beauty of tone. Virtuosity is here at its own service, or rather, the work's strong vitality demands virtuosity in order to be manifest; it overflows in this passage work as the passion and bitterness of the D minor had done in the fierce diminished seventh arpeggios (ex. 259; bars 148–61). The intensity reaches its climax in four heavy chords to which the pianist should give their full measure of weight (bar 162); then, taking breath in a few quiet bars, the movement regains its impetus on a trill whence it starts off afresh as from a springboard (bars 163–8). And again a series of arpeggios alternates with scales, rushing to the onslaught like troops of Titans placing their ladders against the ramparts of Olympus. The waves of sound break more and more generously, with periods of an amplitude hitherto unattained in Mozart (bars 169–93).

---

[1] We exclude those of the D minor, for one cannot call them pure virtuosity.

The balance of the work demands a development of equal breadth for the tutti; so, instead of the usual short transition at the end of the first solo, we hear a prolonged and triumphal affirmation of the march,[1] where the dominant, G major, gives way before a modulation into E flat (bars 198–203), and a restatement of the second part of the great scale passage which had concluded the first tutti, ex. 254 (bars 52–63; here, 205–15). But we have travelled beyond this stage and the time is not yet ripe for returning to it. The expected cadence is dodged, the magnificent self-reliance of the music fades away; we modulate into B minor, and with a stroke of the wand Mozart throws open one of those windows on infinity through which the eye pierces all the more keenly for the opening being so unexpected (bars 215–21). We halt upon a note of wondering and, as before the first piano entry in the D minor, we sense without defining it a new presence.

The *development* opens with a tune which unfolds in groups of three and four sections. Not only does its temper carry us back to the last concerto, but the violin answer (ex. 260) is almost a quotation of the piano left hand part in ex. 237 (bars 222–30). The woodwind restate it with a variation, and the piano adds embroideries; the whole thing is one of those variations, uncommon in Mozart, which keep nothing but the harmonic basis of the theme (ex. 261; bars 231–7). Departing from this subject, so attractive nevertheless, piano and woodwind open fiery speech over a little figure (ex. 262 a), on whose back we travel through new keys. The progression is methodical, from subdominant to subdominant, but the feeling, more and more intense, ends by rising to a state of passion as the phrases are shortened from four to two bars (bars 249–52). A quieter passage begins when E flat is reached and after a long chromatic climb (bars 259–64) the motion breaks into a rapid glissade, with a fleeting sign of weariness; then, hoisting itself up for one last effort, drops degree by degree, decrescendo, on a dominant pedal, to the tonic (bars 265–74). This reprise, like the rest of the movement, is of unwonted breadth; in this respect it is surpassed only by that of the other great concerto in C, K.503, the harmony of whose reprise is similar.

The recapitulation opens, like the movement itself, on a soft note. Again, a long tutti development succeeds an extensive solo. The first nineteen bars repeat those of the beginning; then we modulate suddenly into F major, a vagary all the more unexpected in that Mozart seldom modulates after his middle section (bars 293–5). The fiddles

---

[1] This return of the first subject after the first solo is perhaps an archaism.

again go through their imitation; then the piano reappears. Profiting by the imitation in which it joins, it emits a brief lament, a distant memory, perhaps, in inspiration, of the G minor subject, ex. 257, but in form a development of the ever-present march (bars 297–305).

Save that it is in the tonic, the second appearance of the second subject differs from the first only in details of orchestration. Identical, also, is the great bravura passage that follows it, as far as the chords (bar 161); in their place, four transitional bars lead to the mock second subject, ex. 258, which answers the roll call here as a delegate from the opening tutti (bars 351–4). Its former emaciation is somewhat disguised beneath a richer scoring; then the piano restates it and, without more ado, enters upon its last virtuosity passage, the elements of which are those of the solo at the end of the exposition. There are a few superficial changes and a few additions, notably a fine rising passage in broken sixths, over a dominant pedal, doubled by the woodwind, of a fullness of tone recalling the passage in the same position in the F major concerto, K.459 (bars 375–7).

The rest of the allegro belongs to the march. It opens the way for the cadenza and, after the recall of bars 44–5 of the first tutti, provides the çoda, nearly as original as that of the D minor. We are led to expect a noisy and triumphant exit; instead, the movement dies away in quiet with the same furtive step as it had opened (ex. 263).

Many are the observations prompted by this movement, but we will confine ourselves to three of them. They concern the distribution of the material, the unity of the orchestral part and the richness and novelty of the piano writing.

In the D minor, the important thing was the drama in which piano and orchestra collaborated equally. Here, the game consists in each one saying what it has to say independently of the other, but without contradiction or opposition, for the message is the same for both and there is agreement of thought, although the words are different. In other terms, piano and orchestra seldom give out the same themes; the elements that fall to each are usually distinct. The mock second subject belongs mainly to the orchestra; only at its second and last appearance does the piano take an interest in it, and then not till the orchestra has dealt with it, and it is abandoned immediately. The true second subject, as transitory as many others in these concertos, belongs rather to the piano, although the orchestra restates it. The long solos owe absolutely nothing to the material given out by the tutti. And even the first subject, whose presence haunts the movement so tenaciously, is avoided by the piano most of the time; at the beginning of the first solo, only the second half is expounded, the less characteristic one; it is true that the piano feels bound to resume the imitative use which the violins had made of it (bars 143-4, 297-8, 328-9), but it at once takes refuge in virtuosity and with haughty indifference lets the theme serve as an accompaniment figure in the hands of the tutti. This dividing of the material into two lots, one for orchestra and one for solo, is not peculiar to this concerto; in most of the others there exist themes reserved for one or other of the protagonists; but in no other does Mozart carry so far the separation between the two.[1]

Despite the presence of a more brilliant solo part than in any earlier concerto, the orchestra is not sacrificed. The first tutti and the three other great interludes, veritable symphonic developments thanks to which Mozart balances the respective influences of the opponents, are full of sustained power; their flow is continuous; nothing holds up their progress; scarcely a theme raises its head above the flood and breaks the magnificent, smooth line of their advance; no closes cut up their unity. These tuttis are permeated and dominated by the presence of the first subject or at least of its first four notes, which haunts them as the rhythm ♩♩♪♩♩ haunted the F major concerto. It is always there, ready to slip on to the stage as soon as the other elements relax their watchfulness. Thrice over it takes possession in the first tutti; the mock second subject drives it away for one moment, but it reappears under cover of counterpoint; the great working out of bars 44-63, ex. 254, keeps it away a little longer, but it returns to close the discussion, provisionally at first, at the end of the tutti, then for good and all, when the allegro, alike in this to the D minor, ends with the very motif with which it had begun (ex. 263).

What shall we say of the solo part? Passage work preponderates in it, for the tunes, however personal they may be, are but bridges over which one crosses to more important things. Despite their length—two fifths of the movement—these passages are always sustained by the breath of grandeur and power which fills the whole work, whose heroic soul they express in their own way. They never degenerate into loquacity as in a few bars of the G major or the rondo of the D minor. One constant harmonic device, the subdominant progression, and the great number of runs based on scales, give them cohesion and discipline. The writing shows several traits new in Mozart and the simultaneous use of the two hands is more persistent than in any earlier work including the D minor. The breadth and

---

[1] Not even in K.415.

richness of the piano part harks back to the ambitious prelude of the
C major concerto of 1782; the piano has at last caught up with the
tutti; Mozart has succeeded in making it as capable a vehicle of his
thought as the orchestra.

All this combines to make it a single-minded work, majestic and
strong, which the D minor concerto, alone among earlier compositions,
could have led us to expect. These two concertos proceed unquestionably from the depths of the same soul, though the depths be
different. The D minor was as forceful, but more violent, less broad,
less smooth in rhythm. This one is Olympian, the first work in a
family which includes the great C major works of the next three years
and the first where this side of Mozart's many-sided genius is fully
displayed.[1]

II. The world of the andante is that of the "dream" andantes,[2] a
family which comprises some of Mozart's most beautiful slow movements in earlier years[3] and in the long succession of which it is the
last; but its form is unique.

It is a piano cantilena preceded by a tutti prelude and sumptuously
sustained and adorned by the murmur of the strings and the multi-
coloured raiment of the wind. The tune winds from key to key,
smooth and closely blended; it passes through various moods, some
dreamy, some full of anguish, some serene, but the themes hardly
stand out; it is a river, moving slowly but unceasingly, and only from
time to time does an eddy in the current announce a fresh subject.

Yet it is not a fantasia. There is direction and progress in its emotion and its form. The stream advances, turns back, passes on again,
and though its structure be free, it is never loose. Even though the
ear does not at first distinguish themes, it picks out strains already
heard, places already traversed, and the succession of these places and
strains, as well as of the keys, satisfies our imagination and is also
justified by our analytical faculty.

The movement unfolds in three periods (bars 1–23, 24–72, 73–104),

---

[1] We recognized an "Olympian" inspiration for the first time in Mozart in
the *Sinfonia Concertante*, K.364. At first, the key of E flat expressed in his
work the mood we have described thus; in 1780, C major is still the key of
festal and joyous overtures; it is only in 1785 that, without losing this character,
it becomes the key of those works that scale the mountain of the Gods.

[2] Cf. pp. 36, 39, 40.

[3] Those of the violin concerto in G, of the symphony in C, K.338, and of
the string quartet in E flat, K.428.

in each of which we hear identical material.   The first is that of the orchestral prelude, where this material, at first sight indissolubly welded, is given out alone almost without modulation; in the second, which opens with the solo entry, the elements come in the same order but their succession is broken by the intrusion of a new theme and another is added to them, whilst modulations are numerous; the third continues to modulate but goes over again the tracks of the first one and ends with a coda.

The key sequence in this andante is even more original.   For clarity's sake let us say that the piece belongs to the large group of binary movements, where the sequence can be simplified to:

Tonic—dominant; various keys—tonic.

Through the labyrinth of keys, in fact, it is towards the dominant that we wend our way as soon as we leave F major, in the thirty-sixth bar.   It is true that, when we reach it, we stay there for only four bars, but by utilizing the fragment, which had concluded the opening tutti (ex. 267) and which we therefore associate with stability, to establish the key, and by following up this fragment with one of the few full closes in the movement (bars 54-5), Mozart gives it a relief and a highlight which the other keys, through which his dreamy bark carries us, do not enjoy.

The end of the second period resumes the modulating progress and the next stage is reached with the return of the first subject in A flat (relative major of the tonic minor; bar 73), whence, after a few more turnings, we regain the key of F from which one half of the movement separated us.

To make these remarks more intelligible, we give a diagram of the movement with the *incipits* of the chief elements.

1   Ex. 264 F   7 bars

2   Ex. 265 F   3 bars

3   Ex. 266 F minor 6 bars   1st period
                                       (tutti)
4   Ex. 267 F major 4 bars

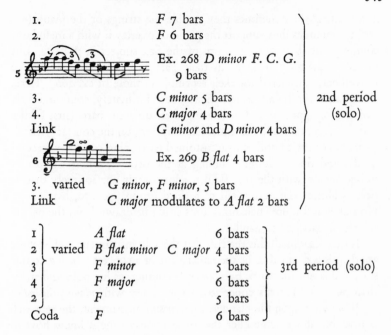

1.		F 7 bars	⎫
2.		F 6 bars	⎪
5	Ex. 268 D *minor* F. C. G. 9 bars		⎪
3.		C *minor* 5 bars	2nd period
4.		C *major* 4 bars	(solo)
Link		G *minor* and D *minor* 4 bars	⎪
6	Ex. 269 B *flat* 4 bars		⎪
3. varied		G *minor*, F *minor*, 5 bars	⎪
Link		C *major* modulates to A *flat* 2 bars	⎭

1		A *flat*	6 bars	⎫
2	varied	B *flat* minor C *major*	4 bars	⎪
3		F *minor*	5 bars	3rd period (solo)
4		F *major*	6 bars	⎪
2		F	5 bars	⎪
Coda		F	6 bars	⎭

But its structure is not the only feature worthy of admiration in this andante and, at any rate on a first hearing, it is not what we notice most. The colour and mass of the various instrumental tones move us more deeply. The scoring, increasingly rich in Mozart's concertos during the last year, reaches here a high level. We have no longer a piece with *obbligati* woodwind; all the instruments[1] collaborate in the work of beauty. The colour is made rarer by the mutes and by the fact that each time the highly characteristic accompaniment figure [♪] sustains the piano, pizzicati replace bows. On the whole, the business of the strings is to provide mass; to them fall the repeated triplets which throb persistently all through the dream and maintain a threatening state of uneasiness. After the prelude, they sing only when doubling the piano (in ex. 267), or when joining forces with the wind (in ex. 266; cf. also ex. 270).

To the colour of the strings enhanced by mutes and pizzicati is added, with profitable discretion, that of the woodwind. Longish rests between their interventions give to each one an impression of novelty. Sometimes the instruments reinforce *sforzandos* with held

---

[1] Except the trumpets and kettledrums, which are silent.

notes (ex. 265); sometimes they double the strings or the piano (ex. 267); sometimes they support the piano or overlay it with a melodious counterpoint (bars 75–81; return of the first subject in A flat). But the most masterly passages in their part and indeed in the whole movement, considered for their scoring, are those of ex. 266. Here, strings and woodwind mingle their groups intimately, confound their harmonies, opposing and interlacing their different parts (first fiddles and flute, second fiddles and first hautboy), or, on the contrary, match members of their families unaccustomed to keeping company (second fiddles and first bassoon, doubling at the octave), whilst the piano, siding openly with the first fiddles, adorns their line so freely that its part is almost the equivalent of a third group (ex. 270, bars 82–7). No richer and more enchanting tints could be drawn from the palette which Mozart had to hand.

Is there not in all this the risk that the solo instrument itself, whose apotheosis is deemed to be the *raison d'être* of a concerto, be left to one side, and is not the work by way of becoming, as has been said more than once of Mozart's concertos, a symphony with *piano principale*?

If we look upon the piano as a percussion instrument, the reproach is just; but if we remember that once upon a time it knew how to sing and was proud of doing so, we shall find that it remains despite everything at the front of the stage. After the prelude it is never silent for more than two bars and its silences are few. Only, except when it uses its left hand to relieve from time to time the strings' triplets, it is confined to singing. No chords, no mass effects; the most massive of Mozart's allegros is followed by the most cantabile of andantes.[1] No opposition, either, to the orchestra, as in the first movement. Never, it is true, does it descend from its position as soloist; yet it often collaborates closely with the other instruments. But there is no interplay; the close knit and continuous nature of the movement does not allow of this. It combines with the others as *primus inter pares*, as a solo singer with other singers. Sometimes, it hears itself supported by the wind and, whenever the unquiet theme, ex. 267, returns, it seconds the first violins without surrendering its independence. And all the time it never stops singing; one feels that its chief contribution here is its tone colour, the pale, delicate colour of the 1780 piano, whose beauty Mozart never set forth more felicitously than in this nocturne.

-----

[1] The concerto in D, K.451, shows with less contrast the same opposition between its first two movements.

We say, nocturne, and in truth the *rapprochement* with Chopin can hardly be avoided. The hazy atmosphere of the mutes, the quivering calm of the ceaseless triplets, the slow, sustained song of the piano—more than all this, the veiled and sorrowfully passionate soul which this music expresses with such immediacy, do we not find them in the work of Chopin and especially in those nocturnes of which this "dream" of Mozart's reminds us? This andante, so placid at first hearing, betrays on further acquaintance an agitated mood. Its perpetual instability, to which its constant modulating and its unsatisfied quest for new places bears witness; its morbid disquiet, thinly concealed now and again under an appearance of calm, breaking forth with heart-rending pathos in the chromaticisms and the discreet yet pungent hues of ex. 270, are unquestionably fundamental elements of Mozart's nature, but they are elements which he shares with Chopin, and indeed they come fully to light as they do here, much less often with him than with the Romantic composer.[1]

III.   These two movements are summits of Mozart's work, witnesses of creative planes as far removed one from the other as those of one same individual can be. After the lovingly analytical study we have made of them, we do not feel inclined to go deeply into the finale. Not that it is unworthy of Mozart, even of the thirty-year old Mozart; but we have just left two movements which he never surpassed, whereas there are a dozen finales in his concertos more interesting and attractive than this one. . . . Yet we are pledged to study each movement of all his greater concertos and we must not shirk the task. Let us then give this one its due.

This finale is a sonata rondo of strict form, as strict as that of K.451. The theme of the refrain, a rough awakening after the glories of the andante, plunges us cruelly in midmost opera buffa and the rest of the movement does not belie it. The finale of the F major concerto, K.459, also began with a skipping subject in 2-4, very similar in character; but the rondo rose later to heights unsuggested by the refrain. Here, there is no such surprise in store; there is not a bar whose nature is not announced by the beginning (ex. 271). The first couplet, starting in C and modulating to G, has first, second and third subjects. It contains much less virtuosity than the allegro but its vitality is also less and it expresses and exhausts itself in less time. The *development*

---

[1] With this andante, the Chopin-like Mozart is best seen in the A minor rondo for piano, K.511, and the slow movement, in F sharp minor, of the concerto in A major, K.488.

couplet is based entirely upon the first notes of the refrain; as in the
rondo of K.451, it is the most interesting part of the movement.
Piano and woodwind banter wittily over their fragment and play
ball with it; the passage recalls a similar one in the rondo of K.450

(ex. 272). When the game is over, the refrain returns complete. The third couplet is the recapitulation and repeats the first with minor changes and without modulating to the dominant. It leads to the cadenza and the last return of the refrain forms the coda.

If the material is commonplace, the realization is nevertheless good Mozart and after less grand first and second movements one would admire this rondo unreservedly. The scoring is sparkling; wind and strings engage in lively rivalry (ex. 273); the accompaniment is often original (bars 128-40, 207-12, 379-92), and exchanges between piano and tutti are more frequent thàn in the allegro (bars 162-9, 413-18, where the piano decorates the woodwind exposition of the third subject with fragmentary arpeggios or scales; bars 314-20, where the piano gives out the refrain and plays in tenths to a fiddle accompaniment; bars 371-5, where it adorns with scales the woodwind exposition of the second subject; and all the last section, where it sustains and enlivens the refrain, given out by the strings, with a brilliant Alberti bass and scales darting like rockets through the last strains of the theme). The development is more interesting than that of K.451, though not the equal of K.450; it recalls both of them and is an excellent example of a Mozartian thematic working-out.

If this chapter stops a little short, it is because this concerto does likewise. After such an opening it was hard to conclude; the C major concerto of 1786, whose allegro is still more majestic, does not hold its head up so well in its rondo. The C major quintet is luckier; but it is only with the *Jupiter* symphony that Mozart hits on the ideal finale with which to rival an Olympian first movement.

3. The Eighteenth Concerto: K.482 in E flat

CONCERTO NO. 18 IN E FLAT (K.482)[1]
Finished December 16th, 1785
    Allegro: C
    Andante: 3-8 (in C minor)
    Rondo: Allegro: Andantino cantabile: Allegro: 6-8
    Orchestra: Strings; flute, two clarinets,[2] two bassoons, two horns, two trumpets, two kettledrums.

THERE are experiences in our life that come to us but once. They seem to arise out of nothingness; no warning allows us to suspect their visit; once over, there is no rediscovering them; they may persist a while as fading memories but no circumstance can revive them; they have vanished as wholly as the minute which brought them.

Other experiences, less haughty, condescend to return. A given state of mind will have become familiar to us from being frequently with us; it is no doubt never identical from one visit to the next; different shades qualify it at each appearance; but in its essence it is the same. The experience comes back, ever richer, ever fuller, affecting ever greater stretches of our being. We end by recognizing its accompanying and determining circumstances; we succeed in foreseeing each of its returns, hoped for or dreaded; it may even come to us so often that it ends by being an almost constant companion.

To these two kinds of experience correspond two kinds of works of art. One kind is unique in the artist's creative history; it is the commoner, no doubt, especially with those who strive after originality before all else and seek to achieve the new at every throw. The other kind, on the contrary, falls into families whose every member is the incarnation of the same type, where the same general lines are drawn again in one individual after another. The work of the older masters, whether writers, musicians or painters, afforded many more

---

[1] *Gesamtausgabe*, no. 22.

[2] Clarinets instead of hautboys; it is their first appearance in these concertos.

instances of these creations in series, extending through the lives of their authors like garlands whose flowers are, at a distance, indistinguishable one from the other. Not only have they the family air that is common to all born of one father; modern works, too, have that; but they have sprung from the same creative plane, from moods so similar that they are but a succession of returns of one same fundamental experience.

These general remarks apply to the work of Mozart. Within the thirteen months from February, 1784, to March, 1785, in compositions like the concertos in E flat, G and D minor there crystallized experiences that either were unique or, if they ever came again to him, left no further trace in his work. No other piece can be likened to them; they have, indeed, the Mozartian family air common to all; but in that family they are isolated. This was not so with the concertos in B flat, D and F, to which we had no difficulty in finding parallels. This is not so, either, with the E flat concerto with which, on December 16th, Mozart opened the 1785-6 season of winter concerts.

In this work a long succession of attempts, expressing with various degrees of intensity and conviction the same state of mind, comes to fruition. From the earliest days of his life as a composer, there is heard an ideal song which the child, and then the youth, tries to reproduce; we hear it in the symphonies of his childhood journeys, in those of his seventeenth year and, by snatches, elsewhere. He has rendered it once for all in its perfection in his eighteenth concerto.

More than a dozen times already its inspiration had taken shape in different compositions. The oldest was his first symphony, written at the age of nine, K.16; the most recent, the E flat quartet of 1783, K.428; between them spread out the two piano concertos, K.271 and 365, the *Sinfonia Concertante*, K. 364, the E flat serenade, K.375, and several other more unassuming pieces.[1] Some began very similarly to our concerto;[2] others, or the same ones, went into C minor for their andante[3] as it does; in others, again, the kinship is less clearly defined but recognizable nevertheless.

Of this chain of works the eighteenth concerto is the culmination. In it we have the clearest proof that Mozart, as it has been said, did what

---

[1] Symphonies in E flat, K.132, 1772, and K.184, 1773; violin sonata, K.302, 1777 or 1778; concerto for wind instruments, Köchel-Einstein 297 b, 1778 (if it is authentic).

[2] K.16, 132; Köchel-Einstein 297b.

[3] K.16, 184, 271, 364; string quartet in E flat, K.171, 1773.

everyone else was doing, but did it better. This is partly true of every great artist, since none, however powerful his individuality, ever withdraws completely from his environment. No doubt, there are in Mozart precursory strains that hark beyond their period, but on the whole his work is the crowning of the closing 18th century, and nowhere better than in this concerto can we see with what art he realized the century's ideal, whilst yet casting aside the shackles of fashion. If, then, this work sings of an experience that others had sung of, this is partly the result of personal circumstances; it is also because the experience was one of those with which the century itself, more or less consciously, was acquainted. After the unflinchingly personal compositions of the beginning of the year, Mozart returns to an ideal more accessible to his public and common to him and them; after two works so individual as to be almost anti-social, here is once again a sociable concerto, a well-bred person, full of savoir-vivre, ingratiating, in contact with its environment.

The autumn and winter of 1784 to 1785 had witnessed, together with fashionable and spritely works like the concerto in F, considerable deepening and enrichment in that life of the soul of which Mozart's music is the expression and the fruit. The C minor sonata, the quartets in A and C and the concertos in D minor and C are the chief products of this change. The process had continued during the spring and summer as we see in the well-known C minor piano fantasia, so perfect a commentary on the sonata of the preceding autumn with which it is always published, and in a strange work, also in C minor, which is revived from time to time as a curiosity, but in reality lights up a fundamental plane of Mozart's nature: the *Masonic Funeral Music* (*Maurerische Trauermusik*).

This work is the only instrumental composition of his with a programme. As its title indicates, it is a lament for the death of two brethren of the lodge to which Mozart belonged, the Duke George-Augustus of Mecklemburg-Strelitz and Prince Franz Esterhazy of Galantha, the grand-master. But it is more than a farewell song to two departed friends. It is a meditation upon death, quiet though sorrowful, and nearer in spirit to the *Magic Flute* than to the *Requiem*. A feeling of other-worldliness pervades it and the music passes effortlessly and without break from this life to that which the musician sees beyond the grave. There is no tragedy and no violence; the beginning and end are expressive of the sadness caused by separation, but the middle portion, into which is woven a psalm tune, contemplates death serenely, without defiance or fear, as a friend in whom the composer sees no mystery.

One single letter has survived the destruction of those Mozart wrote to his father after his initiation as a mason, and though it was written two years later, on April 4th, 1787, it is relevant to this symphonic poem.

> I have made a habit of being prepared in all affairs of life for the worst. As death, when we come to consider it closely, is the true goal of our existence, I have formed during the last few years such close relations with this best and truest friend of mankind, that his image is not only no longer terrifying to me but is indeed very soothing and consoling! And I thank my God for graciously granting me the opportunity (you know what I mean)[1] of learning that death is the key which unlocks the door to our true happiness. I never lie down at night without reflecting that— young as I am—I may not live to see another day. Yet no one of all my acquaintances could say that in company I am morose or disgruntled. For this blessing I daily thank my Creator and wish with all my heart that each one of my fellow creatures could enjoy it.[2]

The intense inner life of which these works are the fruit was active throughout the summer. Written soon after the *Funeral Music*, the first movement of the G minor piano quartet still reflects at times the emotional storms of the past months. A little later, there escapes from his letters the first of those cries of distress which were so soon to succeed each other with harrowing regularity. We hear it in a letter to Hoffmeister, the publisher of this quartet, when Mozart asks him, "just for a moment", to lend him "a little money, for", he says, "I have the greatest need of it just at present." This letter is dated November 20th.

Four weeks later, he enters the E flat concerto in the list of his works.

After nearly one year of highly personal music, Mozart seems now to make an effort to recapture the public he sees slipping from him. Purely galant works reappear among his compositions. Since 1783, there had been no such "drawing-room piece", for instance, as the violin sonata in E flat, K.481, contemporary with our concerto. The allegro is one of his most lifeless sonata movements and the andante lives only through the echoes from the lovely andante of the G minor quartet that sound in it at times. Henceforward, "society" works,

---

[1] This has generally been taken to refer to freemasonry.
[2] E. Anderson's translation, III, 1351.

absent since the concerto in F, K.413, will be frequent and go on appearing till the end of 1788. Galant works before 1783 had been
written with some delight and the gap between them and the more
serious ones was less wide than now; the distance between the little concerto in F of 1782 and the B flat concerto, K.450, of 1784, is less great
than that which separates this sonata and the concerto finished four days
later. It is hard to realize that two such works should be contemporary,
just as it is hard to understand how Mozart, whilst working at his
great symphonies in 1788, could produce such trifles as the trios in
E, C and G and the "easy" sonatinas in C and F. Such condescension
towards an ideal he had transcended and to which he submitted now,
it seems, without joy, can be explained only by the need he felt for
recapturing his public. This need may account also, at least in part,
for the more sociable and accessible character of the E flat concerto
itself and for Mozart's return in it to an inspiration on which he had
already often drawn.

I. Of all his concertos, this one is the queenliest. Combining grace
and majesty, the music unfolds like a sovereign in progress, the queen
of the twenty-three. The work is of ancient lineage and utters what
many earlier works have uttered, but it speaks with the language of
an adult of thirty, whereas they had stammered with the tongues of
children and youths. Thoughts once short-winded are here spread
out with breadth and developed with rich orchestration and easy
counterpoint. This is as true of the first movement as of the touching
C minor andante, also the last of a noble ancestry.

The first six bars of the allegro conform to the same pattern as
the openings of earlier E flat works: a vigorous and rhythmical attack
and a light answer, quiet and tuneful.[1] It is in the childish symphony
K.16, of 1765, that this kind of opening resembles most nearly what
it has become in our concerto (ex. 274). On returning to it twenty
years later, Mozart shortens the second part, thus improving the balance, but keeps the held notes with their syncopated progression, and
sets against their stability a diaphanous dance entrusted the first time
to the bassoon and the second to the violins, which fulfils the same
function as the repeated crotchets of the bass in the symphony
(ex. 275). A development based on a figure given out at first by the
flute and repeated by the clarinets and bassoons links on to this first

---

[1] Its formula is a commonplace in *galant* music. It occurs in particular
in an E flat symphony of Abel which passed for a long time as a work of
Mozart's (no. 18 in Köchel), op. 7, III.

subject, whilst the violins mingle with them a winding counter-
subject derived from it (ex. 276).   This, too, is repeated and a vigorous
passage follows whose most striking feature is the fragment ex. 277.
It leads to a close and a few solemn woodwind chords over a pedal
in the horns open the way for a new theme.   The tune thus heralded
is a close relation to one in the overture of *Figaro* and reminds us that
Mozart had begun that opera about the time he was finishing the
concerto (ex. 378).   In spite of appearances, it is but the mock second
subject; the true one is held back for the solo exposition.   A loud and
energetic passage on a rising bass leads to the conclusion, the last bars
of which are a diminution of its theme and seem to sum up the last
part of the tutti (ex. 279).

Ex. 276

Ex. 277

Ex. 278

Ex. 279

Ex. 280

With this prelude we return to the world of the 1784 concertos. The vital drive, the strong phrases of the two last works are absent; there are no more ample workings out; no more of that thematic unity which conveyed so much power to the C major nor of that concentrated thought and form which, abandoned for a while, is resumed a few months later with the C minor and leads up to the string quintets. In their place we have a succession of subjects, different from each other if not actually contrasted, with restatement instead of condensation. We pass through a variety of interludes; some graceful and tender, some mischievous, some energetic, but all seeking to be acceptable to their patrons. And over all, ensuring unity in spite of these formal differences, the same blend of grace and majesty, the same confidence; the queen not only anxious to please but sure of doing so.

This tutti is the *argument* of the movement in that, except for the second subject, it contains all the chief elements. The solo exposition, nevertheless, repeats only the beginning and end of it (bars 1–12, 58–76); between them, it inserts a new section provided by the piano. It opens with a solo prelude of seventeen bars, whose tunefulness, grace and strength answer faithfully to the nature of the tutti, and when the orchestra re-enters with ex. 275 the piano collaborates in giving out the subject by decorating it (ex. 280).[1] Instead of the working out of ex. 276 there unfolds a passage which modulates to the dominant. Two bars of orchestra introduce the solo subject, a fierce explosion in B flat minor, with massive chords underlined by the stealthy creeping strings (ex. 281). Its angry mood takes some time to subside and the virtuosity passage which follows it, with flute and bassoon taking it in turns to escort the piano, does not shake off the mourning garb of the minor mode till we near the second subject.

This latter bulks larger than in the last concertos. Not only is it in perfect agreement with the general sense of the movement but it is long and leisurely. The piano expounds it, repeating its first half; then, instead of passing it over to the orchestra, it restates it and the instruments' only share is a touching counter-subject in the woodwind, where flute and clarinets, hovering above the joyful restlessness of the piano, move down as if to meet it (ex. 282).

The solo into which it opens is one of those we have called loquacious. Bearable at first, this loquacity becomes tedious when Mozart repeats the chatter unchanged except for an interversion of the hands.

---

[1] The quotation combines both presentations of the theme.

It is true that he had done likewise in the C major concerto, but there virtuosity, much less obvious than here, had in its favour a passion and a vigour which constrained us; one felt that without it and without the precise shape it was taking, the experience could not be translated. Here there is nothing so inevitable.   These runs might be replaced by many others without altering the character of the concerto, and we protest when Mozart, by repeating the same passages twice over, attaches undeserved importance to them. Happily, only a dozen bars are affected and the beauty of the whole is not lessened thereby.

Here we join again the opening tutti. The exposition links on to the development by repeating its last eighteen bars in B flat.   Then the piano, like a kitten who has just spied a bit of thread and decides to play with it, seizes hold of the last notes of ex. 279, modulates into B flat minor and, thanks to them, exchanging the while a few short remarks with the orchestra, enters upon the long bravura passage which constitutes the *development*.

No theme guides its exploration.   This concerto returns to the tradition of the *fantasia developments* of the previous year and carries through sundry keys a number of running figures which appear to repeat themselves but actually are always changing shape.   Sometimes the woodwind, sometimes the strings accompany the piano on its voyage, but neither comes to the fore.   Minor keys predominate and the excursion takes place under a threatening sky which has forgotten the sunny opening and announces the twilight of the andante.   These are grand and powerful bars, devoid of the capricious charm of the *developments* in the D and G major concertos.   The movement puts into port for an instant in A flat with a tune very like ex. 282 and we work back to the reprise with a bridge passage entrusted to the woodwind and brass: a pedal in the horn and second bassoons with a syncopated counterpoint in the rest, and piano scales; there reappear the clashing seconds of the first subject which characterize this allegro and make it sound at times like a wind serenade (ex. 283).[1]

We saw that only the beginning and end were common to both expositions.   The recapitulation has therefore to pick up the material from the first which the second had omitted, and to interest the solo in it.   This is done admirably in what is certainly the finest portion of the movement.   It goes again over the whole first tutti, with important changes in scoring and the addition, for most of the time, of the

---

[1] The reader will have noticed them also in the quotation from K.16, ex. 274.

piano. From the solo exposition it recalls the first half of the second subject, but it leaves out the solo subject, ex. 281, and the passage that followed it; the "loquacious" bravura passage is replaced by a new one, half as short. It is, on the whole, a repetition of the first exposition with the piano part added and the inclusion of only half the second subject.

Never hitherto had Mozart varied his recapitulation with such art. The piano, especially, is determined to make all things new. It decorates the violin answers in exs. 275 and 280 with sparkling two-handed scales. It is in the development of ex. 276 that it shows its genius best. Let the reader turn to the miniature score and take stock of the substitutions Mozart has carried out here, first of all introducing the solo in place of the wind, then reinstating the wind while the piano enriches the score with a new part. The bewitching mock, second subject, roguish and sentimental, tarries longer with us this time and everyone becomes busy with it. The piano gives it out, joined and doubled in the third bar by the flute and clarinet; fiddles and clarinet repeat it, and piano and flute unite in the rippling counterpoint which belonged the first time to the clarinet and bassoon (cf. with ex. 278). This tune is now the fashionable one and the true second subject comes meekly behind, all the spritelier for being shorn of its second half. Save for four additional closing bars, the conclusion is unaltered. There is no coda: another difference with the last two concertos and a point of likeness with those of the previous year.

The piano has unlearnt the lessons of the D minor and C major concertos. Its writing is once again linear and mass effects are confined to the chords of ex. 281. Nearly everything is done in scales. The two hands seldom play both together and when they do it is in octaves. There is nothing like the two-handed passages of the D minor nor the muscular arpeggios in contrary motion of the C major. We have returned to the writing of K. 450 and the piano style is another feature that takes us back at one bound, beyond February and March, to the works of the past year.

II. The andante opens with one of Mozart's themes which speak most to the imagination and kindle our sense of the picturesque. It is a mournful, trailing tune, whose heavy sadness is emphasized by the use of mutes. The strings, with their veiled and muffled tone, unfold a long lament, irregular and tortuous, that moves almost entirely within the compass of an octave (ex. 284). It comes and goes upon itself and calls up the picture of a blind man groping his way towards the light; at times he draws near to it and thinks he has reached it; he holds out his hands towards it, but he is alone and no one comes to help him; at length, worn out by his sobs he lets his arms drop, gives up his quest and sinks down in despair.

The tune, reserved to the strings, belongs mainly to the first violins confined to their lower register, but the accompanying seconds mingle with them at times (ex. 285). A momentary halt on E flat lightens it, but it falls quickly back into the minor, wavering between F, G and C, and expires in C minor. The very Mozartish lengthening of its last strain by two bars more pathetic than the rest is peculiarly moving (ex. 286).

The form of the movement cannot be guessed from these thirty bars. Theme and variations, rondo, sonata: all are possible. The piano entry appears to settle the question. The solo takes up the tune, unaccompanied, and varies it. The instrument's incisive tone illuminates it; no longer do we hear a muttered lament nor glimpse a fumbling, penumbral searcher; it becomes a supplication formulated as clearly as a recitative (ex. 287). Its vitality is suddenly increased; the prayer of ex. 286 pulsates in its new garb (ex. 288); the apparently purely formal change expresses in reality a change of feeling. The strings mark the last bars of each half by underlining the theme beneath the solo ornamentation.

Till now the drama has been enacted between the muted strings and the piano; with the wind entry and a fresh subject in E flat the colour and atmosphere change. So! The movement is to be a rondo and this is the first episode. This subject is a caressing tune with clear, gentle outlines, unfolding in two strains of eight and twelve bars, each one followed by the same four-bar phrase or codetta (ex. 289). The first part modulates into the dominant, the second returns to the tonic; this is the plan of numberless airs and refrains of the time. Its *galant* symmetry contrasts with the almost extemporizing irregularity of the first stanza. It is natural that not only its scoring but also its harmonization (accompaniment in thirds, repeated notes on the horns, first clarinet and first bassoon doubling in octaves, Alberti bass in the second clarinet, echoing from clarinet to flute) should recall the woodwind serenades, especially the andante of the C minor with which it has in common both key and beat.

It is a digression which does not affect the climate of the movement and the piano comes in again at once with a second variation of the subject where the tune is restated almost unchanged over an extremely

agitated bass in demi-semi-quavers (ex. 290). After the first bars of
each half the strings also sustain the theme and the piano then allows
itself to vary it.

The second episode is in C major and consists in a dialogue between
flute and first bassoon, their sharp tones standing out from the dark
mass of the still muted strings. The instruments state and counter-
state, question and answer, after the fashion of the first fiddle and first
viola in the andante of the C major quintet. The symmetry of the
first episode has gone; the melody evolves with ease and breadth,
rising and falling like a garland swaying in the breeze in front of a
misty forest (ex. 291).

This episode is followed by a third variation of the main theme
which draws upon all forces. It treats the subject more freely. It
disintegrates the smooth, sinuous form and crumbles it up into short
exclamations where the tutti attack *forte* and the piano answers softly.
Strings and wind double, or one group gives out the tune, and the
other a counter-subject. Then both groups resume expounding the
theme and the piano adorns it. All this takes place successively and
nothing lasts for long; the flow is irregular and jerky. In the second
half, the wind counter-subject (ex. 292) comes to the fore and is
responsible for modifying and lengthening the part that precedes the
"beseeching" motif, ex. 286. This latter is twice repeated in two
forms. Despite this apparent confusion clarity prevails; the three
groups—strings, wind and piano—mingle, oppose, double and decorate
each other, without losing their individualities; each one contributes
its facet to the sparkle of the whole. Through the agitation a trilling
figure leads like Ariadne's thread, now in the strings, with a descant
in the wind, now in the piano, over the unison strings; finally, it rises
chain-like towards the tonic whilst the line of the strings writhes
beneath it like a wounded snake (ex. 293); then everything relapses
into the sorrow of the "beseeching" motif.

At the end of this variation the strings open a slow drumming of
repeated chords and we feel that the supreme moment is at hand. The
coda which begins here is indeed one of the most magical passages
in all Mozart. The passion rises to tragic intensity. Upon the
throbbing strings there is laid a desolate theme of the clarinets and
bassoons (ex. 294). Its outline is familiar[1] but it seems, as we hear it,
strikingly original and it lifts up like a voice emerging from the
unknown. The very soul of the movement, bereft of all adornment,

---

[1] See ex. 71; p. 173.

stands before us in its nakedness.   As it rises towards its highest point
the flute comes and rounds off slightly the asperity of the other instruments.   Then the piano repeats it.   The theme hovers above the
bassoon's staccato and the crossing curves of violins and violas and
comes to land, to our surprise, on the chord of C major and, for a
second, we expect an optimistic conclusion.   One bar later the minor
mode is re-installed.   The closing phrase unfolds wearily; all feeling
of tragedy has gone and saddened resignation alone remains (ex. 295).
It is divided between piano and woodwind and finds rest at length in
a chromatic rise of the solo which the tutti complete by repeating
thrice its last notes.

This andante is certainly the centre of gravity of the concerto and
the movement by which we remember it.   Its beauty was recognized at once and at its first performance it was encored.   It is the
last scion of a race of Mozartian slow movements in C Minor, belonging to works in E flat,[1] several of which, like it, are in three time,
3-8 or 6-8.   The most significant are those of the string quartet K.157,
of the symphony K.184, the piano concerto K.271 and the *Sinfonia
Concertante*, K.364—this latter a very great piece which, like our
andante, rises an instant to tragedy, whereas the others sing rather of
melancholy or hopelessness, and represents Mozart's art at its highest.
Two vocal works in C minor shed light on the meaning of this
andante.   One is the fine *Kyrie* of the *Missa solemnis*, so-called: in
C minor, K.426; it confirms our interpretation of the "beseeching"
nature of certain bars; the other is an aria of the oratorio *Davidde
penitente*, written for the Lent of 1785.[2]   In 3-8 like the slow
movement of this concerto, its beginning recalls closely that of
the latter, and it happens that the words, "Fra le oscure ombre"
("Through the deep shadows that surround us") justify the simile
of the blind man which these bars had, before we knew the
aria, suggested to us.

In form, this andante is unique in Mozart.   Its plan is not unlike
one often used by Haydn, a blending of rondo and variation,[3] but
none of the many instances of Haydn's that we know resembles it
exactly and its form is as original as its feeling.

---

[1] Or in C major: quartet, K.157; symphony, K.96.

[2] Mozart used the completed numbers of his C minor mass for this oratorio,
but added two new arias, of which this is one.

[3] The Salomon symphonies, nos. 2 in D, 6 in D, 11 in D and 12 in
G; etc.

In spite of its partly episodic structure, the flow of its emotion is unbroken. It progresses towards increasingly clear definition. Confused and uncertain at first, it begins already to know itself in the first variation; the E flat episode defines it by its contrary, by showing what it is not. The second variation with its greater vigour is the result, and a heightened consciousness of what it is. A further manifestation of its opposite, the C major episode, is followed by an outburst of wrath; then, in the "tragic" song of the coda, ex. 294, it possesses itself and is fully revealed. After which, exhausted, having uttered itself wholly, the emotion dies away in the slower snd slower steps of the last bars.

"Mozart's work is the opposite of his life. The life was all suffering and the work, almost all of it, breathed nothing but happiness." When writing this, Camille Bellaigue did but repeat what was usually said half a century ago. It is at the end of a movement like this andante that one is most astounded when one unearths this judgement of a period which knew not Mozart. Is it possible to see "happiness", or indeed anything but deep suffering, rising from variation to variation to the stress of the coda, in this song where sorrow, tragedy and collapse follow each other with, it is true, two serene but ever so ephemeral interludes? We have learnt better. Mozart who, truly enough, could sing of happiness when he wished, though never as full-heartedly as Beethoven, is a great poet of sorrow, a fact which could not be perceived by a century for whom sorrow did not express itself without shouting, for whom the violence with which an emotion proclaimed itself was the measure of its depth and intensity.

III.   The refrain of the rondo is a stiffer version of that of the B flat concerto, K.450, but it is more of a dance than a gallop (ex. 296). The piano gives out the first part and the tutti repeat it. The second half (ex. 297) belongs exclusively to the piano and a longish transition, braced by woodwind and horn calls, brings back the first part. This is the usual ABA design of rondo refrains. A very long ritornello follows it, the chief elements of which are an alternating motif, given out by clarinet and bassoon (ex. 298), and an active figure (ex. 299), quivering with the bassoon, chirping with the flute, which plays a part later on.

The piano's entry in the second couplet is more arresting than usual. It is preceded by nearly three bars where the silence is broken only by chords in the strings, lightly repeated, and when it occurs

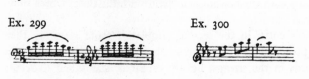

Ex. 301

Ex. 302

Ex. 303

Ex. 304

the piano does not start with a well-marked theme[1] but with a faltering
figure, a reminiscence of ex. 298 (ex. 300), all the clearer for being
followed, as the piano grows bolder, by ex. 299, on the vaultings of
which the solo instrument sets sail for its first cruise.   The solo, long
but varied, and sustained by strings and wind in turn, evolves into the
second subject whose seesaw rhythm is well suited to 6-8 time.   Given
out at first by the piano, it is repeated by the clarinet and bassoon,
accompanied by the piano bass (ex. 301).   Near the end of a second
solo occurs one of the most perilous sketchy passages in these concertos—perilous in that it is even more absurd than usual to play
it as it is written (ex. 302).[2]   Is it in order to hear the pianist
pick circumspectly, with one finger, first at the top, then at
the bottom of the treble of his keyboard that the instruments
hold their peace or lower their voices to an impersonal murmur?
Obviously not.   We have here a kind of cadenza *in tempo*, an
extemporization in which only the starting-point in each bar
is given but which can take no other form than that of arpeggios
and scales.

---

[1] As in all other concerto rondos except those of K.271 and 449—both, let
it be noticed, in E flat.

[2] Reinecke draws attention to these bars in his little work: *Zur Wieder-
belebigung der Mozart'schen Klavierkonzerte*, but in his Breitkopf edition he
leaves them as they are, although in similar places elsewhere he suggests
completions on an extra stave.   In the only recording of this work the soloist
unfortunately makes the usual mistake of playing the bare minims.

According to custom, only the first part of the refrain, ex. 296, is resumed after this couplet and the orchestra modulates swiftly through various minor keys to A flat major, where a pause on a dominant seventh chord leaves us an instant in suspense, awaiting the second episode.

What ensues is one of the most curious examples of the way in which Mozart's musical ideas are associated with keys. Consciously or not, our rondo behaves at this point like that of his first E flat concerto, K.271, eight and a half years earlier[1] and as no other rondo had behaved since. Instead of a *development* there unrolls a spacious minuet in A flat. The likeness, it is true, goes no further; the minuet of the Salzburg concerto was followed by five variations; this one is made up of two symmetrical halves, each one given out by the wind and the piano doubled by strings, and of a coda where the piano's staccato and the violins' pizzicato are reminiscent of the arpeggios of demi-semi-quavers in the last variation of the minuet of K.271 (exs. 303 and 304). In the repeats, Mozart uses only the right hand of the piano, doubling the first fiddles; his intention is clearly to treat the piano as an orchestral instrument and to mingle its tone with the others on a single line, as if it were a flute; this effect is destroyed if chords are added in the left hand as is sometimes done. It is an effect of the linear tone of the instrument and not of its mass which he intends.[2]

The episode culminates on a pause where the soloist should insert a short cadenza to bring back the refrain.

The third couplet corresponds to the recapitulation. The return of the refrain in the tutti brings back ex. 299 in the bassoon, then in the flute, as before, and the piano receives it from the lips of the latter. The solo is shortened; the second subject returns in the tonic and the cadenza follows it closely.

The refrain comes back complete after the piano's reappearance and is followed by a coda where exs. 298 and 299 are the main elements; a witty dialogue takes place between bassoon, clarinet and piano anent the second of these. There then sounds a flourish which appears to conclude the movement.

Here occurs perhaps the most original, certainly the most mis-

---

[1] And where, too, the slow movement was in C minor.

[2] Eric Blom points out the close likeness between this episode and the theme of the round, "Nel tuo, nel mio bicchiero", in the finale of the second act of *Cosi fan tutte*. The theme of the round is a variation of the concerto$_8$.

chievous, incident in this lively rondo. With the humour of a small boy hiding behind a chair to say Boo! to his elders as they go by, Mozart lets his flourish die away; as at the beginning of the solo, which these bars reproduce, the strings repeat softly the triad and the wind sustain; this appears to be the closing chord of the movement. This goes on for three bars. Then comes the surprise. Quietly, almost wheedlingly, the piano puts forward a little phrase recalling ex. 300. After thinking we were at the end, we fancy (if we enter into the spirit of the game) we are back at the beginning.[1] The little phrase unfolds in three bits, roguish and wily; then the flourish is repeated and the movement winds up with speed and noise.

The very Mozartish form of humour seen here is one we come across in his correspondence. The following lines from a letter to his father of January 22nd, 1783, is an instance of it. "Last week, I gave a dance in my apartment. . . . We started at six in the evening and finished at seven. What? only one hour? No, no! . . . seven in the morning. . . ." In both instances, there is a transparent misunderstanding, an innocent trick; the same spirit is at work in both concerto and letter. Seldom can one find so exact a parallel between the music and the words of a composer and seldom can the same mental feature be so clearly recognized in both orders of expression. The sentiment behind letter and coda is identical.

E flat is one of the keys that Mozart, like many composers of the 1700–1800 period, has used most often. Counting from his majority, there are more than twenty sonata-form works in it, as well as nearly as many andantes and adagios of works in B flat, G minor and C minor. Not all these compositions are important; not all stand out clearly enough for us to say that the key always has with him the same character. The technical limitations of the horn, for instance, led him to use it in three of the concertos and the quintet he wrote for his friend Leutgeb and the same cause was responsible for the choice of E flat in a wind serenade, K.375, and in the quintet for wind and piano, K.452. But there remain some fifteen E flat works which make up a spiritual family and thanks to them we can determine the features which seem to accompany the key in his allegros and finales. (The andantes form a group of their own and their nature depends

---

[1] A like device is used at the end of the first movement of K.413, but less humorously.

mainly on their relation with the rest of the work to which they belong.)

Among them there is a far from negligible work which one cannot bring into any category: the highly personal concerto of February, 1784, K.449. If we leave it to one side, we shall see that, generally speaking, E flat is, for Mozart as for all the *galant* period, the key of grace and happiness.   A carefree joy, usually with elegance and lightness, sometimes with energy, but without depth: this is what we find most often, sometimes unmixed, as in trifles, sometimes linked with other qualities in his more serious compositions.[1] In some works with piano, like the concerto K.365, this one and the piano quartet K.493, this joy is expressed with majesty: the work we have been studying is the best embodiment of this conception. At one period of his life Mozart chose this key to render an emotion we have called "heroic" or "Olympian"; in this he was following a convention to which Beethoven also conformed sumptuously in his third symphony and his E flat concerto. It can be noted in parts of the two pianos concerto and the serenade K.375; it is in the powerful allegros of the violin sonata K.380 and the *Sinfonia Concertante* that Mozart has expressed most fully this lofty sentiment in the key of E flat.[2] Already, at the same date (1779), it is found in a symphony in C major and later he always expresses it in this latter key.[3]

There remains a rather different sentiment of which E flat is the vehicle late in his life. It is a kind of refined and rarefied state of the light joy which characterizes this key in most *galant* composers. The term "blithesomeness" suits it better than "joy"—a disembodied blithesomeness, a play of happy spirits, or, as Adolphe Boschot puts it in speaking of one of the works we mean, "une allégresse franciscaine". This other-worldly feeling is in touch in some cases with the musician's Masonic experience. We meet it in 1788 with the symphony K.543 and the divertimento for string trio, K.563, still mixed with joy and marked in the symphony by a certain heroic tone which reminds us of the *Sinfonia Concertante*. It reaches its most rarefied state in the string quintet of his last year; the music still sings of play, but it is the play of Botticelli's Graces, not that of an

---

[1] Saint-Foix calls E flat in Mozart "at once gentle, sensuous and energetic" (op. cit., III, 179).

[2] Cf. pp. 120 and ff.

[3] Cf. p. 341.

aristocratic Viennese ballroom.[1]   And finally, in parts of the overture and finale of the *Magic Flute* it is frankly allied with an awareness of unearthly things.   The use of E flat, not only for important parts of this opera but also for two other Masonic works, the cantatas *Dir, Seele des Weltalls* and *Die Maurerfreude*, helps us to characterize still more precisely the nature of this quasi-mystical inspiration which the key serves to embody in the last years of Mozart's life.

---

[1] Cf. pp. 491 ff.

4. The Nineteenth Concerto: K.488 in A

Concerto No. 19 in A major (K.488)[1]
Finished March 2nd, 1786
    Allegro: C
    Adagio: 6-8 (in F sharp minor)
    Allegro assai: ¢
Orchestra: Strings; flute, two clarinets, two horns, two bassoons.

THE family of Mozart's works in A major is both smaller and more select than that of his E flat compositions. These latter, besides cultured personalities, comprised some rather ordinary members—undistinguished menials, wearing the livery of the key, good enough, and no more, to line up for the passage of personages of mark like the eighteenth concerto, the symphony or the string quintet; young men with urbane faces, shaven and inexpressive, in whom good manners made up for an absence of individual feeling and intellect, whose society was not unpleasant, but whose lustreless chatter allowed us to interchange them without gain or loss.

The works in A major, on the other hand, fewer in number, are all creatures of quality. Their fully formed personalities, with sharp outlines, characteristic gestures and feelings which are not interchangeable, forbid anyone of them being confused with its kinsmen. They compose a race of individualists, as well bred as those in E flat but provided with an ego of which they are aware and which they carefully cultivate. Belonging to a small family, they have been able to grow up more freely, have enjoyed more elbow room, whereas in the house of the E flats, where the inmates were legion, air and space were lacking, overcrowding prevailed, and only the sturdiest off-spring profited fully from life.

After his return from Paris, the event from which his maturity may be dated, Mozart composed only six whole works in A

---

[1] *Gesamtausgabe*, no 23. The autograph and earliest edition have Adagio and Allegro assai; all subsequent editions have Andante and Presto.

major.¹ Two of them are piano concertos; three are chamber works—
a violin sonata, K.526, a quartet, K.464, and the clarinet quintet, K.581
—and the last is a clarinet concerto, K. 622. All are works of the
first order.

Of these six works, the best beloved, with the clarinet quintet, is
this concerto—the best beloved and, with the D minor, the most
played of his twenty-three piano concertos. It enhances the technical skill of the executant less than most; it is the least virtuoso of the
lot; but its loveliness is such that.it attracts the notice of all pianists
anxious to measure their talents with the master.

I. We recognize certain general features in it which we meet in
other A major works, yet it stands quite apart from them and, like all
the 1785-6 concertos, is one of its creator's most personal productions.
Its first movement is simple in structure and engaging in disposition.
It is remarkably homogeneous and all its themes have a similar character, perceived in its very first bars (ex. 305). Under the transparent
disguise of a cheerful exterior, the heart of the work is sad and its
mood hovers between smiles and tears.

> His luminous genius has so often sung the beauty of life and so often
> replied to his daily trials with songs of love and hope, that one does not
> discover at once the sadness which is veiled behind his geniality; in his
> soul and his music, even the shadows are shot through with light and the
> reflection of the sky makes them diaphanous.²

Of this intimate blending of joy and care, the flattened leading note
of the second chord is an early witness; the discreet chromaticisms of
the eighth bar and the second subject (ex. 306), the falterings between
major and minor in the passage which follows this latter (bars 46-52)
are others; and the light in the movement is one of a March day—the
month in which it was composed—when a pale sun shines unconvincingly through fleeting showers. It is a commonplace to say that
Mozart unites features of German and Italian music, and we may
recognize here a Mediterranean brightness tempered and moistened
by Northern sensibility. Very pre-Romantic, but *à la Rousseau*

---

¹ We say whole, because of an unfinished quartet whose first allegro is
almost complete, Köchel-Einstein no. 464 a (170 bars), a prelude and fugue
(or sonata) for piano and violin, where the prelude (the only part in A major)
is finished but half the fugue (in A minor) is missing, K.402, and the rondo
for piano and orchestra, K.386.

² Adolphe Boschot: *Chez les musiciens* (2ᵐᵉ série, p. 19).

rather than after the wise of the *Sturm und Drang*, it is at the same time one of Mozart's most authentic movements.

Its scoring, like its size, is on a humbler scale than in the works of the previous year. Trumpets and drums are lacking. The first subject, ex. 305, given out *piano* by the strings, then repeated by the woodwind in a shorter form, links on to a *forte* passage for all[1] which in turn leads to a dominant close.

The second subject, ex. 306, is more tearful than the first; its sadness is more marked; its pathetic and rather wilting tenderness is a trifle morbid. Again, exposition by the strings, restatement by the woodwind, doubled by the first violins. There follow the passage already mentioned that alternates between major and minor (bars 46-52) and a threefold call tossed from woodwind to violins and back; then, *forte*, but without any rise in the emotion, without a *strepitoso* close, we reach the common chord which precedes the concluding subject. This latter, only four bars long, returns to *piano*; only the last chords are *forte*.

In the three great concertos of the previous year and in those that follow this one in 1786, the piano enters with a prelude of its own which is sometimes important enough to be recalled later on.[2] Here, with almost studied simplicity, it comes forward with the first subject, restated literally at first, then discreetly decorated and sustained by a very light string accompaniment. How far we are from the pompous, dramatic or mysterious entries of the other concertos of this period! The tutti come in with the strain which had followed the first subject (bars 18-22): an ancient device, simple and conventional, universally used in the aria, that form whence the *galant* concerto is partly derived. After a few bars the solo takes the words from the orchestra's mouth as the voice would in the aria. Here, in most concertos, the piano strikes out along new paths, brings in its own subject, launches out into bravura. But to-day it is content to follow the lines traced by the orchestra, with very moderate virtuosity, and, lengthening by only a few bars the transitional passage, just enough to modulate without haste to E major, it gives out the second subject, ex. 306. When the instruments have restated it with occasional collaboration on the piano's part, it resumes control of affairs and, dialoguing with wind and strings, repeats almost unchanged the major-minor passage of bars 46-52, tarries an instant to play with the fiddles,

---

[1] Note once again the *piano* to *forte* opening.

[2] K.466 and 491.

Ex. 305

Ex. 306

Ex. 307

Ex. 308

and, after a very short solo, different from the end of the tutti but hardly any longer, stops on the usual trill which concludes the exposition.

We have met with several argument tuttis whose function was to give out the chief elements of the movement in the order in which they were to reappear, amplified, in the solo exposition.[1] But never, not even in the D major, K.451, have we found one where the solo exposition followed so exactly, so timidly the lines laid down by the tutti. What it adds is insignificant; whereas in most of Mozart's concertos the relation in length between tutti and first solo is two to three, here they are of almost equal size.[2] The piano confines itself to decorating most discreetly the orchestra's speech—an unheard-of fearfulness in a companion work of those in C and E flat. It

---

[1] See K.451, 456, 466, 449.

[2] The solo is four bars longer. The concertos which diverge most widely from this 2-3 ratio are, with this one, the very heterodox K.449, where the tutti is even longer than the solo exposition (eighty-eight bars to eighty), K.413 (fifty-five bars to a hundred and eight) and K.467 (sixty-eight to a hundred and twenty-five).

may be explained, perhaps—if, however, there can be any explanation outside the critic's mind!—by Mozart's wish to vary the relations of the protagonists from one concerto to the next.

The band comes in with the beginning of the passage which had followed the first subject, but at once sounds a D natural which threatens to bring back the tonic key, an unprecedented act of daring at the end of an exposition. The work changes its mind after three bars; then, quickening slightly with a few upward scales in the violins, suddenly breaks off. A rest; then the strings give out, softly, a new theme (ex. 307). New it is in its outline, but its spirit is that of the rest of the movement. Recollected and meditative, perhaps, it appears to dream of all that has happened, and its start on the third of the scale,[1] its irregular rhythm and its counterpoint in contrary motion give us the impression that it continues a discourse begun elsewhere instead of being itself a beginning. The piano, still imitative, repeats it, but this time in the form of a free variation[2] which nevertheless retains the counterpoint (bars 149–56). This kind of pianistic writing, new in the concertos, recurs in the finale of the next work. On this theme is built the *development*, an admirable example of piano and orchestral intercourse, where the instruments compete on equal terms without either obliterating or duplicating each other.

The variation having ended in E major, clarinets and bassoons recall in E minor the first two bars of ex. 307. The piano interrupts them with some irritation and substitutes a passage based on a wriggling figure in which fiddles and violas sustain (bars 156–60). The woodwind, reinforced by the flute, return to the beginning of ex. 307, but in C major; the piano again counters them crossly and a third time the woodwind go back to their theme; the key is now A minor. Quietened and won over, the piano answers in F major; interpellations give way to brotherly intercourse and there ensues a passage new in character in Mozart's concertos but of which two later works offer examples.[3] Clarinet and flute engage in a dialogue in free canon at the fourth upon ex. 307 whilst the solo's right hand bewreathes their two lines and binds them loosely one to the other with a decoration of broken scales (ex. 308). Thrice the clarinet starts its contrapuntal walk, dropping each time by one degree without

---

[1] And, especially, the chord of the sub-dominant ninth in its second note.

[2] The *development* of K.467 also began with a new theme followed by a variation of it in the piano.

[3] K.503 and 595.

leaving the region of A minor, and thrice the flute follows it; a fourth time, the walk is at once interrupted and all stop on the dominant of the key with an almost sinister sense of foreboding.[1] The idyll turns to drama. Suddenly from the depths surges up the *daimon* of Mozart. Wind and piano relapse into frightened silence and over throbbing basses the first violins sing a fragment of the theme, all the more questioning and threatening for being inverted, whilst second violins and violas complete the harmonies of a dominant ninth, one of Mozart's red-letter-day chords, reserved for moments of intense yet restrained emotion. Piano and wind answer the strings, maintaining the chord; the piano's broken chromatic scale adds the presence of a hunted suppliant to the mass of the instruments, which have suddenly become impassive (ex. 309). We know of no more poignant instance of the lightning appearances of Mozart's *daimon* in the midst of his least dramatic works.

The strength of such moments is a function of their brevity. Having half-opened the jaws of Tartarus, he shuts them immediately and scatters the piled-up emotion in a piano cadenza. This cadenza, accompanied by held notes in the tutti, brings back the first subject in a dozen bars and introduces the recapitulation. We know how close is the relationship in Mozart between keys and formal features. Once before he had led us to the reprise on the back of a cadenza, also in a concerto in A.[2]

After this *development*, at once one of his most individual in thought and one of his most firmly constructed, the concerto returns to regular ways. For this allegro, ironically, so original both in the simplicity of its first solo and the details of its *development*, is the only one of the series which obeys the "rules" of the classical concerto as textbooks state them! Alone in Mozart, it abides by the laws which make the concerto an adaptation of the symphony and sonata and which were laid down after the event when 19th-century Aristotles drew up statutes for a genre which had never had any and which, at that time, was declining.

Docile, then, to the teaching of posterity, Mozart repeats his exposition unaltered, managing to keep his second subject in the tonic and changing a few details in the scoring and the sharing of parts

---

[1] In all this passage (bars 169–78), it is most important to hear the flute and clarinet, beside which the piano part is but decoration, and subordinate to them. The wind should play out *forte* and the soloist should not rise above *mp*.

[2] K.414.

between piano and tutti. We thus come quite uneventfully in sight
of the last trill, when, only a few bars off it, the solo, seized with a
belated desire for emancipation, wends its way towards the rising
violin scales which had preceded ex. 307. The reason is that the
theme on which the *development* had been built up is too important
to be missed out in the recapitulation. The piano, on its own re-
sponsibility, states it exactly as we heard it on the strings; then clarinet
and bassoon take it up and Mozart treats us to a retrospect of the fairest
moment of the day. While the wind start up a four-part counterpoint, the piano again entwines them with its garlands. The game
becomes animated and reaches quickly a pitch of excitement like that of
ex. 309, but with no sinister intention, in three bars of a dominant pedal
where the piano's left hand awakens for the first time and does its best
to give body to the whole, if only with an Alberti bass (bars 267–75).[1]

Once this homage paid to the departed and all the forces having
been reviewed, the solo concludes with a few bravura bars and reaches
its trill. The tutti announce the cadenza and after the execution of
this latter, concerning which we will confine ourselves to repeating
Beethoven's recommendation in his G major concerto "*La cadenza
sia corta*",[2] the orchestra restates the conclusion of the first tutti and
adds a short codetta.

II. There is generally more contrast than likeness between the first
allegro and the andante of a work in several movements. In this
concerto it is not so. The andante maintains the same mood as the
allegro, but deepens and clarifies it. The melancholy which shim-
mered through the smiles in the allegro and shared our attention

---

[1] This original recapitulation calls for some comparisons. The sonata
for two pianos also brings in a new theme in the *development* and works it
out, but less fully; at the close of the recapitulation the theme reappears.
(There is a well-known instance of an important thematic element introduced
at half-time in the first movement of the *Eroica*.) Bars 261–75 are a kind of
premature coda and hint at the great coda of the quintet in C, also followed by
a conventional conclusion which closes the movement by repeating the end
of the exposition after the coda. Regarding the dynamic marks, we make
the same recommendation as for bars 169–78. Some pianists make a slight
rallentando in bar 261; this is right provided they remember that the wind
restate the theme, so that, once their exposition is over, they must not hurry on
again with their semi-quavers, otherwise the balance between them and the wind
will be destroyed; the pace must be steady throughout the section (bars 261–75).

[2] Mozart's cadenza for this concerto has one merit—that of being short.
It is often played but might be omitted with advantage. Its existence shows
perhaps that the master taught this concerto to a pupil. It is uninteresting.

with them now takes possession of the stage and draws the whole movement to itself. The work had hitherto remained astride joy and sorrow; its nature was somewhat uncertain; there is no longer any doubt; with the first strains of this *danse triste* in F sharp minor, a key Mozart uses here for the only time in his life, the superficial affability disappears and the sombre *daimon* of ex. 309 reigns unchallenged.

As often happens in lyrical andantes, the piano gives out the cantilena and by so doing appears no longer to represent the musician's emotion but to identify itself with it; the instrument's voice becomes the very voice of Mozart's grief. The rhythm is that of a siciliana and is instinct with that melodious sorrow which so readily expresses itself in that form. The long phrase which opens it is in two parts: the first, of four bars; the second, with an unsymmetrical outline, of seven. Mozart often divides thus the cantabile themes of his andantes; after the square-cut rhythm of the first half the irregularity of the rest is a pleasing surprise. The E sharp of the second bar (ex. 310) belongs to the tune and not to the bass; the leap of three octaves and a third imitates, as Tovey has pointed out, the leaps in arias which enhanced the contrast of timbre between two registers of the voice; it is a vocal effect found also in violin and clarinet music which is in danger of appearing meaningless on a keyboard. The pianist should give the impression of carrying off a difficult feat, as if he were a singer; to that end, it may be found helpful to cross the hands and play the E sharp with the right hand.

The orchestra continues with a still more sorrowful song, heavy with beauty, given out in three-part imitation by first violins, clarinet, bassoon and flute, ex. 311 (bars 12–20). The music passes from *piano* to *forte* and the solo repeats the theme, decorating it; but soon diverges with a new subject which leads for a moment to A major. There is a fresh vocal leap in the right hand in bar 50. Then, for the space of a few bars, it wavers between major and minor and the violins echo its wistful strains;[1] finally the major wins, but unconvincingly (bars 20–34).

A brighter theme is heard in the flute and clarinet; it announces the trio, "*Ah! taci ingiusto core!*" in *Don Giovanni*, but without the latent irony (ex. 312); beginning in the wind, it passes to the solo and is followed by a codetta shared between the three groups of

---

[1] How magical an effect when the strings resume their accompaniment at the precise moment when the major appears for the first time (bar 25)!

Ex. 309

Ex. 310

Ex. 311

Ex. 312

Ex. 313

Ex. 314

strings, wind and piano (ex. 313). Two transitional bars in the wind are enough to recall the mourning hues of F sharp minor and the first subject (bars 50-1)—two bars full of the pathetic overlapping harmonies beloved of Mozart, where the spirit of Chopin seems to hover near us.

The recapitulation follows regular paths, with a dramatic extension of the first subject, till the piano re-enters with the variation of ex. 311. Instead of giving out again the A major section, the melody clouds itself more deeply in dusky hues and the stress rises to the point of suffering. In the background, flute and clarinet accompany with a figure which is a kind of augmentation of ex. 311; in the foreground, the piano's left hand and the bassoon engage in a dialogue over which the right hand traces "on the wall" mysterious signs, the emaciated outline of a theme (ex. 314).[1] The languorous Sicilian grace of the opening has vanished and there reigns a stark mood, with almost physical pain. After reaching a climax[2] (bar 83), the pain subsides and, as in the andante of the last concerto, the coda unfolds wearily, rather than peacefully, in an atmosphere where resignation turns to quiet hopelessness and where the strings' pizzicato accompaniment, with its serenade associations, is well-nigh uncanny. The piano tune, unfortunately, is merely sketched out; it is as indispensable to give it life by decorating it as it is needless to say that no soloist ever thinks of doing so—an omission which deprives it of all sense and turns this conclusion into a pompous one-finger progress from top to bottom of the keyboard.[3] Finally, the sorrow dies away little by little with a threefold recall of the beginning of ex. 311 in which the piano takes part and then, once the woodwind has finished echoing the last piano chords, nothing more is heard.

Not only its key but also its beat make this andante unusual in Mozart's work. From 1778 till his death we do not find more than a dozen 6-8 andantes and very few of these have a siciliana rhythm. In fact, the movement which most resembles this one is the F minor

---

[1] Which should not be decorated, for once, we think. The motion is ensured by the basses; to enliven the treble would be to counteract it.

[2] The likeness of this passage with bars 193-200 of the andante of K.482 will be recognized.

[3] In the *Breitkopf* edition, Reinecke proposes a realization; we suggest another (ex. 315); but the ideal is that each soloist should extemporize his own, according to his understanding of the movement. When one plays this movement in the solo piano arrangement, the bareness of the treble is less apparent because one's attention is taken up by the liveliness of the bass.

adagio of the piano sonata in F major, K.280, of 1774, composed at eighteen. Across the fourteen years that separate them, the thought is picked up afresh; the concerto extends and deepens the sonata; the emotion of the young man is expressed in it with the fullness of the man of thirty.

This is the last minor andante that Mozart will write for a concerto and, except for a few pieces, either separate or else in a special form,[1] the last minor slow movement in his work. It is perhaps the one where we perceive most clearly the union of passion and formal beauty which gives such a price to his music. Abert has written one of his best pages on this matter.

> The best pianists have always recognized that behind (Mozart's) apparent clarity lies an inner life of the greatest variety and complexity. Others—very mistakenly of course—have complained that it lacks passion, allowing only that it possesses the qualities of symmetry, beauty and euphony. They make the great mistake of equating the free expression of passion with passion itself and thus, at the very start, block their own approach to an art like that of Mozart. For, while he cannot be reckoned as a true son of the Rococo age, eager to sing even his sorrows in graceful strains, yet he was no *Stürmer und Dränger*. With unbridled excitement, the chief thing for the latter, he was concerned only inasmuch as it lent itself to artistic control, that is, to form. His interest was not in Nature but in Culture. That does not mean, however, at all that he renounced the artistic presentation of passion in all its forms in favour of a vague and colourless ideal of beauty. Even had he wanted to do this, it would have been downright impossible, for we are well enough acquainted with the daemonic, nay, volcanic side of his nature and we should be underrating his originality as an artist if we considered him capable of being so false to this essential side of himself as to deny it expression in his art. On the other hand, of course, the Storm and Stress that seethed and rioted in his blood was not, in itself, capable of satisfying him completely. Rather did he feel a constant urge to master this raw material of the spirit by giving it form, adding, incidentally, some things as well as eliminating much that a later age was to value more highly, eager throughout to attain a higher standard of clarity and transparency. The most noble fruits of this urge are these adagio themes. Their importance lies, not in the perfection of their formal finish, and in their sensuous beauty, splendid as these secondary features are, but in the deep feeling from which they spring, the feeling that covers the whole wide field of inner life and that, while very far from concealing the inward glow of passion, yet lends it expression without as much as a trace of unhealthy ferment or pretentious subjectivity. To appreciate this, one needs only to compare his work with that of the later Romantics, say, of the young Schumann. With them, everything is

---

[1] B minor adagio for piano, K.540; C minor adagio for strings, K.546; F minor adagio in the first organ fantasia, K.594.

movement, excitement, unbridled passion, such as may well present itself to youth as the highest ideal of art. With Mozart, on the other hand, form, the completed activity, is the main thing, and not the activity for its own sake.[1]

The interplay of the three groups, strings, wind and piano, is particularly delicate and masterly. The woodwind are used much less by themselves than in the andante of the last concerto and much more in collaboration with the other groups. Thus, in the second subject, ex. 311, twice given out by the orchestra, the clarinet and flute do not do much more than double, one after the other, the first fiddles, while the bassoon provides one of the essential parts. The little phrase that follows the third subject, ex. 312, is given out first by the clarinets and bassoons, with a piano echo; but when it is repeated (ex. 313) it is shared by the piano and strings according to the usual plan; the theme for the latter, a variation for the former; the echo is provided by the instruments that had given out the theme the first time. These two bars (46–7) are an admirable instance of Mozart's art of combining his instruments while leaving to each one almost a soloist's independence, and of the thoroughly concertante quality of his style. Some composers are content to write for their piano as concerto writers and for their orchestra as symphonists; Mozart realizes that the concerto principle must extend also to the orchestra. Spohr called Mozart's concertos symphonies with *piano principale*; they are rather *sinfonie concertante* where first violins and first woodwind are soloists, in addition to the piano. Hence, the only half unjust criticism that they are concertos for wind instruments with piano obbligato.

The strings, also, behave less egotistically than in the andante of K.482, where they expounded alone the long refrain. They preponderate in ex. 311 and they echo back the piano with originality in the third subject (bars 29–31); their most personal contribution is their pizzicato at the end, where they accompany the solo's unquiet wanderings like tormented spirits.

III. The contrast we expected between allegro and andante is found between andante and rondo. The charm of the first two movements came largely from their drooping airs and their touch of morbidity. The rondo, on the other hand, is one of the most exhilarating and the most infectious ever sprung from Mozart, overbrimming with

---

[1] H. Abert, op. cit.: II, 227–8.

life and energy. It is the most successful and strongest finale of the whole series; its only possible equal is that of the concerto in F, K.459. A true *moto perpetuo*, it keeps up the irrepressible go of its opening bars without a break, with subtle changes in the length of its phrases. Tune follows on tune; song is more prominent than rhythm; Mozart uses up an incredible number of melodies; but all the time the race is maintained through the kaleidoscopic series of themes. Beneath this sparkling motley, the flow of thought remains more powerfully homogeneous than in some other rondos, such as that of the D minor, for instance, where the opening torrent of fire is quenched long before the end.

After the dying away of the siciliana, the onslaught of the refrain, bouncing with health, is one of the most brutal awakenings in all Mozart and also one of those that bring most relief.[1] That of K.482, at the same moment, was less abrupt, because the rondo opening was less decided. The theme is given out by the piano (ex. 322) and followed by the long tutti usual in those rondos where the refrain is expounded by the solo.[2] After the refrain has been restated by the orchestra, no fewer than five separate motifs can be counted; none of them comes back before the final grand review. The stream flows with irresistible rush and there is no interruption between these different subjects; each one links on inevitably to the next.

Is this not bad organization, one is tempted to ask? A passage of such length, no element of which plays any part in the body of the movement, is surely just wasteful improvisation? To this we would reply that the initial tutti of a rondo, once the main stanza of the refrain has been given out, is not like the exposition of an allegro and does not aim at introducing the chief characters in the play. In a rondo the only character is the hero, the refrain, whom we know already.

The function of these long tuttis is different. Their justification is found, not in the matter expounded, as in an allegro's initial tutti, but in the expounding instruments; the orchestra, rather than the music, is the important thing. The solo has asserted itself by capturing

---

[1] The *Mozarteum* contains two fragments for piano and orchestra in A which may be sketches for the finale of this concerto (Köchel-Einstein, nos. 488 b and e). The first, resembling the theme of the finale of the A major quartet, K.464, heralds a movement similar in mood to the opening allegro; the other, in 6-8, appears to be a theme for variations; it is rather like a major version of the finale of the D minor quartet, K.421.

[2] K.415, 450, 456, 459, 466, 482.

the refrain first; the orchestra has lost its primacy and has to make up for this loss by the length of its subsequent speech. It failed to put in the first word; at least, once its turn has come, it will speak lengthily. Hence the multiplicity of its themes, thanks to which it impresses us as deeply as its rival. When the instruments open the debate, they feel less keenly the need of counterbalancing the solo and their prelude is nearly always short.[1]

In the present concerto, moreover, the refrain demands a numerous following lest, slight and quick as it is, it be overwhelmed by the many other themes that fill the movement. Its escorting motifs are courtiers whose purpose is to draw our notice to it and enable us to recognize it when it returns—an important point for, characteristic though it appear to us, the other main subjects are no less so.

The impetus of these sixty bars flows a little more calmly in the less seething waters of the subject with which the piano opens the first couplet (ex. 317). It does not dally with this theme. Hardly have its first bars been repeated by horns and clarinets when the piano completes it and resumes full flight with one of those ascending scale themes which return so often in Mozart's prestos.[2] This one carries out the regulation transfer into E major; after which, it vanishes in its turn never to be seen again, and the new key is established by a short bravura passage culminating in a trill.

The race comes to a sudden halt and for three-quarters of a bar complete silence reigns. Three-quarters of a bar is not much, but after so inexhaustible an outpouring of animal spirits, the shortest silence becomes dramatic. The flute and bassoon, with string accompaniment, break it with what may be called the rondo's second subject —the subject which, like a sonata second subject, generally occurs in the key of the dominant. Here, it does indeed occur in E, but in E minor (ex. 318). It is interestingly scored. When Mozart subordinates his strings to his wind, he generally keeps only one or two parts of the former; here, it is the whole quartet of strings which sustains the flute and bassoon playing in octaves. When the piano restates the theme, it breaks away from it towards the end with a short digression to C major; then returns to E minor and concludes abruptly in the major (bars 114–29).

There follows a long solo, playful and high-spirited, in which

---

[1] K.467 is an exception.

[2] Ex. 317 itself is based on a tag of ascending scale. We shall hear another later (ex. 319). See also the finale of the E flat piano quartet, K.493.

now one group, now another participates; like several other solos
arising from the second subject, it pretends to stop on a trill and sets
off again more spirited than ever (bars 130-75). Its effervescence
crystallizes at length in a theme which serves as conclusion, another
fragment of an ascending scale, set on a long horn pedal. When
the wind reiterate it after the piano (in the whole movement, the
strings give out no tunes but those of the refrain, and even so they
share most of them with the wind!), the solo muddles it with a
witty counterpoint derived from the motif just given out (ex. 319).
The game closes with a fragment (ex. 320) which the piano uses to
bring back the refrain.

As usual, only the first part of the refrain is repeated. As soon
as the tutti intervene, the music diverges abruptly and modulates to
F sharp minor, the key of the siciliana. But there is no suggestion
of the mood of this movement. The minor passage which opens
the second couplet is no return to sadness. At most does the movement gain for an instant in vigour and earnestness. The solo figure
is an impersonal one much favoured by Mozart at this time; he had
used it already in the allegro of the E flat concerto and returns to it
three months later, less felicitously, in the finale of the E flat piano
quartet. Here, it is completed by an answer in the woodwind (bars
230-45). After its repeat, the same answer, instead of returning to the
dominant chord whence we had started, jumps sharply into D major.

There is nothing unnatural in the appearance of this key in a work
in A; what is astonishing is the perfunctoriness with which Mozart
does not even modulate from one key to the other, but merely juxta-
poses them (ex. 321).

Such a juxtaposition, not only of keys but also of the moods for
which they stand, is something of a shock. The unprepared substitution of a waggish tune (ex. 322) for a passionate and earnest one
seems to us to savour of frivolity or, if we confine ourselves to considerations of form, of a lack of organization, a faulty architecture
where straight jointing replaces bonding. Such abrupt transitions
are not uncommon in Mozart; there is one quite as brusque in the
finale of another concerto in A, that for clarinet (bars 157-8), and yet
another in the finale of the C minor (on the appearance of the A flat
variation).

These changes remind us of one of the most pronounced characteristics of later 18th century music: its strophic build. Reduced to its
simplest expression, a *galant* work consists of three or four successive
themes or strophes, well contrasted, separated rather than connected

Ex. 315

Ex. 316

Ex. 317   Ex. 318

Ex. 319

Piano

Vents

Ex. 320   Ex. 321

Ex. 322

Ex. 323a

Hautbois
et
Clarinettes

Quatuor
et
Bassons

by less important ornamental passages. First tune; passage; second tune; passage; third tune—and so on: such is, with extreme but not deforming simplification, its outline. Between these different parts there are the same breaks as between the strophes or verses of a

poem. We can put the same idea rather differently and say, with
Bernard Shaw, that 18th century music is dancing music—a music
beneath the progress of which is found a small number of fundamental
rhythms, common to all dancing: 2-4, 4-4, 6-8, and the assembling
of phrases in symmetrical groups as in the dance.

But comedy, even more than dancing, sheds light on passages
like this one. Opera buffa has, indeed, deeply impregnated the
orchestral music of the latter part of the century and between it and
the concerto the common element of the soloist establishes a close
link. Of the instrumental forms of the *galant* period, the quartet
is without doubt the furthest from opera, the concerto the nearest.
It is true that Mozart, in his soaring flight of the last three years, has
left farther and farther below him the dramatic models whence he
started, like all his South German contemporaries; yet the proximity
of comedy elements—overtures, arias, finales—is still perceptible in
his early concertos, whatever their solo instrument. This is also true
of certain works of 1784: the D major opens like an opera seria overture; the F major is a sublimation of comedy and certain codettas
and closes in both its allegros have stepped straight out of opera buffa;
but the E flat and the second B flat of the same year, the D minor,
the two first movements of the C major and the andante of the 1785
E flat owe little or nothing to dramatic practice. Nor do the allegro
and andante of this concerto. In the finale, the most conservative of
the three movements, a return is often made to dramatic origins. The
only operatic echoes heard in the D minor are in the rondo; after
two serious movements, the C major has a 2-4 finale whose tunes
might have come from comedy, and in the finale of the E flat we
found an interlude which was to reappear in *Cosi fan tutte*. Here,
despite a slighter likeness with opera buffa, the cascade of tunes in the
opening tutti recalls on a broader scale the coda of an overture, and
the first couplet and especially the second are operatic finales transposed for piano and orchestra.

Looked at in this manner, a change of front like that in bar 260
comes to appear as natural as the abrupt entry of a new character,
shedding new light on the situation, would be in a comedy. A
moment in the finale of the second act of *Figaro* reminds one of this
passage. The countess, Susanna and Figaro have just been singing
the moving trio (in C) where they beseech the count to give, without
delay, his consent to the marriage of the barber and maid. The
hesitations of the nobleman, who is reckoning largely on Marcellina's
arrival to get him out of his fix, adds to the fullness of the ensemble;

it is one of the most serious and most poetic moments in the score. Hardly is the trio over when the gardener rushes in to complain that a man has fallen out of the window on to his flower-bed. At one bound, the music jumps into F major and becomes as frivolous and clownish in its bustle as it was meditative and grave a moment earlier. Yet nothing offends us; the appearance of the gardener, stammering with anger, is reason enough for the change.

We have the equivalent of this here. Mozart's public, for whom the language of opera buffa was the musical language *par excellence*, recognized it and behaved in presence of this concerto as it would have done in the theatre. Since then, the parts have been reversed; opera has become the tributary of symphony and we no longer respond to the allusions to dramatic music that we hear in the instrumental works of the 18th century.

Each of the two halves of ex. 322 is given out by the clarinets and flute with piano accompaniment[1] and repeated by the solo, doubled by the violins in a simplified version (bars 262-93). The tune does not evolve into a passage but vanishes as unceremoniously as it had come, like a comrade who is shown out as soon as he is no longer needed. A few bars of dialogue between piano and wind and a solo passage bring us back to the key of A, but the pace of the movement is so swift that its impetus carries it, so to speak, beyond its point of arrival and when we regain a footing we are in ex. 317, the first subject of the recapitulation couplet. The refrain has been skipped altogether.[2]

As usual in the sonata rondo, the third couplet is the recapitulation. It differs from the recapitulation of a first movement in that, not having to collect material which had been scattered over the first tutti and the first solo, it is generally shorter than the exposition, whereas in an opening allegro it tends to be longer. The part which follows the reprise is at once modified and shortened. Ex. 317 itself, given out by the piano, is darkened by the woodwind who restate it in the minor and its last notes are repeated and exchanged two or three times by them and the piano. We pass immediately to the second subject, ex. 311; the previous theme had concluded in the minor and this one is expounded by the wind in the major. When

---

[1] Ex. 302 in the finale of K.482 had been treated likewise.

[2] A similar device had been used in another "irrepressible" rondo, K.459. It occurs more than once, notably in the piano quartets and in K.456. Beethoven uses it in his concerto in G.

the piano gives it out after them, it returns to its original mode. From it evolves the graceful dialoguing passage we noticed earlier.[1] The bravura passages and concluding subject are repeated with no changes except that of the key, and after a rather more spacious "bridge" the refrain comes back for the last time.

The coda is worthy of the rest. The last return of the refrain is followed by all the motifs we have not heard since the first tutti. Mozart shares them out between orchestra and solo in the order of their first appearance, but he interrupts them once to recall his concluding subject, ex. 319. He brings in the whole of it, developing the dialoguing section, and in the key of D, unexpected so near the end; after which he resumes the catalogue of the material from the first tutti. Then, at the last moment, the piano remembers ex. 320, the continuation of the previous theme, and with this late-comer it whips its cream and sets going the indispensable *strepitoso*. Thanks to this frisking figure, the last bars are among those which produce most vividly in all Mozart the sense of physical strength. All the end is admirable for the manner in which the composer transforms the material of the opening tutti. Now he replaces the orchestra by the piano in the whole of one phrase (bars 464–8; cf. with bars 24–8), adapting the phrase to his new instrument; now he gives the solo the larger share, but leaving a small one to a group of the tutti (bars 468–71; cf. with bars 28–31); now the orchestra keeps the main part and the piano takes over the line of a single instrument (bars 502–5; cf. with bars 46–9); and even in the purely orchestral bars Mozart varies the general effect with imperceptible touches (bars 473–6; cf. with bars 33–6; bars 496–9; cf. with bars 40–3). Never was the accusation of reproducing unchanged whole sections of his movements less deserved than here.

We have already mentioned the importance of A major in Mozart; it is a key he uses seldom during his mature period and only for first-rate works. Those we enumerated at the beginning of this chapter are all related in one or more of their movements to our concerto. Nearly all show that mingling of joy and tears which characterizes the first movement and which is certainly the family sign of the key. The only one in whom this kinship is not apparent, the violin sonata, K.526, comes near our concerto in its rondo which is, both in form and inspiration, a kind of second version of the concerto rondo—a fine one, no doubt, but borne forward with a less

---

[1] Ex. 1.

irresistible spirit than the original.[1] This mingled feeling, expressed with a caressing sweetness that reminds us how close voluptuousness is to regret, is kindled in Mozart by the dusky, passionate tones of the clarinet; two of his three works for this instrument are in A. Chromatic themes, a tendency to hover between major and minor are the most recognizable means of expression of this mood. It is hard to find preferences in this bunch of great works, where deep emotion is never accompanied by violence or murkiness, where the texture is always diaphanous, and if we owned to a greater liking for one than for the other it could be but an irrelevant personal confession.

---

[1] The theme of the refrain comes from a sonata of C. F. Abel, op. V, 5. Abel, whom Mozart, as a child, had met in London, had died in that city on June 22nd, 1787. Mozart's sonata is dated August 24th of the same year. Saint-Foix (op. cit., V, 319–20) suggests that the use of Abel's theme was a tribute to the memory of the old composer. A similar tribute to the memory of John Christian Bach may be recognized in the andante of K.414 (see p. 140, note 2).

5. The Twentieth Concerto: K.491 in C Minor

CONCERTO No. 20 IN C MINOR (K.491)[1]
Finished March 24th, 1786
  (Allegro): 3-4
  Larghetto: C (in E flat)
  (Allegretto): C
Orchestra: String, flute, two hautboys, two clarinets, two bassoons, two
  horns, two trumpets, two kettledrums.

IT is customary to wonder at the fruitfulness with which Mozart, during the summer of 1788, composed his three great symphonies in twice as many weeks, and this feat is indeed admirable. But there is as much reason to marvel at this month of March, 1786, during which, at three weeks' distance, he produced two works as fine and as different as the concertos in A and C minor. And our wonder is still greater when we remember that the writing of these concertos was not his only occupation. *Idomeneo*, composed six years earlier, was to be revived on the Vienna stage and he was busy overhauling it and even writing a new aria and duet to replace those which the taste of the Austrian capital was likely to find too simple. These numbers were finished between the completion of the concerto in A and that of the C minor.

Such fruitfulness rivals that of the Lents of 1784 and 1785. Like the latter, the Lent of 1786 presents two great twin works, conceived simultaneously or nearly so, which light up opposite aspects of their composer's soul. The difference between them, however, is less great than between the D minor and C major concertos of the previous year, and it is now the more sorrowful of the two which follows the other.

The C minor concerto is the last but one of the great twelve which spread over these three years. With its companion in C major, K.503, which was to crown the series the following winter, it is the glorious culmination of Mozart's work as a concerto writer. In these two we

---

[1] *Gesamtausgabe*, no. 24.

find united the most admirable of the features which characterize it as a whole but which had hitherto not been found in one single concerto. Lofty thought, breadth of structure, close and well-balanced collaboration between tutti and solo, rich scoring, thematic *developments*, finales rivalling first movements in importance: these characteristics, which had appeared separately in one or other concerto, are all present in the C minor and C major of 1786.

Like the D minor, this concerto is isolated in Mozart's work. But we will not make in its favour the exception we made for the former and call it Beethovenian. Unconnected with any particular composition, it is nevertheless in the main stream of Mozartian inspiration. Tempest-tossed it certainly is, but with less intensity and less obsession than the D minor. It expresses a soul driven hither and thither by the storm; the D minor was itself the storm. For one instant only, in the short *development*, does it attain the stress and compelling force of the elder work; the rest of the time, its predominating mood is elegiac rather than dramatic. It is the rule to speak of both works as if they formed a closely related pair and it is no doubt natural to wish to liken one to the other the two concertos Mozart wrote in the minor mode; but the attempt is idle. The fact that they are so different from the rest of his work is almost all they have in common.

I. The evolution of music at the end of the 18th century and the beginning of the 19th carries it away from the sectional and strophic design of the *galant* style towards a closer structure where the joins between the parts of a movement are less clearly distinguishable. To borrow a metaphor of Ernest Newman's, it is less and less like a table and more and more like a tree. This is, of course, merely the start of an evolution which has gone on to our own day and appears to culminate in the symphonies of Sibelius.

Mozart was too susceptible to the influence of his time for this evolution not to affect him. Beside movements like those of many a sonata,[1] where the quasi-autonomous divisions are marked off one from the other by emphatic cadences, themselves often preceded by noisy bars of tonic and dominant harmony,[2] he has left pieces like most of his quartets and quintets where the sections are joined by

---

[1] The allegro of the duet sonata in C, K.521, is the most successful of these movements in *galant* style, with well-marked-off divisions.

[2] Wagner's "clatter of dishes at princely banquets".

bridge passages almost as significant as the groups of main themes themselves. It is no doubt in his chamber music that he moves farthest away from *galant* conventions, whilst the sonata and the concerto, genres more fashionable because involving the honour of an executant, are those where he remains most faithful to them. But his greatest concertos possess themselves of so vast an extent of his personality, they reflect it so fully, that it was impossible they should not be influenced by this tendency. We recognize it in the works of these three years: first, in exceptional movements like the finale of K.449; then, in the allegro of the G major, the allegro and andante of the C major and, to a lesser degree, in the allegro of the D minor. Beside these more unified movements we continue to find, mixed with them, others built strophically, such as the allegros of K.482 and 488. And, in spite of the progress in unification proved by many works, movements with separate sections continue to occur to the end of his life. His last concerto and his last quintet both let us hear once more the clamorous cadences of *galant* music.

On the whole, however, the twelve concertos of 1784 to 1786 bear witness to progress towards a homogeneity which reaches its highest point in the C minor. The noisy, expressively vigorous cadences of the D minor have gone and the groups of themes link on to one another unbroken. In this the work recalls the C major, K.467, the twin of the D minor, from which it is very different in most other respects.

The opening theme resembles no other first subject of Mozart's; the only one which might recall it a little would be that of K.449, ex. 74. It takes us as far as the D minor did from the marches and flourishes with which most of his concertos begin. The ternary beat, seldom used by them, strengthens the impression of originality (ex. 323 a). It unfolds in unison,[1] without a clear-cut outline at first, unstable and chromatic; with no definite key, it seems to return to the same place and yet in reality moves forward; in the ninth bar it gains a little in concentration; though it ends by coming back to the tonic, one feels it is not compelled to do so and might pursue for a long time its wandering course.

Of the conventional *galant* opening Mozart keeps here nothing but the *piano* to *forte* plan.[2] In the thirteenth bar the orchestra

---

[1] Notice the expressive held note in the hautboys from the eighth bar onward.

[2] See p. 240.

enters *ff*—the largest orchestra in all these concertos, the only one with both clarinets and hautboys. The theme is repeated and its instability is now blended with an increasing strength, especially noticeable in the prolongation and insistence of the last bars. Instead of concluding with a return to the tonic, without interrupting its march it is quickened by the "fluttering seconds" of the violins and when it rests, for a brief moment, on a dominant chord, it is not replaced by a new, contrasted subject but sets off afresh with heightened vitality.

The bars that follow appear in their own right and not as heralds, and yet they turn out to be a bridge to ex. 324. Without a change of discourse, but softly, as at the opening, the woodwind trio rises one degree at a time, exchanging and opposing two tags of the first theme (ex. 323 b); nothing warns us that their climb is near its end when suddenly there glides down from the sky a new figure, just a scale of a little over an octave, whose desolate gentleness defines more clearly the mood of the beginning (ex. 324). It has the shape of a canon at the octave between flute and bassoon. It is not the second subject but one of those engaging snares thanks to which Mozart avoids casting his concertos in the mould of orthodoxy; it will not reappear till the recapitulation. It lengthens and loses itself in a budding of a fragment from ex. 323 b. This latter opens out and brings back the first subject, which rumbles in the bass, where it is confined, and tries to rise through the repeated notes of the violins and the held notes of the woodwind, seeming to conclude. But now, at a turning, we fall suddenly into the beseeching sweetness of the subdominant of the relative major, a surprise all the greater that Mozart seldom modulates in his initial tuttis. We stop an instant, whilst violins and flute call to each other; then resume our march, return to C minor, and a chain of ascending scales, suspended between flute, clarinet and bassoon above a fragment of four notes from ex. 323 a which had already served in the transition, ex. 323 b, leads to a new *forte*, and the concluding subject, a rhythmical and wrathful phrase in which we recognize the leaps of the first theme.

This stirring tutti is comparatively one of the shortest[1] and contains but a small part of the movement's material. If we omit the mock second subject, ex. 324, and the concluding theme, which return only at the end, it is all an exposition and development of the initial strain which, in the shape either of a simple statement (bars 1-27,

---

[1] A little more than one half the solo exposition.

63–73), or of a working-out (28–44), or of a passage based on one of
its fragments (74–87), is almost constantly present. No theme of
Mozart's is so rich in possibilities of elaboration for no other is as
fluid, no other leaves the door as wide open behind it. Its transformations throughout the movement are many and diverse (ex. 325),
and through them it permeates the whole allegro. We have met
with passages where one rhythmical feature from the first persisted
throughout,[1] but here it is the melodic outline—the leaps of a sixth
and a seventh, the four descending notes, the chromatic rise at the
end, as well as the characteristic rhythm ♪| ♫♫| ♩ ♩ which pene-
trates and unifies the work. Mozart has given up the more primitive
and formal method, inherited from the aria, of using "link themes"—
secondary motifs gathered from the opening tutti which reappeared
like familiar faces to reassure us and act as landmarks. He had indeed
made little use of them since 1784.

This tutti is therefore an introduction and not an argument. It
is like the tutti of the E flat, K.482, in that the solo exposition takes
from it only the opening theme and that more than half of it, given
out by the solo or restated by the orchestra with piano decoration,
reappears in the recapitulation. These concertos are not the first
where Mozart repeats thus passages already heard, with piano ornamentation; in those in D and G of 1784 he had done so at the very
beginning of the first solo; but the postponement of the reunion
between piano and orchestra till the end of the movement is a step
forward, since it heightens the dramatic sense of the work.

These first hundred bars, by insisting on the main theme, have
fixed the bounds to the field on which the movement will open out.
With the piano entry, the action itself is engaged.

The monologue with which the solo introduces itself unfolds in
three strains, like so many Mozartian themes; the third is prolonged
and crumbles away into a succession of sighs, collapsing on the tonic.
The general line of the music, starting from the dominant, rises little
by little, to drop abruptly at the end with a gesture of discouragement
(ex. 326). Like the tutti, this prelude announces an elegy rather than
a drama (bars 100–18).

The orchestra re-expounds the first subject harmonized by the
brass; the woodwind take it from the strings at the fourth bar and
the piano from them at the sixth (ex. 325 a). But the piano takes it

---

[1] For instance, the dotted quaver of K.459, the march of K.467.

over only to deform it, to exaggerate its leaps which, from sevenths, become twelfths and fourteenths; then, enlivening it, transforms it into a scale passage which in a few bars leads to B flat, the dominant through which we approach the key of the relative major (bars 118–47).

A new tune starts (ex. 327); it seems to sing of peace after strife but recalls in its outline the lament of the first tutti, ex. 324. Its serenity is but apparent; the lowering of the leading note at its third repetition and the B natural betray instability and remind us of the proximity of C minor. It occupies the place of the solo subject and the piano gives it out; but instead of continuing with a bravura passage, the solo becomes silent and the woodwind repeat the theme, enriching it with imitations in hautboy and clarinet (bars 148–64). It would therefore be a true second subject, were it not that the presence later on of another subject in E flat prevents us from fitting this movement into the framework set up by the textbooks.

The wind have not done when the mood changes suddenly and the idyll turns to tragedy. Passion speaks out, though still piano, with the entry of the solo instrument which cuts off the last notes of the theme and hovers a moment in the key of F minor (ex. 325 b; ex. 328). The alarm is sudden but short and we soon regain E flat; but the excitement keeps up; it is a far cry from the piano's plaintive note in its first solo to the fiery race on which it has now started. Whilst its right hand keeps a very lively "Alberti bass" going in the treble, its left rises from the deep with wrathful scales which remind us for the briefest of instants of the angry runs in the D minor. The harsh tones are to some extent belied by the graceful interlacings of the flute and hautboy (ex. 325) which round off the rough outlines. After three smoother bars (175–7), uncertainty again envelops us; we oscillate between B flat, A flat and E flat; in each of these keys piano and violins repeat a panting figure (ex. 329) which resolves into a lightning train of arpeggios and scale fragments whose curving line rises and drops and finally carries off the E flat trill in a triumphant onslaught.

Thereupon, hautboys and clarinets give out another subject caressed by a wavy violin figure (ex. 330 a); from third to third, it percolates to the depths of the bassoon whence its second half rises (ex. 330 b). The piano repeats it and decorates the line of descending thirds, whilst the strings repeat them as they were.

The major mode now appears to have set in for good and the first bar (220) of a fresh working out section seems to confirm it. No doubt we are about to hear some of those bravura passages which conclude the solo exposition and are laid entirely in the complementary key. Yet the reviving agitation, marked by repeated notes in the strings, should put us on our guard. Moreover, we should remember how precociously the major had banished the minor on the piano's appearance. Too mild a February heralds frost in the spring. And true enough, the chord of E flat, punctuated by the strings, which concludes ex. 330, turns out in its second bar to be but the beginning of the initial subject, ex. 323 a, which had lorded it over the first tutti and was hibernating since the start of the solo. Enunciated in the upper register of the flute, it is harmonized by the quivering fiddles and violas and whipped along by the piano's arpeggios (ex. 331)—all this in E minor. In the seventh bar it breaks away from its original form and enters the key of F sharp minor, so exceptional in Mozart. Here the storm rages. Again idyll and elegy yield to an atmosphere of strife; the piano part runs tersely up and down the keyboard, escorted by the sketchy arpeggios of the wind and the syncopations of the strings (ex. 332). Then the waves of sound become less ample, shorter phrases appear, and with some of Mozart's beloved subdominant modulations and a last thrust of the minor, the rhythm breaks up and slackens and we return to the peaceful zone of E flat.

This time the calm seems to be final. The restless tutti accompaniment is silent and the piano disports itself alone for a few bars with ingenuous and limpid passage work (bars 241–8). But its energy is not exhausted. It makes sure of its victory in a well-scanned dialogue with the wind in which the strings double it; all three seem to be congratulating each other on having passed unscathed through such redoubtable alarums (bars 249–56).

Except at the beginning of the stormy section, ex. 331, the initial theme has been much less discussed than in the opening tutti. It now falls to it to provide the material for the second tutti, but illumined and glorified by its transposition into E flat major and the inversion of its sinister leaps (ex. 325 d). This short passage of eighteen bars breathes a certain humour for, beginning with ex. 323 a, with its claws drawn, it concludes with the final bars, also transposed, of the first tutti; it is therefore a miniature in bright hues of that dusky opening.

The second solo promises to be similar. It begins, like the first, with ex. 325 a, translated into the major. But at the very first repetition of the fragment the assertion turns into a question, the wind echo dreamily, and the question is put a third time, then a fourth, in the minor. It is perhaps a memory of his other minor concerto which leads Mozart to open his *development* with the first notes of the solo;[1] at any rate, he does not make the same use of this device as in K.466; the hour is not for pathetic questions or sighs but for action, and from elegy the work, with a brusque movement, passes once again to tragedy.

It is the return of ex. 323 a, in F minor, which lets loose the strife. After the orchestra has restated its first bars, the piano takes its leap from the top of the keyboard and swoops down on the strings with its usual weapons of arpeggios and mutilated scales. It rushes to the onslaught in four bar phrases, thrice repeated in different keys: G minor, C minor and E flat, while the instruments defend themselves with a fragment of ex. 323 a (ex. 325 e). The contact with E flat does not bring any relaxation and the scales continue tracing their angry wake against the troubled background of strings and wood-wind. At the moment of greatest struggle, the orchestral defence gives way and the piano comes hurtling down three octaves. With the simplest technical means, Mozart produces a poignant effect; in these few bars, we feel the firmament collapsing better than in the most chord-laden passages of Liszt or Tchaikovsky (ex. 333). The power of the effect is due largely to the skill with which the moment has been prepared.

The section which now opens is one of the few in Mozart where passion seems really unchained. Ex. 334 is an appeal to physical sensation most exceptional with him. There is here an attempt to move us by the sheer force of the attack, to take us by the shoulders and shake us; an attempt which still succeeds, provided the conductor realizes and renders the composer's intention.[2]

To the quivering instruments there answers an upward rush on the piano; it is now the attacked party that takes the offensive. The duel starts four times, each time in a different key;[3] at the fifth, we witness a kind of reconciliation and piano and wind travel together over the registers in great strides full of anger (ex. 325 f, for the bass),

---

[1] They are the only concertos of Mozart's which, like Beethoven's op. 61, behave thus.

[2] Saint-Foix (*Les symphonies de Mozart*, p. 167) points out the likeness between these bars and the climax (also in C minor) of the *development* in the great E flat symphony. Here, nevertheless, the wildness is more aggressive, the physical appeal more direct. In both works, the formal nucleus is nothing but the "fluttering seconds" so common in Mozart at moments of intense emotion, but so transformed by its context and by the passion with which the composer charges it that we do not at once recognize it.

[3] Progression by fourths, once again.

Ex. 330

Ex. 331

Ex 332

Ex. 333

Ex. 334

enlivened by a torrent of breathless arpeggios in the treble. Then, dropping its voice to *piano*, the solo returns to the tonic via the dominant; behind the line of its scales can be perceived an echo of the ever-present first subject, bounding from one wind instrument to the other (ex. 325 g).

This *development*, as short as most of Mozart's, is certainly one of his most eventful. From the moment when, with an impatient gesture, it rid itself of the "elegiac" tune, we have not stood still one instant. Often, Mozart's *developments*, after a few expressive bars, are but a wending back towards the first subject and the recapitulation. Often, too, they toy with a fragment of a theme already heard. And in his concertos, we have noted the preponderance of the fantasia[1] and virtuosity. Thematic *developments*, which appear as early as K.271, become commoner after 1784 and reveal the heart of the drama as in the D minor and A major concertos, and here. Of the three, the C minor's is the most varied. Recall of the first subject in F minor, fierce piano onslaught (bar 309) swooping down on the orchestra like an eagle on its prey, shattering collapse of ex. 333, shock tactics in the tutti in ex. 334, new adventure of the piano and wind (bars 346–53) and finally a gliding back over the light swell of the accompaniment: so many episodes stamped, truly enough, with one same passionate spirit, but diverse in their degrees of stress, in the passing of the initiative from one instrument to the other, in the particular mood—yearning, wrath, aspiration—which is lighted up, and in their constant modulation. None of the keys through which we pass is as remote as F sharp minor in the first solo; we remain in the zone of C minor and its relative major; but the motion is unceasing and Mozart, with limited means, wins as much variety as if he was exploring less closely related keys. In no other concerto is the ceaseless passing to and fro, from one key to another, kept up so long. Hence the impression that this work is not only one of his strongest but also one of his most highly coloured.

Between the tutti and solo expositions there is the same difference as in the concertos in C, K.467, and E flat, K.482. One subject only is common to both; the second exposition, instead of repeating and amplifying the material of the first,[2] introduces entirely fresh elements. The recapitulation's task will be to link up the two and to recall all their themes. It will perform this task as concisely as possible, without allowing any leisure for virtuosity.

---

[1] Cf. K.414, 450, 451, 453, 456, 459, 467, 482.
[2] As do K.451, 466 and 488, for instance.

It is as if, after the passionate outburst of the *development*, everything had been said: great vital energy has been expended and the life of the movement is limited. Certain it is that all this last part expresses profound depression. Its somewhat defeatist spirit consents, it is true, to recall the serene and almost happy themes of the first solo, exs. 327 and 330; but, according to Mozart's invariable practice, it does so in the minor; moreover, it changes their order, so that the more pathetic of the two, ex. 327, follows the other. And, in order to insist with finality on the meaning of the movement, to this latter there links on at once the lament, ex. 324, which we had not heard since the opening tutti. Though there are no more explosions of fury as in ex. 334 or certain angry bars of the *development*, the atmosphere grows ever darker and a sadness, where elegy triumphs again over tragedy, prevails more and more deeply till the magnificent coda.

The first subject is repeated *forte*, as after the solo prelude, and we follow at first the solo's and not the tutti's exposition. We part from it in the codetta added by the piano and come back with the conclusion which had followed in the first tutti (bars 28-33 and 381-6). Without closing, this passage acts now as a bridge to the third subject, ex. 330, given out with no change other than the transposition into C minor. Drastically cutting out all virtuosity, the movement links it up with the second subject, ex. 327, very affecting in its new mourning garb. The piano gives it out as before, but, when the wind restate it, interposes between each repetition a touching ascending phrase; this is one of the loveliest moments in the concerto. The theme is profoundly transformed by these tragic parentheses of the piano's. The fine modulating passage, ex. 328, succeeds it (bars 165-8 and 428-34), quickly modified, and loses itself in a variation of the first subject. The scoring is completed and the line of melody decorated and enlivened by the piano and suddenly there falls from the sky ex. 324. The working-out which prolongs it is also reproduced with piano co-operation and, at the same point as in K.482, exhibits at its highest the art with which Mozart introduces the piano into a passage originally entrusted to the orchestra, without disturbing the instrumentation or upsetting the balance of tone. Compare bars 35-62 with 435-62; to within a few details, the scoring is laid out in the same manner and Mozart no longer relies exclusively on the trick of giving the solo the former flute or hautboy part; he adds it to the wind in ex. 323 b and to wind and strings together in ex. 334, to thicken the bass with its lively arpeggios, to emphasize a particular bar with some detail, to decorate with one hand the treble or bass; for four bars, finally, he uses the replacement device already described.

Again we leave the paths of the first tutti and a bravura passage— the only one in the recapitulation—short but powerful, concludes for the nonce the piano's part. A last statement of ex. 323 a ushers in the cadenza. Mozart has not written one for this concerto but the return of the tutti shows that it should not close with a trill but link on to what follows. Then comes a repetition of bars 80–99, leading up to the conclusion.

Mozart is not content to finish thus, although he had done so elsewhere, even in his greatest and most personal works; he adds a coda, the only true one in these concertos.[1] The music drops to *piano* at the end of the quotation from the opening tutti and, softly, the solo makes its last entry. It moves swiftly over a tonic pedal in a mysterious twilight of diminished sevenths, whilst violins and wind keep going from one to the other a light-footed accompaniment figure, maintaining the first subject's rebounding semi-quavers which give such spring and such vigour, despite its quietness, to this superb close (ex. 335). At the very end, the *nuance* drops to *pianissimo*.

This recapitulation is shorter than most and its absence of virtuosity is noteworthy. There is no trace of those torrents of notes with which the soloist seems to try and stamp his image deeply on the minds of his hearers at the last moment; on the contrary, the piano part now does honour to the composer rather than to the pianist. Playwright prevails over actor; intent upon fulfilling its mission, the music hastens towards its conclusion. Only at the end, when all has been said, does Mozart remember he is a *virtuoso* and in his coda combine both functions.

Beethoven's admiration for this concerto is well known. He never imitated it but he certainly remembered it in his own concerto in C minor, composed, like this one, at thirty, and, in his own way, he felt and expressed the same mood, as far as a mood can be identical from one man and from one work to another. However Beethovenian this concerto be—of a very young Beethoven—it is not fanciful to consider it as a homage to Mozart; it is perhaps not by chance that its major subject is one of the most Mozartish in all Beethoven, and the general tone of the work is much nearer Mozart than usual with him. When Beethoven is not just himself, he comes nearer to Haydn

---

[1] But which had a humble forerunner in K.271.

or Clementi than Mozart; but for once we recognize in his third concerto a composition which would perhaps not have seen the light of day without this latter's C minor work.

This is probably the best place to speak of an important problem to which we have already alluded in an earlier chapter.[1] Although it is of a general nature, we have preferred to postpone discussion of it till the diligent reader has neared the end of the greater works of Mozart's Viennese period and is familiar through them with the character of his concerto form. As this problem is solved with most consummate art in the C minor, the time appears ripe for dealing with it.

It is this.

The tutti exposition, the solo exposition that follows it, and the recapitulation are three parts of a first allegro into which enter identical elements. Hence the danger of some monotony, especially in the recapitulation which runs the risk of merely reiterating the solo exposition. Does Mozart avoid this danger, and how does he avoid it?

The question is really twofold. What difference does a concerto make between the tutti and solo expositions? How does a recapitulation differ from these and especially from the solo exposition? Though they are distinct, the success with which a classical composer solves the second of these questions depends on the way in which he has already solved the first.

Some concertos distinguish the first tutti from the solo that follows it only by the inevitable introduction of passage work. They repeat tutti elements in the solo, in the same order, modulating to the dominant, and adding the piano part to that of the orchestra, or more often substituting it for the latter. The majority, however, bring in a subject reserved for the solo and this is usually the chief difference between the two expositions. The majority, also, omit a few less important fragments which they usually, but not always, reinstate in the recapitulation; the concluding subject is often among these. Such differences are trifling—far less noteworthy than those resulting from the presence of the piano and the reshuffling in the orchestration which it necessitates.

But in a few concertos the differences, though no greater, are more significant. The number of secondary motifs which appear in the first tutti to be left out in the solo exposition may be increased and the presence of the mock second subject in one and its replacement in the

---

[1] I, 2; pp. 33, 34.

other by the true second subject emphasizes the difference all the more in that its apparent importance makes its future absence more noticeable.

Finally, in a few others, most of them works of the great period,[1] the first subject, present on both occasions,[2] and the conclusion are the only elements common to the two expositions, and even the latter is sometimes new in the solo. In the concerto to which this chapter is devoted and in the C major, K.467, the importance of the first subject, both before and after the piano entry, connects tutti and solo, in spite of the small number of details common to both. Such a procedure is obviously the most interesting because it is the richest in possible new combinations in the last part of the movement.

As the *developments* of Mozart's concertos generally take none of their material from both expositions, the novelty of the recapitulation will depend on the use it makes of the material drawn from either of them. When there is little difference between them, the recapitulation will tend to be largely a repetition of both. When the difference is great, the recapitulation has the chance of holding surprises in store for us. There are exceptions, but this is true of three-quarters of the concertos.

In the early and late works, and even in a few belonging to the great period, the recapitulation is content with repeating the first solo with the necessary transpositions. It is then with changes in the order of the material, in the solos, harmonization, scoring, distribution of themes between solo and tutti, and at least once with a heightening of the passion, that Mozart prevents it from merely reiterating the solo exposition. The concerto in A, K.488, renews its last part by introducing a theme from its *development*; this felicitous device does not occur elsewhere.

When the difference between the expositions is perceptible without being great, the recapitulation can bring together all the important elements of both, and the order in which it reviews them offers chances of variety of which several concertos have availed themselves.

Finally, when the difference between them is very wide, it would entail too great a length in the recapitulation to include in it all their elements. A choice is therefore needed. Here, five concertos act in a particularly interesting manner and their devices are not repeated.

---

[1] K.365, 415, 459, 467, 482, 491, 503.

[2] One of the horn concertos, K.417, even introduces a new first subject in its solo exposition.

That for two pianos drops its mock second subject which had re-appeared in the *development*, and a part of the solo subject, but calls up again a secondary theme and a codetta from the first tutti. The F major, K.459, leaves out the whole of the solo subject, modifies the solos and repeats several secondary motifs from the initial tutti. The C major, K.467, acts likewise and, moreover, recalls its mock second subject. The E flat, K.482, at first sets out as if to bring back every-thing; actually, it omits half its second subject and the whole of the solo one; moreover, its bravura passages are modified and cut down and all the part of the first tutti that the solo exposition had left out is put back into the movement at this stage. Finally, the C minor brings together all the important themes of both expositions, but the solos are so much reduced that in reality only a small part of the solo exposition is repeated, and here, as in K.482, the recapitulation is a kind of *revanche* of the first exposition over the second.

In this respect, the 1784-6 concertos are the most interesting to study, although two earlier ones, K.271 and 365, had managed to vary greatly these three sections and although several works com-posed during these years had been content with repeating the second exposition as it was or had sought to renew their recapitulations in some other way. In the two concertos of 1788 and 1791, the problem ceases to interest Mozart; one of them dwells especially on virtuosity; the other pours out its originality in its *development*. The three chief formal problems of a concerto are those of the relations between expositions and recapitulation, and between orchestra and piano (inter-play), and that of the *development* (this last one common, of course, to all subdivisions of sonata form). If there is any concerto of Mozart's which has faced and solved them all in an equally masterly manner, it is certainly the C minor. And, if we remember that the very essence of a work of art, its inspiration, is here of the loftiest, it will be granted that the first movement of this concerto is the high-water mark of Mozart's concerto art.

II. The plan of the larghetto is as simple as the allegro's was com-plex. A refrain—aba—a couplet in the relative minor; the return of the first part of the refrain—a; a couplet in the subdominant; a third return of the refrain, entire—aba—a short coda. The plan of each couplet is similar: two four-bar phrases, given out by the orchestra, repeated and varied by the solo; moreover, the second couplet links on to the refrain with a bridge of four tutti bars.

The feeling appears as simple as the design but its simplicity is that of a complex soul at rest and not of an artless one. All melodic beauty defies analysis in the last resort but that of this refrain laughs at it even more contemptuously than most; all that one can say is that the wavy accompaniment adds to the magic of the canto, especially when the tutti take it up. The theme is at first sight implacably symmetrical; in reality, its fourth bar contains an element of surprise; the first two bars had accustomed us to the familiar opposition of a rhythmical motif and a melodic and expressive one; in the last bar, instead of the expected singing phrase, a purely rhythmical bar is followed by another no less so (ex. 336).[1] But that is not all its secret and we make no claim to disclose it. Out of the well-worn progression: tonic—dominant—tonic—dominant seventh—tonic—never had there been struck such loveliness.

The second part of the refrain, reserved for the solo, is but a sketch which the pianist must at all costs fill in; to play it as it is printed is to betray the memory of Mozart. As it returns at the end of the movement the soloist will have to draw on his imagination to adorn it a second time.

The refrain once given out, we pass without transition into C minor. The first movement finished such a short while ago that this feels like a return; we rediscover the principal key of the work rather than enter a new one. Like a great part of the allegro, this couplet has an elegiac tone, and the rising arpeggios in the flute and piano remind us of the piano echo in the recapitulation of ex. 327. It is a fragment of a woodwind serenade; hautboy and flute share the tune or co-operate in enriching it, and the lively bassoon part borrows its best features from the treble instruments (ex. 337). The strings are confined to sustaining the piano when it follows the wind's lead and varies their exposition. Once again we observe how skilfully Mozart gives expressive beauty to an apparently quite formal decoration and renders deep feeling through the medium of ornament.

After the four bars of refrain, we again leave E flat, which clearly is but the official key of the movement, and plunge into the warm, relaxing atmosphere of the subdominant as abruptly as we plunged just now into the relative minor. To elegy and lamentation succeeds a soft, voluptuous melody (ex. 338). But, though the feeling changes, the wind remain none the less masters of the field; the strings join in only to add their warmth to the piano by doubling it at the lower

---

[1] The alteration of A flat to A natural the second time the piano gives out the tune (bar 17), and on all later occasions, will be noticed.

Ex. 335

Ex. 336

Ex. 337

Ex. 338

Ex. 339

Ex. 340

octave.[1]   At the beginning of the second half, we touch on the minor;
then voluptuousness reaches an almost painful pitch of intensity (bars
50–4).   The feeling survives a while in the strings which lead to a
pedal over which float airy thirds and sixths in bassoons, hautboys

and flutes, the last echoes of the figure ⟨figure⟩ which is the
motto of the passage.[2]

---

[1] Bar 48 is but a sketch (ex. 339).

[2] The reader will remember at this point the transition pedal, so close in
feeling to this passage, in the A flat larghetto of the E flat piano quartet,
K.493, a contemporary of this concerto.

One word of advice. Some conductors and pianists tend to slow down in this second couplet and to decrease the speed even further in the passage which leads back to the refrain (bars 59-62). When the soloist repeats this latter, he returns to *tempo primo* and a rough unseating of the rhythm is the result. To avoid it, the couplet should not have a rallentando and the refrain should not be speeded up. The secret is to keep an equal tempo in the different sections of the larghetto and above all not to drag in bars 59-62 or hurry in ex. 336.

When the whole refrain has been restated,[1] the woodwind build up the coda on two figures: one, descending, in clarinets and bassoons; the other, ascending, in the piano, crossed by a scale in the hautboy. The strings are still confined to accompanying and the last bars belong to the piano, seconded by a very active bassoon and adorned by the comments of hautboys and flute.

III. The commonest form for a concerto finale is the rondo. But Mozart dislikes completely minor rondos. He has left only three, all in sonatas;[2] a fourth rondo which begins in the minor, that of the concerto K.466, concludes in the major. Elsewhere, in minor works, he uses either the fugue,[3] the sonata form[4] or, as here, variations.[5] The theme of this finale is certainly one of the most personal of those he has "varied". Measured but not slow, spare but not dry, it reminds us both of a march and a hymn. It is composed of two halves of eight bars each, with repeats, and modulates from tonic to dominant and not, like so many minor pieces, to the relative major. It remains throughout in the shadow of grief and is only distantly connected in feeling with the two earlier movements; less melodious and more reserved than the allegro, it has nothing of the serenity and voluptuousness of the larghetto (ex. 340).

However austere be this theme and its harmonization, the scoring is exquisitely subtle. The tune is given out from end to end by the first violins, *piano*, with an accompaniment in the other strings which

---

[1] Including the sketch passage!

[2] K.304 for violin in E minor; K.310 for piano in A minor; K.457 for piano in C minor.

[3] K.173, string quartet in D minor.

[4] K.183 and 550, symphonies in G minor.

[5] K.388, serenade in C minor; K.421, string quartet in D minor; K.491, this concerto. The G minor piano quartet and string quintet, K.478 and 516, have finales in the major.

shows independence only in the last bar of each half.   The rhythm,
on the other hand, is as full of contrasts as the outline of the tune is
smooth.   Marked at first with crotchets (a), it broadens into minims
and semibreves (b); then follows the line of the tune with crotchets,
legato (c).

All the wind help to mark (a); in (b), the flute doubles the fiddles
at the octave; in (c) (bars 5-6), the bassoon doubles the horns; in
bars 7-8, all four woodwind double or complete the string harmonies.
Comparable but not identical behaviour occurs in the second half,
with the result that, in a theme almost bleak with austerity, there
prevails a glistening colour to which every instrument in the orchestra, even the kettledrums, contributes something at one moment or
another.

This theme is followed by eight variations.[1]   The first has double
bars; nos. II, III, IV, V and VI are "double" variations; VII is a
single one, without repeats; VIII is in different time and is followed
by a coda.

As in other variations in these concertos, the piano takes no part
in the theme.   The first variation belongs to it exclusively; the strings
provide a reticent accompaniment to the *melismas* with which it
decorates the tune.   The woodwind expound the second variation,
a literal repetition of the theme with new harmonies and rhythm
but without the original contrasts; despite its smoothness, the bassoon
quavers betray a slight rise in emotion.   The piano repeats each half
in semi-quavers, using scales the first time and arpeggios the second;
the strings sustain it with a simplified reading of the tune.

A greater intensity of feeling corresponds to the third variation.
The mark rises to *forte*.   The piano attacks alone.   With the right
hand it repeats the substance of the theme, but lashes every second and
fourth beat with a dotted quaver; with the left hand, it climbs up the
lower register in triplets, falling back and starting up again after each
ascent.   This is the first appearance of a rhythmical element in the
tune itself.   The dotted quaver persists in the tutti repeat in which the
whole orchestra plays, and the place of the triplets is taken by the
second fiddles which keep up a rapid, undulating accompaniment
on their lower strings.   The impression produced by strings, woodwind, brass and drums, emphasizing repeatedly the ♩♪♩ ♩♪♩

---

[1] Not numbered in the text.   Here are the bars at which each one begins:
I, 16; II, 32; III, 64; IV, 96 (A flat); V, 128; VI, 164 (C major); VII, 200;
VIII (in 6-8), 221.

rhythm which now invades the whole theme, is powerful and warlike, not in the manner of some popular rondo militaire, but like Beethoven's C minor violin sonata. Such purely physical effects, we said in speaking of the allegro, are not common in Mozart and all the more impressive when they occur.

This fanfare stops suddenly and in its stead clarinets and bassoons sing out a gentle tune which opens in A flat, full of sub-dominant softness, a variation which retains neither the outline nor the rhythm nor the harmonies nor the spirit of the original, and is more of an interlude (ex. 341). The rhythm is still military, but neither warlike nor fierce. The piano repeats it almost exactly, doubled by the strings in their lower registers. Only in the second half does it allow itself a few runs in scales and broken chords.

The fifth variation which, like the earlier ones, links on to its predecessor is one of the most moving. It returns all at once to the elegiac inspiration we recognized so often in the other movements and which had been missing hitherto in this one. It belongs wholly to the piano; the only intervention of the orchestra consists in the held notes of the strings towards the end of each section. The first part begins with a true variation, and no longer an interlude, in free four-part counterpoint, melodious and very Mozartian in its diaphanous texture (ex. 342). Somewhat unexpected here, it is the kind of writing one meets in the *minore* of a series of major variations. Its second part recalls the pugnacious dotted quaver rhythm in the treble, whilst from the bass surges up wave after wave of scales rising one degree at a time with occasionally modal resonances (ex. 343). The other half is similar, except that the counterpoint is mostly in two parts.

Again the mood becomes serene, and this time the transparent key of C major announces a heavenly peace, very different from the warm caresses of the A flat interlude (ex. 344). It is a conversation between hautboy, flute and bassoon that reminds us, both in its inspiration and its writing, of the C major episode in the andante of the E flat concerto, K.482. The violins take possession of the tune when the piano relinquishes it to soar upwards; right at the end, the wind take their place and the conclusion is a dialogue between the solo and them.

This is the last genial moment in the concerto. Henceforward, attempts at pacification having failed, the work gives itself up to suffering. The seventh variation opens like the theme, but an interruption by the piano and woodwind between fragments (a) and (b) (cf. ex. 340) brings us at once close to passion, whose realm we enter when at (c) the solo adds a quivering two-handed accompaniment of arpeggios and Alberti bass. This variation where piano, strings and woodwind interplay constantly has no repeats; it seems to hasten onward towards the issue. Instead of letting it finish, the piano adds three bars of flourishes like those of ex. 335 which lead to a dominant chord and the cadenza.

As in the allegro, the cadenza does not end in a trill but links on to the next variation without intervention of the tutti. This last variation is in 6-8 time like the conclusions of many rondos and arias, but the mode remains obstinately minor. The piano speaks alone (ex. 345). Not only its dancing rhythm but also the preponderance of the treble for both hands gives it a light-footedness which contrasts with the gravity of its thought and heightens the feeling of grief and almost of tragedy. We often find these deliberate contrasts between matter and manner in the 18th century, and in Mozart in particular. They are the musical equivalent of the use of a short, skipping verse for the utterance of sorrow. Programme notes usually draw attention to the haunting presence of the so-called Neapolitan sixth[1] in this variation and the coda which flows from it (bars 225-6, 233-4, etc.; ex. 345 a). The emotion is now that of the first movement with a return of that physical appeal which we heard in its *development*; and yet something raises it above the ordinary world of passion and bears it far away into planetary space. One feels this more strongly still when, dwelling on a motif derived from the variation, the piano rushes up to the higher octave and, doubled lower down by the strings (a favourite scoring device in this concerto), attacks furiously a chromatic succession of sixths, grating enough to set one's teeth on edge (ex. 346).

To mark that this passage is the climax of the movement and the concerto's final message, Mozart repeats it (bars 240-56, 257-73); then, having sounded for the last time the fragment (a) of ex. 345, he throws himself with the orchestra into the concluding fanfare which proclaims with desperation the triumph of the minor mode.

This concerto is in all respects one of his greatest; we would fain say: *the* greatest, were it not impossible to choose between four or five of them. We have tried to analyse the chief elements of its greatness or at least to draw attention to them; there remains one of which we have not spoken.

---

[1] Chord on the subdominant composed of a minor third and a minor sixth.

It concerns the collaboration of piano and orchestra.

The *interesting* complexity of such collaboration is the element *par excellence* of the concerto. A concerto whence it is absent may be good music but cannot be a good concerto, for it is because of the co-operation of the solo and the orchestral instruments that a work is a concerto and not a symphony. It is a *formal* ideal, but one inseparable from certain possibilities of expression which are the sole property of the genus. A concerto which does not set this ideal before it may be, we repeat, a beautiful work, but does not deserve the title it bears.

Now, this ideal is kept in mind and attained very unequally by Mozart's twenty-three piano concertos. Remote from it in his first nine, he draws nearer to it in 1784, in which year those in D, G and F attain it fully. But their success in this exceeds their emotional importance, and when with the D minor he expresses in concerto form a greater depth of passion than he had expressed hitherto in any instrumental composition, he moves away from the ideal of co-operation to return to that of alternation and opposition between the protagonists. He loses in *concertante* complexity and richness what he gains in earnestness of thought.

We saw that he won back a good deal in the concertos in E flat (recapitulation) and A (*development* of the allegro and andante). In the C minor, all the lost ground is regained; about to withdraw from the concerto stage, he excels here equally in greatness of inspiration and richness and variety of interplay between piano and tutti.

Let us say at once that the piano scarcely ever plays alone in the allegro and larghetto. The prelude which marks its entry (ex. 326) is the only entirely solo passage of any length;[1] at other times the orchestra is sometimes silent for three or four bars, either to allow it to sing more clearly the temporary serenity of the end of the exposition (bars 241–4), or so that its isolation may make the outburst of passion at the climax of the movement, ex. 333 (bars 325–9), more dramatic because more personal. In the larghetto, the first and third expositions of the refrain (bars 1–4, 63–6) are given by the unaccompanied piano. For the rest of the time in both movements, representatives of the orchestra play with it.

Yet the constant presence of the tutti by the solo's side does not constitute in itself the merit of a concerto. The resulting complexity must be *interesting*. Now, the C minor concerto surpasses

---

[1] Eighteen bars.

all its predecessors and two out of the three that come after it by the large number of original and expressive accompaniments and the abundance of moments of masterly collaboration. There is no need to enumerate them.[1] Well-worn formulas, held or repeated notes, are uncommon and, when present, are in situations which restore all their forcefulness to them.[2] Mozart prefers here expressive and melodious figures: the woodwind "question and answer" over the restless piano runs (ex. 325 c; bars 170-4), the breathless violin echoes in ex. 329. But, above all, the instruments are no longer content with accompanying in the strict sense; they complete the tones or line of the solo: its tones, by doubling it and adding the warmth, sharpness or softness of their *timbres*; its line, by sustaining it with one or other of the fragments from the first subject with which the movement is shot through. Here, examples are obvious at almost every page of the score and we must refer the reader to passages from which we have quoted a few bars such as exs. 328 and 335.[3] Strings or wind sustain the piano semi-quavers constantly and at moments of stress their diverse figures and rhythms raise the whole to a fine degree of power.[4] We mention only as a reminder the device of a tutti passage enriched at its repetition by the piano's presence, of which bars 435-62 in the recapitulation are an impressive example. Here, and in several of the passages we have instanced, one protagonist is no longer subordinated to the other, but co-operates on equal terms; piano and orchestra both subdue their egotism to the common ideal of the work, without obscuring their personality or turning the concerto into a "symphony with piano".

The piano writing itself retrieves something which had vanished and unites two features hitherto separate. It combines the D minor's varied line and quick use of different registers with the massive virtuosity of the C major, almost entirely missing from K.482 and 488. Blending the wiry strength and the fire of the one with the weight and mass of the other of the two great concertos of the previous winter, this one, with the three other piano works in C minor, marks the limits of the emotional power Mozart ever drew from his favourite instrument.

Spohr's oft-quoted expression is no juster here than elsewhere, but the semi-humorous description: concerto for woodwind and

---

[1] We have tried to classify Mozart's *interesting* accompaniments in I, 3.

[2] Held notes in the strings in ex. 325 a (bars 125-33, 369-80); repeated notes, especially in ex. 331 (bars 220-7).

[3] Also, bars 239-40, 252-6, 310-24, 388-90, 463-8.

[4] Ex. 332; bars 346-54, 355-61, coda.

piano, is perhaps more suitable. This concerto, already so many-hued in its harmonies and keys, so fruitful in constant and sometimes daring modulations, is also one of the richest in *timbre* colour, thanks to the number of its woodwind and their importance. In no other concerto has Mozart treated his woodwind so generously. Not only is it the only one with seven woodwind instruments, but they have frequently true *concertante* parts. On several occasions they play alone; in the larghetto they do it to such an extent that we called some parts of it "woodwind serenades". Both times the strings are excluded from participating in the second subject of the allegro, ex. 327; and as for the third subject, ex. 330, whereas the flute and hautboy give it out each time, the strings do but accompany them and are allowed to repeat it after them only together with the piano. The mock second subject, ex. 324, belongs also to the wind; the strings mix with them but keep an inferior position, and when, in the recapitulation, flute, clarinet and bassoon yield up some of their pre-eminence, the piano and not the violins profits thereby. When there is a melody, whether to be given out or to be accompanied, Mozart prefers frankly his hautboys, clarinets and flute.

The allegro and finale of this concerto, the andantino of K.271 and the andante of K.482 are the only movements of his piano concertos for which Mozart used the key of C minor. This key is as uncommon in the rest of his work. This concerto, the wind serenade, K.388, the piano sonata, K.457, are the only sonata-form works which use it; with the first interlude in *King Thamos*, the two piano fantasias, the *Masonic Funeral Music* and the prelude and fugue, K.546, they complete the list of his instrumental compositions in this key.

C minor is clearly exceptional with him. Exceptional because of its infrequency; exceptional, too, in the value of the works that use it. As with all minor keys, Mozart uses it only when he feels deep emotion, and most of the compositions mentioned are among his masterpieces. But for this reason it is hard to generalize about its character in his music, for in many respects each one of his "C minors" is unique. We have already said this in speaking of this concerto and it is as true of his other works in this key. The fiery passion, uttering itself through rhythmical rather than melodic effects, carrying us away rather than overcoming us with the magic of its song, which was a character of the D minor concerto and the finale of the G minor symphony, belongs also to the *King Thamos* interlude, the C minor sonata and some parts of the serenade. One should therefore not argue from the fact of its non-predominance in our concerto that it is foreign to the key. On the other hand, the singing and often elegiac tone which is heard in all three movements prevails also in the D minor quartet which has not the stormy nature of the concerto in the same key and is nearer in feeling to this one. It is therefore perilous to generalize about the characters the key of C minor may, or may not, have in Mozart's music.

Neither sonata nor serenade have the dignified melancholy, yielding only occasionally to violence, of this concerto. Both proceed by violent oppositions, causing a calm, singing phrase to follow an incisive, rhythmical one. If Beethoven remembered our concerto, one wonders whether he did not also remember the serenade, for the first movement of his op. 37 advances by contrasts like that work, and its Mozartish E flat theme bears cousinly, if not brotherly, likeness to its second subject. His concerto comes near to Mozart's, as we have said, in its coda, and here is also the point of contact between Mozart's concerto and sonata, for the last bars of the sonata express more tersely the feeling with which the concerto closes its first movement.

We end, therefore, with a thought that had come to us at the beginning of this chapter: this concerto, like the D minor, is isolated in its author's work. About to forsake the genre which had given him his chief means of expression for three years, Mozart embodied in it the passionate sorrow that dwelt in him, which has left witnesses in many of his works, but had only occasionally permeated a whole composition. Before concluding the series of his twelve masterpieces with a song of triumph in December of this same year, he lets us hear his song of grief. When, eighteen months later, he composes his last symphonies, he will do likewise and pass through the valley of tears with the G minor to reach victory with the C major.

6. The Twenty-first Concerto: K.503 in C

CONCERTO NO. 21 IN C MAJOR (K.503)[1]
Finished December 4th, 1786
    Allegro maestoso: C
    Andante: 3-4 (in F)
    (Allegretto): 2-4
Orchestra: Strings, flute, two hautboys, two bassoons, two horns, two
    trumpets, two kettledrums.

DURING more than two years now, for Mozart the composer and virtuoso, the piano concerto has been holding the first place in his musical consciousness. During more than two years, neither symphony nor chamber music nor even opera has been able to compete with it. The first is quite eclipsed; only at distant intervals does he return to the second[2]; as for opera, which was so often his favourite, except for the curtain raiser, *Der Schauspieldirektor*, he leaves it to one side almost as completely as the symphony. He does not come back to it till the end of these two years; if Lorenzo da Ponte is right in saying that the music of *Le Nozze di Figaro* was written in six weeks, this opera must have been begun a short while before the completion of the concerto in C minor.

And we too, for a long time, for more than two years perhaps, have been living with these great works. It is a long time, it seems to us, since we resumed with fresh zest the study of his concertos when our progress through his life brought us to the threshold of those years, 1784, 1785 and 1786, with the E flat, K.449. From one work to the next, we have followed the young master with an interest, nay more, with a love easy to imagine; we have watched him growing ever more clearly conscious of the problems raised by the genre and which he hardly suspected in his earlier concertos, attacking them and solving them separately at first, then all together after the great

---

[1] *Gesamtausgabe*, no. 25.

[2] Quintet for piano and wind and B flat string quartet in 1784; quartets in A and C early in 1785, in G minor during the summer.

step forward of the D minor, triumphing at length over all the difficulties they presented in the very great concerto the pages of which
we have just closed.

These two years were a fine day in his short maturity and it is
with sadness that we see them draw to their end.   Twelve masterpieces in the same genre in thirty-three months should be enough
to assuage the most voracious appetite; but every end brings sadness,
however long the life, and the splendour of the sunset does not console
us.

Splendid, at any rate, this sunset will be, and it is with a work
which is not only one of the two or three peaks of the whole series—
at once the rival and the complement of the C minor—but also one
of the greatest works of his life, that Mozart the concerto writer
makes, as the saying goes, "his last appearance".[1]   Let us then take
courage; night is not yet come; once more we may admire the way
in which he faces and solves the problems of the game and makes the
game itself an opportunity for expressing, as never hitherto, the
"Olympian" nobility of his soul.

Lent having come to an end, the Viennnese concert season is over
and Mozart does not appear again on the platform till the winter.
Moreover, the composition of *Le Nozze di Figaro* and the various
preparations for this opera occupy him fully till May 1st.   The
creation of this work, the first in date of his great opere buffe and the
first opera he had written since *Die Entführung*, four years earlier, is
a turning point in his life in that the concerto, without disappearing completely, soon ceases to be the genre which expresses him
fully and into which he pours what is most precious.   Henceforward,
opera, then the quintet and the symphony, take its place.

1786 is one of his most fruitful years.   Usually, we notice a
falling off or a stop in his composing during the months when his
patrons leave Vienna and concerts are suspended.   But this year the
output does not cease.   The great effort of *Figaro* is followed in
June by the second of the six piano quartets ordered by the editor
Hoffmeister, a partly derivative work, full of reminders of other
E flat compositions, embodying a unique experience only in its
moving larghetto.   In spite of its charm, the editor greeted it with
the words one knows: "Write more popularly!" and it is not
surprising that Mozart preferred to forgo the rest of the order.

---

[1] All virtuosi, as we know, make several "last appearances" and Mozart
confirms the rule, since he composed two other concertos a few years later.

To the end of the same month belongs the last of the horn concertos written for Leutgeb. It has the same character as the others;
the great piano concertos have passed but have left no mark upon
it.[1] In July arrives the first work of a genre that Mozart had scarcely
cultivated hitherto: the trio for piano and strings.[2] Its only example
in his work had been a divertimento, K.254, an undistinguished
bauble composed years ago in Salzburg. The genre will never be
one of those into which his genius puts of its best, except for brief
instants. Actually, the andante of this trio is one such instant; a
profound *Seelenleben*, under the apparent calm, is discovered through
the imitative arabesques of its one and only subject. This return
to a genre attempted in his youth is followed by another when he
turns to the duet sonata, a form in which he had produced two little
works thirteen or fourteen years earlier. He goes back to it with
enthusiasm and one might think it was to replace the concerto, for
he treats his grand F major work, K.497, with a breadth and power of
thought and dimensions that are unparalleled in his works for two
hands. A great adagio introduction, worthy of his last symphonies,
opens the allegro; in the andante, he uses again with a slight alteration
in time the theme of the romance in his last horn concerto; it is instinct
with that yearning which is so personal to him, which remains on
this side of elegiac melancholy and shines through the second
movements of the G minor quartet and the concerto in D, K.537.
In the rondo, the middle couplet contains passionate rushes
of ascending scales, ending in space, which haunt Mozart at this
period and occur in the allegros of the G minor quartet and the
G major trio.

Early in August there comes a fresh trio, this time for friends,
the Jacquin family. It is the first of a family of three—trio, quintet
and concerto—which friendship, and also admiration for the clarinet,
drew from him. The humblest of the three, it attains nevertheless
a sombre grandness in its minuet, with the disquieting and demonic
trio. A fortnight later Mozart completes a string quartet in D,
K.499, the first since the six dedicated to Haydn. As beautiful as
any of them, it is very different; the only work of his which it recalls
is the quintet in the same key of 1790; in the adagios, especially,
there is close relationship; both belong to the rich line of meditative

---

[1] Not so with the G minor quartet, the beginning of which is "quoted"
in the romance (bars 55-6).

[2] K.496 in G major.

slow movements[1] which stretch from the harpsichord concerto of 1773 to the quintet. The minuet, tartly concise, records, like that of the clarinet trio, a step towards those of the quintets, symphonies and quartets still to come, so full of meaning, so far from being mere "diversions."

And still his activity continues! A piano allegro, the first movement of an unfinished sonata,[2] the original conception of which comes perhaps from a sonata of Clementi's, op. 10, III; then, a second attempt at a duet sonata, K.357, consisting of a strange allegro, original rather than beautiful—one of Mozart's few attempts of which this can be said—and a finale where the piano writing announces (or recalls, for the date is not certain), the most original bars in the rondo of K.503, and where he tries to combine in a single movement andante and rondo. This experimental work, like so many others, remained incomplete.

After some variations in B flat for piano two hands, K.500, his infatuation for duets is expressed, less ambitiously, early in November in other variations, K.501. They are followed at a fortnight's distance by another trio, in B flat, K.502, a second cousin of the violin sonata in the same key of two years earlier, K.454, more substantial than that in G and the finest, perhaps, of the series of trios. This is the last work before the C major concerto.

We have dwelt at some length on the output of these few months because of its abundance and diversity. It is mainly concerned with chamber music, which is natural since concerts were in abeyance, but within its limits it deals with five or six different combinations,[3] producing a significant work in each of them. The diversity of material is no doubt responsible for the diversity of content. It is

---

[1] Cf. I, 2; p. 40.

[2] Left unfinished by Mozart, but not by publishers, thanks to an andante which is but a *pasticcio*, or a travesty, of that of K.450, to a magnificent minuet, certainly by Mozart and as certainly conceived for orchestra, and to a rondo which apes that of the same concerto K.450. In this form, it figures in several modern editions. The allegro is no. 498 a in Köchel-Einstein. Dr. Einstein upholds the authenticity of the allegro which has been impugned by Richard S. Hill (*The plate numbers of C. F. Peters' predecessors*, in *American Musicological Society*, 1938, p. 129). Einstein maintains that it is quite foreign to the style of A. E. Müller to whom it is attributed by some editions (and by Hill). See *Music Review*, vol. 2 (1941), p. 330.

[3] And even so, we have not mentioned the group of little duets for bassett horns, K.487, which Mozart dates August 1st but which he had perhaps composed at various times.

absolutely impossible to characterize in a few words the emotional streams of these nine months as we tried to do with those of the previous year. It is a transition epoch in that, among its genres, there are some that Mozart is using for the last time; others to which he is returning after leaving them for a period; others, again, which he had given up so many years ago that on returning to them he could consider them as new. The string quartet alone had figured constantly in his work for four years, and alone, also, with the opera, it is still to provide important works. The others either will be given up in the course of the next year or else, like the trio, will survive awhile but never be employed for great ends. One word only can apply to such a period: that of experimental; we adopt it to characterize the months that separate the twentieth concerto from the twenty-first, on condition, however, that it imply no judgement of inferiority for the three or four finest compositions that fall within its confines.

In the course of November Mozart began at approximately the same time a big piano concerto and a symphony. He completed them at two days' interval, the concerto on December 4th, the symphony on the 6th.

In this concerto his power is raised to its highest pitch; with the C minor, it is the climax of his development during the last three years. Except in the quintets of the next year and in the finale of his C major symphony, he never attained elsewhere such breadth and might. But the might has nothing stiff about it and does not exclude sweetness. Like the quintet in C, to which it is near, this concerto is one of his most melodious works and its many tuneful themes are gentle and caressing as well as strong; spacious and self-assured, with a broader and more pliant rhythm than usual, they are also indulgent. They are the creatures of a great man in the prime of life who, trusting in his vigour, does not disdain to be tender.

The three concertos of this year have been likened by Tovey to the symphonic trilogy of 1788, and the analogy is partly true. Though it may be a rather far cry from the concerto in A to the symphony in E flat, the second works in each group start from more neighbouring planes in Mozart's soul, and as for those in C, they both express that blend of sweetness and "Olympian" power which made an unknown Romantic call the symphony *Jupiter*. Of the two, it is certainly the concerto that deserves the title best; its first movement is permeated throughout by the heroic inspiration we associate with the ruler of Olympus; or, if one prefers, the same idea can be expressed by calling it Mozart's *Eroica*, or his *Emperor* concerto.[1]

Like the C minor, it brings together all the best in the art of concerto writing that its predecessors contained. Its orchestra is one of the largest; the C minor's alone surpasses it by including clarinets.[2] Its first movement—four hundred and thirty-two bars in common time—is the longest in all Mozart[3]; its themes, the broadest and most supple; its developments, the most sustained; its modulations the freest. The collaboration between piano and orchestra is equalled for interest and continuity only by the C minor; its middle section, the so-called *development*, entirely thematic, is close-knit and masterly; other *developments* are more dramatic, but drama is foreign to this serene work. The thought moves constantly in lofty regions and the earnestness of the first movement is found again in the rondo which is one of Mozart's few concerto finales whose scope is that of an initial allegro. Only the finale of the *Jupiter* shows Mozart the symphonist in full possession of his powers better than this work, and the public's ignorance of this king of his concertos hinders it from seeing his full stature and realizing of what calm, sustained might he is capable. To those who look on him as a pretty trifler, if any yet breathe, there is no better answer than this concerto's opening tutti.

I. Few of Mozart's compositions show themselves to the world with as original a frontispiece and none open in such bold tones. Its heroic nature is apparent in its first bars—not the sham heroism of an overture for which a few impersonal formulas suffice, but that which expresses greatness of spirit. The C minor concerto was a conflict which no victory had ended. Here, now, comes the *revanche* —a triumph whence every shadow of strife has vanished, where the display of the might, without which no strife could have been waged, is the only remains of the conflict.

A succession of majestic chords in which the whole orchestra takes

---

[1] But, *au fond*, all such names are best discarded altogether!

[2] The same orchestra is used in K.451, 466, and 537, and, with clarinets instead of hautboys, in 482.

[3] Beethoven's C minor concerto has the same length (444 bars); that in G, 370; that in E flat, 583. Mozart's longest allegro after this one is the first movement of the quintet in C.

part opens the first movement.[1]   Built upon the triad of C major,
they descend with slow stateliness from realms above, hastening a
little as they draw near us, then rise again to beyond their starting-
point (ex. 347).   After this proud assertion of serene power, the
work reveals at once the other aspect of its greatness: tenderness and
love; the music drops to *piano* and bassoon and hautboy exchange
two touching little complementary phrases (ex. 348).   Then, symmetrical yet quivering with life, as sumptuous as an emperor's suite,
the succession of chords resumes its progress, unfolding now in the
dominant, and again all take part in it.   Once more the movement
turns its gentler face towards us, and hautboys and bassoons again
exchange their confidential phrases.   Then, with a lowered third which
is a *coup de theâtre*, everything changes; the day clouds over, and
the happy, triumphant face shows itself as that of a soul which has
suffered and remembers it.   It is a memory, indeed, rather than the
expression of a present sorrow, but the memory is tenacious, and
we have to sojourn awhile in its shadow before the cloud passes.

As soon as the little phrase ex. 348 which introduced us into this
new landscape is repeated, we hear a rhythmical fragment which
passes all through the movement and is like its signature.   Here it
is, as it comes forward on its first appearance, in its two shapes, at the
foot of a mysterious ascent where only the harsh, disembodied voices
of the flute and hautboy trace a smooth line above the panting mur-
murs of the violins (ex. 349).

This ascent, like the triumphal downward progress at the beginning, comes back to its starting-point on the tonic; after which, the
work rediscovers the broad daylight of the major as simply as it had
lost it.   But the rhythmical fragment does not stop on this account;
it is not the servant of any one mood but of the whole work and is
to be present at every incident of the day.   Confined for the nonce
to basses and bassoons, it resumes the climb, *forte*, against the chords
of woodwind and brass, and on its shifting bass there builds up a proud
train of scales, a display in action of the power pent up in the opening
chords (ex. 350).   Half-way up, treble parts and basses change over;
the latter now take the scales whilst the former hammer out the three
repeated notes whose rhythm is enriched by the flute imitations (ex.
351).   The sense of strength grows when we enter the field of the

---

[1] Which is marked *maestoso* and not *brillante*; the memory of an unfortunate experience obliges us to insist on this point.   The work is majestic,
not festive; if it is taken too fast the majesty vanishes and breadth of line
gives place to something skimped and curtailed.   We suggest ♩ = 132.

dominant and the rhythmical fragment turns into a series of repeated quavers enlivened by octave leaps in the violins and basses (ex. 352).

Reaching the summit of its power, the energy suddenly overflows in a stream of quavers in the second violins, but firsts and basses still maintain the imitative sport of ex. 351. All this is finally summed up in a downward rush of two octaves and three powerful G major chords which carry over into the proclamation of the authentic rhythm: ♫♩, in unison in the whole orchestra. Thereupon, everything rests awhile.

No other work of Mozart, we said, opens with a grander page. Its only possible rival, which has no close likeness to it, would be the quintet in C with which this concerto has such affinity. Grand this beginning is, but not as immutable as one might at first think. The slow descent of the chords may call up a majestic baroque portal, with all the frigidity such an association implies; but, once the little hautboy phrase is repeated in the minor, the portal opens wide and lets us view, not the circumscribed cella of the god, but a boundless horizon. We were in port, moored in sight of a fine spectacle; now we are at sea, bound for some unknown but certainly heroic adventure, sailing on waters where none has ever preceded us. Everything, to the very rhythm of the movement at the point at which we have stopped—a broad period decomposing into the wavelets of fragment (a)—suggests this comparison.

And now, this great development over, we wait, full of expectancy. The change is complete and of all that has gone before only the persistent rhythm (a) with which the new theme begins, is left. From far away, it seems—so different is what follows—the fiddles fetch one of Mozart's simplest and most moving tunes, a fairy march whose scoring, at first slender, becomes richer as it goes on. The beauty of the melody is most strikingly enhanced by its preparation; the ancient device of contrast has seldom been used more freshly (ex. 353). This theme, given out at first in C minor, is not the second subject but is nevertheless destined to play an important part later on. Hautboys, horns and bassoons restate it, transposed into C major, and thus confirm the main key which we do not leave again till the end of the tutti; the flute crowns the tune with an undulating counter-point, the elements of which enter into the *development* (ex. 354). After a fanfare, one of the three or four appearances which Handel's *Alleluia* makes in Mozart's music, a secondary theme, sinuous and caressing leads the prelude towards its end on a more lyrical note (ex. 355).

We recognize the rhythm of (a) in it, and the same rhythm blossoms out again in the concluding theme, a song rising from the depths of the heart and whose apparent levity disguises thinly its intensity of feeling (ex. 356).[1] Many are the bars where Mozart has sustained a tune with Alberti basses in his seconds or violas, but there are few in which this well-worn formula is as significant as here, it sets off the gossamer lightness of the dancing tune above it.

The experience of earlier concertos[2] has taught us to await the piano entry with emotion. This dramatic moment happens sometimes quite simply, and even in some of his most personal concertos Mozart brings his piano in straight away with the first subject.[3] But, in most instances, the concertos of the great period, especially in 1785 and 1786, find original shifts for calling the solo on to the stage. Sometimes it makes itself heard as the spokesman of a more intimate feeling;[4] sometimes, as a new character ready to show off.[5] In the other C major concerto of these years, K.467, after an imposing prelude, its voice had been lifted up timidly and it was only with hearing itself speak that it gathered courage. The charm of these varied entries after the long orchestral introduction is a source of beauty of which post-Beethovenian concertos have deprived themselves by bringing their piano in at the very beginning of the movement.

Here, the tutti has been so massive and so sumptuous that the piano cannot hope to equal it at one stroke and, far from imposing itself, it waits to be called in, almost to be fetched, before it dare appear, like a little child acting for the first time in a nursery play who waits in the wings when his turn comes, crying and refusing to advance on to the stage. His nurse goes to fetch him; here, the strings fulfil this function and invite the solo to appear with a most winsome sighing trill. Fearfully, the right hand of the piano responds, with a fragment complementary to that of the strings, in the treble, but steps forward no further (ex. 357). A second invitation follows, similar to the first; a second response is a little bolder, for semi-quavers replace quavers; finally, a third time, the strings, feeling their mission

---

[1] From its third bar on, hautboys and bassoons complicate the motion with an imitative answer, like that of the flute in ex. 351.

[2] Notably of K.271, 450, 466, 467, 482 and 491.

[3] K.451, 453, 488 and others.

[4] K.466, 482, 491.

[5] K.271, 450.

to be at an end, change their sighing motif into a cadence and are silent.   After this threefold appeal,[1] the piano seeks its way alone, in short trial runs at first, and repeating its first motif three times; then, quickly, it grows bold and soars up into flight like a butterfly whose wings have expanded and dried; carried up by its scales and broken octaves, it goes and perches triumphantly on the heights of the first subject which looms up in the orchestra (bars 92–112).

Adopting now the plan of several earlier concertos, the movement resumes the whole of its stately opening, enriching it with the piano part.   Never had this device been used so sumptuously.   The first six bars belong to the tutti and it is at the first *piano*, with the little phrase ex. 348, that the solo is again heard; it decks out the woodwind confidences with lavish embroidery, typical of this concerto, in a stepped outline (ex. 358).   Then, the series of chords having been resumed, we remain at *piano*[2] and only the wind represent the tutti and alternate their chords with the solo's.   Thus, with close collaboration, with a touching union of gentleness and mass, we reach ex. 349, around which the piano again embroiders its festooning counter-subject.

The working-out passage in C minor is gone through again for some eight bars, but without the support of the wind.   Against the hammering rhythm of (a), the piano rises and falls in scale fragments whose graceful waves recall ex. 351.   The opposition and reconciling of the strings' sharp rhythm and the solo's supple caresses is a fresh manifestation of this great work's rich, many-sided nature.

The delicate sport comes to an end and the piano forges ahead alone, climbing up from the bass with an amplification of the wavy figure with which it was accompanying the strings.   A cadential figure concludes the passage; wavering between C minor and G major, it chooses the latter key but is uncertain of the mode, and a tutti phrase, on the incisive three quaver rhythm thrown thrice from first violins to the rest of the orchestra and back, remains in the same undecided frame of mind.

The piano releases us from it by modulating with mischievous simplicity into the key of E flat, the natural and yet unexpected exit from the C minor into which we were involved, and starts upon its own subject.   The majestic tenor of the movement is nowise broken

---

[1] May we once again point out Mozart's love for threefold divisions and repetitions?

[2] Soloists and conductors should be careful to obey this mark.

Ex. 357   Ex. 358

Ex. 359

Ex. 360

Ex. 361

Ex. 362

Ex. 363

by this change of direction; indeed, to have got rid of the orchestra
appears to have made it freer, for the solo theme opens out with an
ease, almost a carelessness, in rhythm most uncommon in Mozart's
allegros. The first part, lightly harmonized, spreads itself with a
mixture of pride and indolence (ex. 359). But oneness, not contrast,
is the hallmark of the movement and into this easy rhythm there
intrudes the three quaver figure, first of all as it was, then, enlivened
by Mozart's "fluttering seconds". The figure makes the phrase
firmer but does not trammel its flight; the progress of the theme is
merely a little hastened thereby before it breaks up into a long
chromatic scale (ex. 360). The end of the passage is discreetly sustained by strings and wind in turn.

With increasing excitement the movement hurries now towards
the second subject into which it opens out a few bars later. This
is not the march, ex. 353, but a new theme, as stiff as that of the solo
was loose and melodious (ex. 15 c); its rhythmical gait is softened a
little by the held notes with which the strings shade off its contour.
Most of the orchestra take no part in it; only flute, hautboys and
bassoons repeat it to a busy piano accompaniment. It is in G major
but its closing bars hesitate between major and minor; it contains a
possibility of development which is exploited in the recapitulation.
It is the representative of a type we have met with in two earlier C
major concertos, K.246 and 415.[1] The end of the solo consists of
ascending scales in tenths and a great display of octave passages in
both hands, of a technique heavier than anything we have heard
since K.467. Twice over the octaves are held up in their race by the
quiet but decisive intervention of the wind in the upper registers;
the second time, yielding for an instant to this spirit of recollection,
the solo gathers towards the middle of the keyboard, then ascends
once again and culminates on the final trill with a chromatic phrase
of seven quavers which straddles across three bars with complete
disregard of bar lines.

This solo exposition, like that of many an earlier concerto, has
carried us far away from that of the tutti. After the twenty-four
bars of the first subject, it has forsaken entirely the paths trodden by
the orchestral prelude. After these bars, too, the piano predominates
and the orchestra, satisfied with showing itself the solo's equal on its
first appearance, falls back and delegates to the woodwind the task
of speaking for it in the second subject. But, though the instrumental

---

[1] See pp. 93 and 152.

centre of gravity has changed, the spirit remains the same; no contrast in mood comes to break the lovely, smooth line of the music, comprehensive enough to hover at times between major and minor and incorporate the key of E flat with those of the tonic, dominant and tonic minor without disrupting the whole, so that this exposition, which modulates further and longer than that of any other concerto of Mozart's, is also one of his most homogeneous.

After the first subject, we said the exposition made no allusion to the material of the opening tutti. To this latter Mozart now turns for his *development*. To introduce this part of the movement, he repeats the transition he has already used; he goes again over bars 26–30 and 41–50, transposing the former into G minor. The latter, on the other hand, being already in G major, he leaves them as they were (cf. ex. 350 and the latter part of ex. 352). And so we arrive at the downward rush of three octaves and the three G major chords prolonged by the proclamation of the ♩♩♩ ♩ rhythm and followed by the same silence.

This close had originally heralded the wistful, roguish "march" in C minor. Now, two bars of minims in the strings, punctuated by the same rhythm on the piano, slip down to E minor, and ex. 353 is given out in this key, the relative minor of the dominant.

The fifty bars that follow busy themselves exclusively with this theme which they restate and break up, and on whose fragments they end by erecting a complex contrapuntal structure.

Once the piano has given out the march, and after two transition bars where the parts of solo and instruments are reversed, the wind repeat it in A minor. The "authentic" rhythm is again asserted; there is a fresh downward slide, and the piano begins the tune again, in F major. This time a tactful but firm intervention of the woodwind holds it up half-way through and it starts once more, one degree higher up, in G minor. There is a fresh wind interruption, whereupon there opens the game which is the central portion of this *development* and one of the most original moments in all Mozart.

Let us glance at ex. 354. Subject and counter-subject, seemingly so united, are to break up, alternate, superpose, mingle with the solo's arpeggios and scales. We distinguished the three fragments into which the subject was to split up. To piano, hautboys and bassoons devolves (a); to the flute (b) and (c), parts of its original counterpoint. The first three make their entries in canons at the sixth and the octave beneath the flute's garlands; once their fragment over, the piano pours out the overflow of its energy in arpeggios; the first hautboy joins the flute; the others remain silent. Then, the figure starts again with the piano; this time (a) belongs to hautboys and flute; (b) and (c) to bassoons. The round starts in A minor and closes in D minor.

The second round is a repetition of the first in the major. The players go through the same movements, but in G and C. During this time, the strings, kept in the background, mumble in unison or in octaves a modification of (a). All this diversion, so transparent in performance, is really in eight-part counterpoint (ex. 361).

The game now grows freer, and bases itself on imitation: imitation of (b) by hautboys and bassoons, of (a), modified, by violins and lower strings—somewhat disconnected figures held together by the rockets of scales ceaselessly let off by the piano. In a few bars we climb up to the pedal of G which announces the climax of the movement and the approach of the reprise. This latter takes place with an increase of power and a display of piano arpeggios in contrary motion which recall ex. 259 in K.467; then, while the piano's broken octaves descend, a scale in the wind rises to the chord of C, proclaimed *forte* by the whole orchestra, with which the first subject opens (ex. 347).

Our study of Mozart's concertos has shown us that their *development* is generally a kind of fantasia where virtuosity runs freely. As the concerto in his work grew in poetic import, so expression won the day over pure virtuosity, and in the works in D and G of 1784 the middle part witnessed the complete release of the spirit of adventure. Yet, as well as the fantasia, some of Mozart's concertos know also the true *development*, so-called "thematic", of which Philip Emmanuel Bach's concertos afforded several examples. Already the E flat, K.271, was one of these. Yet, with the doubtful exception of K.449, we had to wait till the D minor to find a second. There, almost everything was drawn from the opening bars of the two expositions. The C major, K.467, and the last of the E flats, K.482, had returned to the fantasia. In the A major, the *development* was again thematic; the theme in question had appeared, it is true, only after the first solo, but it was important enough to figure in the recapitulation. That of the C minor, without being actually thematic, was so near to the rest of the allegro in the spirit which infused its runs and the form of its accompaniments that it belonged to both kinds.

Here, finally, the *development* is the strictest we have found since K.271. A *development* based on a theme from the exposition always adds to the formal unity of a movement; here, this result is still more marked. The absence of ex. 353 in the first solo was one of the chief differences between it and the first tutti; by returning to it and giving it so important a part, the *development* reintegrates it into the work and at the same time wipes out the distance between the two expositions.

> In Mozart's great works the repercussion of such *developments* on the rest of the piece is so weighty that, even if the recapitulation is similar to the beginning, its components are transfigured by it; there is a hidden, inexpressible power, a kind of rebounding of the elements stirred up by the powerful, sovereign rudder.[1]

This happens here; the sense of triumph in the first subject is glorified by the *development* which precedes it and by the pedal point, with its powerful virtuosity, which brings it back.

Yet it returns unchanged. The bringing together of tutti and first solo, a task which generally falls to the recapitulation, having been accomplished by the *development*, there is no reason why this last part should differ much from the first solo. So we find that all the beginning (bars 290–322) reproduces faithfully the corresponding part of the exposition (bars 112–54), with a few trifling changes.[2]

Only when the solo subject arrives do we leave the beaten track. Instead of reaching G major through D minor, the theme suddenly rises and, modulating enharmonically, traverses swiftly E flat minor, B major, B minor and G minor, before returning via G major to the tonic—a most poetic excursion which adds to the breadth of the section. The second subject unfolds at first with no change but that of key; then, again, Mozart's instability asserts itself and just as we think it is to close in C the theme ventures forth through unexpected modulations, borne on the wings of its last four notes, while the piano, completing the harmonies, strings out arpeggios full of pitfalls for those unwary pianists who think that Mozart's technique can be summed up in a few formulae.

We regain the tonic, as before, via G minor, and a reminder of ex. 353 links on to the last runs of the second subject. The reminder is more ephemeral than is usual with mock second subjects, for this

---

[1] Saint-Foix: *Les symphonies de Mozart*, 224–5.

[2] Note that bars 298 and foll. are *piano*.

one has already enjoyed a good innings; only its second half is repeated, under a piano trill which breaks before the end into joyful fountains.

The rest reproduces the end of the first solo, with slight modifications; the tutti which concluded the latter is repeated; then we diverge for a few bars for the cadenza, after which the *Alleluia* fanfare and exs. 355 and 356 return rather shortened, and the movement ends, without a coda, like the first tutti, an extra bar being added to show that the end is really come. Should we have preferred something else—the equivalent, in the sunny light of C major, of the coda of the C minor?... Mozart has judged otherwise.

Although this concerto belongs on the whole to those which oppose piano to orchestra, mass to mass, the *development* afforded an instance of collaboration unequalled in its complexity. The work unites, therefore, two ways of considering the relations between tutti and solo; one, in its second exposition; the other, in its *development*.

The lack of marked change in the recapitulation expresses its static nature. Several other concertos expressed something dramatic, in varying degrees, even though the drama were a happy one, and the renewal of their last section emphasized this. Here, the world is as abiding, as far removed from crises and catastrophes, as that of the B flat, K. 456; it is the world of fugue and cathedral, not that of tragedy.

Another work in the same key had shared in this nature: K.467, the first in date of those C major compositions we called Olympian and of which the concerto we are considering is the grandest. The kinship between the two is clear; but K.503 surpasses the earlier one not only in its greater size and breadth, in its more sustained inspiration, in the beauty and organic character of its *development*, but also in strains of sweetness and poetic flights which were much rarer in the other. K.467 could be called "marmorean"; the term might suit K.503 too, perhaps; but it is a marble of Attica, with lines as chaste, it is true, as a Greek temple's, but warmed, like the temple, by the rays of the sun. Mozart's passionate temperament is here quite near the surface; it comes constantly to light in the sudden falls (or shall we say "flights"?) into the minor and in the caressing outlines of nearly all its themes. In Mozart's work, this allegro is a giant, but a giant as warm-hearted as he is powerful.

II. We meet again in the andante the same breadth of conception, the same spacious lines, the same sustained motion of the themes, losing themselves one in the other instead of splitting up into separate sections. We find the same calm, lofty inspiration, more tender, however, as is befitting, and without the shadows which the frequent intrusions of the minor cast over the first movement.

Its form is that of a sonata where the *development* has been reduced to a few bars of transition—a form occurring at all periods of Mozart's life but which appears to have attracted him particularly during these months for he has made use of it in three of his most spacious compositions: this concerto and the two string quintets of the following spring. A few examples of it were to be found in his early concertos but the only other one of the great period to use it was K.459.

The andante consists of two halves, the second of which reproduces the first with superficial differences, preceded by a tutti containing the chief themes. It begins with a group of short phrases whose meaning does not become clear for some bars. Repetition and variation play a great part within the group; bars 3 and 4 are a variation of 1 and 2; 7 and 8 repeat 5 and 6, varying the run; 9 and 10 give out the same phrase on different degrees and 11 repeats it, linking it up with the concluding cadence. The whole is made up of two-bar phrases. But the feeling which inspires them is so homogeneous and their outlines, consisting in rises and falls, are so similar, that they make up but one *song*; within it, the subtle variations of rhythm are such that no monotony has yet been felt when the uniformity is broken by a third bar added to the concluding strain (ex. 362). The violins double in the first four bars; elsewhere, the main work falls to the wind instruments from one to another of which, with great care for colour, Mozart passes the different fragments of his theme.

Hardly is the theme complete when a rustling of semi-quavers in the second violins opens a fresh section. With alternations of loud and soft it lasts for four bars. Its outline takes us back to the concerto for three pianos where a very similar motif had occurred in the same place.[1] Against this background there stands out a fragment which begins *piano* with the first violins and closes *forte* with the whole orchestra; like the previous ones, it is repeated, then extended by a long descending scale which leads, *piano*, to the depths of the G string whence, on the lips of flute and hautboys, the tune rises again and concludes almost at once (ex. 363). Whereupon the final strain unrolls its threefold curve in a dialogue where first fiddles, horns and bassoons answer the other strings, and to which the flute, doubled by the bassoon, adds one last touch (ex. 364).

---

[1] Cf. p. 90.

Such is the essence of the movement. The greater part of this
tutti reappears in each of the two halves, with rearrangements in the
scoring caused by the presence of the piano. In the first subject,
only the horns keep their original part almost unchanged; the other
instruments are excluded by the solo. The piano inserts its own
theme between exs. 362 and 363; its rhythm is as diverse and as supple
as the rest but it is more melodious and thus contrasts with the tutti
where mass predominated over line. Not content with this solo,
the piano takes over ex. 363 and, encouraged by the example of its
fellows in the concerto for three pianos, appropriates the rustling
accompaniment which suited the strings so well. It wants also to
play the bass and, as its right hand is taken up with the trilling theme,
the left hand part is rather heavy. The last fragment is extended by
one bar and links on to a new subject which replaces ex. 364. This
latter is certainly one of the queerest children of Mozart the melodist
(ex. 365). It is an outline rather than a theme. Clearly Mozart
wished to express something unusual and we experience at first the
kind of surprise that we would like to be admiration, which overtakes
us on hearing certain passages in Beethoven's late quartets. But the
mystery is cleared up when flute and hautboy, then bassoon, repeat
it, modifying its skips, and the piano throws over it the graceful
streamers of its scales and arpeggios (ex. 366).

The trill and C major close mark the end of this exposition. Between it and the reprise, instead of a *development*, there extends an
ample transition which carries us back to F major, as in the andante
of the C major quintet—a movement which gives us the feeling of
expressing horizontally, in discursive melody, the mood that this
andante expresses vertically and in mass. The transition is longer
in the concerto and amounts to one seventh of the movement.

Its base is a pedal on C, held at first by the strings, then by the
horns reinforced later by the piano. It is an idealized example of
those extemporizations on A with which organists enable an orchestra
to tune up before a concert. Over this foundation the piano disports
itself with happy majesty.[1] The movement's concentrated thought
reaches its fullest utterance in the chords that follow this display of
nimble energy; here, the effort, once scattered, gathers itself together;

---

[1] The great leaps in the first bars must be filled in by the soloist; Reinecke's
edition indicates upward runs between the dotted crotchet and the quaver;
it is quite possible, however, to leave the octaves bare and insert the run on the
way down, between the crotchet and the dotted crotchet.

the introduction of the chords by the tutti causes their repetition in the solo to sound like a piano transcription of an orchestral passage. The solo instrument—the cantabile piano of 1780—recovers its true personality when it spins out their power in a flexible line of triplets whose wingspread ends by covering all the upper register and whose impetus flows over into the first bar of the reprise (ex. 367).

The recapitulation leaves out the solo subject and remains in the tonic; otherwise, it reproduces faithfully the first half of the solo. But the limits of the keyboard compel Mozart to modify the detail of ex. 365. The movement ends with ex. 364; the woodwind give it out; then the piano and the other instruments repeat it with the original scoring, or nearly; the concluding upward scale in demi-semi-quavers belongs to the piano alone.

We have seen by what qualities this andante shows that it draws upon the same inspiration as the allegro. But certain features are its own and make it one of Mozart's most original slow movements. Despite its broad sweeps, its thought is concentrated; this is visible in the incessant changes of rhythm in the first and solo subjects, in the sometimes epigrammatic brevity of the other themes whose elements are always very short fragments repeated two or three times. We are conscious in it of a deep feeling which has some difficulty in uttering itself, and a good performance, while it should make the movement intelligible, will yet keep this sense of effort.

This andante, whose form is less easy to grasp at first sight than that of most of Mozart's movements, runs the risk of putting off executants, with its changing rhythms and its lack of sharply marked and melodious themes. It is most important not to hurry it; it is nearer adagio than andantino.[1] The expression of its dignity and breadth depends on its pace remaining even. The only place where a slight accelerando is permissible is in the solo subject, but a return must be made to the original speed with the rustling theme, ex. 363. It is especially disastrous to hurry the descending quavers in the first subject, which above all, should be *lasting*. The main difficulty lies in keeping the parts together; this once overcome, the rest will follow easily.

III. The finale is one of Mozart's most serious-minded rondos. Refrain and episodes have nothing of the merry tone of the usual rondo; one feels that the composer wished to end his concerto with a movement in keeping with the other two. We find the same breadth in the themes and their developments as in the allegro and andante, the same monumental conception and, in the mood, the same vacillation between certainty and doubt, expressed by hesitations between major and minor. The chief difference between this movement and the first is the absence of heroic accents; on the other hand, the middle couplet attains a degree of passion which has no counterpart in the allegro.

Mozart has gone five years back, to the ballet music of *Idomeneo*, to find his refrain. Its first eight bars reproduce almost literally the opening of the gavotte, transposed from G to C. By omitting the

---

[1] We suggest ♪ = 100.

portamento of demi-semi-quavers which, in the original, connected
the first and second notes, he has made his theme less sentimental,
but it remains none the less tinted with melancholy, serious, almost
brooding, and full of a languishing grace unexpected in a concerto
finale. It is only too easy to falsify its character, either by playing
it too fast or by not respecting the phrasing which runs across the
beat. The mark *piano* confirms the impression of gentle sadness.

The refrain is rather long and its plan irregular. After the gavotte
itself, given out by the strings (ex. 368), the wind let us hear a march
fragment, then the first violins repeat the last bars of the gavotte
which seconds and violas complete with a cadential phrase (ex. 369).
The 'cellos then do likewise, but in the minor, whilst firsts and seconds
repeat ex. 369. The wind join in and after two bars the same phrase
is repeated once more in the major (ex. 370). This passage is comparable to bars 15-18 of the first movement—a restatement several
times over of the same motif, in major and in minor, a device more
typical of Beethoven than of Mozart, and very characteristic of this
concerto. A short ritornello in the whole orchestra concludes this
refrain in which the piano plays no part.

The solo instrument comes on with the first couplet and the orchestra at once withdraws to the background. After an introductory
theme, it launches out into a long and grand virtuosity passage where
we notice the same care for varying the rhythm as in the other movements. It begins hesitatingly, like an unskilful walker picking his
way gingerly in the midst of pitfalls (ex. 371). Then it grows more
daring; the left hand engages in semi-quaver triplets, a formula which
predominates in the piano part of this rondo. The strings mark the
strong beats; the right hand punctuates the weak ones with chords,
ending by taking possession of the triplets, and the music falls into its
final stride, a firm, moderate gallop, whose majestic grace is in no way
lessened by its impetus. The figure ex. 372 is prominent in it. Soon
the triplets pass back to the left hand; the right hand accompanies
them while it converses with the strings and a short pedal on D
announces the second subject which the piano gives out alone (ex. 373).
As in the allegro, the wind restate it while the piano, still faithful to
its triplets, climbs down and up more than three octaves with scales
and arpeggios. The theme once enunciated, the solo enters on a
magnificent transition passage, the most sustained and perhaps the
grandest in all Mozart (twenty-two bars, 91-113). It is based entirely
on a dominant pedal adorned by scales and fragments of arpeggios.
The triplets remain hard at work; the orchestral accompaniment

grows livelier (ex. 374). Towards the end, we enter the minor and the intensity reaches passion. At this point the whole orchestra intervenes and the wind weave a web of colour round the piano's untiring gallop (ex. 375).

The piano gives out the gavotte; the tutti repeat it *forte*, hammering out the last part. Then follow the little march and exs. 369 and 370, but in this latter the 'cellos repeat the figure in the major and only fragment (b) is in the minor.

The piano opens the second couplet—the *development* of the sonata rondo—with an aggressive theme[1] in A minor, the key in which we had stopped. The theme is repeated and is followed by a few bravura bars as a coda. As soon as it is over, three vigorous chords in the whole orchestra settle its fate and that of its key by removing us, without possible protest, into F major.

The piano now gives out one of Mozart's simplest and most personal tunes. At first sight, it seems almost inert, so calm is it. Many other themes of his are simple but usually their simplicity goes with ingenuousness; behind this one's reserve one feels the experience of maturity (ex. 376). It will be noticed that the true bass is given by the double-basses and not by the piano's left hand. Hautboys and flute restate it, decorating it slightly; the piano accompanies them with an "Alberti" figure; both this and the true bass differ from the bass lines of ex. 376.

The second part is more lively and the return of the triplets in the accompaniment betrays some restlessness (ex. 377). This time the 'cellos alone give out the bass. Hautboys and flute repeat the tune over the piano triplets, and here too there is a change. To express the gradually rising emotion, Mozart adds the warm tone of the bassoon to the double-basses. The advance does not stop at the end of the tune and we modulate quickly through a few bars into C minor. Thereupon the strings enter and oppose the wind and the piano accompaniment becomes more excited. We are on the threshold of the most stirring passage in the rondo.

What follows—a transfiguration of the French rondeau's *mineur* —is profoundly dramatic. The pensive grace of the refrain, the calm assurance of the first solo vanish before a sorrowful and passionate conflict which carries us for an instant into the world of the last concerto. And, as so often happens with Mozart, the moment of

---

[1] It is a transposition of the theme with which the piano had opened the first couplet.

the most poignant emotion is also that of the most complex and closely woven technique.

As in the *development* of the allegro, the kernel of the passage is a figure of a few notes derived from a theme already heard, and the working-out takes a contrapuntal form.   As in the allegro, too, and

Ex. 370

Ex. 371

Ex. 372

Ex. 373

Ex. 374

Ex. 375

Ex. 376

indeed whenever Mozart combines closely instruments and solo,
the woodwind are to the fore; the strings are reduced to sustaining or
to keeping silence.   Flute, hautboy and bassoon share the exposition
of the drama.   Once the key of C minor reached, the flute repeats
the first four notes of ex. 376 which the bassoon takes up in a canon

at the octave (ex. 378).[1]   The flute starts again; then the hautboy gives
out in its turn the beginning of ex. 376; the augmentation of one degree
in the leap betrays heightened stress.   The flute replies with an imperfect
canon at the fourth (ex. 379; bars 206-10).   Then the bassoon opens
a further episode with a third exposition of the same fragment; the
leap increases to an octave and the figure climbs swiftly from the
bassoon to the hautboy and thence to the flute (ex. 380).   As in the
preceding episodes, the phrase is repeated, but this time, instead of
passing on to the flute, the fragment returns from the hautboy to the
bassoon (bars 210-16) and the flute starts a last episode, the subject of
which is still the beginning of ex. 376, but inverted, and moving
downwards.   The answers follow each other more closely and the
threefold canon at the octave is compressed now into two bars (ex.
381).   This episode, like the preceding, is given out twice, but nothing
more follows; the orchestral part finishes *en echelon* as each one of
the three instruments withdraws in turn (bars 216-20).   The basses
hold on their fundamental G for two bars more; then, the piano
continues alone and, in a long passage of broken sixths in triplets
which drops and rises two octaves, the passion evaporates and the
emotion returns to the level of the refrain.

Like all very dramatic passages in Mozart this one is short, but in
every respect it is the most significant moment in the finale.   Never
had Mozart used the canon to express such passionate feeling.   The
growing intensity is perceptible, not only in the extending to a
fourth, then to an octave, of the leap in the original figure, but also
in the length of the different episodes.   The two first, in two-part
imitation, decompose into periods of two bars each; the third is also in
two-bar periods, but the counterpoint is now in three parts; it forms
a miniature stretto.   The overlapping phrases and episodes, the
increase in length of periods and in number of parts, and the compression of the last episode, is exhilarating.   No passage reveals more
intimately the perfect union in Mozart between form and thought;
in it we grasp admirably the manner in which one is at the service
of the other, without either of them lording it.   No passage
shows better the meaning of the expression: to think, or feel,
musically.

------

[1] We meet this figure again at the most dramatic moment (end of the
development) of the B flat quartet, K.589, first movement.

And the piano, it will be asked? Has Mozart forgotten that he is writing a concerto and is he sacrificing his solo instrument upon the altar of his woodwind? Not at all. The lines of the design belong to them but the task of evoking the atmosphere, the impressionistic function, is the piano's. We have found in several concertos places where it accompanied a theme which was given out by the clarinet or the flute.[1] But here we have more than an accompaniment. The source of these bars is in the bravura passages of the concertos of John Sebastian and Philip Emmanuel Bach and their contemporaries, where the solo runs were punctuated in the strings by figures derived from the main themes. Already with the Bachs the orchestra's contribution was tending to become as important as the piano's; nevertheless, virtuosity remained the *raison d'être* of the passage. Here the centre of gravity has passed from the piano to the three representatives of the tutti.[2] Its presence is nevertheless indispensable. The waves of its triplets, breaking regularly bar by bar, fill out the slender lines traced by the instruments and punctuate each degree in the great ascent. This use of the piano for mass effects during a whole passage is new in Mozart for he is a conservative in this respect and, at a period when Clementi had been using it for some ten years in a manner resembling Beethoven, confined himself to a purely linear technique. We find similar piano writing in two almost contemporary sonatas: that in two movements in F, K.533, at the end of the following year, and that in G, unfinished, for piano duet, whose kinship of style with this finale is such that Saint-Foix and Einstein both date it from this period.

Only the gavotte is repeated at the reprise; however, the orchestra repeats it after the piano and thus gives the refrain a breadth unusual at this stage of the movement where several other rondos leave it out altogether. This breadth is significant; it stresses the exceptional character of the stormy episode which has just closed. It raises in some sort a barrier between it and the rest of the movement which prevents it from contaminating the recapitulation and shows how foreign the normal nature of this finale is to such outbursts.

The third couplet repeats the first, abridging it; the beginning of the solo is omitted and the long bravura passage shortened. Ex.

---

[1] E.g. the finales of K.482 and 488.

[2] Who should play out, and *espressivo*, all through this passage.

373 is given out in the tonic and the great transition which followed it is replaced by a new and briefer passage, which retains, however, the hesitations between major and minor; it also (bars 301-2) contains a foretaste of the C major quintet.[1]

At the refrain's last appearance piano and tutti join forces. The refrain is given out entire; after the little march the woodwind are silent; the piano takes over the first violin part in ex. 369, that of the basses and wind in ex. 370, decorating them with gruppetti. It adds a rather long solo which it repeats; triplets preponderate in it and the writing recalls earlier solos; the orchestra stands quite in the background. After which, the tutti conclude the movement unceremoniously with the ritornello which had ended the first exposition of the refrain.

The problem with which a composer is presented in a concerto first movement occurs also in a finale when the latter's form is the sonata rondo: to wit, how to ensure that the last part of the movement shall be more than the mere repetition of the exposition. We have seen how Mozart solves it in an allegro. In most of his rondos he deals with it as felicitously as in his first movements. But here, the third couplet is really but a shortened version of the first with precisely the best parts left out. The coda consists in a long solo where virtuosity runs to seed and stifles the thought and the last bars repeat unchanged the commonplace ritornello we know already. As a result, the last quarter of the movement is frigid and we listen to it with some impatience. In spite of the general superiority of the sonata rondo, this is a case where the use of the two part rondo would have been more suitable. The dramatic central section does not dispose us to hear a second time what went before it; we would like to skip the recapitulation and pass at one bound from bar 229 to bar 308. Moreover, the coda, all in runs, is worthy neither of the finale nor of the work as a whole. It is clear that, after his superb *development*, Mozart had nothing more to say and grew tired of the work.

This concerto is the last of the four that Mozart composed in C major. We have connected it with its 1785 predecessor and the string quintet which was to follow it a few months later, and, of course, the word Olympian, which we have used of it, evokes inevitably the so-called *Jupiter* symphony, although that work belongs more

---

[1] Allegro, bars 270-2.

to the allegiance of Apollo than of Zeus. The key of C major, with those of F, B flat and D, is the key which Mozart has used most often; he is alike in this to all his contemporaries. Only, whereas the most used keys are not generally those in which he wrote his most distinctive works, some of his C majors do make up a well characterized family.

It is true that he used this key for many pieces about which there is little to say and, sometimes, in which there is not much to enjoy —works which reflect the personality of his period rather than his own. This is especially true of many youthful masses and symphonies, but also of many a sonata for piano, two or four hands, and for piano and violin, of late years.[1] The flute and harp concerto is no doubt the most successful of these drawing-room pieces since, whilst it keeps the impersonal exterior of the well-bred gentleman, it expresses something which is Mozart's own. But our concerto does not enter into this group.

C major is also the festal key, the key of pompous marches and overtures. It is the key with which he likes to begin and end his operas.[2] Used in this way, it often acquires strength and nobility,[3] and thus it becomes, in the last six years of the master's life, the key which expresses what we have called the Olympian quality of his inspiration. It takes by degrees the place of E flat which, at that period and down to Beethoven, is the essentially "heroic" key[4] and was so with Mozart at the time of the *Sinfonia Concertante* and the wind serenade, K.375. His first C major work where we recognize an unmistakable Olympian inspiration is the symphony K.338 which he composed at Salzburg a year or two before his final departure. Later, he turned to this key for some of his noblest contrapuntal pieces: the fantasia and fugue, K.394, the overture and fugue in the suite, K.399, and above all the massive choruses of the C minor mass: *Cum sancto Spiritu, Sanctus* and *Hosanna*. We have noticed the same inspiration in the grand tutti with which the concerto K.415 opened. We find it especially after 1785, spaciously expressed, in the family of works to which our concerto belongs: in the quartet K.465, the two concertos, the quintet and the symphony. After this last work, he gives it up and returns to it only in opera; the

---

[1] K.296, 303, 309, 330, 521.

[2] *Die Entführung, Der Schauspieldirektor, Cosi fan tute, Titus.*

[3] Strength in the *Schauspieldirektor* overture, nobility in that of *Titus.*

[4] Cf. p. 366.

overture of *Titus* is undoubtedly connected with the same stream of emotion as the concertos and quintet.

In spite of our strictures on the end of the rondo, this concerto is a very great work, one of the master's greatest. It is regrettable that, in the Mozart revival of recent years, the composer's trifling works should have received as much attention as his important ones, and even more. No one can maintain that his best violin concertos are not heard as often as they should be, but who will dare say as much of the great piano concertos, far superior to those for violin, which count among the most valuable part of his creation? We know only too well the piano sonatas; those for violin are not neglected; but performances of the string quintets, the peaks of his chamber music, and of the three wind serenades,[1] are still exceptional, whereas one station or another broadcasts every day the tiresome *Kleine Nachtmusik*.

With the concerto in C we reach the end of the period in Mozart's life when the concerto was his favourite means of expression. Two days after finishing it, the guard is changed and the symphony, in the person of the so-called Prague, K.504, takes over duty. This taking over may even date from before the completion of the rondo; it is perhaps because the symphony he was composing had drawn all his vitality to itself that the conclusion of the concerto was so uninspired. However it be, henceforward the master's instrumental personality takes shape in the symphony and the quintet; other genres, including the concerto itself, survive as exceptions and none of them bear fruits as rich as those they have already produced. The period of his piano concertos is over.

SCENA WITH RONDO FOR SOPRANO WITH PIANO OBBLIGATO: *"Ch'io mi scordi di te"*; *"Non temer, amato bene"* (K.505).
Finished December 27th, 1786
Orchestra: Strings, two clarinets, two bassoons, two horns.

A few days before the end of this same year, Mozart completed a curious and beautiful work in which the piano plays with the orchestra, the recitative and aria *"Ch'io mi scordi di te"*, written for soprano and piano obbligato, with orchestral accompaniment. The

---

[1] Recently recorded, for the first time, by Les Discophiles Français.

piano part is brilliant and strongly redolent of the neighbourhood of the chamber works with piano and the great concertos.

Earlier in the year he had hoped to have *Idomeneo* produced in Vienna. The hope was never realized but a private concert performance was given at the mansion of Prince Charles von Auersperg in March, and on that occasion he altered the opening of the second act. Originally, it had begun with a scene in recitativo secco between Idomeneo and Arbace. For this was substituted one between Idamante and Ilia, and the latter was given an aria, on words which had not figured in Varesco's libretto (K.490). In December, he again set the text of the solo, but with different words in the recitative that preceded it, for Nancy Storace, the Susanna of *Le Nozze*, who was leaving Vienna and returning to her native city of London. The MS. of this new aria, K.505, bears the remark: "*Composto per la Sigra Storace dal suo servo ed amico W. A. Mozart Vienna il 26 di decbr 786*" (sic) and the entry in his catalogue confirms the dedication: "*Für Mselle Storace und mich.*"

A solo for voice and orchestra with piano obbligato was not in Mozart's time the curiosity it would be to-day. John Christian Bach had composed in 1774 a scena con aria, on words from *Rinaldo ed Armida*, in which there figured obbligato parts for piano and hautboy. At some later date, he played in it with Gainsborough's son-in-law, the hautboist John Christian Fischer and the castrato Tenducci.[1] He and Tenducci were both in Paris in 1778, during Mozart's stay there, and Mozart was asked to write a scena for the singer. He did so, and the work, now lost, had four obbligato parts: piano, hautboy, horn and bassoon;[2] it was probably modelled on Bach's.

In the aria for Nancy Storace, the piano is the only obbligato instrument.[3] The aria proper is preceded by twenty-seven bars of

---

[1] A MS. copy of this scena in the British Museum bears the title: "The Favorite Rondeau sung by Mr. Tenducci accompanied on the Pianoforte by Mr. Bach and on the Hautboy by Mr. Fisher" (C. S. Terry: *John Christian Bach*, p. 250). The piano part is an accompaniment throughout. The scena is published in Landshoff's edition of *Twelve Concert Arias by J. C. Bach* (Peters, 1929).

[2] Köchel-Einstein 315 b. Cf. his letter to his father of August 27th, 1778.

[3] The earlier setting, K.490, had an obbligato violin part, which was played by Mozart's friend, Count August von Hatzfeld. In spite of a certain superficial likeness in the figuration between the solo violin and piano parts, there is little in common between the two settings, and the latter is greatly superior to the earlier one, which is mainly showy virtuosity.

recitative, accompanied only by the strings. The rondo begins with an andante of seventy-three bars, consisting of refrain, couplet, and repetition of the refrain, and an allegretto of a hundred and forty-one bars, with three returns of the refrain, two couplets and a long coda. The refrain in the allegretto, different from that in the andante, may, at a pinch, be considered a free variation of it. In its allegretto form it is very close to the main subject of the finale in the clarinet trio, K.498, composed four and a half months earlier.

The combination of piano and soprano is constant and varied. The writing, we have said, is close in style to the piano parts in both concerto and chamber music, especially in such concertante works as the quintet for piano and wind, K.452, the brilliant B flat violin sonata, K.454, the piano quartets and the clarinet trio. Only twice does the piano give out the theme before the voice, each time in the refrain (bars 4-12 and 73-81).[1] Elsewhere, save for an occasional bar of transition, it never plays alone. Since its presence is our only justification for mentioning this work, we will confine our remarks to the relations between obbligato and solo.

In their intercourse, the piano is either subordinate to the voice or collaborates with it. It is often the solo's equal but never its superior. Twice, in bars 202 and 207,[2] it supports the vocal line a third below. In each of the expositions of the andante refrain, where the voice has a tenuto of a couple of bars (bars 18-19 and 62-63), the piano weaves over it a rococo line of gruppetti, themselves of a coloratura character and not unlike a passage that occurs in the voice part towards the end of the aria (bars 208-9).[3] But as a rule its behaviour to the voice in those passages where it is not collaborating on equal terms consists in harmonizing the vocal line with arpeggios or, once, with an "Alberti-bass" figure in both hands,[4] recalling certain passages in the allegro of K.467[5] or the coda of the first movement of the G minor quartet. The most original instance of such harmonization occurs in a place, which is repeated, where the voice has a slow descending chromatic scale (bars 26-32 and 134-40). On the first occasion the piano superimposes arpeggios over the vocal line; the result is an entrancing chain of diminished sevenths (ex. 381 a). When the text ("*l'alma mia mancando va*") returns in the

---

[1] Our numbering goes from the beginning of the andante.
[2] Bars 205-9 are cut in the *Breitkopf* piano score.
[3] Bars 205-9 are cut in the *Breitkopf* piano score.
[4] Bars 94-5.   [5] Bars 253-8.

allegretto the bass falls to the piano and the harmonization is different; the voice part is now enveloped in the piano arpeggios (ex. 381 b). These are among the most expressive bars in all Mozart's vocal music.[1]

We have classed these bars as accompaniment, but accompaniment of such originality and beauty easily becomes the equal of the solo. In those moments where piano and voice interplay on equal terms we

Ex. 381a

Ex. 381b

Ex. 381c

Ex. 381d

---

[1] Cf. with ex. 181 b, from the allegro of K.456.

Ex. 381c

may distinguish between those when they succeed or answer each other, and those in which they combine.

The most dramatic examples of question and answer occur when a balanced phrase is divided between the partners. There is no more moving strain in the rondo than at the setting of the words: "*Tu sospiri?*" (bars 141–4), where they alternate with a minor two-bar phrase, one of those stylized imitations of sighing beloved of the rococo age (ex. 381 c; the example joins on to ex. 381 b). Sometimes the voice speaks first and the piano replies; it is then, as a rule, in semi-quavers that the instrument rejoins, just as it did in the allegro of the C minor concerto.[1] There is a particularly beautiful example of this treatment in the coda of the rondo (bars 165–70; ex. 381 d).[2]

---

[1] Bars 420–3 of the concerto; it is the return of ex. 327 in the recapitulation.

[2] See also K.452, first movement, bars 8–11 of the allegro moderato.

There are also a few instances of echoes.[1]   Such bars are nearer to concerto than to chamber music style.

Another moment when the concertos are close is in the main couplet of the allegretto, the counterpart of the *development* couplet of a concerto rondo.   Here, in bars 111-18, the piano right hand comes tumbling down the keyboard in broken chords, while the voice gives out the melodic thread in crotchets, just as, in the finale of K.451 (ex. 146), the wind had toyed with their skeletal theme and the piano had "accompanied" with similar figures.   There is an analogy here with other *developments*[2] and with the coda of the first movement of the C minor concerto.

It is, on the other hand, of the chamber works that we think when we hear the piano part rise and fall in runs of semi-quavers— scales or broken scales—under the sustained dotted minims and crotchets of the voice (bars 21-5, 89-93),[3] particularly in the return to the refrain (bars 151-5, ex. 381 e), a most euphonious passage which recalls several rentrées in chamber music rondos.

None of these devices is used for more than a few bars and the incessant shifting of emphasis, the setting off now of piano now of voice must be heard (or seen in the score, alas! since this shapely work never leaves the sheath of the *Gesamtausgabe*) to be appreciated. Mozart has at least a dozen ways of enhancing the soprano tone with the piano's, the piano's with the soprano's, and he passes constantly from one to the other.   We, to whom such a combination is foreign, can best realize the effect by imagining an orchestral background added to a lied for voice and piano.   The work is very far from being a curiosity or a rhetorical exhibition of instrumental and vocal technique; it is a vital, moving piece, where the music rises generously to the emotional theme: that of the love and fellow-suffering which Ilia feels for Idamante and the assurance she gives him of her fidelity. The few quotations we have given will, we hope, send readers to the score or to the almost unobtainable piano arrangement in the selection of Mozart's concert arias published many years ago by Breitkopf and Härtel.

---

[1] Bars 173, 185 ; cf. ex. 3.

[2] First movements of K.451, 453, 482 and 493; middle couplets of rondos in K.386 and 456 (ex. 200).   Note also bar 204, which is almost identical with 92-5 in the first movement of K.365.

[3] Cp., among others, with bars 37-41 in the first movement of the G minor piano quartet and the end of the *development* in the same movement of the E flat piano quartet.

PART V

1. The Twenty-second Concerto: K.537 in D

CONCERTO NO. 22 IN D MAJOR (K.537)[1]
Finished February 24th, 1788
    Allegro: C
    Larghetto: ¢ (in A major)
    (Allegretto): 2-4
Orchestra: Strings, flute, two hautboys, two bassoons, two horns, two
    trumpets, two kettledrums.

"Short-sighted minds, I mean those which are narrow and shut up
in their own little spheres, are unable to understand the universality of
talents that one sometimes observes in one individual; where they see what
is agreeable, they rule out what is substantial; where they think to discover bodily grace, agility, nimbleness, dexterity, they refuse to allow the
gifts of the soul, depth, reflection, wisdom; they erase from the story of
Socrates the fact that he danced."[2]

How well these words of La Bruyère apply to the opinion on
Mozart current in the last century and the beginning of this
one and still surviving here and there! It saw in him above all an
entertainer—a "divine" one, possibly, but an entertainer all the same.
Comparable opinions saw in Beethoven nothing but the "Titan",
in Bach, the "mathematician", in Haydn, the "Papa", in Chopin,
the elegiac author of certain nocturnes. That Bach and Beethoven
should have "danced", that Haydn and Mozart may have wept, that
Chopin should have sung of energy and warlike spirit: this was cut
out of their story.

When one undertakes to study a great figure who is the victim
of such a simplification (and almost every great figure is), one feels
a keen delight on discovering how varied and even how contradictory
his personality may be. Beethoven's minuets and écossaises, Bach's
gavottes, lyrical arias of Handel, mournful adagios of Haydn, martial
polonaises of Chopin come and remind us that these men, like all of
us, knew the most diverse moods, and that posterity's choice, rather

---

[1] *Gesamtausgabe*, no. 26.
[2] La Bruyère: *Les Caractères*, chap. II: *Du mérite personnel.*

than the nature of their work itself, has imposed on us the idea we
have of them.

It is impossible to study any of the genres into which Mozart
put himself most fully without noticing at every turn how changeful
and manifold was his soul. We have recognized it many times while
going through our beloved concertos. His variousness is not met
with only from one work to another; it strikes us also when we pass
from one period of his life to another. Nothing is less true than
Lenz's assertion that, though the artist in him had grown, the man had
never done so. The study of his Viennese concertos alone, from 1782
to 1786, is enough to prove the contrary, but if their example did not
suffice, the works of the two years on the threshold of which we
now stand would serve to refute this contention.

The psychological evolution of these years is unmistakable. If
we consider the most significant works of 1787 and 1788,[1] among
which, alas! his only concerto composed during this period cannot
be numbered, we recognize two streams in his inspiration. To one
of them correspond powerful, unified works, of the race of the two
last concertos: some of them bright and serene (quintet in C, symphonies in E flat and C), others gloomy (quintet and symphony in
G minor); but having all of them a frank, straightforward nature,
with no other mystery than that which all work of beauty bears in
it. To the other stream belong certain movements in which new
strains are heard. To find ancestors for these we have to return to
the days of Mozart's last stay in Salzburg.[2] The earliest of them is
the andante of the Prague Symphony. This work, absolutely contemporary with the great concerto in C, has nothing in common
with it. The first movement, less broad and more quivering, has
moments of tense strength, of keen feeling, which make one think
of the *Don Giovanni* overture. But the andante is the most original
piece. Few slow movements of Mozart's are so uneven in progress.
We perceive in it a kind of dialogue where the voices, half confused,
are those of his daïmon, his divided personality, languishing, caressing,
groaning, yielding and striving in turn. The emotional instability
of the movement is great; it passes ceaselessly from one mood to

---

[1] Symphony in D, K.504; rondo for piano in A minor, K.511; string
quintets in C and G minor, K.515 and 516; violin sonata in A, K.526; piano
sonata in F, K.533; adagio for piano in B minor, K.540; adagio for strings in
C minor, K.546; the three last symphonies, K.543, 550, 551; divertimento for
string trio in E flat, K.563.

[2] Cf. pp. 119-23.

another without ever settling down.[1] More than anywhere else, Mozart is here what a contemporary called him: "Stürmer und Schmeichler" ("stormer and caresser"). The opposition between the tuneful sweetness of the opening strain and the dry, almost mocking tone of the second is typical of the piece.

With its occasional exacerbated chromaticisms, it is the first of those andantes and adagios with discordant passages which now make their appearance and sound a strange, disquieting note in his work. In the B minor adagio—a most unusual key with him—the presence of the voices is clearer; this adagio and the one which he composed as prelude for his arrangement for strings of his fugue for two pianos, K.426, are the movements where the elements of his soul, conversing or struggling, are most dissociated.[2]

In a less acute degree, the same character is found in several other slow movements of this period—in those of the G minor quintet, of the violin sonata in A, whose bleak moorland landscape takes us far away from Mozart to the greyest regions of Brahms, of the F major sonata, where harsh, rasping phrases, laden with chromaticisms, clash with bitter cacophony, and where we again recognize Mozart's power for "thinking musically", since, though so emotional, they are the result of a desire for extreme formal compression. This inspiration appears for the last time in the adagio of the string trio where the very concise *development* has a few bars of almost physical cruelty.

A kindred inspiration flows through the A minor rondo, but is more languishing—we are tempted to say: wilting, if the word be not too strong for Mozart. The feeling which dominates this rondo is on the whole that of all our composer's works in A. Long ago, Reinecke pointed out the likeness between it and some of Chopin's compositions where an exasperated sensibility revels in an orgy of melismas.[3]

As for the quintets, we have already said that they belong to the

[1] It is impossible to bring out this basic character of the movement if it is taken, as some conductors take it, as a siciliana or a berceuse, in 2-4; the beat is 6-8 and the speed should not exceed ♪ = 100.

[2] The affecting minuet for piano in D, K.355, of unknown date, comes from the same plane of his consciousness and is perhaps contemporary with this group.

[3] *Zur Wiederbelebung der Mozart'schen Klavierkonzerte*, 1936 edition, p. 40. The andantes of the concertos in D, K.451, and C, K.467, can also be likened to Chopin, for the same reason. It should be added that the breadth of certain periods in the A minor rondo betray the neighbourhood of the concerto K.503 and the C major quintet.

same line of growth as the last two concertos. With the allegro of
the F major sonata, they are the works of Mozart where the form
spreads itself with greatest breadth. The new stage brings it back
to the dimensions of earlier works. Never more does Mozart undertake anything as vast as the allegro of the quintet in C. The likeness
of its andante to that of the last concerto has been noted; its finale is a
more generous edition of that of the C major quartet, K.465; even
the characteristic modulation into A flat of the earlier movement
occurs in it. It has less variety than the rondo of the concerto but
interest is kept up in it more successfully and it has no dead patches.

The two years 1787 and 1788 are without doubt the most glorious
in the story of Mozart's work and every fervent admirer of the master
should be able to gaze on them with unmixed joy. But one for whom
the concertos have become the favourite children of his genius cannot
suppress a feeling of melancholy, for their sole representative at this
period, although popular, is one of the poorest and emptiest. We
allude to that in D which Mozart composed for the Lent of 1788 and
which is dated February 24th. (The fact that the composer played
it at Frankfurt in 1790 at the Coronation festivities of Leopold II has
earned for it the high-sounding but irrelevant title of Coronation
concerto.)

The end of the great concertos corresponds to the end of the
period when Mozart was a fashionable pianist and composer. His
financial position had never been brilliant; it soon became bad and
for the last four years of his life he was often in great want. The
stories of his poverty are well known but, to have an immediate
impression of it, nothing equals a perusal of the heart-rending notes
he sent to his brother mason Puchberg.

When after more than a year he had again the opportunity of
coming before the public as a virtuoso composer, it looks as if he made
a determined effort to fall in with his listeners' taste and "write popularly". But the gap between the average *galant* taste and his ideal
had grown too wide for him to bridge it in so important a work.
He could still condescend to what was asked of him for short moments,
in trifles like his trios and some of his last sonatas;[1] in a composition
of the scope of a concerto, he could do so no longer. The mask
stifled him; from time to time he would lift it up to breathe, then put
it back more or less correctly; the result was something factitious

---

[1] K.521, 545, 547.   K.570 and 576 are not trifles.

which is neither Mozart nor a work quite in the *galant* style of his younger days.

Between the growth in breadth of the C major concerto and the quintets and the growth in concentration of his last symphonies, the concerto in D is, then, a manifestation of the *galant* taste of the time. But it is not a perfect work such as had been in their narrow field the divertimenti and cassationen of Salzburg and the showy concertos of 1784, still near to their public's level. There, the brilliance was the effect of a spontaneous urge of their author, in sympathy with his public and glad to please it. Here, the urge is lacking and this is what saddens us most. In all his other concertos the joy of the maker in the act of creation is present, even in the most insignificant, even in the drooping, resigned work of 1790; only here is it absent.

It is very significant that at the time when Mozart was most ignored, alone among all his piano concertos this one remained on concert programmes, on the Continent at any rate. When in 1891 Reinecke attempted to revive these works and brought out his valuable booklet on how to play them, he drew nearly all his examples from this one. To-day its popularity is not so marked, but it is still more often played than others which are greater.

We shall gain nothing by analysing it with the care we bestowed on the study of its predecessors. We will merely distinguish what belongs in it to the return to *galanterie* and what still bears witness to the ideal that Mozart was unable entirely to forsake.

I. The tutti opens with a mysterious phrase over a repeated bass, portending grave and sombre things (ex. 382). This, however, is bluff; nothing in the movement recalls it and it is in as striking contrast with what follows as the minor adagios which Haydn prefixed to his most joyous symphonies. The *piano* is followed by a *forte*, according to the usual plan of openings in *galant* concertos, and we enter on a chain of subjects and motifs which leads after eighty bars to the piano's entry. One is at once struck by the square, rigid outline of the phrases, subdivided into periods of two and four bars. The only passage which breaks this uniformity is the first violin solo which precedes the second subject. The scoring is much less resourceful than in the previous concertos; the strings preponderate and the woodwind does no more than double them from time to time. The extent to which Mozart seems to have unlearnt his woodwind craft, here and in the solos, is astounding; the work has to be known for so entire a renunciation of his riches to be believed.

Except for the solo subject the prelude contains all the elements of the movement. Their emotional significance is slight; they are amiable, impersonal words; their step is quick, but skipping, not winged.

The piano makes its bow with ex. 382 but the Alberti bass which replaces the repeated notes deprives the subject of its former gravity. As if to emphasize that he renounces all that he had adored in his earlier works, Mozart has recourse to a device borrowed from the aria and found only in his first concertos; he repeats a part of the tutti conclusion after the first solo run—a device which appears quite archaic here.

The impertinent and irrelevant virtuosity which at once overruns the movement in great force makes it mark time instead of carrying us on towards weightier matter. It has not even formal originality in its favour; pianistically, it is more archaic than the piano writing of the concertos in C major. It consists in scales, now in one hand, now in the other, seldom in both together. The lack of all interplay (except in ex. 384) is particularly distressing; no concerto since 1782 had been so devoid of it. Of the ambitions of past years there remains only the movement's great size, for after K.503 it is the longest of Mozart's allegros. But, though the outside be spacious, the inside remains empty.[1]

The solo subject brings us nearer to the true Mozart (ex. 383). its chromaticisms, especially the unexpected flattening in its third bar, and its modulation from A major to D minor, are echoes of the A minor rondo, K.511. The bravura passage which evolves out of it resounds with vigorous strains at first, but the energy soon expends itself in a few bars of scales. When repeating the second subject, strings and solo collaborate an instant (ex. 384) and the little contrapuntal working-out of the piano which follows it (bars 176–87) is Mozart at his best; it recalls the *development* in the two pianos sonata and the fifth variation in the finale of the C minor concerto.

The tutti which concludes the exposition repeats without any marked change some twenty bars of the first tutti[2]; we are far from

---

[1] "The autograph shows the piano part incomplete; thus, the larghetto gives only the tune; the left hand stave is blank. In the finale, the solo is often only sketched out; it is most complete in the first movement" (Köchel-Einstein, p. 687). The first edition was published by André in 1794; it is not known what source he used to complete the solo. "He may even have completed it himself" (id.).

[2] Bars 13–23 and 71–8.

the grand exposition closes where piano and orchestra co-operated in preparing the *development*.

The *development* here is thematic, but on what a theme! With an utter lack of seriousness Mozart catches hold of the last fragment of the ritornello and gives it first to the piano, then to the strings, then once again to the piano, after the fashion of the E flat concerto, K.482. Then, the piano having launched out into runs, sundry members of the strings accompany it with the same figure (ex. 385) and now we think of the D minor concerto, where in the *development* a thematic fragment had likewise followed the piano in its excursions. But, though the device be the same, what a difference in the artistic import of the figures and the use made of them! Here, it is all a joke, without the slightest dramatic content; what is needed is to kill time and fill in the framework of sonata form.

Yet one cannot go on for ever doing the same thing, so after a few bars the orchestra stops its commentary and the piano forges ahead almost alone. The section (bars 261-9) which begins in B minor is one of the best in the movement. It modulates freely and resembles a recitative—one of those "voices" of which we spoke just now—but it finishes poorly and the stream of its emotion becomes sanded up in passage work.

The recapitulation is scarcely different from the first solo; only towards the end do the strings, and then the piano, recall a part of the concluding subject which had been omitted (bars 381-92). It is in D major, like the rest of this third solo, but just as it is about to conclude, a *fp* chord on the piano, followed by a torrent of scales and arpeggios, breaks out in G minor like a bolt from the blue. Two more claps follow, each one a degree higher; after which the solo ends in D major as if nothing had happened (bars 393-9). These few bars are the most truly Mozartish moment in the whole movement. Letting loose demonic passion, they show that the lion was only slumbering in its court dress and are a revenge of Mozart's genius for the restraint put upon it by its master. But nothing further reveals its existence and the allegro closes with the same bars as the first tutti. The brevity and triteness of the seven bars that follow the cadenza[1] are depressing in a movement of such size; they fully deserve to be covered by the applause of a public carried away by the soloist's performance in the cadenza.

II. Within the restricted limits of the larghetto, the composer has known how to reconcile *galant* taste and individual expression. It is the best movement of the three, neither great nor deep, but true Mozart, and it deserves the popularity it has always enjoyed and to which many separate editions bear witness.

We find again in it the soft voluptuousness of certain A major arias. Very near to vocal music, it mirrors the same mood as Bel-

---

[1] Mozart has left no cadenza for this concerto; the cadenza sometimes printed with it belongs to K.451.

mont's "O wie ängstlich, o wie feurig!", the duets "S'io no moro" in *Idomeneo*, "Un' aura amorosa" in *Così fan tutte*, and "Ah! perdona!" in *Titus*, and, in instrumental works, the andantes of the D major violin concerto, K.218, and string quartet, K.575. In some pieces in this key, mockery mingles with sensuousness, as in "La ci darem la mano" and "Ah! taci, ingiusto core!" in *Don Giovanni*, but here there is no trace of it. It breathes the gentle voluptuousness, tinted with melancholy, so typical of the end of the Old Regime.

The refrain is a winding tune where theme and accompaniment entwine (ex. 388). Given out by the piano, it is restated by the whole orchestra. The second period belongs to the piano solo, then the first is repeated and the tutti add a coda instinct with true Mozartish yearning; it is the most deeply felt part of the movement (ex. 387). The middle section is a cantilena for piano solo whose general outline and rhythm make us think of the same section in the romance of the D minor and the larghetto of K.595. Some of its bars are sketchy and gain by being filled out (49-53, 63-7), but it is less grievous here than elsewhere to play them as they are written. The last part recapitulates the whole refrain, without repetition, and in ex. 387 the piano adds a few runs to the orchestral song.

III. The finale is a rondo with a plan we have not yet met. This plan is, indeed, its most interesting peculiarity, for its musical content is even slighter than that of the first movement.

In several sonata rondos Mozart, and after him Beethoven, leaves out the refrain between the *development* and recapitulation couplets.[1] The result is to reduce to two the sections of the movement included between the returns of the refrain. This is one simplification. In more than one of the rondos of 1787, notably those of the quintets, the simplification is carried still further and the development itself is reduced to a few modulatory bars or a passing theme and the recapitulation begins almost at once after the second return of the refrain. The finale is then in reality a two-couplet rondo, comparable to the binary sonata andantes.[2] In the Coronation concerto, the second couplet begins with the same subject as the first, but modulates, and these modulations are all that is left of the development. Such a movement may be called a binary sonata rondo.[3]

---

[1] K.456, 459, 488; 478, 493; Beethoven's op. 58.
[2] K.503; 515, 516.
[3] Other binary rondos occur in K.428, 575, 576.

The theme of the refrain in this finale is neither more nor less interesting than those of many other rondos of the time (ex. 388). It comprises a second section and a longish orchestral ritornello; it spreads itself widely and indeed the whole movement is on as spacious a scale as the allegro.

We will not follow it in detail. The same ineffective virtuosity occurs as in the first movement, the same almost complete absence of interplay between piano and orchestra, the same lack of independence in the wind parts. Occasionally, however, the true Mozart reveals himself. The second theme of the couplet brings us a surprise by starting in the minor (ex. 389); it enters the major only when the piano takes it up. On the whole, the movement modulates more freely than the allegro; at the beginning of the second couplet, in particular, we pass swiftly through the keys of B minor, F sharp minor, B flat (an expressive enharmonic modulation), B flat minor, A minor and B minor to land in G minor, whence by slow stages we wend back to the tonic. This inroad of fancy into a prosaic piece lasts unhappily but twenty-five bars.

There comes another most poetic moment, worthy of the master's best works. Twice, at the end of each couplet (bars 136–43 and 287–94), the virtuoso withdraws and the musician lifts his mask. There unfolds then one of those exquisite passages where strings, wind and piano work together, without surrendering their individualities, in a melodious, ethereal counterpoint (ex. 390). The little rising figure with which the string and flute tune ends is a favourite of Mozart's; it occurs again in the E flat symphony,[1] in the finale of the D major quartet, K.575, and elsewhere. And, since beauties are scarce in this concerto, we will draw the reader's attention to the bassoon part in bars 361–2—an unexpected counter-subject which is lost in the piano solo arrangement.

The key of D major, much used at all times by Mozart, is the favourite key for overtures and occasional pieces—divertimentos and serenades—in *galant* music. Its superficial majesty has not the martial strains heard in many a C major composition, capable in certain chosen works of attaining to the expression of heroism, and it easily passes over to showiness and virtuosity. It is the concerto key *par excellence* and in those which Mozart has written in D virtuosity plays a great part. In his violin concertos, the most difficult are in

---

[1] First movement, second subject.

this key;[1] his D major flute concerto is more *virtuoso* than that in G;
it is in D that he writes that one of his three flute quartets which most
resembles a concerto; his four piano sonatas in D,[2] especially the first
two, are works of technical display, and this is true also of his only
violin sonata in this key.   Finally, two out of his three piano concertos in D are those where the display of technique enters most deeply
into the personality of the work.

Yet all Mozart's music in this key has not this character.   Though
the pomp of D major never rises to heroism, it sometimes gives us
glimpses of sombre depths, as towards the end of the overture of

---

[1] K.218 and Köchel-Einstein, 271 i.

[2] Including that for two pianos, the most brilliant of all.

Idomeneo. A feeling akin to this, less tragic but quite as serious, runs through the joyous vigour of the Prague symphony and the overture of *Don Giovanni.* His finales in D are bursting with physical energy and sometimes make use of close counterpoint.[1] Finally, a few very individual pieces like the opening allegros of the quartets K.499 and 575 and the *Ave verum* cannot be brought under any classification. On the whole, the key shows so many different features in his work that the only general judgement one can pass on it is the rather commonplace one that it contains some of his finest movements.[4]

---

[1] Prague symphony; quartet K.499; quintet K.593.

[2] Overtures of *Idomeneo, Figaro, Don Giovanni*; piano concerto K.451; quartets K.499 and 575; quintet K.593; Prague symphony; *Ave verum.*

2. The Twenty-third Concerto: K.595 in B flat

CONCERTO NO. 23 IN B FLAT (K.595)[1]
Finished January 5th, 1791
    Allegro: C
    Larghetto: C (in E flat)
    Allegro: 6-8
Orchestra: Strings, flute, two hautboys, two bassoons, two horns.

JUST as the period of the concertos had come to a glorious close with the magnificent work in C, so that which followed and was summed up in the quintets and symphonies of 1787 and 1788 culminated in a masterpiece in this same key of C major in which Mozart had so often expressed the "heroic" and "Olympian" sides of his inspiration. The finale of his last symphony, the only movement of the four to which the name of Jupiter is really suited, crowns gloriously his orchestral work, as the concerto in C had crowned his achievements as piano composer and virtuoso.

The symphony was finished on August 10th; in September, Mozart wrote his one string trio, the divertimento in E flat, K.563, the inspiration of which links it with the period just closed. Then comes the great silence of the two saddest years of his life. It is not complete, since now and again it is broken by a chamber work and, once, by an opera, but it is a silence nevertheless when one compares these months with the fruitful periods which had preceded them since he had come to Vienna.

It is good to dwell on this paucity of important works in order to gainsay once more the legend of his miraculous productivity. According to this legend, the young musician was ceaselessly pouring out compositions of all sorts, with the utmost facility and often with a deplorable lack of self-criticism. When one lives at all continuously with his work, one realizes that, during his maturity, instead of being spread over the eleven years of his life in Vienna, his moments of great productiveness are compressed within a few periods. Within these,

---

[1] *Gesamtausgabe*, no. 27.

it is true, his fruitfulness is prodigious, but between-whiles he does not write much. The earliest of them comes in February, March and April, 1784, when there appear the first four of his great concertos, a violin sonata and a quintet: six major works in two and a half months. The second is at the end of the same year and the beginning of the next, when in a little under six months he gives forth four important concertos, three quartets and the finest of his piano sonatas: eight major works. Then, in the middle of the year, 1788, which we are about to leave, come the celebrated seven weeks in which he inserts trios and sonatinas between his three great symphonies after the fashion of light interludes between the acts of a drama. Finally, in the last year of his life, from December, 1790, to March, 1791, two string quintets, a piano concerto and two fantasias for mechanical organ follow quickly one upon the other: five works of which three were composed in one month; and this, incidentally, destroys another legend, according to which, at the time of his death, he was spiritually as well as physically exhausted. Surely this is enough to arouse our admiration, without our making him live at constant high pressure ![1]

In the spring of 1789, Mozart started on the first large-scale journey he had undertaken since his return from Paris eleven years earlier. Invited by Prince Lichnowsky to accompany him to Berlin, he set out almost without warning on April 8th, yet not without having written a line to a friend, Franz Hofdemel, to borrow the necessary money. The prince and his suite stopped on the way at Prague, Dresden and Leipzig and reached Potsdam at the end of the month. The visit which Mozart made to the aged Doles, a pupil of Bach's and one of his successors at St. Thomas's, Leipzig, has often been told; he extemporized so beautifully on the church organ that Doles exclaimed: "It is my old master come back to earth!" To reward his visitor, he made his choir sing the motet: "Singet dem Herrn ein neues Lied". According to Rochlitz, Mozart listened to it with rapture and declared: "That is something one can learn from!" He had the parts of Bach's other motets brought out, set them on the floor all round him, studied them with enthusiasm and asked for copies.

If this visit to Northern Germany had ever raised hopes in his breast, they were soon dispelled. King Frederick-William II of

---

[1] The basic state of emotional natures is indolence, according to Bain. Mozart's is an "emotional nature" which works only under the stimulus of an occasion, "an irritation, a shock, acting upon a Nirvanic basis", as Julien Benda says in speaking of himself.

Prussia was a keen musician and a good 'cellist, but all the places round him were occupied. Among his court musicians was a certain French 'cellist Duport whom Mozart disliked and whom, it is said, he blamed in insulting terms for "being settled in Germany and eating the bread of Germans" without troubling to learn the language of the country. The king did not even allow him to give a concert of his works. Yet he presented him with a purse of a hundred gold fredericks and ordered six string quartets and six easy sonatas for his daughter, the Princess Frederika.

Mozart tried to hide his disappointment from his wife by writing witty and affectionate letters. It was in joking terms that he informed her of the unprofitable outcome of his journey. "My dear little wife, you must rejoice at my return for love of me rather than for the money." His only earnings were the king's purse and a hundred ducats which a concert in Dresden had brought him, and even so he lent a part of this sum to a friend. Six weeks after his return we find him again writing to the faithful Puchberg: "I am in a state in which I would not wish my worst enemy to be! If you, my excellent friend and brother, abandon me, I am lost, as unhappy as I am innocent, with my poor sick wife and my child!" And as Puchberg did not answer at once, he repeated his request five days later.

This journey and its resulting disappointments separate the period of the quintets and symphonies from that which opens at this point and at the end of which comes his last piano concerto. His financial situation had not been improved by his absence from Vienna. In the fall of 1787 he had succeeded Gluck as court composer, but the re-muneration was slender and the duties uninteresting. He had merely to provide dances for the court balls and on a receipt for his salary he wrote: "Too much for what I do, too little for what I would like to do!" His wife's health was bad and cures at Baden, near Vienna, added to the household's expenses.

A second journey in the autumn of the next year was no more remunerative than the Berlin one had been. Early in 1790, Leopold II had succeeded his brother Joseph on the Imperial throne and he went to Frankfurt to be crowned in October of the same year. He took with him a suite which included some fifteen musicians, Salieri, his Kapellmeister, being among them, but Mozart was left behind. The composer determined thereupon to go to Frankfurt at his own expense and set out with his brother-in-law, the fiddler Joseph Hofer. They were absent six weeks and Mozart visited not only Frankfurt but also Munich and Mannheim. He gave only one concert in the

Imperial capital; the programme consisted entirely of his own works and he appears to have played the concertos in F, K.459, and D, K.537; the latter owes its name of Coronation Concerto to this performance. He met old friends in both places, the Wendlings at Frankfurt, the Ramms and Cannabichs at Munich, renewing acquaintances which went back to the great journey he had made to Mannheim and Paris thirteen years earlier. His letters give proof of the joy he felt in coming again into touch with these witnesses of a bygone period, yet such an experience must have brought home more vividly and more sorrowfully to him the difference between past and present. The man of thirty-four, undermined by cares, beginning to suffer in body and spirit from the privations and disappointments of recent years, must have compared himself with bitterness with the stripling of twenty-one, sallying forth from Salzburg full of hope, on the threshold of his independent life.

This journey was as unsuccessful as the Prussian one. However, on his way back, the Elector of Bavaria asked him to take part in the concert given in honour of the King of Naples, and the musician triumphed at this, for the king had recently passed through Vienna without Mozart having been asked to play before him. "A great honour," he wrote to his wife, "for the Vienna court, that the king should have to go to foreign parts to hear me!"

His material poverty ended by telling on the very nature of his work. We find no more the fullness and spaciousness of the compositions of 1787 and 1788 and his inspiration reflects the cares which oppress him. It is not inferior to that of earlier years, but joy, strength and passion no longer preponderate in it.

If we omit *Cosi fan tutte*, which perforce reveals his mood less than purely instrumental works, the important compositions of these two years are six in number. Soon after returning from Berlin, he set about fulfilling the orders he had received; he composed his last sonata, in D, K.576, the only one of the series for the Princess Frederika which was ever written and which is far from being "easy",[1] and the first of the quartets for the king her father, also in D, K.575. At the end of the summer, his friendship with Stadler called forth the quintet for clarinet and strings; then, in the following spring, after the months devoted to *Cosi fan tutte*, he completed two more quartets, the last he was ever to write, in B flat and F, K.589 and 590. Finally, after

---

[1] The writing in its finale recalls that of the finale of K.503.

more than six months' silence, an order from an Hungarian music lover made him return to the string quintet with the work in D, K.593. This year, 1790, is the most barren in his life.

Through these six works runs a somewhat diverse but characteristic inspiration, proving how thoroughly the master's genius had been affected by the wretched conditions of his existence. We can distinguish in it three elements which sometimes alternate in a single work but never mingle in the same movement.

Of the three, we will put first that which lies closest to the circumstances of his life. It is a spirit of weariness and exhaustion, instinct with a melancholy resignation which saddens us when we remember the superb self-assurance of earlier times. It predominates in the allegros of the B flat sonata, K.570, and the D major and B flat quartets, and in the larghettos which open and close the first movement of the D major quintet. The word "wilting" is hardly too strong to characterize the spirit of the allegro and especially of the larghetto of the B flat quartet ; in the latter movement, the long winding semi-quavers unfold like bands of mourning crape.

The sonata in D, the quartet in F and the allegro of the first movement of the quintet in D reveal another strain of his inspiration, seen most clearly in the quartet. This work has a whimsical character which has put off certain commentators but was well grasped by Abert. It is a sport of the intellect, almost a witticism, in that key of F which is Mozart's joking key. No deep feeling should be sought in it,[1] not even that of discouragement; Mozart has solved the problem set him by the clash between his ideal and reality by turning his back on it. As a result, this quartet leaves an impression of renunciation and detachment, evident also in the preponderance of rhythm over tune in its minuet and in the skeletal outline of the themes in the first movements of sonata and quintet. We think of certain movements in Beethoven's last manner which also seem to be pure sports of the intellect.

These two strains exclude each other and the second may be a defence against the painfulness of the first. The third, on the contrary, combines with melancholy and renunciation. We cannot depict it better than by calling it a thirst, a yearning for beauty. Yearning, indeed, a part of Mozart's music always has been, but the longing of 1789 and 1790 fills whole movements with a more poignant aspiration than anything heard hitherto. It is the "wilting" mood raised

---

[1] We refer, of course, to the allegro, not to the meditative andante.

to a positive plane, and the movements infused by it leave us deeply satisfied. The loveliest of them and at the same time one of the loveliest in all Mozart is the allegro of the clarinet quintet. Here, the longing has been allayed by utterance and the movement bears the mark of triumphant serenity. Nevertheless, the sorrowful feeling at the heart of it is still recognizable, and makes this music, however serene, different from the equally tranquil music of the following year. The andante of the quartet in D belongs to the same climate.

These three strains do not exhaust the emotional content of this group of works. The quartets, languishing or dry in their first movements, awaken in their finales with a nervous, energetic life, prone to find an outlet in counterpoint. The minuets of the B flat and the F and the finales of all three[1] have a breadth and diversity which take us back to the happy days of the "great" concertos; the minuets in particular are as unique in their way as those of the quintets of 1787. This contrapuntal inspiration is present also in the little jig for piano, K.574,[2] a masterpiece of condensation, in the finale of the D major quintet and the allegro of the first organ fantasia, K.594.

Finally, twice over, right at the end of 1790, the yearning grows deeper and evolves into a more contemplative mood, producing two surprisingly introspective adagios: those of the quintet in D and of the first organ fantasia. In the first, the minor episodes, with their threatening repeated triplets, are like a return of the "voices" of earlier times and seem to arise from a conflict, but the serene gravity of the rest calls up rather the andantes and adagios of Beethoven's third manner, which this penultimate year of Mozart's life recalls, therefore, in more ways than one. In the adagio of the fantasia K.594, with its rasping chromaticisms, anguish and serenity are blended as never hitherto, as if Mozart were reaping the harvest of his suffering. And, if it be not fanciful to seek the presence of kindred inspirations in artists separated in time, we would say that through the andante variations of the other fantasia, K.608, there passes a breath of César Franck—the Franck of the larghetto of the string quartet.

Weariness, resignation, detachment, yearning, vigour, introspection: all these are found in the moods of these strange works, whose beauty is somewhat forbidding and un-Mozartish in the ordinary sense. Of this group, the concerto in B flat is one of the last representatives.

.   .   .   .   .   .

---

[1] The monothematic nature of the finales of K.589 and 590 and of the first and last movements of K.614 is another aspect of this spirit of renunciation.

[2] Written probably as a pastiche of Bach after Mozart's visit to Doles.

It is because some of these streams flow through his last concerto that we have dwelt so long on the compositions that precede it. This concerto is the finest and fullest of those works to which we applied the perhaps unjust term "wilting". Its form is simple; it shows neither the complexity nor the curious details of its great predecessors, but its inspiration is unique among its kind.

Its immediate foregoer was the most showy and superficial of the series, whilst it, on the other hand, is the most reserved. The intimate nature of its feeling makes almost chamber music of it and renders it unsuitable for performance in a large concert hall; its proper environment is a circle of lovers of music . . . and of Mozart, gathered in the house of one of them. We do not know for what occasion it was written. It is generally agreed that Mozart composed it for his own use, but there is no proof of this and the existence of cadenzas and its introspective character would lead us to think that it had been produced for a pupil.[1] If Mozart had had to play it himself, it seems to us that he would have written a more brilliant work, like the concertos composed for his own use in 1784, 1785 and 1786, and the Coronation.[2] But all this is supposition.

The resignation and nostalgia which infuse the works of these two years are present in all three movements, even in the 6-8 rondo. It spreads not only a veil of sadness over the whole concerto; it also casts on it at times as it were an evening light, announcing the end of a life; the larghetto in particular has the quality of a farewell. Needless to say, we do not look upon this as a forewarning of Mozart's own death; even if he had not been destined to pass away eleven months later, his mood at the close of 1790 would have inspired him with these strains; moreover, most of his works written after this concerto and therefore nearer his death have not this character; nothing, for instance, is further from it than the E flat quintet. This resignation is not present all the time; now and again, his soul remembers its rebelliousness of former years and more passionate notes are sounded, but they do not last and weariness soon reigns supreme again, and is responsible for the noteworthy drops into the minor mode that occur in the allegro and rondo.

I. The allegro begins with a bar of accompaniment—an apparently

---

[1] It will be remembered that the most intimate concertos of 1784 were those he wrote for others.

[2] It is true that he played it himself at the concert given by the clarinettist Beer, but that was two months later, on March 4th.

insignificant detail; but the fact is that, with the allegro of the G minor symphony, this is the only movement of Mozart's that starts thus. It is as if the composer had wished to prepare the ground and induce in his hearers a placid mood before bringing in his first subject.

This latter, as in most classical concertos, expresses the sentiment that predominates in the movement. It unfolds in three strains of unequal length separated by two interruptions of one bar each. The ease and freedom of its rhythm make it one of the most personal and expressive of all Mozart's concerto openings. The three strains, given out by the strings, with their rise and fall, betray the resignation born of weariness which fills the whole movement. Under their heavy yet supple line, the accompaniment keeps up a rocking motion. Twice over, the wind break into the progress of the theme with a warlike unison call; on its third appearance, the call is taken up by the strings and extends into a run which reproduces a figure from the finale of the Jupiter (ex. 391).

Then strings and wind separate again and discuss a motif whose charm lies in its contrast of tone (ex. 392). It leads to a formal close on the dominant and three soft bars usher in the second subject. This expresses much the same feeling as ex. 391, but the way it hovers between major and minor when it is repeated makes it more tearful. It recalls the beautiful demi-semi-quaver passages in the andante of the G minor quartet and, nearer to us, certain bars in the larghetto of the B flat quartet, K.589; but here the motion gives a little more vitality to the long trailing scales (ex. 393).[1]

A very simple decorative figure, based on an ascending scale, which is to return unchanged in the piano, follows the second subject; it rises from *pp* to *forte*. Its semi-quavers introduce some excitement, but we soon fall back to the mood of the beginning with a sudden drop into the minor, all the more unexpected as it links on to a little, innocent-looking cadential figure, ex. 394, on which the tutti exposition appears to be about to close. This excursion into the minor is but momentary; when it is over, the strings expound a long, winding tune on which falls the slanting light of evening; both in outline and feeling it is akin to ex. 391. Then comes the usual noisy close and on it, no doubt, the tutti of a normal concerto would end. But this one adds a very Mozartish wistful phrase which reminds us of the end of the andante in the E flat serenade, K.375.

---

[1] This figure occurs also in the allegro of the B flat symphony, K.319, but in 3-4 time and with a different accompaniment and context.

The twilight atmosphere in which this beginning is veiled takes us far from the concertos of 1784-6, whilst its construction goes back to an earlier stage than they. It is true that its mood is as homogeneous and as sustained as in the most single-minded concertos of that period, but its form is more strophic, more articulated, and its progress is broken by closes. In spite of the personal nature of the feeling, this gives it an archaic appearance beside its predecessors; a cursory glance might lead one to think it earlier than they.

The first solo confirms the hints of the tutti: Mozart is no longer interested in structural problems as in the days when the concerto was his principal means of expression. The solo exposition does not rejuvenate that of the tutti; it follows the same lines and is content with introducing an important piano passage between the first and second subjects, and with modifying and shortening the end to join it on to the *development*. No doubt some earlier concertos had not been more enterprising, but in 1784 to 1786 they were exceptions.

The piano entry has nothing of the dramatic character of more passionate works; it does not in any way disturb the mood. The solo instrument gives out the first subject with a few discreet additions of scales and gruppetti; in the "calls", the strings replace the wind. The subject completed, we hear the *Jupiter* figure sounded by the whole orchestra. The piano repeats it and at once adds a bravura passage—a very simple one, only a few bars long; the orchestra then intervenes with the formal close which had preceded the second subject in the tutti.

The piano advances alone with a touching strain in F minor, more dramatic than what has gone before, where the trailing scales again appear (ex. 395); it becomes almost poignant when the piano rises high into the treble and reiterates thrice a pathetic phrase against which the flute[1] and later the hautboy outline a restrained but expressive counterpoint (ex. 396). Never had Mozart's moderation and reserve betrayed so heart-rending an emotion.

After another formal close in the tutti, asserting for an instant the key of F minor, the emotion gradually quietens down in a characteristic passage. Elsewhere, such a passage would be virtuosity, but here the technique is so simple and the feeling so intimate that the term is out of place. A single hand in the piano, now the right, now the left, sketches delicate filigree patterns beneath which we discern

---

[1] Surely one of the most poignant strains in all flute music! Flautists, play it out!

at first the design of the beginning of ex. 395, and then the rising
and falling line which is the movement's signature. Now the fiddles,
now the violas and 'cello accompany pizzicato, picking out the line
of which the piano part is a decoration; the tone of the combination
is very personal in its wistful haziness.

F major ousts F minor and the last piano filigree loses itself in
ex. 392, given out in dialogue by piano and wind. We now follow
the tracks of the first tutti but in F major. The second subject, ex.
393, is expounded by the strings; in the modulating section the piano
doubles the first violins with broken octaves and completes the
theme. Devoid of all personal ambition, it does not undertake a
bravura passage as in nearly all the other concertos; it confines itself
to reproducing the unpretentious decorative passage which the
strings had given out in the tutti; alone at first, it is escorted by the
wind and then by the strings when it reiterates the section; the last
part is livelier and leads to a dramatic interruption to which the pianist
should give emphasis by animating and quickening slightly the bars
that precede the break. One bar's silence follows; then the wind
give out a figure in semibreves twice repeated. To their harsh,
hollow voices the piano adds a series of G's, the last of which is held
for nearly two bars and is followed by a B natural two octaves higher
up; the soloist should trill the first of them and fill up the interval with
a scale in the second;[1] played as it is written, the passage is meaningless (ex. 397). In these bars the movement as it were holds its breath
and we welcome like a deliverance the few very simple runs which
lead us to the customary trill.

As the *development* draws near, Mozart takes interest again in the
concerto form. Instead of repeating the conclusion of the tutti
and starting the *development* after its last notes, as in the Coronation
concerto (where his interest in form was no greater and its absence
was not compensated by a personal inspiration), he brings in his
orchestra with a new passage. Commonplace to begin with, it soon
makes for ex. 394, the figure which, in the tutti, with its innocent air,
had called forth the surprise modulation into B flat minor. Its
nature is to behave unexpectedly and now, cut down to its first notes
and starting from F major, it modulates swiftly and puts us down at
the gates of B minor, which the piano unlocks (ex. 398).

The *development* is not only the most noteworthy part of the movement; it is also one of the three or four most masterly developments

---

[1] Or fill up both bars with a chromatic scale, as in the Steingräber edition.

in all Mozart's concertos.   This is saying a lot, especially of a work so
unambitious and unrenowned.   Before accusing us of exaggeration,
let the reader cast a glance with us at the score.

The orchestra is silent and the piano unfolds ex. 391 in B minor.
Thus transposed, this theme, once so resigned, becomes elegiac.
The unison call, thrown out by the strings, points to E minor, but a
bar of modulation in hautboys and bassoons ushers in C major
where the piano repeats its exposition.   This time the call is in the
same key the first time, but drops at once into C minor, and when
the piano repeats it after the strings, it does so in E flat.   It has not
finished when the hautboy steals its theme from it, reduced to the
first two bars and modified (ex. 399), and the bassoon replies.   This
hints at what is coming.

The piano regains the upper hand and gives out ex. 399 in E flat
minor.   After these searchings, this is the beginning of the *development* proper.   For a little more than thirty bars, wind and strings
keep up a conversation on the subject of this fragment and the unison
call of ex. 391, modulating constantly but generally in the minor,
whilst the piano is almost always excluded from taking part in the
discourse and wreathes round the orchestral parts an unbroken line
of arabesques, now close to the line of the melody, now far from it
(ex. 400).   Save for one moment, the instruments remain to the fore,
but their number is never great enough to veil the slender piano
filigree.   The solo technique is as simple and transparent as elsewhere;
there is no trace of the mass effects and two-handed passages of the
last two C major concertos; the piano style has become as archaic
as the structure and the novelty of the emotion and of the collaboration is all the more obvious.

These thirty bars are among the most interesting in all the concertos.   The dialogue which unfolds, at first between the woodwind,
then between the violins, on the score of ex. 399, is in counterpoint
and takes the shape of two-part imitation.   The unison call stands
out now against the piano's broken chords and loses its combative-
ness; it is shared impartially between wind and strings.   When it is
the violins' turn to lead the game, they alter ex. 391 a second time
and give it out in a canon at the fifth (ex. 401).

We said that the music modulated unceasingly.   Without ever
stopping for more than two bars in the same key it travels through
E flat minor, F sharp minor, A flat, F minor, G minor, C minor, F
minor, B flat, E flat (ex. 400), F minor, C minor and G minor.   Here
the piano breathes awhile and gives out a third alteration of the first

subject (ex. 402), accompanied by a single held note in the bassoon. Once again the emotion is sorrowful and it reaches for a moment an acute pitch in what is the climax of the movement. The reprise is negotiated via D minor and a series of imitations between hautboys and bassoons; the piano's arpeggios unroll in triplets over a space of two octaves (ex. 403); we drop gently back to B flat major, and the first subject, which had never really left us, is again in our midst.[1]

There is no need to insist on the originality of this passage. There had been other thematic *developments* in Mozart's concertos,[2] and very grand ones, but in none of them did the orchestra keep up a continuous discourse over which the piano glided carelessly with independent passages. Its closest predecessor would be in K.503, but the sequences on which this latter was founded do not occur here; the music keeps an elasticity which does not tolerate any regular form. It is true that it seems to advance mainly in canon, but, except in ex. 401, none of these canons is regular and ex. 391, which makes up nearly all the substance of the discourse, is really modified several times, so that we feel a slight relief when we meet it in its original state at the reprise.

This movement is one of those which do not seek to vary their recapitulations. We may deplore it, but we must recognize that no work could be further than this one from the world of catastrophes. Nothing is more static than its climate. The variations in its emotional pitch are slight; it recalls in this its B flat predecessor of 1784, K.456. We do not deny that a renewal of the last part enriches any concerto allegro, whatever its substance, but it is certain that dramatic movements require it most urgently. Here, the tenor is so even that only on analysis does one perceive the identity of the two expositions, and no monotony is felt on that account. Moreover, after so original a *development* it would be ungracious to complain.

The first important change in the recapitulation occurs after the reappearance of ex. 397 (now in B flat). After the piano trill, the orchestra continues with ex. 394; the piano completes it, then reinserts the C minor parenthesis which had vanished from the first solo and

---

[1] We would urge conductors to make their violins, flute, hautboys and bassoons play out all through this development. It is absolutely necessary, not only that they should be heard, but that one should feel them to be what matters most and the piano to be but subordinate. For lack of this, the passage loses most of its point. The weakness of the H.M.V. recording lies in that one has to have the score in hand to hear the orchestral parts.

[2] K.271, 466, 491, 503.

the winding theme with its evening light.[1] Then comes the cadence which followed this passage in the first tutti, and the cadenza. This return of material which had not been heard since the first tutti just before the cadenza is another archaic device which Mozart had scarcely ever used in his "great" concertos.[2]

The movement closes with the cadence of the solo exposition and the last bars of the opening tutti which let it die, *piano*, on the note of depression and renunciation on which it had begun.

We have referred to the simple technique of this movement. We would go further and say that virtuosity is almost entirely absent. No other concerto is so devoid of it, not even the A major of 1786, to such an extent that Mozart appears to renounce his very conception of the genre and bring his piano down to the level of an orchestral instrument. Not a breath of opposition separates the protagonists; on the other hand, the closest unity reigns between them. In other concertos, too, it is true, K.451 and K.466, piano and orchestra collaborated to the same end, but the solo's intervention always increased the intensity of the emotion and modified the affective tone of the movement. There is nothing like this here. The piano's entry alters in nowise the intensity of the gentle melancholy of which this allegro is the expression. All that belongs exclusively to the solo is the theme exs. 395 and 396, and the eight bars that follow it, with their pizzicato accompaniment. At the end of the first exposition and of the movement, when one expects the concluding solo which was not missing in any other concerto, it repeats an orchestral passage. In the *development*, finally, it finds a new function for itself which brings this concerto still nearer to the "symphony with piano" and looks forward, not to Beethoven's concertos, as Abert says, for in them no such *development* occurs, but to those of Liszt and Brahms. This concerto, so simple in plan and at times so archaic, opens surprising views towards the future.

Its chief interest, however, is in its inspiration. Before all, it is a *Tondichtung*, where the nature of the emotion is more important than the relations between protagonists. Its sorrow does not break forth with the rebellious passion of the D minor nor collapse with the despair of the G minor quintet or the adagio in B minor, K.540; no less deep than formerly, it is more reserved and more dreamy; it is so strongly tempered by the spirit of resignation that one might

---

[1] A single bassoon acts as a funeral escort to it.

[2] We have already mentioned that Mozart has left cadenzas for this concerto.

take it at times for mere tearfulness. But its classical restraint hides a sorrow as sincere as that of more vehement music. And above all, this sentiment, which might have been so selfish, is fragrant with that spirit of kindness and love breathed by so much of Mozart's art and for the utterance of which B flat is his favourite key. As we listen to this allegro where there is so little *allegrezza* and which we quit, nevertheless, with a light heart, we are reminded of what one of his forgotten contemporaries wrote of his work, as he heard it in his exile:

> "This music, so harmonious and so lofty in inspiration, so pure, both soft and sorrowful . . . made me forget as I listened to it my past woes and those that the future held perhaps in store for me . . ."[1]

II.   The E flat larghetto[2] dwells in the same mood as the first movement. The emotion is no more intense; on the contrary, the few passionate strains heard in the allegro have no counterpart here; the music keeps within the limits of an elegy and the light that illumines it is constantly that of the evening. We insist on this feature, for it gives this concerto, so unambitious in size, its unique place in the series of the twenty-three; in this, too, the work belongs to its period and represents a stage in its author's life.

The refrain which opens the larghetto, a kind of romance, is like a farewell. It sings of an irrevocable parting. When a musician has not spoken it is always rash to attribute a precise meaning to any passage in his work; we naturally do not assert that Mozart felt himself, as he composed this refrain, in the mood which accompanies a painful separation; yet the likeness in melody and harmony between this theme and the beginning of Beethoven's *Farewell* sonata may allow us to think that our impression is not wholly unfounded.

The piano gives it out alone (ex. 404); the tutti repeat it, harmonizing it richly and alternating *fortes* and *pianos*. Between its version and that of the solo there is a trifling difference which persists throughout the movement. Whereas the ascending motif in

---

[1] Abbe Martinant de Préneuf, 1797; quoted by Baldensperger: *La sensibilité musicale et le romantisme*, p. 44.

[2] Mozart, towards the end of his life, was fond of this mark which was uncommon before 1786 (but see K.413, 447 and 452); in 1786, cf. K.491, 493, 502; in 1788, K.537; in 1789, K.581; in 1790, K.589 and 593; in 1791, this concerto—the Breitkopf edition for piano solo—has andante by mistake. In the H.M.V. recording the soloist has made the worst possible mistake by taking this larghetto as if it were an adagio molto; the movement is completely deformed thereby.

the second bar is in semi-quavers in the piano, it is in demi-semi-quavers in the orchestra. The second part of the refrain belongs to the piano only and is clearly but a sketch. The outline returns four times in all; it is permissible to give it out as it is the first time, but on the three other appearances it must be decorated; the decoration should of course be in keeping with the spirit of the movement.[1] This larghetto has no cadenza and it is within the limits of these few bars that the soloist's extemporizing talent should be displayed.

The piano repeats the first part; as it finishes, the horns sound reiterated B flats, a tonic pedal with which the coda begins. Climbing up the degrees of the chord of the seventh and passing from *piano* to *forte*, the melody rises with some power and eventually comes to rest on the tonic. A trilling figure in the second violins animates pleasantly its ascent. Then, over a wavy motif in the seconds, the firsts outline the fragments of a new theme; on its repetition, the violas join the seconds and the woodwind add held notes (ex. 406). A third figure, a succession of winged sighs in violins and flute (ex. 407), leads the refrain to its conclusion.

The only couplet in this rondo consists in a piano cantilena sustained by a somewhat varied tutti accompaniment. It decomposes into a series of short phrases, each one of which is repeated, usually with slight changes in the tune or the scoring. This part modulates less than certain *developments* of Mozart's; we start from the tonic and pass into B flat and G flat, where we remain for eight bars. The last part unfolds in the minor and the end brings us back to the tonic.

For the first half, the accompaniment consists in repeated notes; when we reach G flat these give way to a marching bass that punctuates each beat with a quaver; the space between the basses and the piano (both hands of which play in the treble clef) is filled by a held note in the first bassoon, a sober but expressive detail of scoring (ex. 408). Towards the end the first violin part becomes so important melodically that it predominates over the piano; we hear an undulating theme whose chromaticisms recall the andante of the D major concerto, K.451; the piano imitates it freely a third above (ex. 409). The weary, "wilting" mood is obvious here. We make our way back to the refrain with a poetic phrase, thrice repeated, ascending in semi-tones from B flat to the tonic; the piano enlivens it with trills.

The first two parts of the refrain are restated almost unaltered, but in the last appearance of ex. 404 the piano's right hand is doubled

---

[1] In ex. 405 we suggest a realization of this passage.

by the flute and first fiddles. Each instrument sticks to its own version of the little figure we have mentioned, which provokes a piquant
contrast in the rhythm. Moreover, as fiddles and flute are playing,
the latter in unison with the piano, the others an octave lower,
sensitive ears will perceive here a succession of octaves and fifths!
But the chief interest of the passage lies in the tone which is the
product of this collaboration of percussion, wind and strings—an
unusual mixture which gives a weird, hollow sound, very un-
Mozartish, caused not only by the blending of the timbres but also
by the lack of bass, since the violins play below the piano's left hand.[1]
We have here a further instance of the renewal, in Mozart the composer of concertos, of the innovating, adventurous spirit which was
lacking in the Coronation concerto.[2]

The coda returns without much change in the melody and harmonization, but the presence of the piano brings about one of those
re-scorings we meet in certain allegro recapitulations[3] which afford
Mozart an opportunity for displaying much ingenuity. In ex. 406,
the line of the seconds and violas is doubled and distributed between
the two hands of the piano; the tune falls to the hautboys; the bassoons
receive a new part and the flute sketches a counter-subject, also new,
whilst the strings are out of the picture. Their substitution by the
wind, in collaboration with the piano, is quite in order, since the
more distinctive wind instruments are the essentially concertante
members of the band.

Finally, after a four-bar insertion for the benefit of the solo, ex.
407 shows us how piano and wind rejuvenate the original part with
two new lines. In these last five bars the flute and first violins seem,
gracefully but firmly, to be leading the piano off the stage.

III. The refrain of the finale takes us back to the "hunts" of former
times[4] by its form, but its spirit is no longer the same as theirs. It
certainly sings of joy, but not the carefree joy of the Salzburg days,
nor the sturdy love of life and success which filled the Viennese

---

[1] A somewhat similar effect occurs in the opening bars of Vaughan
Williams's *Flos Campi*, where flute and first viola play in octaves.

[2] In the finale of K.450 (bars 82–6 and 262–6), flute, piano and violins
also combine in giving out a theme, but the effect is less weird because the
left hand of the piano and the rest of the orchestra accompany them.

[3] Among others, K.482 and 491.

[4] K.450, 456, 482.

Ex. 413

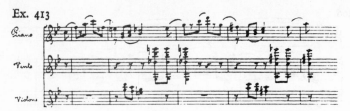

Ex. 414

Ex. 415

Ex. 416

Ex. 417

concertos of the three "great" years. Its joy is more ethereal; it is a foretaste of the disembodied bliss of the E flat quintet.

It begins like a Lied written a few days later:[1] "Komm, lieber Mai, und mache die Baüme wieder grün" (Come, sweet May, and make the trees green again), and it is significant that the title of this Lied contains the word "Sehnsucht". Yearning: this has been one of the chief sentiments in Mozart's music for the last two years, and, in spite of the freshness of its refrain, it inspires parts of this rondo.

The piano gives out the first stanza (ex. 410) and the orchestra repeats it. If the opening reproduces a Lied, the fragment (a) recalls an aria: "E l'amore un ladroncello", from *Cosi fan tutte* (at the words: "Come gli piace al cor," after the pause); the whole refrain is indeed very close to this air both in feeling and form. This fragment is the only chromatic part in a diatonic tune and later on it turns out to be an important element of the movement. The piano gives out the second stanza (ex. 411) and returns to the first, to which the tutti add a conclusion incorporating a reminder of (a) and ending with the habitual clamorous close.

As usual the first couplet is opened by the piano; it starts with a familiar Mozartian figure (ex. 412)[2] and leads to a dominant close. Another concerto would at once admit us into F major where we are in any case destined to arrive some day; this one, in its rondo as in its first movement, takes us along the byways of several minor keys. Using for this purpose a fragment of the refrain, modified, ex. 413, the piano flits from F major to F minor and G minor, urged on by light repeated woodwind chords which continue even when the piano part has spread out into arpeggios and broken scales whose ripples detain us for awhile in the realms of G minor. At length, via F minor and D flat major, we enter F major through its dominant, C, and even so the bit of the refrain which brings in this key hovers between major and minor with a see-saw motion typical of this concerto (ex. 414). A short imitative dialogue between piano and flute precedes the main theme of the couplet, brother to the refrain, equally light-footed and quite as ignorant of the lower registers of the piano. The butterfly flittings of its second bar, one of the last appearances of Mozart's beloved "fluttering seconds", occur several times, in diverse

---

[1] "Sehnsucht nach dem Frühlinge" (Yearning after spring), itself based on a folk-song. Cf. Köchel-Einstein, no 596. This indicates the speed of the rondo which should not be played faster than the voice can sing the song.

[2] See the finales of the Linz symphony, K.425, the horn concerto K.447 and the clarinet concerto.

shapes, in the course of the movement. The wind restate it and the piano accompanies with delicate gestures (ex. 415). An arpeggio passage, an ascending scale on a tonic pedal, leads to a pause where the soloist is expected to improvise a short cadenza; it is followed by the return of the refrain.

The first part only is repeated, first by the solo, then by the tutti, but when we reach fragment (a) (ex. 410), it breaks off; hautboys, bassoons and horns continue alone and, repeating the fragment softly, echo shyly what went before. It is as if the whole orchestra discovered suddenly that it had committed a blunder and stopped, horror-struck, still muttering unconsciously the unfortunate words it had just spoken.

The piano is braver; nevertheless, it is in the minor that it repeats the figure upon which all had stopped, and the executant will do well to introduce a momentary hesitancy into his playing.[1] Then, the solo becomes bolder and finally launches forth into a run. The *development* couplet begins in B flat minor and its starting-point is the fragment (a) of the refrain. This heralds a thematic *development*, and indeed the first part of the refrain is present, in one shape or another, almost all the time.

A bravura passage follows (a); urged on by a restless, wandering impulse, the solo explores the various zones of the upper register with a bold, sweeping flight, brushing past several keys without settling in any. The orchestra at first lets it play alone; then, as if to fix its thoughts, the fiddles recall softly the beginning of the refrain; flute and hautboy likewise (ex. 416). Beneath the solo arpeggios which have replaced the undulations and climb rapidly up and down the two registers of the keyboard, a conversation in an undertone between violins and woodwind keeps the first notes of the refrain[2] constantly before us; this dialogue, which begins in F minor, carried away by the piano's modulations, starts each time in a fresh key: C minor, G minor, D minor, stopping without closing, together with the piano runs, on a chord of the seventh whose resolution is delayed by a pause, then by three questioning chords sounded by the representatives of the orchestra. The piano breaks in roughly upon our expectancy; the harmonies pivot on their bass in an enharmonic modulation and we come out into the clear daylight of E flat major (ex. 417).

---

[1] The Steingräber edition rightly marks: quasi cadenza.

[2] And which reminds us of the dialogue between 'cello and violin at the same point in the finale of the string trio in E flat, K.563.

In this key the refrain makes its third appearance. This return to the first subject or its equivalent in the key of the subdominant is an archaism uncommon in Mozart; an earlier example is found in the allegro of the little sonata in C, K.545. It is not only the key which is irregular here, but also the very form of this return. At the end of the sixth bar (end of [a]), the piano breaks off suddenly, as the orchestra had done earlier, and delegates its authority to the wind who continue, but in the minor. Thereupon opens a little development in the course of which we work up a scale fragment and at each step piano and fiddles recall (a), which clearly has become the chief figure in the movement. Thus, we pass by D flat minor and E flat minor and reach the tonic after a sojourn in the key of the dominant where we again notice the hesitation between major and minor so characteristic of these years (cf. ex. 414). All this passage may be looked on as a continuation of the *development* couplet as well as a new version of the refrain; we have here a cross between the regular sonata rondo where the refrain recurs between the second and third couplets and the other kind where it is omitted;[1] at the end of his life, Mozart rejuvenates once again this rondo form which is the realm of musical architecture where he experimented most freely.[2]

The third couplet begins with ex. 412; when it has been given out piano and woodwind discuss ex. 413 with the usual transpositions. The violins join in wittily. (We quoted their answers in ex. 413; these should now be read a fifth lower.) As in the first couplet, the minor extends nearly to ex. 415. After this latter subject and the short passage which prolongs it, a few tutti bars usher in the cadenza, the last of the collection left by Mozart and one of his prettiest.

The piano restates the whole of the refrain and the tutti add their ritornello. We then enter the coda, consisting in a bravura passage very brilliant for this work and in one last echo of the beginning of the refrain, thrown from fiddles to wind, with piano arpeggios, as in ex. 416. The last bars cast off all morbidity and resound with a joyful unison fanfare in the orchestra, based on the first bar of the movement.

There is not quite the same unity of feeling in this rondo as in the first movement. The inspiration of the refrain corresponds only

---

[1] See also the rondos of the G minor quartet and the clarinet concerto where the refrain is left out but where nevertheless we hear a hint of it before the beginning of the third couplet.

[2] This part of the finale is treated in a similar manner in the adagio and rondo for flute, hautboy, viola, 'cello and harmonica, K.617, composed a few months later.

partly to that of the rest. If we knew nothing more of the finale, we would think it sang of joy—the joy we sought to define a few pages back. The two other themes, exs. 412 and 415, would confirm us in this idea, and so would the witty flute and piano dialogue and the virtuosity passage that precedes and follows it, and the coda. But other passages express a different mood: the minor digressions which separate the two main subjects exs. 413 and 414, the short working-out of ex. 410 which follows the refrain's return in E flat and, above all, the middle couplet which begins with the dramatic interruption of the refrain and unfolds entirely in the minor. On the whole, if the refrain and the two bright spots, exs. 412 and 415, sing of happy thoughts, four times over the music turns from joy and, leaving sunlit avenues, passes into the shade of doubt. At such moments we encounter something like the sadness experienced in the allegro and larghetto. And even in the brighter bars of the refrain, those which, with the opening, attract Mozart's attention most are just the only ones where chromaticism enters, the fragments (a) which we have heard him work out several times. The note of weariness, however, is absent; at no stage does the rondo belie the vigour of its beginning and as a result its minor passages are more dramatic than those of the first movement.

The constant reappearance of fragments of the refrain (exs. 413, 414, 416) and the fact that the whole *development* couplet, except in the bravura bars, is built on its first notes and fragment (a) gives this rondo a thematic unity uncommon, if not unique, in the finales of these concertos.[1] It is akin in this respect, not to its predecessors in the same genre, but to contemporary chamber works, to the two last quartets and especially the E flat quintet, the most unified of all Mozart's compositions.

The piano style is more brilliant than in the allegro; in the coda virtuosity is for a moment an end in itself, but elsewhere it is always at the service of the emotion and is less prominent than in other concerto finales. The writing is constantly linear and never returns to the mass effects that Mozart renounced in his concertos after K.503. It is also very homogeneous. The runs, which are always short, belong to a small number of types, of which the principal are the wide spread arpeggio (exs. 415 and 416), the broken descending scale and, especially, the broad, wavy line; this latter, which is predominant, is typical of this rondo. The unimportance of the virtuosity and

---

[1] No, not unique, for we remember that of K.449.

its subordination to feeling, which is as noteworthy here as in the two other movements, separates the work from the other concertos and brings it nearer to the symphonies and chamber music.

Mozart has taken more interest in structural problems in this finale than in the other movements. Rondo form always stimulated most strongly his taste for innovations and the plan of this one is among his most distinctive. Piano and orchestra, moreover, collaborate more continuously than in the allegro. Ex. 415 is shared between them when it is repeated; there are many moments when both discuss a fragment of the refrain and when the tutti quicken the piano with an original accompaniment: for instance, the woodwind interruptions in ex. 413, the conversation between wind, strings and solo in ex. 416, the intervention of the wind and the violins in ex. 417. After the listless scoring of the D major concerto, it is consoling to rediscover here the Mozart of the great concertos, eleven months before his death. The discourse is constantly shared by both wind and strings, and the interest kept up by numberless details in the instrumental parts.[1] From whatever angle it is examined, except that of piano technique, this concerto, till recently so neglected, is in every point the equal of the finest and deserves fully to be added to the twelve great works of 1784-6 as one of its author's most personal compositions.

B flat is a favourite key with Mozart. In his mature period, besides the four piano concertos, he used it for two quartets, one trio, two piano sonatas, two violin sonatas, a wind serenade, a duet for violin and viola and a symphony—only one, and that not important. It is in the concerto, the sonata and chamber music that the mood he generally associates with this key should be sought. If we leave aside the three B flat works of 1789 and 1790, and especially if we bring in the ten or twelve slow movements in this key, we recognize that it expresses before all a state of serenity, as absolute a calm as Mozart's restless soul can experience. It calls up a benedictory spirit; applying to it what has been written of an andante of Beethoven, we would say that its mildness is like "grace falling on the soul of a saint". A typical B flat work of Mozart's leaves behind it a feeling of moral well-being the expression of which is accompanied by playfulness in the first movements and gaiety in the finales. We

---

[1] There is not room to say everything! Let us point out only the place where the wind, in the first enunciation of the refrain, give up their function as accompanists and join in the tune when fragment (a) is reached.

perceive it at its clearest in the concerto K.450, the Hunt quartet and the Strinasacchi sonata K.454, but it is as obvious in lesser compositions like the Paris sonata K.333 and the trio K.502. Mozart's most significant B flat andantes are those of the D minor concerto, the G minor quartet,[1] the F major duet sonata and the E flat string quintet; in the latter, the joy has that unearthly quality that permeates so large a part of the master's music in his last year. In 1789 and 1790, mildness persists, but serenity gives way for a while to weariness and disheartenment.

The B flat concerto comes at the end of a period in Mozart's musical development. We shall not meet again the inspiration which gives it life and which had predominated in him for the last two years, save perhaps in the andante of the second organ fantasia, K.608, completed in the following March. The years 1789 and 1790 spoke of sadness and renunciation; 1791, his last, on the other hand, witnesses the surging up in his music of a new growth of spring, the herald of a summer that was never to mature.

This growth is already apparent in the second of the two fantasias that he wrote, against his will, for the mechanical organ—"ein Orgelwerk in einer Uhr"—which a certain Müller, calling himself Count Deym, had set up in an exhibition of curiosities. We know nothing of this instrument but it must have been a sorry tinkle, for Mozart groaned: "Oh! if only it were a big clock, if the mechanism were to produce an organ tone, it would interest me; but the instrument is just a little reed and its tone is shrill and too childish for my liking." [2]

But he could not prevent his imagination hearing the instrument he would have liked and it is indeed for a cathedral organ that these fantasias were conceived. At distant intervals one hears them performed by organists; one would really prefer to hear them in an orchestral arrangement; several such exist but none has been published.

The first of these fantasias dates from the preceding autumn and is still tributary of the inspiration of that period; in the partly fugal allegro of the second, the strength and fullness of the quintets and great concertos are again apparent in the master's art. In the short but distinguished list of his polyphonic movements this allegro takes one of the highest places; in the humbler family of his variations the andante does likewise.

---

[1] Very typical, with its voluptuous and nostalgic figure of trailing scales.
[2] Letter to his wife, October 3rd, 1790.

But it is with the E flat string quintet that the spring proclaims itself fully.

This quintet, his last instrumental work,[1] is indeed a culmination. It is complete and self-sufficient. In it an ideal is attained, and whilst we do not claim that Mozart would have remained at this point if he had lived, we acknowledge a perfection in it which befits the closing act of a fruitful life. The spirit that inspires it and blossoms forth in it so sumptuously is the same which will inspire the "mystical" parts of the *Magic Flute*, that is, precisely the most original parts of that opera.[2] This quintet has been almost completely neglected by performers and even by critics; only in recent years has any appreciation worthy of it been written.[3] As our book is entitled, not: *Mozart's Piano Concertos*, but: *Mozart and His Piano Concertos*, we consider we have the right to dwell upon it at some length, even though we have got beyond the last of our composer's concertos.

The first impression it makes is one of a pure *jeu d'esprit*. Beethoven's last quartet makes the same impression. Both owe it to their detachment, to the fact that no breath of passion or even of emotion appears to touch them, except in the andantes; they are like intercourse between disembodied spirits. In the chronological study of Mozart's compositions we are tempted at first to class the E flat quintet with works of the last years like the quartet in F where we thought we recognized traces of spiritual dryness. And we do indeed feel that there is an evolutional link between them and it. Its mood does indeed grow out of theirs, but it is not the same. We might express the same idea by saying that the quartet in F had sought, but failed, to embody the ideal embodied by the quintet.

Its true spirit, despite its apparent simplicity, is even less easy to grasp at a glance than that of more normal Mozartian music. Its basic ideas are simple, even mean, if we compare them with other themes of its composers; neither the first subject of the allegro nor the refrain, which is really the only subject in all the finale, are distinctive tunes; one of them is not much more than a rhythmic figure, the other,

[1] With the little quintet K.617. The clarinet concerto, which figures as a completed work at a later date in Mozart's catalogue, had been composed in part earlier.

[2] We mean the Temple scenes; Papageno and the Queen of Night derive from other inspirations, already often met with in his work.

[3] Adolphe Boschot, Henry Ghéon, Eric Blom. The Pro Arte quartet recorded it before the war in America, but the recording has never been on sale in Britain.

almost a jingle. It is true that the way in which they are set forth
compensates to some extent for their poverty; this quintet is much
more a conversation than its predecessors and the substance is divided
equally between the different parts. A contrast in colour is thus
provided which strikes us in the very first bars where the shrill note
of the fiddles answers the husky tone of the violas. In no other
quartet or quintet of Mozart does anything similar exist.

It is none the less true that its thematic material is meagre. But
its spiritual abundance is in inverse proportion to its material poverty.
Its nudity and lack of passion are neither dessiccation nor hyper-
intellectuality; our first impression is rectified as we become more
familiar with it. It is the soaring flight of a strong personality rising
through sheer fortitude above daily cares and finding the appeasement, but not the forgetfulness, of its sorrow in itself and its art.
Serene, this quintet certainly is, but with the rich sereneness of a
spirit that has suffered and not the passiveness of a being apathetic
or incapable of strong feelings. It is the sanctuary into which
Tamino and Pamina enter after the trial by fire and water. As Boschot
expresses it, a "Franciscan blitheness" ("une allégresse franciscaine")
reigns in it; we hear "the song of a heart living beyond visible things
. . . an ethereal, luminous murmur, like the rustling of a grove full of
twittering birds conversing with the Poverello of Assisi".[1]

This is particularly true of the allegro and finale. The trio of the
minuet, a Viennese waltz, brings a more earthly joy. As for the
andante, in it lies a more physical feeling, grace, love, even a touch of
longing. If the allegro makes us think of Giotto's frescoes, the
andante is redolent with the spirit of Botticelli; it is haunted by the
three Graces from the *Primavera*, and the gruppetti which accompany
the refrain on its last appearance and persist to the end, call up the
flowers that flutter round the goddess in the *Birth of Venus*.

This quintet lives in the same climate as the *Magic Flute* but its
kinship with other E flat works is more distant. Very few features
recall the symphony of 1788. The finales of both works, it is true,
arise in part from the same vein and there is a formal likeness in the
"stiff" violin passages which occur in both. But the first movement of the symphony has more warmth and passion; its atmosphere
is less rarefied and its majestic introduction has no counterpart in the
quintet. There is more likeness in the contrast, in both andantes,
between the rather prim rhythms and the fullness of the emotion, and

----

[1] Ad. Boschot: *Chez les Musiciens* (2me série, pp. 22 and 38).

the minuets, both of them haughty with different shades of arrogance, both of them having waltzes for trios, recall one another.

Do we find more relationship between this quintet and its great predecessors, the "Heavenly Twins" of 1787? The two quintets of Mozart's last year are indeed less imposing than those in C and G minor. But they have none the less their own place which nothing else fills. His last quintet in particular is duplicated by no other work. The C major and G minor quintets affect and stir a larger surface of our being, but the corner which the E flat has marked as its own belongs to none other and it is a corner which Mozart alone has explored with success. The 1787 quintets belong to a much more numerous category of works; their ideal is in reality that of most of the great 19th century composers; their climate is nearer that of Beethoven or Brahms than that of the quintet of 1791. With the important reservation that every genius is unique, we would say that in the musical literature of the 19th century there are more compositions of the same character as the quintets in C and G minor than of that of the E flat. Some tastes may prefer the sumptuous, spacious beauty of the former, but there is no doubt that the beauty of the latter is more rare.

We therefore end with this quintet the journey we have undertaken through Mozart's work, a journey in which we chose his piano concertos as our chief landmarks. It is indeed his last instrumental composition. His catalogue, it is true, enters the clarinet concerto after a cantata the date of which is September 28th, but the conception and partial realization of its first movement, at any rate, go back several years, when Mozart had intended it for a bassett horn, so that it does not represent the inspiration of his last months.[1]

What of the *Requiem*? Does it not belong authentically, in its completed portions, to Mozart's last days? Certainly; but its history is so special, as much on account of the feeling imposed by the very words of the Mass for the Dead as of the disturbing circumstances in which it was ordered, that we must consider it as a parenthesis in his life. Fate ordained that the parenthesis should never be closed; it is the *Magic Flute* and not the *Requiem* which concludes the year and which explains and crowns the growth of Mozart's thought since 1787. And the *Magic Flute*, as we have said, in the most personal part of its content, mingles its waters with the stream which, a few months earlier, had flowed through the quintet in E flat.

---

[1] See Köchel-Einstein, nos. 584 b and 622.

Conclusion

THE increasing enthusiasm of our time for Mozart's concertos is far from being accompanied by performances which bring out all their beauty. In the course of many hearings, certain traps have come to appear to us as particularly dangerous and we would like to point them out at the risk of repeating what has been said elsewhere.

There are two common forms of bad Mozart playing. One consists in making him graceful, elegant and gentle; the other, lively and dashing.

These two kinds of style are not always out of place, but they are insufficient. There are indeed passages which should be rendered with elegance and grace and others which should be dashing, but none of Mozart's works demands a performance where both styles, or one of them, preponderate. To interpret him as he deserves other qualities than elegance and brio are needed.

As a matter of fact, the graceful, delicate style is seldom desirable and there are few torments for a keen Mozart lover equal to that of hearing a whole concerto played in this way. Some of his least arresting sonatas may be suited by it, but it should be excluded from his greater works. It has the power of belittling a piece and making a bauble of it; those who favour such a way of playing should therefore confine themselves to the few genuine baubles that he has left.

The dashing style is more often opportune. It is excellent, for instance, in certain concerto rondos, energetic, witty, superficial, eminently suited to a performance con brio. But it is as disastrous to be "smart" in his initial allegros as it is to be "graceful" in them. We have insisted on the witless sacrilege of turning into a *brillante* the *maestoso* with which he sometimes heads his opening movements.

By the light of sudden flashes we get glimpses of depths which open for a moment and close up again at once; the "dashing" performer leaps over them like a mountaineer over a crevasse, without looking into its glinting darkness, and a rich, manifold work becomes sparkling and commonplace.

One of the mannerisms of those who cultivate this style consists in giving rising scales a kind of push by putting down the loud pedal at the beginning and emphasizing the last note with a sforzando, thanks to which the scale goes off like the uncorking of a bottle. Mozart's line, treated thus, loses all breadth and serenity and the composer is turned into a species of anæmic Liszt. One longs for more of those linear, warm-hearted and sensitive performances which Gieseking and Wanda Landowska give us, where we feel the beautiful runs quiver, clean and full of life, under the pianist's fingers.

In reality, no single style is peculiar to Mozart. His music should be played as it is and the pianist should be like it, vigorous, graceful, delicate, merry, witty, sombre, sparkling, deep in turn, and always clear. Clarity is the one quality which is always in season. There is no special technique to adopt; it is the very sensibility of the composer that the executant must assimilate. Which is true of every great musician whose works we play! All this, then, boils down to saying that there is no peculiar Mozart style of playing; the advice given for the performance of any good music applies to his, and that is all!

We have already dwelt on the need for completing those bars which are merely sketched out. The 18th century soloist was a creator; he was associated with the composer and in concertos he had limited scope for extemporization. There is nothing like this in sonatas, for the sonata was not the preserve of the soloist; the amateur who played it was not a creator but a mere executant; he only reproduced the composer's thought and this thought was given him in its perfect state. But certain bars in sonatas give us useful hints how to complete sketchy passages in concertos. For instance, the andante of Mozart's C minor shows how the refrain of a slow rondo should be varied at each return. Reinecke's valuable pamphlet, *Zur Wiederbelebung der Mozart'schen Klavierkonzerte*, was reprinted some ten years ago and we refer the reader to it; every pianist who plays a concerto of Mozart's period should take its advice to heart.[1]

One last piece of advice. Mozart's piano writing is generally linear. From time to time, however, we meet with mass effects. We repeat once again that their exceptional character should compel the pianist to give them their full value. An exaggeration in the direction of heaviness is better than the opposite and is truer to the composer's intention.

---

[1] Let him take as a model the way in which Wanda Landowska plays the larghetto of the *Coronation* concerto in the H.M.V. recording.

Many hearings of these concertos and a few performances in an orchestra have convinced us that a good execution depends still more on the conductor than on the soloist. An intelligent conductor and a good orchestra with a mediocre pianist will give a better result than a first class soloist with a conductor and a band which are not his equals. For each instrument in turn is treated as a soloist and should be conducted accordingly. These concertos make more demands upon the instrumentalists' qualities than many symphonic works: they exact a personal understanding, sensitiveness, a good tone— more, that is to say, than can be obtained by merely adequate conducting. All the parts, when they are not accompanying, should be played with as much care and in the same spirit as solos.

The woodwind, especially, should stand out. In our modern orchestras, where the strings preponderate, the balance between them and the woodwind runs the risk of being broken if the conductor is not aware of the danger. It is principally in those numerous passages where one or other of the wind gives out a theme whilst the solo adorns or accompanies it that the instrument to which the band has momentarily handed over its powers should be heard. Some conductors are so impressed by the difference in strength between the modern orchestra and the piano as Mozart wrote for it that they never allow their players to rise above *mp*; the result is that parts which ought to be heard are unnoticed, whereas one hears only too well everything the piano has to say, even when its discourse is less important than the orchestra's. Many a performance and a recording have been spoilt in this way.

We have at length reached the end of the pilgrimage that we have been making through Mozart's life from the date when his piano concertos first appeared to act as landmarks. The fruit of this pilgrimage is the first book ever wholly devoted to these concertos. We do not in anywise claim that it is definitive, even in the very un-absolute sense in which one can apply this term to sublunary works of learning. For the glory of the master to whom it is dedicated, we ask for nothing more than that further studies, worthier of him, should succeed and displace it. For many a year the twenty-three works with which we have been living will not be exhausted, and we realize that, however bulky our book may be, there are aspects of them we have not touched upon and others, at which we have glanced, that deserve more thorough treatment.

Into the conclusions drawn by a study where a subject as impalpable as the nature of an inspiration plays a large part, an element of arbitrariness is bound to enter. We do not expect that all the different appreciations we have given will be approved by everyone; we do not even hope it, for the diversity of the impressions which a work of art produces on those who contemplate it is a sign of its greatness. There is less disagreement over second and third rate artists than over the great masters. In their presence, our reactions are as different from one man to the next as in presence of the beauties of Nature. Admiration is sometimes their only common element.

One indisputable fact, nevertheless, we believe, results from our study: in Mozart's artistic existence there was not only development of technique; there was also growth in thought. We are far from thinking that no one before us had noticed the organic quality of his work, considered in time; no one who has soaked himself in the composer's music has failed to recognize it. But the opinion that Mozart never grew up and merely repeated himself, with an unconsciousness that some profess to find charming, all through his life, is so slow in dying that we are glad to carry yet another slab to its grave.

Following him through his fifteen most fruitful years has shown us once again to what extent his musical being gained in depth and power from stage to stage, to what extent it discovered new realms for itself and transformed its inspiration from the period of the *galant* concertos with which we began, to the E flat quintet, the *Magic Flute* and the *Requiem*. We saw that, if at certain moments there was a kind of withdrawal and apparent retrogression, under the influence of new surroundings when he settled in Vienna, under that of material worry in 1789 and 1790, there was never decadence nor lack of renewal; to each year of his maturity correspond fresh shades of inspiration and this is true to the very end. Even if this study of his work in his great concertos has only served to make this once more evident, our task will not have been in vain.

The greatness of the concertos themselves no longer needs demonstrating; neither does the pre-eminence of their place in Mozart's output. In them are seen aspects of his genius unperceived elsewhere or more visible here than elsewhere. The constructive power, the architectural side of this musician who was looked on so long as a pure melodist, reveals itself as it does nowhere else except in the two 1787 quintets. No allegro of his symphonies reaches such vast dimensions nor shows so complex a structure as his concertos of the three great years; in no other genre did he carry so far the development of rondo form—the form in which he experimented most,

and most successfully. Only a few exceptions like the quartet in
A and the Jupiter symphony possess finales whose masterly construction equals that of his best concerto rondos.

And nowhere else, not even in his operas, did he work out contrast
of tone with so much skill. His concertos display most clearly
his ability to handle the woodwind, to contrast them one with the
other, with the strings and with the solo. The presence of a foreign
body, the piano, stimulated him and showed him combinations of
tone of which he never thought in his symphonies and overtures.
It appears paradoxical; but in order to see his absolute mastery of the
orchestra, we must turn to his concertos rather than to his works for
orchestra alone.

As for his thought, it will be enough to recall what we have
already written: it is in the concertos that the Olympian and tragic
strains in his inspiration are manifested with greatest power and
depth.

Starting from the divertimento conception of the genre, he ended
by putting as much of himself into it as into his chamber music and
symphonies. Of almost all his concertos composed after he had
settled in Vienna it is true to say that each one corresponds to a
mood. With many of them it is possible to live continuously. The
choice of these is, of course, a matter of taste; yet it seems to us that
everyone will grant that the two works in A major, and those in G,
D minor, C minor, C major K.503 and B flat K.595 allow us to frequent them intimately without exhausting them, without wearying
of them, and that is the test of greatest art.

What is precious in Mozart is the perception he affords us of beautiful and powerful motion, at once delicate and sure-footed, seeing
whither it goes and following its aim unflinchingly, with the effort-
saving spareness of a tiger bounding towards its prey. This motion
is all the more precious for being at the service of a nature belonging
to the little band of those artists or thinkers "who seem rather to
have come down into the flesh from above than to be straining
upwards to free themselves from its limitations."[1]

The revival of Mozart since the opening of the century is one
form of the reaction against Romanticism. Yet he is not the "pure"
musician, untainted by emotion, whom some thought they saw in him
twenty years ago; our study of the concertos has, on the contrary,

---

[1] Lawrence Hyde: *The prospects of humanism*, p. 162. It is we who apply
his words to Mozart.

striven towards setting forth the fullness of the affective life in his music. We have come to love in him one of the healthiest and most imaginative natures in all art. He is discreet, not because he has nothing to say, but because he speaks with a moderation and a sense of form that few artists have so consistently exhibited. Let us no longer judge him from his minor works, sonatas or trios. His true face is shown in his best quartets and quintets, his last symphonies and his Viennese concertos, his operas, his C minor and *Requiem* masses. There, he throbs with as intense a life as Bach or Beethoven, and if we compare his last fifteen years with any fifteen years of theirs, we shall have to admit that he is as manifold and as profound as they. His inner life is of the richest and most communicative; his work, a personal revelation which never falls into a series of self-centred confessions. It is as much a testament as that of the greatest masters, capable of affording unfailing comfort and support.

When we first laid the foundations of this study, a few years after the 1914–18 war, the rediscovery of Mozart had begun but had not reached his concertos. Since then, many of them too have re-entered the field of concerts, especially that of broadcasts and amateur performances. Our study is itself but a sign among many of his value for the inter-war generations. A few great concertos are still absent from our programmes; their revival is surely only a question of time. Between the years in which we set out on our labours and that in which we complete them, executants and public have discovered for themselves the greatness of these works; our book does not come forward as the herald of a new thesis but simply as an attempt to explain a few points and to co-ordinate thoughts and sentiments common to all Mozart lovers which it may be convenient to find assembled in the same volume. In all humility, it offers itself as a homage of devotion to him of whom it treats.

Appendix I

CADENZAS TO K.365

I

2

3

4

Appendix II

CADENZAS TO K.413

I

2

Appendix III

LIST OF COMPOSERS MENTIONED IN THIS WORK

Schumann, 14, 48, 57, 61, 74, 378.
Sibelius, 390.
Spohr, 213, 412.
Steibelt, 53.

TCHAIKOVSKY, 229, 396.

VIVALDI, 219.

WAGENSEIL, 20, 109.
Wagner, 34, 73.
Weber, 165.
Williams, R. Vaughan, 482.

LIST OF WORKS BY MOZART, OTHER THAN PIANO CONCERTOS, MENTIONED IN THIS WORK

MASSES, MOTETS.

K.317 in C, 105.
K.337 in C, 105, 148.
K.427 in C minor, 119, 123, 126, 148, 160, 168, 308, 324, 330, 360, 443.
K.626: Requiem, 17–19, 123, 176, 301, 308, 330, 331, 350, 493, 497.
K.341: Kyrie in D minor, 105, 119, 122, 123, 330, 331.
K.618: Ave verum, 464.

CANTATAS.

K.429: Dir, Seele des Weltalls, 366.
K.469: Davidde penitente, 360.
K.471: Die Maurerfreude, 366.

OPERAS AND BALLETS.

La Finta Semplice, 75.
Mitridate, 75, 123.
Ascanio in Alba, 75.
Lucio Silla, 75, 123, 167.
La Finta Giardiniera, 82.
Il Rè pastore, 82.
King Thamos, 330, 331, 413
Les Petits Riens, 103.
Idomeneo, 17, 123, 125, 167, 175, 210, 227, 330, 331, 389, 435, 436, 445, 461, 464.
Die Entführung aus dem Serail, 126, 160, 167, 416, 443.
L'Oca del Cairo, 160, 167, 168.
Lo Sposo deluso, 160, 167.
Der Schauspieldirektor, 174, 415, 443.
Le Nozze di Figaro, 167, 174, 353, 385, 415, 416, 445.
Don Giovanni, 167, 330, 331, 375, 454, 455, 461, 464.

Così fan tutte, 167, 240, 254, 315, 364, 385, 443, 461, 468, 485.
The Magic Flute, 17–19, 101, 115, 122, 176, 188, 310, 333, 335, 350, 366, 491–493, 497.
La Clemenza di Tito, 443, 444, 461.

ARIAS, DUETS, LIEDER.

K.294: Non so d'onde viene, 106.
K.369: Misero, dove son! 167.
K.416: Mia speranza adorata, 167.
K.489: Spiegarti non poss'io, 389.
K.490: Non più, tanto ascoltai, 389, 445.
K.505: Ch'io mi scordi di te, 444–449.
K.528: Bella mia fiamma, 247.
K.596: Sehnsucht nach dem Frühlinge, 485.

PIANO SOLO.

Sonatas:

K.279 in C, 83.
K.280 in F, 83, 378.
K.281 in B flat, 83.
K.282 in E flat, 83.
K.283 in G, 83.
K.284 in D, 83, 463.
K.309 in C, 109, 114, 443.
K.310 in A minor, 111, 323, 407.
K.311 in D, 463.
K.330 in C, 127, 250, 443.
K.331 in A, 44, 127.
K.332 in F, 127, 290.
K.333 in B flat, 127, 490.
K.457 in C minor, 34, 43, 239, 278, 280, 323, 328, 332, 407, 412–14, 495.

K.533 in F, 31, 300, 301, 441, 454-6.
K.545 in C, 37, 352, 456, 487.
K.570 in B flat, 52, 456, 468, 469.
K.576 in D, 456, 461, 463, 468, 469.

Fantasias:

K.394 in C (with fugue), 127, 148, 212, 443.
K.396 in C minor, 412, 413.
K.397 in D minor, 330.
K.475 in C minor, 316, 350, 412, 413.

Variations:

K.398: *Salve tu, Domine*, in F, 167.
K.455: *Unser dummer Pöbel meint*, in G, 167, 268.
K.500 in B flat, 418.

Rondos:

K.485 in D, 173.
K.494 in F, 301.
K.511 in A minor, 345, 454, 455, 458.

Various:

K.399: Suite in the style of Handel, 148, 443.
K.E.453a: Funeral March, 178.
K.E.498a: Allegro and minuet in B flat, 418.
K.540: Adagio in B minor, 42, 318, 327, 328, 378, 454, 455, 478.
K.574: Jig in G, 470.
K.355: Minuet in D, 455.

PIANO DUETS.

For One Piano:

Sonatas:

K.497 in F, 173, 300, 417, 490.
K.357 in G, 55, 418, 441.
K.521 in C, 390, 456.

Variations:

K.501 in G, 418.

For Two Pianos:

Sonata:

K.448 in D, 52, 126, 127, 277, 374, 463.

Fugue:

K.426 in C minor, 148, 413.

VIOLIN SONATAS.

K.296 in C, 37, 443.
K.302 in E flat, 134, 349.
K.303 in C, 443.
K.304 in E minor, 126, 323, 407.
K.306, in D, 89, 463.
K.378 in B flat, 37, 261.
K.376 in F, 126.
K.377 in F, 41, 42, 46, 123, 126, 160, 268, 300, 301, 330.
K.379 in G, 43, 126, 160, 256.
K.380 in E flat, 32, 41, 42, 43, 126, 160, 366.
K.402 in A, 148, 369.
K.454 in B flat, 211, 257, 258, 279, 303, 418, 446, 490.
K.481 in E flat, 351.
K.526 in A, 369, 387, 454, 455.
K.547 in F, 37, 352, 456.

TRIOS.

Strings:

K.E.404a: Preludes, 42.
K.563: Divertimento in E flat, 31, 32, 52, 239, 268, 277, 366, 454, 455, 465, 486.

Piano and Strings:

K.254 in B flat, 417.
K.496 in G, 417.
K.498 in E flat (with clarinet), 417, 446.
K.502 in B flat, 211, 418, 480, 490.
K.542 in E, 352.
K.548 in C, 52, 352.
K.564 in G, 352.

DUETS.

Violin and Viola:

K.423 in G, 256.
K.424 in B flat, 489.

Bassett Horns:

K.487 in C, 418.

QUARTETS.

Strings:

K.155 in D, 75.
K.156 in G, 75.
K.157 in C, 38, 75, 97, 360.
K.158 in F, 43, 75.
K.159 in B flat, 75.
K.160 in (E) Flat, 75.
K.E.Anh.210-213 in B flat, C, A and E flat, 75.
K.171 in E flat, 349.
K.173 in D minor, 44, 330, 331, 407.
K.387 in G, 43, 48, 80, 147, 160, 161, 169, 256, 289, 290, 292, 293.
K.421 in D minor, 34, 45, 46, 123, 161, 169, 278, 328, 330, 331, 380, 407, 414.
K.428 in E flat, 169, 278, 341, 349, 461.
K.458 in B flat, 34, 113, 211, 264, 279, 280, 289, 303, 415, 490.
K.464 in A, 46, 48, 268, 269, 278, 280, 302, 350, 369, 380, 415, 498.
K.E.464a in A, 369.
K.465 in C, 40, 48, 278, 289, 302, 350, 415, 443, 456.
K.499 in D, 40, 91, 417, 418, 464.
K.575 in D, 137, 146, 264, 461, 462, 464, 468, 469, 470.
K.589 in B flat, 45, 52, 191, 278, 289, 440, 468-470, 472, 480, 488.
K.590 in F, 34, 278, 301, 468-70, 488, 491.
K.546 in C minor (prelude and fugue), 41, 42, 148, 378, 413, 454, 455.

Strings and Wind:

K.285 in D (flute), 96, 234, 463.
K.298 in A (flute), 44.
K.370 in F (hautboy), 330.

Piano and Strings:

K.478 in G minor, 34, 54, 218, 256, 264, 277, 289, 327, 351, 386, 407, 415, 417, 446, 449, 472, 487, 490.
K.493 in E flat, 52, 277, 366, 381, 382, 386, 406, 446, 449, 480.

QUINTETS.

Strings:

K.174 in B flat, 81.
K.515 in C, 31, 32, 34, 40, 45, 48, 227, 237, 278, 289, 302, 332, 347, 374, 419, 420, 432, 442-44, 455-57, 493.
K.516 in G minor, 31, 33, 34, 40, 43, 45, 48, 96, 270, 274, 278, 289, 302, 319, 327, 328, 332, 407, 419, 432, 444, 454, 455, 457, 478, 493.
K.593 in D, 31, 34, 40, 48, 417, 444, 464, 469, 470, 480, 493.
K.E.613a in E flat, 273.
K.614 in E flat, 31, 34, 38, 45, 48, 52, 191, 208, 293, 366, 444, 471, 488, 490-93, 497.

Strings and Horn:

K.407 in E flat, 169, 365.

Strings and Clarinet:

K.581 in A, 32, 137, 188, 198, 369, 417, 468, 470, 480.

Piano and Wind:

K.452 in E flat, 199, 238, 257, 277, 365, 415, 446, 448, 480.

Harmonica, flute, violin, hautboy, and 'cello:

K.617 in C, 42, 487, 491.

SYMPHONIES:

K.16 in E flat, 349, 352, 356.
K.96 in C, 360.
K.132 in E flat, 349.
K.183 in G minor, 83, 85, 407.
K.184 in E flat, 38, 97, 349, 360.
K.297 in D, 103.
K.319 in B flat, 472, 489.
K.338 in C, 109, 119, 123, 168, 341, 366, 443.

A CATALOGUE OF
SELECTED DOVER BOOKS
IN ALL FIELDS OF INTEREST

A CATALOGUE OF SELECTED DOVER
BOOKS IN ALL FIELDS OF INTEREST

CELESTIAL OBJECTS FOR COMMON TELESCOPES, T. W. Webb. The most used book in amateur astronomy: inestimable aid for locating and identifying nearly 4,000 celestial objects. Edited, updated by Margaret W. Mayall. 77 illustrations. Total of 645pp. 5⅜ x 8½.
20917-2, 20918-0 Pa., Two-vol. set $10.00

HISTORICAL STUDIES IN THE LANGUAGE OF CHEMISTRY, M. P. Crosland. The important part language has played in the development of chemistry from the symbolism of alchemy to the adoption of systematic nomenclature in 1892. ". . . wholeheartedly recommended,"—Science. 15 illustrations. 416pp. of text. 5⅝ x 8¼.
63702-6 Pa. $7.50

BURNHAM'S CELESTIAL HANDBOOK, Robert Burnham, Jr. Thorough, readable guide to the stars beyond our solar system. Exhaustive treatment, fully illustrated. Breakdown is alphabetical by constellation: Andromeda to Cetus in Vol. 1; Chamaeleon to Orion in Vol. 2; and Pavo to Vulpecula in Vol. 3. Hundreds of illustrations. Total of about 2000pp. 6⅛ x 9¼.
23567-X, 23568-8, 23673-0 Pa., Three-vol. set $32.85

THEORY OF WING SECTIONS: INCLUDING A SUMMARY OF AIR-FOIL DATA, Ira H. Abbott and A. E. von Doenhoff. Concise compilation of subatomic aerodynamic characteristics of modern NASA wing sections, plus description of theory. 350pp. of tables. 693pp. 5⅜ x 8½.
60586-8 Pa. $9.95

DE RE METALLICA, Georgius Agricola. Translated by Herbert C. Hoover and Lou H. Hoover. The famous Hoover translation of greatest treatise on technological chemistry, engineering, geology, mining of early modern times (1556). All 289 original woodcuts. 638pp. 6¾ x 11.
60006-8 Clothbd. $19.95

THE ORIGIN OF CONTINENTS AND OCEANS, Alfred Wegener. One of the most influential, most controversial books in science, the classic statement for continental drift. Full 1966 translation of Wegener's final (1929) version. 64 illustrations. 246pp. 5⅜ x 8½.(EBE)61708-4 Pa. $5.00

THE PRINCIPLES OF PSYCHOLOGY, William James. Famous long course complete, unabridged. Stream of thought, time perception, memory, experimental methods; great work decades ahead of its time. Still valid, useful; read in many classes. 94 figures. Total of 1391pp. 5⅜ x 8½.
20381-6, 20382-4 Pa., Two-vol. set $17.90

YUCATAN BEFORE AND AFTER THE CONQUEST, Diego de Landa. First English translation of basic book in Maya studies, the only significant account of Yucatan written in the early post-Conquest era. Translated by distinguished Maya scholar William Gates. Appendices, introduction, 4 maps and over 120 illustrations added by translator. 162pp. 5⅜ x 8½.
23622-6 Pa. $3.00

THE MALAY ARCHIPELAGO, Alfred R. Wallace. Spirited travel account by one of founders of modern biology. Touches on zoology, botany, ethnography, geography, and geology. 62 illustrations, maps. 515pp. 5⅜ x 8½.
20187-2 Pa. $6.95

THE DISCOVERY OF THE TOMB OF TUTANKHAMEN, Howard Carter, A. C. Mace. Accompany Carter in the thrill of discovery, as ruined passage suddenly reveals unique, untouched, fabulously rich tomb. Fascinating account, with 106 illustrations. New introduction by J. M. White. Total of 382pp. 5⅜ x 8½. (Available in U.S. only)   23500-9 Pa. $5.50

THE WORLD'S GREATEST SPEECHES, edited by Lewis Copeland and Lawrence W. Lamm. Vast collection of 278 speeches from Greeks up to present. Powerful and effective models; unique look at history. Revised to 1970. Indices. 842pp. 5⅜ x 8½.   20468-5 Pa. $9.95

THE 100 GREATEST ADVERTISEMENTS, Julian Watkins. The priceless ingredient; His master's voice; 99 44/100% pure; over 100 others. How they were written, their impact, etc. Remarkable record. 130 illustrations. 233pp. 7⅞ x 10 3/5.   20540-1 Pa. $6.95

CRUICKSHANK PRINTS FOR HAND COLORING, George Cruickshank. 18 illustrations, one side of a page, on fine-quality paper suitable for watercolors. Caricatures of people in society (c. 1820) full of trenchant wit. Very large format. 32pp. 11 x 16.   23684-6 Pa. $6.00

THIRTY-TWO COLOR POSTCARDS OF TWENTIETH-CENTURY AMERICAN ART, Whitney Museum of American Art. Reproduced in full color in postcard form are 31 art works and one shot of the museum. Calder, Hopper, Rauschenberg, others. Detachable. 16pp. 8¼ x 11.
23629-3 Pa. $3.50

MUSIC OF THE SPHERES: THE MATERIAL UNIVERSE FROM ATOM TO QUASAR SIMPLY EXPLAINED, Guy Murchie. Planets, stars, geology, atoms, radiation, relativity, quantum theory, light, antimatter, similar topics. 319 figures. 664pp. 5⅜ x 8½.
21809-0, 21810-4 Pa., Two-vol. set $11.00

EINSTEIN'S THEORY OF RELATIVITY, Max Born. Finest semi-technical account; covers Einstein, Lorentz, Minkowski, and others, with much detail, much explanation of ideas and math not readily available elsewhere on this level. For student, non-specialist. 376pp. 5⅜ x 8½.
60769-0 Pa. $5.00

THE SENSE OF BEAUTY, George Santayana. Masterfully written discussion of nature of beauty, materials of beauty, form, expression; art, literature, social sciences all involved. 168pp. 5⅜ x 8½.   20238-0 Pa. $3.50

ON THE IMPROVEMENT OF THE UNDERSTANDING, Benedict Spinoza. Also contains *Ethics, Correspondence,* all in excellent R. Elwes translation. Basic works on entry to philosophy, pantheism, exchange of ideas with great contemporaries. 402pp. 5⅜ x 8½.   20250-X Pa. $5.95

THE TRAGIC SENSE OF LIFE, Miguel de Unamuno. Acknowledged masterpiece of existential literature, one of most important books of 20th century. Introduction by Madariaga. 367pp. 5⅜ x 8½.
20257-7 Pa. $6.00

THE GUIDE FOR THE PERPLEXED, Moses Maimonides. Great classic of medieval Judaism attempts to reconcile revealed religion (Pentateuch, commentaries) with Aristotelian philosophy. Important historically, still relevant in problems. Unabridged Friedlander translation. Total of 473pp. 5⅜ x 8½.   20351-4 Pa. $6.95

THE I CHING (THE BOOK OF CHANGES), translated by James Legge. Complete translation of basic text plus appendices by Confucius, and Chinese commentary of most penetrating divination manual ever prepared. Indispensable to study of early Oriental civilizations, to modern inquiring reader. 448pp. 5⅜ x 8½.   21062-6 Pa. $6.00

THE EGYPTIAN BOOK OF THE DEAD, E. A. Wallis Budge. Complete reproduction of Ani's papyrus, finest ever found. Full hieroglyphic text, interlinear transliteration, word for word translation, smooth translation. Basic work, for Egyptology, for modern study of psychic matters. Total of 533pp. 6½ x 9¼. (USCO)   21866-X Pa. $8.50

THE GODS OF THE EGYPTIANS, E. A. Wallis Budge. Never excelled for richness, fullness: all gods, goddesses, demons, mythical figures of Ancient Egypt; their legends, rites, incarnations, variations, powers, etc. Many hieroglyphic texts cited. Over 225 illustrations, plus 6 color plates. Total of 988pp. 6⅛ x 9¼. (EBE)
22055-9, 22056-7 Pa., Two-vol. set $20.00

THE STANDARD BOOK OF QUILT MAKING AND COLLECTING, Marguerite Ickis. Full information, full-sized patterns for making 46 traditional quilts, also 150 other patterns. Quilted cloths, lame, satin quilts, etc. 483 illustrations. 273pp. 6⅞ x 9⅝.   20582-7 Pa. $5.95

CORAL GARDENS AND THEIR MAGIC, Bronsilaw Malinowski. Classic study of the methods of tilling the soil and of agricultural rites in the Trobriand Islands of Melanesia. Author is one of the most important figures in the field of modern social anthropology. 143 illustrations. Indexes. Total of 911pp. of text. 5⅝ x 8¼. (Available in U.S. only)
23597-1 Pa. $12.95

THE PHILOSOPHY OF HISTORY, Georg W. Hegel. Great classic of Western thought develops concept that history is not chance but a rational process, the evolution of freedom. 457pp. 5⅜ x 8½. 20112-0 Pa. $6.00

LANGUAGE, TRUTH AND LOGIC, Alfred J. Ayer. Famous, clear introduction to Vienna, Cambridge schools of Logical Positivism. Role of philosophy, elimination of metaphysics, nature of analysis, etc. 160pp. 5⅜ x 8½. (USCO) 20010-8 Pa. $2.50

A PREFACE TO LOGIC, Morris R. Cohen. Great City College teacher in renowned, easily followed exposition of formal logic, probability, values, logic and world order and similar topics; no previous background needed. 209pp. 5⅜ x 8½. 23517-3 Pa. $4.95

REASON AND NATURE, Morris R. Cohen. Brilliant analysis of reason and its multitudinous ramifications by charismatic teacher. Interdisciplinary, synthesizing work widely praised when it first appeared in 1931. Second (1953) edition. Indexes. 496pp. 5⅜ x 8½. 23633-1 Pa. $7.50

AN ESSAY CONCERNING HUMAN UNDERSTANDING, John Locke. The only complete edition of enormously important classic, with authoritative editorial material by A. C. Fraser. Total of 1176pp. 5⅜ x 8½. 20530-4, 20531-2 Pa., Two-vol. set $16.00

HANDBOOK OF MATHEMATICAL FUNCTIONS WITH FORMULAS, GRAPHS, AND MATHEMATICAL TABLES, edited by Milton Abramowitz and Irene A. Stegun. Vast compendium: 29 sets of tables, some to as high as 20 places. 1,046pp. 8 x 10½. 61272-4 Pa. $17.95

MATHEMATICS FOR THE PHYSICAL SCIENCES, Herbert S. Wilf. Highly acclaimed work offers clear presentations of vector spaces and matrices, orthogonal functions, roots of polynomial equations, conformal mapping, calculus of variations, etc. Knowledge of theory of functions of real and complex variables is assumed. Exercises and solutions. Index. 284pp. 5⅝ x 8¼. 63635-6 Pa. $5.00

THE PRINCIPLE OF RELATIVITY, Albert Einstein et al. Eleven most important original papers on special and general theories. Seven by Einstein, two by Lorentz, one each by Minkowski and Weyl. All translated, unabridged. 216pp. 5⅜ x 8½. 60081-5 Pa. $3.50

THERMODYNAMICS, Enrico Fermi. A classic of modern science. Clear, organized treatment of systems, first and second laws, entropy, thermodynamic potentials, gaseous reactions, dilute solutions, entropy constant. No math beyond calculus required. Problems. 160pp. 5⅜ x 8½. 60361-X Pa. $4.00

ELEMENTARY MECHANICS OF FLUIDS, Hunter Rouse. Classic undergraduate text widely considered to be far better than many later books. Ranges from fluid velocity and acceleration to role of compressibility in fluid motion. Numerous examples, questions, problems. 224 illustrations. 376pp. 5⅝ x 8¼. 63699-2 Pa. $7.00

THE AMERICAN SENATOR, Anthony Trollope. Little known, long un-available Trollope novel on a grand scale. Here are humorous comment on American vs. English culture, and stunning portrayal of a heroine/villainess. Superb evocation of Victorian village life. 561pp. 5⅜ x 8½.
23801-6 Pa. $7.95

WAS IT MURDER? James Hilton. The author of *Lost Horizon* and *Good-bye, Mr. Chips* wrote one detective novel (under a pen-name) which was quickly forgotten and virtually lost, even at the height of Hilton's fame. This edition brings it back—a finely crafted public school puzzle resplendent with Hilton's stylish atmosphere. A thoroughly English thriller by the creator of Shangri-la. 252pp. 5⅜ x 8. (Available in U.S. only)
23774-5 Pa. $3.00

CENTRAL PARK: A PHOTOGRAPHIC GUIDE, Victor Laredo and Henry Hope Reed. 121 superb photographs show dramatic views of Central Park: Bethesda Fountain, Cleopatra's Needle, Sheep Meadow, the Blockhouse, plus people engaged in many park activities: ice skating, bike riding, etc. Captions by former Curator of Central Park, Henry Hope Reed, provide historical view, changes, etc. Also photos of N.Y. landmarks on park's periphery. 96pp. 8½ x 11. 23750-8 Pa. $4.50

NANTUCKET IN THE NINETEENTH CENTURY, Clay Lancaster. 180 rare photographs, stereographs, maps, drawings and floor plans recreate unique American island society. Authentic scenes of shipwreck, light-houses, streets, homes are arranged in geographic sequence to provide walking-tour guide to old Nantucket existing today. Introduction, captions. 160pp. 8⅞ x 11¾. 23747-8 Pa. $7.95

STONE AND MAN: A PHOTOGRAPHIC EXPLORATION, Andreas Feininger. 106 photographs by *Life* photographer Feininger portray man's deep passion for stone through the ages. Stonehenge-like megaliths, forti-fied towns, sculpted marble and crumbling tenements show textures, beau-ties, fascination. 128pp. 9¼ x 10¾. 23756-7 Pa. $5.95

CIRCLES, A MATHEMATICAL VIEW, D. Pedoe. Fundamental aspects of college geometry, non-Euclidean geometry, and other branches of mathe-matics: representing circle by point. Poincare model, isoperimetric prop-erty, etc. Stimulating recreational reading. 66 figures. 96pp. 5⅝ x 8¼.
63698-4 Pa. $3.50

THE DISCOVERY OF NEPTUNE, Morton Grosser. Dramatic scientific history of the investigations leading up to the actual discovery of the eighth planet of our solar system. Lucid, well-researched book by well-known historian of science. 172pp. 5⅜ x 8½. 23726-5 Pa. $3.50

THE DEVIL'S DICTIONARY. Ambrose Bierce. Barbed, bitter, brilliant witticisms in the form of a dictionary. Best, most ferocious satire America has produced. 145pp. 5⅜ x 8½. 20487-1 Pa. $2.50

HISTORY OF BACTERIOLOGY, William Bulloch. The only comprehensive history of bacteriology from the beginnings through the 19th century. Special emphasis is given to biography-Leeuwenhoek, etc. Brief accounts of 350 bacteriologists form a separate section. No clearer, fuller study, suitable to scientists and general readers, has yet been written. 52 illustrations. 448pp. 5⅝ x 8¼.   23761-3 Pa. $6.50

THE COMPLETE NONSENSE OF EDWARD LEAR, Edward Lear. All nonsense limericks, zany alphabets, Owl and Pussycat, songs, nonsense botany, etc., illustrated by Lear. Total of 321pp. 5⅜ x 8½. (Available in U.S. only)   20167-8 Pa. $4.50

INGENIOUS MATHEMATICAL PROBLEMS AND METHODS, Louis A. Graham. Sophisticated material from Graham *Dial*, applied and pure; stresses solution methods. Logic, number theory, networks, inversions, etc. 237pp. 5⅜ x 8½.   20545-2 Pa. $4.50

BEST MATHEMATICAL PUZZLES OF SAM LOYD, edited by Martin Gardner. Bizarre, original, whimsical puzzles by America's greatest puzzler. From fabulously rare *Cyclopedia*, including famous 14-15 puzzles, the Horse of a Different Color, 115 more. Elementary math. 150 illustrations. 167pp. 5⅜ x 8½.   20498-7 Pa. $3.50

THE BASIS OF COMBINATION IN CHESS, J. du Mont. Easy-to-follow, instructive book on elements of combination play, with chapters on each piece and every powerful combination team—two knights, bishop and knight, rook and bishop, etc. 250 diagrams. 218pp. 5⅜ x 8½. (Available in U.S. only)   23644-7 Pa. $4.50

MODERN CHESS STRATEGY, Ludek Pachman. The use of the queen, the active king, exchanges, pawn play, the center, weak squares, etc. Section on rook alone worth price of the book. Stress on the moderns. Often considered the most important book on strategy. 314pp. 5⅜ x 8½.
20290-9 Pa. $5.00

LASKER'S MANUAL OF CHESS, Dr. Emanuel Lasker. Great world champion offers very thorough coverage of all aspects of chess. Combinations, position play, openings, end game, aesthetics of chess, philosophy of struggle, much more. Filled with analyzed games. 390pp. 5⅜ x 8½.
20640-8 Pa. $5.95

500 MASTER GAMES OF CHESS, S. Tartakower, J. du Mont. Vast collection of great chess games from 1798-1938, with much material nowhere else readily available. Fully annotated, arranged by opening for easier study. 664pp. 5⅜ x 8½.   23208-5 Pa. $8.50

A GUIDE TO CHESS ENDINGS, Dr. Max Euwe, David Hooper. One of the finest modern works on chess endings. Thorough analysis of the most frequently encountered endings by former world champion. 331 examples, each with diagram. 248pp. 5⅜ x 8½.   23332-4 Pa. $3.95

THE COMPLETE BOOK OF DOLL MAKING AND COLLECTING, Catherine Christopher. Instructions, patterns for dozens of dolls, from rag doll on up to elaborate, historically accurate figures. Mould faces, sew clothing, make doll houses, etc. Also collecting information. Many illustrations. 288pp. 6 x 9. 22066-4 Pa. $4.95

THE DAGUERREOTYPE IN AMERICA, Beaumont Newhall. Wonderful portraits, 1850's townscapes, landscapes; full text plus 104 photographs. The basic book. Enlarged 1976 edition. 272pp. 8¼ x 11¼. 23322-7 Pa. $7.95

CRAFTSMAN HOMES, Gustav Stickley. 296 architectural drawings, floor plans, and photographs illustrate 40 different kinds of "Mission-style" homes from *The Craftsman* (1901-16), voice of American style of simplicity and organic harmony. Thorough coverage of Craftsman idea in text and picture, now collector's item. 224pp. 8⅛ x 11. 23791-5 Pa. $6.50

PEWTER-WORKING: INSTRUCTIONS AND PROJECTS, Burl N. Osborn. & Gordon O. Wilber. Introduction to pewter-working for amateur craftsman. History and characteristics of pewter; tools, materials, step-by-step instructions. Photos, line drawings, diagrams. Total of 160pp. 7⅞ x 10¾. 23786-9 Pa. $3.50

THE GREAT CHICAGO FIRE, edited by David Lowe. 10 dramatic, eye-witness accounts of the 1871 disaster, including one of the aftermath and rebuilding, plus 70 contemporary photographs and illustrations of the ruins—courthouse, Palmer House, Great Central Depot, etc. Introduction by David Lowe. 87pp. 8¼ x 11. 23771-0 Pa. $4.00

SILHOUETTES: A PICTORIAL ARCHIVE OF VARIED ILLUSTRATIONS, edited by Carol Belanger Grafton. Over 600 silhouettes from the 18th to 20th centuries include profiles and full figures of men and women, children, birds and animals, groups and scenes, nature, ships, an alphabet. Dozens of uses for commercial artists and craftspeople. 144pp. 8⅜ x 11¼. 23781-8 Pa. $4.50

ANIMALS: 1,419 COPYRIGHT-FREE ILLUSTRATIONS OF MAMMALS, BIRDS, FISH, INSECTS, ETC., edited by Jim Harter. Clear wood engravings present, in extremely lifelike poses, over 1,000 species of animals. One of the most extensive copyright-free pictorial sourcebooks of its kind. Captions. Index. 284pp. 9 x 12. 23766-4 Pa. $8.95

INDIAN DESIGNS FROM ANCIENT ECUADOR, Frederick W. Shaffer. 282 original designs by pre-Columbian Indians of Ecuador (500-1500 A.D.). Designs include people, mammals, birds, reptiles, fish, plants, heads, geometric designs. Use as is or alter for advertising, textiles, leathercraft, etc. Introduction. 95pp. 8¾ x 11¼. 23764-8 Pa. $4.50

SZIGETI ON THE VIOLIN, Joseph Szigeti. Genial, loosely structured tour by premier violinist, featuring a pleasant mixture of reminiscenes, insights into great music and musicians, innumerable tips for practicing violinists. 385 musical passages. 256pp. 5⅝ x 8¼. 23763-X Pa. $4.00

TONE POEMS, SERIES II: TILL EULENSPIEGELS LUSTIGE STREICHE, ALSO SPRACH ZARATHUSTRA, AND EIN HELDEN-LEBEN, Richard Strauss. Three important orchestral works, including very popular *Till Eulenspiegel's Marry Pranks*, reproduced in full score from original editions. Study score. 315pp. 9⅜ x 12¼. (Available in U.S. only)
23755-9 Pa. $8.95

TONE POEMS, SERIES I: DON JUAN, TOD UND VERKLARUNG AND DON QUIXOTE, Richard Strauss. Three of the most often performed and recorded works in entire orchestral repertoire, reproduced in full score from original editions. Study score. 286pp. 9⅜ x 12¼. (Available in U.S. only)
23754-0 Pa. $8.95

11 LATE STRING QUARTETS, Franz Joseph Haydn. The form which Haydn defined and "brought to perfection." *(Grove's)*. 11 string quartets in complete score, his last and his best. The first in a projected series of the complete Haydn string quartets. Reliable modern Eulenberg edition, otherwise difficult to obtain. 320pp. 8⅜ x 11¼. (Available in U.S. only)
23753-2 Pa. $8.95

FOURTH, FIFTH AND SIXTH SYMPHONIES IN FULL SCORE, Peter Ilyitch Tchaikovsky. Complete orchestral scores of Symphony No. 4 in F Minor, Op. 36; Symphony No. 5 in E Minor, Op. 64; Symphony No. 6 in B Minor, "Pathetique," Op. 74. Bretikopf & Hartel eds. Study score. 480pp. 9⅜ x 12¼. 23861-X Pa. $10.95

THE MARRIAGE OF FIGARO: COMPLETE SCORE, Wolfgang A. Mozart. Finest comic opera ever written. Full score, not to be confused with piano renderings. Peters edition. Study score. 448pp. 9⅜ x 12¼. (Available in U.S. only)
23751-6 Pa. $12.95

"IMAGE" ON THE ART AND EVOLUTION OF THE FILM, edited by Marshall Deutelbaum. Pioneering book brings together for first time 38 groundbreaking articles on early silent films from *Image* and 263 illustrations newly shot from rare prints in the collection of the International Museum of Photography. A landmark work. Index. 256pp. 8¼ x 11.
23777-X Pa. $8.95

AROUND-THE-WORLD COOKY BOOK, Lois Lintner Sumption and Marguerite Lintner Ashbrook. 373 cooky and frosting recipes from 28 countries (America, Austria, China, Russia, Italy, etc.) include Viennese kisses, rice wafers, London strips, lady fingers, hony, sugar spice, maple cookies, etc. Clear instructions. All tested. 38 drawings. 182pp. 5⅜ x 8.
23802-4 Pa. $2.75

THE ART NOUVEAU STYLE, edited by Roberta Waddell. 579 rare photographs, not available elsewhere, of works in jewelry, metalwork, glass, ceramics, textiles, architecture and furniture by 175 artists—Mucha, Seguy, Lalique, Tiffany, Gaudin, Hohlwein, Saarinen, and many others. 288pp. 8⅜ x 11¼. 23515-7 Pa. $8.95

THE CURVES OF LIFE, Theodore A. Cook. Examination of shells, leaves, horns, human body, art, etc., in *"the* classic reference on how the golden ratio applies to spirals and helices in nature . . . ."—Martin Gardner. 426 illustrations. Total of 512pp. 5⅜ x 8½. 23701-X Pa. **$6.95**

AN ILLUSTRATED FLORA OF THE NORTHERN UNITED STATES AND CANADA, Nathaniel L. Britton, Addison Brown. Encyclopedic work covers 4666 species, ferns on up. Everything. Full botanical information, illustration for each. This earlier edition is preferred by many to more recent revisions. 1913 edition. Over 4000 illustrations, total of 2087pp. 6⅛ x 9¼. 22642-5, 22643-3, 22644-1 Pa., Three-vol. set **$28.50**

MANUAL OF THE GRASSES OF THE UNITED STATES, A. S. Hitchcock, U.S. Dept. of Agriculture. The basic study of American grasses, both indigenous and escapes, cultivated and wild. Over 1400 species. Full descriptions, information. Over 1100 maps, illustrations. Total of 1051pp. 5⅜ x 8½. 22717-0, 22718-9 Pa., Two-vol. set **$17.00**

THE CACTACEAE,, Nathaniel L. Britton, John N. Rose. Exhaustive, definitive. Every cactus in the world. Full botanical descriptions. Thorough statement of nomenclatures, habitat, detailed finding keys. The one book needed by every cactus enthusiast. Over 1275 illustrations. Total of 1080pp. 8 x 10¼. 21191-6, 21192-4 Clothbd., Two-vol. set **$50.00**

AMERICAN MEDICINAL PLANTS, Charles F. Millspaugh. Full descriptions, 180 plants covered: history; physical description; methods of preparation with all chemical constituents extracted; all claimed curative or adverse effects. 180 full-page plates. Classification table. 804pp. 6½ x 9¼. 23034-1 Pa. **$13.95**

A MODERN HERBAL, Margaret Grieve. Much the fullest, most exact, most useful compilation of herbal material. Gigantic alphabetical encyclopedia, from aconite to zedoary, gives botanical information, medical properties, folklore, economic uses, and much else. Indispensable to serious reader. 161 illustrations. 888pp. 6½ x 9¼. (Available in U.S. only) 22798-7, 22799-5 Pa., Two-vol. set **$15.00**

THE HERBAL or GENERAL HISTORY OF PLANTS, John Gerard. The 1633 edition revised and enlarged by Thomas Johnson. Containing almost 2850 plant descriptions and 2705 superb illustrations, Gerard's *Herbal* is a monumental work, the book all modern English herbals are derived from, the one herbal every serious enthusiast should have in its entirety. Original editions are worth perhaps $750. 1678pp. 8½ x 12¼. 23147-X Clothbd. **$75.00**

MANUAL OF THE TREES OF NORTH AMERICA, Charles S. Sargent. The basic survey of every native tree and tree-like shrub, 717 species in all. Extremely full descriptions, information on habitat, growth, locales, economics, etc. Necessary to every serious tree lover. Over 100 finding keys. 783 illustrations. Total of 986pp. 5⅜ x 8½. 20277-1, 20278-X Pa., Two-vol. set **$12.00**

GREAT NEWS PHOTOS AND THE STORIES BEHIND THEM, John Faber. Dramatic volume of 140 great news photos, 1855 through 1976, and revealing stories behind them, with both historical and technical information. Hindenburg disaster, shooting of Oswald, nomination of Jimmy Carter, etc. 160pp. 8¼ x 11. 23667-6 Pa. **$6.00**

CRUICKSHANK'S PHOTOGRAPHS OF BIRDS OF AMERICA, Allan D. Cruickshank. Great ornithologist, photographer presents 177 closeups, groupings, panoramas, flightings, etc., of about 150 different birds. Expanded *Wings in the Wilderness*. Introduction by Helen G. Cruickshank. 191pp. 8¼ x 11. 23497-5 Pa. **$7.95**

AMERICAN WILDLIFE AND PLANTS, A. C. Martin, et al. Describes food habits of more than 1000 species of mammals, birds, fish. Special treatment of important food plants. Over 300 illustrations. 500pp. 5⅜ x 8½. 20793-5 Pa. **$6.50**

THE PEOPLE CALLED SHAKERS, Edward D. Andrews. Lifetime of research, definitive study of Shakers: origins, beliefs, practices, dances, social organization, furniture and crafts, impact on 19th-century USA, present heritage. Indispensable to student of American history, collector. 33 illustrations. 351pp. 5⅜ x 8½. 21081-2 Pa. **$4.50**

OLD NEW YORK IN EARLY PHOTOGRAPHS, Mary Black. New York City as it was in 1853-1901, through 196 wonderful photographs from N.-Y. Historical Society. Great Blizzard, Lincoln's funeral procession, great buildings. 228pp. 9 x 12. 22907-6 Pa. **$8.95**

MR. LINCOLN'S CAMERA MAN: MATHEW BRADY, Roy Meredith. Over 300 Brady photos reproduced directly from original negatives, photos. Jackson, Webster, Grant, Lee, Carnegie, Barnum; Lincoln; Battle Smoke, Death of Rebel Sniper, Atlanta Just After Capture. Lively commentary. 368pp. 8⅜ x 11¼. 23021-X Pa. **$11.95**

TRAVELS OF WILLIAM BARTRAM, William Bartram. From 1773-8, Bartram explored Northern Florida, Georgia, Carolinas, and reported on wild life, plants, Indians, early settlers. Basic account for period, entertaining reading. Edited by Mark Van Doren. 13 illustrations. 141pp. 5⅜ x 8½. 20013-2 Pa. **$6.00**

THE GENTLEMAN AND CABINET MAKER'S DIRECTOR, Thomas Chippendale. Full reprint, 1762 style book, most influential of all time; chairs, tables, sofas, mirrors, cabinets, etc. 200 plates, plus 24 photographs of surviving pieces. 249pp. 9⅞ x 12¾. 21601-2 Pa. **$8.95**

AMERICAN CARRIAGES, SLEIGHS, SULKIES AND CARTS, edited by Don H. Berkebile. 168 Victorian illustrations from catalogues, trade journals, fully captioned. Useful for artists. Author is Assoc. Curator, Div. of Transportation of Smithsonian Institution. 168pp. 8½ x 9½. 23328-6 Pa. **$5.00**

SECOND PIATIGORSKY CUP, edited by Isaac Kashdan. One of the greatest tournament books ever produced in the English language. All 90 games of the 1966 tournament, annotated by players, most annotated by both players. Features Petrosian, Spassky, Fischer, Larsen, six others. 228pp. 5⅜ x 8½. 23572-6 Pa. $3.50

ENCYCLOPEDIA OF CARD TRICKS, revised and edited by Jean Hugard. How to perform over 600 card tricks, devised by the world's greatest magicians: impromptus, spelling tricks, key cards, using special packs, much, much more. Additional chapter on card technique. 66 illustrations. 402pp. 5⅜ x 8½. (Available in U.S. only) 21252-1 Pa. $5.95

MAGIC: STAGE ILLUSIONS, SPECIAL EFFECTS AND TRICK PHO-TOGRAPHY, Albert A. Hopkins, Henry R. Evans. One of the great classics; fullest, most authoritive explanation of vanishing lady, levitations, scores of other great stage effects. Also small magic, automata, stunts. 446 illustrations. 556pp. 5⅜ x 8½. 23344-8 Pa. $6.95

THE SECRETS OF HOUDINI, J. C. Cannell. Classic study of Houdini's incredible magic, exposing closely-kept professional secrets and revealing, in general terms, the whole art of stage magic. 67 illustrations. 279pp. 5⅜ x 8½. 22913-0 Pa. $4.00

HOFFMANN'S MODERN MAGIC, Professor Hoffmann. One of the best, and best-known, magicians' manuals of the past century. Hundreds of tricks from card tricks and simple sleight of hand to elaborate illusions involving construction of complicated machinery. 332 illustrations. 563pp. 5⅜ x 8½. 23623-4 Pa. $6.95

THOMAS NAST'S CHRISTMAS DRAWINGS, Thomas Nast. Almost all Christmas drawings by creator of image of Santa Claus as we know it, and one of America's foremost illustrators and political cartoonists. 66 illustrations. 3 illustrations in color on covers. 96pp. 8⅜ x 11¼. 23660-9 Pa. $3.50

FRENCH COUNTRY COOKING FOR AMERICANS, Louis Diat. 500 easy-to-make, authentic provincial recipes compiled by former head chef at New York's Fitz-Carlton Hotel: onion soup, lamb stew, potato pie, more. 309pp. 5⅜ x 8½. 23665-X Pa. $3.95

SAUCES, FRENCH AND FAMOUS, Louis Diat. Complete book gives over 200 specific recipes: bechamel, Bordelaise, hollandaise, Cumberland, apricot, etc. Author was one of this century's finest chefs, originator of vichyssoise and many other dishes. Index. 156pp. 5⅜ x 8. 23663-3 Pa. $2.75

TOLL HOUSE TRIED AND TRUE RECIPES, Ruth Graves Wakefield. Authentic recipes from the famous Mass. restaurant: popovers, veal and ham loaf, Toll House baked beans, chocolate cake crumb pudding, much more. Many helpful hints. Nearly 700 recipes. Index. 376pp. 5⅜ x 8½. 23560-2 Pa. $4.95

ILLUSTRATED GUIDE TO SHAKER FURNITURE, Robert Meader. Director, Shaker Museum, Old Chatham, presents up-to-date coverage of all furniture and appurtenances, with much on local styles not available elsewhere. 235 photos. 146pp. 9 x 12. 22819-3 Pa. $6.95

COOKING WITH BEER, Carole Fahy. Beer has as superb an effect on food as wine, and at fraction of cost. Over 250 recipes for appetizers, soups, main dishes, desserts, breads, etc. Index. 144pp. 5⅜ x 8½. (Available in U.S. only) 23661-7 Pa. $3.00

STEWS AND RAGOUTS, Kay Shaw Nelson. This international cookbook offers wide range of 108 recipes perfect for everyday, special occasions, meals-in-themselves, main dishes. Economical, nutritious, easy-to-prepare: goulash, Irish stew, boeuf bourguignon, etc. Index. 134pp. 5⅜ x 8½. 23662-5 Pa. $3.95

DELICIOUS MAIN COURSE DISHES, Marian Tracy. Main courses are the most important part of any meal. These 200 nutritious, economical recipes from around the world make every meal a delight. "I . . . have found it so useful in my own household,"—N.Y. Times. Index. 219pp. 5⅜ x 8½. 23664-1 Pa. $3.95

FIVE ACRES AND INDEPENDENCE, Maurice G. Kains. Great back-to-the-land classic explains basics of self-sufficient farming: economics, plants, crops, animals, orchards, soils, land selection, host of other necessary things. Do not confuse with skimpy faddist literature; Kains was one of America's greatest agriculturalists. 95 illustrations. 397pp. 5⅜ x 8½. 20974-1 Pa. $4.95

A PRACTICAL GUIDE FOR THE BEGINNING FARMER, Herbert Jacobs. Basic, extremely useful first book for anyone thinking about moving to the country and starting a farm. Simpler than Kains, with greater emphasis on country living in general. 246pp. 5⅜ x 8½. 23675-7 Pa. $3.95

PAPERMAKING, Dard Hunter. Definitive book on the subject by the foremost authority in the field. Chapters dealing with every aspect of history of craft in every part of the world. Over 320 illustrations. 2nd, revised and enlarged (1947) edition. 672pp. 5⅜ x 8½. 23619-6 Pa. $8.95

THE ART DECO STYLE, edited by Theodore Menten. Furniture, jewelry, metalwork, ceramics, fabrics, lighting fixtures, interior decors, exteriors, graphics from pure French sources. Best sampling around. Over 400 photographs. 183pp. 8⅜ x 11¼. 22824-X Pa. $6.95

ACKERMANN'S COSTUME PLATES, Rudolph Ackermann. Selection of 96 plates from the Repository of Arts, best published source of costume for English fashion during the early 19th century. 12 plates also in color. Captions, glossary and introduction by editor Stella Blum. Total of 120pp. 8⅜ x 11¼. 23690-0 Pa. $5.00

THE ANATOMY OF THE HORSE, George Stubbs. Often considered the great masterpiece of animal anatomy. Full reproduction of 1766 edition, plus prospectus; original text and modernized text. 36 plates. Introduction by Eleanor Garvey. 121pp. 11 x 14¾. 23402-9 Pa. $8.95

BRIDGMAN'S LIFE DRAWING, George B. Bridgman. More than 500 illustrative drawings and text teach you to abstract the body into its major masses, use light and shade, proportion; as well as specific areas of anatomy, of which Bridgman is master. 192pp. 6½ x 9¼. (Available in U.S. only) 22710-3 Pa. $4.50

ART NOUVEAU DESIGNS IN COLOR, Alphonse Mucha, Maurice Verneuil, Georges Auriol. Full-color reproduction of *Combinaisons ornementales* (c. 1900) by Art Nouveau masters. Floral, animal, geometric, interlacings, swashes—borders, frames, spots—all incredibly beautiful. 60 plates, hundreds of designs. 9⅜ x 8-1/16. 22885-1 Pa. $4.50

FULL-COLOR FLORAL DESIGNS IN THE ART NOUVEAU STYLE, E. A. Seguy. 166 motifs, on 40 plates, from *Les fleurs et leurs applications decoratives* (1902): borders, circular designs, repeats, allovers, "spots." All in authentic Art Nouveau colors. 48pp. 9⅜ x 12¼. 23439-8 Pa. $6.00

A DIDEROT PICTORIAL ENCYCLOPEDIA OF TRADES AND IN-DUSTRY, edited by Charles C. Gillispie. 485 most interesting plates from the great French Encyclopedia of the 18th century show hundreds of working figures, artifacts, process, land and cityscapes; glassmaking, paper-making, metal extraction, construction, weaving, making furniture, clothing, wigs, dozens. of other activities. Plates fully explained. 920pp. 9 x 12. 22284-5, 22285-3 Clothbd., Two-vol. set $50.00

HANDBOOK OF EARLY ADVERTISING ART, Clarence P. Hornung. Largest collection of copyright-free early and antique advertising art ever compiled. Over 6,000 illustrations, from Franklin's time to the 1890's for special effects, novelty. Valuable source, almost inexhaustible.
Pictorial Volume. Agriculture, the zodiac, animals, autos, birds, Christmas, fire engines, flowers, trees, musical instruments, ships, games and sports, much more. Arranged by subject matter and use. 237 plates. 288pp. 9 x 12. 20122-8 Clothbd. $15.00

Typographical Volume. Roman and Gothic faces ranging from 10 point to 300 point, "Barnum," German and Old English faces, script, logotypes, scrolls and flourishes, 1115 ornamental initials, 67 complete alphabets, more. 310 plates. 320pp. 9 x 12. 20123-6 Clothbd. $15.00

CALLIGRAPHY (CALLIGRAPHIA LATINA), J. G. Schwandner. High point of 18th-century ornamental calligraphy. Very ornate initials, scrolls, borders, cherubs, birds, lettered examples. 172pp. 9 x 13. 20475-8 Pa. $7.95

GEOMETRY, RELATIVITY AND THE FOURTH DIMENSION, Rudolf Rucker. Exposition of fourth dimension, means of visualization, concepts of relativity as Flatland characters continue adventures. Popular, easily followed yet accurate, profound. 141 illustrations. 133pp. 5⅜ x 8½.
23400-2 Pa. $2.75

THE ORIGIN OF LIFE, A. I. Oparin. Modern classic in biochemistry, the first rigorous examination of possible evolution of life from nitrocarbon compounds. Non-technical, easily followed. Total of 295pp. 5⅜ x 8½.
60213-3 Pa. $5.95

PLANETS, STARS AND GALAXIES, A. E. Fanning. Comprehensive introductory survey: the sun, solar system, stars, galaxies, universe, cosmology; quasars, radio stars, etc. 24pp. of photographs. 189pp. 5⅜ x 8½. (Available in U.S. only)
21680-2 Pa. $3.75

THE THIRTEEN BOOKS OF EUCLID'S ELEMENTS, translated with introduction and commentary by Sir Thomas L. Heath. Definitive edition. Textual and linguistic notes, mathematical analysis, 2500 years of critical commentary. Do not confuse with abridged school editions. Total of 1414pp. 5⅜ x 8½.   60088-2, 60089-0, 60090-4 Pa., Three-vol. set $19.50

Prices subject to change without notice.

Available at your book dealer or write for free catalogue to Dept. GI, Dover Publications, Inc., 31 East 2nd St. Mineola., N.Y. 11501. Dover publishes more than 175 books each year on science, elementary and advanced mathematics, biology, music, art, literary history, social sciences and other areas.